Sex and the Marriage Covenant

A Basis for Morality

Sex and the Marriage Covenant

A Basis for Morality

John F. Kippley

The Couple to Couple League International, Inc.
Cincinnati, Ohio

Publisher
The Couple to Couple League International, Inc.

Location
3621 Glenmore Avenue
Cincinnati, Ohio

Mailing address
P. O. Box 111184
Cincinnati, Ohio 45211
U.S.A.

Nihil obstat
Rev. Ralph J. Lawrence
1 May 1991

Imprimatur
Most Rev. James H. Garland, V.G.
Auxiliary Bishop of Cincinnati
7 May 1991

> The *Nihil obstat* and *Imprimatur* are a declaration
> that a book or pamphlet is considered to be free from
> doctrinal or moral error. It is not implied that those
> who have granted the *Nihil obstat* and *Imprimatur*
> agree with the contents, opinions, or statements ex-
> pressed.

Cataloging data
Dewey: 176.

Kippley, John F.
Sex and the Marriage Covenant: A Basis for Morality

1. Birth Control   5. Marriage
2. Contraception   6. Sexual Morality
3. Family Planning   7. Theology
4. *Humanae Vitae*

ISBN O-9601036-9-4

Table of Contents

Acknowledgements

I wish to express my deep gratitude to my manuscript reviewers—Father Edward Bayer, STD, William May, Ph.D., Father Donald McCarthy, Ph.D., Father Steven Rohlfs, STD, Janet Smith, Ph.D., Monsignor William B. Smith, STD, and Father Robert Zylla, STL. Their constructive criticism was extremely helpful and was responsible for many an improvement. Also very important to me was their encouragement to bring this project to a conclusion.

I am also very grateful to Betty Schwartz who, as a volunteer, typed the entire first draft and then the many changes; to Ann Gundlach who did the layout work and managed the printing process; to Dorothea Farrell, Virginia Niehaus, and Rosemary Olding who did the proofreading; and to Joe Kneip for his copyediting.

I thank also the following publishers for permission to quote as needed:

The Documents of Vatican II, Abbot-Gallagher edition; reprinted with permission of America Press, Inc., 106 West 56th Street, New York, NY 10019, ©1966 All Rights Reserved.

Scripture quotations are from the Revised Standard Version Bible, copyright 1946, 1952, 1971 by the Division of Christian Education of the National Council of Churches in Christ in the USA. Used by permission.

Humanae Vitae, translated by Marc Culegari, S.J., © Ignatius Press, San Francisco, 1978.

Harvey Cox, *The Secular City,* 1965; reprinted with permission of Macmillan Publishing Co., New York, Copyright ©1965, 1966 by Harvey Cox.

John Ford, S.J., and Germain Grisez et al, *The Teaching of Humanae Vitae: A Defense,* © Ignatius Press, San Francisco 1988.

Sigmund Freud, A General Introduction to Psycho-Analysis, translated by Joan Riviere, 1935; with permission of Liverwright Publishing Corporation, New York.

Germain Grisez et al., "Every Marital Act Ought to Be Open to New Life," *The Thomist,* July 1988; with permission of *The Thomist,* Washington, D.C.

Brian Harrison, "*Humanae Vitae* and Infallibility," *Fidelity,* November, 1987; with permission of *Fidelity,* 206 Marquette Avenue, South Bend, IN 46617.

Thomas J. O'Donnell, S.J., "Repentance following directly willed contraceptive sterilizations," *The Medical-Moral Newsletter,* January 1989; with permission of Ayd Medical Communications, Baltimore, MD.

Karl Rahner, *Nature and Grace,* 1964; used with permission of Sheed and Ward, Kansas City, Missouri.

Dedication

Up until 1930, Christian churches had been unanimous in teaching that it was immoral to use unnatural methods of birth control. On August 14, 1930 the bishops of the Church of England broke away from this teaching. On December 31, 1930 Pope Pius XI reaffirmed the previously universal teaching in his famous encyclical, *Casti Connubii,* (Concerning Chaste Marriage).

This book, published shortly after the sixtieth anniversary of *Casti Connubii,* is dedicated to its brave and holy author, Pope Pius XI.

It is dedicated also to Pope John Paul II who has been singularly courageous and unprecedented in his frequent but always varied affirmations of the teaching of *Casti Connubii, Humanae Vitae,* and his own *Familiaris Consortio.*

Introduction

In the immediate aftermath of *Humanae Vitae,* I scanned the Catholic newspapers and periodicals looking for the announcement that a recognized theologian was writing a theological defense of the teaching reaffirmed by the encyclical. I found none. There were good things being written by Germain Grisez, Mary Joyce, and Dietrich von Hildebrand, but they all wrote from the perspective of philosophy as distinct from theology.

I had been teaching adult education classes on the Roman Catholic faith since 1963, and I had faithfully transmitted the Church's teaching about the immorality of using unnatural methods of birth control in each one of my regular courses of instruction in the Faith. I used the arguments that were then available, especially the argument about the wrongful use of a basic human power and the analogy with gluttony and the vomitorium.

However, whatever their intrinsic merits, such arguments were not making much of an impression and were under constant attack by Catholic pro-contraceptionists in the mid-1960s. Thus, I looked for another way to defend the teaching, a way that was more personalistic, a way which married couples could relate to their own marriage relationship.

I reflected on the two realities that 1) marriage is the result of unreserved giving—for better and for worse—and that 2) contraception is sex with very serious reservation—for better but positively excluding the imagined worse of pregnancy. Marriage comes into being by a couple unreservedly entering God's covenant of marriage; contraception contradicts the very essence of the marriage covenant. From these considerations I developed the covenant theology of sex described in this book.

I was also appalled by the "arguments" people were using to "justify" using unnatural methods of birth control. Otherwise sane people were saying things such as "It must be okay to use the Pill because God gave us the brains to make it." Christians who, if asked, would remember the words of Christ about the necessity of carrying the cross daily were arguing that because periodic abstinence was a daily cross for some, it therefore couldn't be the will of Christ! Such nonsense and other more serious questions called for an answer, and Part IV of the present book deals with such issues.

In 1969 when I was writing the predecessor of this book,[1] the outlook for the practical survival of the teaching of *Humanae Vitae* in North America was so gloomy I had utterly no hopes of making any practical impact. My chief hope was that my book might find its way into some library archives so that researchers in the late 21st century would realize that not everyone had jumped on the contraception bandwagon.

What's the outlook twenty-two years later? In the Preface to the 1981 printing of *Birth Control and the Marriage Covenant,* I was mildly optimistic that there would be a growing acceptance of *Humanae Vitae* during the 1980s, but I was mistaken. As of this writing in 1991, there are few signs of any such growth.

With hindsight, this is not surprising. Put yourself in the shoes of a typical young engaged couple of the 1980s and ask yourself: What would there be in your background to lead you to believe that it is immoral to use unnatural methods of birth control? If you are from a typical home, your parents—Catholic, Protestant, or whatever—have most likely been using unnatural methods of birth control for years and are quite likely to be sexually sterilized. If you went to a Catholic high school, you probably found no teaching that supported *Humanae Vitae,* and if you went to a "mainline" Catholic college, you probably were instructed in the art of dissent. If you went to other colleges and universities, you found that use of unnatural methods of birth control was simply taken for granted.

What seems clear to me now is that things will not improve until individual bishops make it evident to all concerned parties that they are truly serious about education in chastity. The sincere, orthodox bishop is going to have to do what he can to reverse the scenario described above. He will have to reclaim Catholic education within his jurisdiction to insure its orthodoxy and prudence. He will also have to reclaim marriage preparation, and he will have to make a truly Catholic education in marital chastity and natural family planning an ordinary and required part of preparation for marriage. Fortunately, there are signs that individual bishops are starting to make these efforts.

Such bishops will need the help of dedicated priests and laity. It is my hope that such priests and laity will find this book useful for confirming themselves in the truth of the Church's teaching, in developing insight, and in conveying the truth, the beauty and the challenge of marital chastity to engaged and married couples.

Part I

The Covenant Proposal

Chapter 1 is the key chapter of this book because it states the basic covenant theology on which the rest of the book is based. In the first part of Chapter 1, the basic covenant theology of sex is set forth. In the second part of the chapter, the usefulness of this theology is explained. Then Chapter 2 applies the covenant theology to sex outside of marriage; Chapter 3 applies it to marital sex; and Chapter 4 develops an analogy between the worthy reception of the Eucharist and the worthy marital embrace.

1

A Covenant Theology of Human Sexuality

I: The Basic Concept

1. Introductory notes about theology

The fundamental meaning of theology is still summed up in the brief expression of St. Anselm, "Faith seeking understanding" (fides quaerens intellectum). The most obvious implication of that statement is that theology is not identical with faith, and certainly no theology is identical with God's revelation. What God has revealed is contained in Sacred Scripture and Sacred Tradition, and its content is presented to us and clarified for us by the teaching authority established by Jesus Christ himself in his Church.

Theology uses the data of God's revelation and attempts to explain certain aspects of it. For example, God's revelation says very clearly, "Thou shalt not commit adultery," but God does not say **why**. Theology starts with the commandment and attempts to explain why.

Once you recognize that theology is not identical with the content of faith, then it is easy to understand that there may be more than one way of seeking to explain the faith, i.e., more than one theology. That doesn't mean that every theology is equally good; any given theology may be more or less adequate for explaining the faith. In fact a theology may be quite adequate at one point in history but less adequate at another. For example, one theology may explain the evil of adultery primarily in terms of the injustice done to the innocent party. At a time when mutually agreed upon adultery was unthinkable, that explanation may have been very helpful. However, at a time of moral degradation as evidenced by mutual spouse-swapping, that explanation may be no less true but it may be less helpful than a theology which focuses on the divinely intended marital meaning of sexual intercourse.

A limited comparison can be made between theology and scientific theories. Moral theology seeks to explain the natural moral law; scientific theories seek to explain the natural physical law. The comparison will read more easily if we treat any specific theology as a theory—an effort to explain non-physical reality.

A theory has value insofar as it applies to the greatest number of cases. A major purpose of a theory, whether it be in the field of physics or morality, is to show a unifying theme, principle, or "law" which is applicable to all of the observable cases. In the physical sciences, a theory is first of all derived from observation. Then if more and new data are observed which do not fit into the previous formulation of the theory, an effort will be made to modify the theory or to replace it with a new one. However, the new theory still has to explain the older data; it cannot rest content with an explanation which is suited only to the new observation. From the point of view of the "laws of the universe," a theoretical law attempts to account for the regular occurrences observed. If the statement of a "law" is changed, it is not because there was a change in nature but because new observations enabled the scientist to see more of nature and then forced him to account for the new observations as well as the old. The statement of a physical law is nothing more than a theoretical expression which has gained universal acceptance. It is an effort to explain that which *is* in the physical order, and the discovery of greater detail about *physical being* may well force the revision of previous theoretical statements which did not account for all that was there but only for that part which was initially observed.

A theory is more valuable if it is simple. The simpler it is, the more universal it will be, and the more universal, the more of *being* it will explain. The natural scientist yearns for the ultimate physical theory which will explain and unify everything. This, of course, will never eliminate the more complex and detailed explanations which are subordinate to, dependent upon, and congruent with the more general theory.

The above comparison may be helpful to explain why there can be different theologies. Furthermore, just as insight can be gained into the physical laws of the universe by witnessing ecological disasters, so also insights can be gained in moral theology by witnessing the moral disasters that have followed widespread disobedience to God's laws. Such insights help to explain why there can be progress in moral theology.

There are, however, real limitations to this comparison because of very real differences in the subject matter of the natural sciences and theology. To conclude this comparison quickly, let us simply note that the physical sciences are based on the human experience of repeated observations, but sound moral theology is ultimately based on God's revelation including that He created man and woman in His own image and likeness.

God has already revealed the answers to the great problems of man—who created the universe, the nature of God, the nature and destiny of man, and salvation. He has revealed that He is the Creator, that He is Love and that man is made in His image and likeness. However, after these matters have been accepted on faith as the great realities of life, we are still left with the duty of showing how various forms of behavior either are loving or are not loving, either do or do not enable man to live up to his calling to perfection in the likeness of Christ. The prime statement about man being made in the image and likeness of God who is Love does not spare us from the duty of trying to construct lesser statements to cover both specific actions and whole areas of related activity. That's what moral theology is all about.

Or at least that's what good moral theology should be doing. However, it is possible for moral theologians to get off track and to work their way into blind alleys; and probably the easiest way for this to happen is for theologians to concentrate their attention so exclusively upon their fellow human beings that they lose sight of God and His order of creation. I think that's what has happened all too commonly in the moral theology dealing with birth control, i.e., in the writings of the dissenters from *Humanae Vitae*.

In the entire birth control controversy, there has been such emphasis on the "problem of contraception" for married people that this problem has been isolated from the over-all "problem of sexuality." (Is there any age group over childhood and before senility for which sex does not provide some sort of a challenge or problem?) One serious aspect of this narrowing of perspective is that it impedes the development of a theology of sexuality that can be applied to the widest possible scope of sexual problems. Another serious aspect of this restricted vision is that instead of seeing contraception in the light of an over-all theology of sexuality, theories are developed to solve only the problem of contraception and are then applied to other problem areas. For example, if one theorizes that suppression of the tendency to express affective love in intercourse is evil, the theory is very quickly applied to pre-marital relations as well. Thus, while seeming to "solve" one problem, the theory creates more.

One of the weaknesses inherent in much of the theorizing that has taken place about birth control is that it has proceeded from the less known to the better known. That is, it has been centered around contraception (a less known) and then is applied to the better known (fornication, adultery, sodomy), having the effect of undermining the traditional teaching on these as well (or at least not being able to show why they are evil).

Any good moral theology must first of all be true to God's revelation; it must make some aspect of the Lord's order of creation a bit more understandable by those who are called to live and love in the image and likeness of God. Secondly, any good moral theology must be true to man. Therefore it will challenge what stems from greed, laziness, lust, etc. within us. We may not like it because it reflects the challenge of walking with the Lord, but we have to admit within ourselves that it has the ring of truth. It will come as no surprise that I hope that such will be your judgment about the covenant theology of sex.

2. A covenant theology of sex

Let us start with a section from *Familiaris Consortio* in which Pope John Paul II called for theology to explain and uphold the teaching against marital contraception:

I feel it is my duty to extend a pressing invitation to theologians, asking them to unite their efforts in order to collaborate with the hierarchical magisterium and to commit themselves to the task of illustrating ever more clearly the biblical foundations, the ethical grounds, and the personalistic reasons behind this doctrine. Thus it will be possible, **in the context of an organic exposition**, to render the teaching of the Church on this fundamental question truly accessible to all people of good will . . . .(emphasis added).

A united effort by theologians in this regard, inspired by a convinced adherence to the magisterium, which is the one authentic guide for the people of God, is particularly urgent for reasons that include the close link between Catholic teaching on this matter and the view of the human person that the Church proposes: **doubt or error in the field of marriage or the family involves obscuring to a serious extent the integral truth about the human person** in a cultural situation that is already so often confused and contradictory. In fulfillment of their specific role, theologians are called upon to provide enlightenment and a deeper understanding, and their contribution is of incomparable value and represents a unique and highly meritorious service to the family and humanity (n.31; emphasis added).

In 1983-1984, the Pope gave a series of lectures in which he developed his "theology of the body" to provide an answer to his own request, but his statements above make it clear that he did not intend to rule out other efforts. As a point of historical fact, I developed the covenant theology of sexuality in the mid-Sixties, and I have been encouraged by the fact that in many ways it corresponds very closely with the theology of the body developed by Pope John Paul II.

What I intend to do now is to express a basic theological statement which is at the heart and core of the covenant theology of sex, and then explain it. Then, after I have shown how this covenant theology is rooted in Sacred Scripture and Christian personalism, I will explain how this reaffirms Christian teaching 1) about authentic love and sex, and 2) against the various forms of sexual immorality including contraception. Please note that the morality of birth control is not considered in isolation. Rather, I contend that unnatural forms of birth control are immoral for the same basic reason that adultery, fornication, and sodomy are immoral. I believe that such a unified approach is in accord with the call of Pope John Paul II for a theological effort "in the context of an organic exposition" as quoted above. In short, while the consequences of various sexual sins may be different, I believe that the ultimate reason for the objective evil of all sexual sins is the same. They all fail, in one way or another, to be a sign of the committed and caring love pledged at marriage; they all fail to be a renewal of the marriage covenant.

3. The core statement

The core statement of the covenant theology of sex is simplicity itself:

"Sexual intercourse is intended by God to be at least implicitly a renewal of the marriage covenant."

It can be embellished slightly by rephrasing the last part of the statement:

"Sexual intercourse is intended by God to be at least implicitly a renewal of the faith and love pledged by the couple when they entered the covenant of marriage."

It can be rephrased further in **secular** terms:

"Sexual intercourse is meant to be a renewal of the couple's own

marriage covenant, a symbol of their commitment of marital love."

Or, in its most secular form:

"Sexual intercourse is meant to symbolize the self-giving commitment of marriage."

Secular phrasing is helpful for conveying the idea to students in schools where religion is not taught and/or where it cannot be taught that sexual intercourse is truly a marriage act and is honest and finds its meaning only within marriage. As an aside, I want to respond to the easily imagined challenge that this concept could not be taught in an American public school because it might be seen as reflecting a religious belief. The response is threefold. 1) Most just laws reflect the **natural moral law** which has been codified in the Ten Commandments, so there is no difference in teaching that man is not meant to steal from others or the government and teaching that man is not meant to have sex outside of marriage. 2) The ordinary language of cultures all over the world—both in time and in place—support the notion that sexual intercourse is meant to be a marital act. Any culture which has a taboo on adultery or which sees pre-marital sex by engaged couples as less good than marital sex supports the notion that sex is meant to symbolize the commitment of marriage. 3) Such basic non-sectarian norms of human behavior simply must be taught at every level and place of education, or alleged education is simply not human education, and that, of course, is the problem with much education today.

4. Marriage is the key

The Catholic faith teaches that sex is a gift from God even though that gift is frequently misused. Any reading of the Bible or even secular literature quickly shows how frequently and in how many ways men and women have misused the gift of their sexuality, and from the biblical statements we can arrive at the core statement that sex is intended by God to be a renewal of the marriage covenant.

There is no direct biblical statement that sex is intended by the author of creation to be a renewal of the marriage covenant. However, we can arrive at the statement by deduction. As will be shown in Chapter 15, "Biblical Foundations," adultery, fornication, homosexual behavior, contraception, masturbation, and bestiality are all condemned by Sacred Scripture. Thus the only form of sexual intercourse not condemned by Sacred Scripture is non-contraceptive intercourse between a man and woman who are married to each other. I will use the term "honest sex" or "honest sexual intercourse" to designate the sex act taught by Scripture and Tradition to be good: mutually voluntary, non-contraceptive intercourse by a validly married couple.

That leads to an obvious question: what is there about marriage that makes morally good the same physical act that is morally evil outside of marriage? Or to put it the other way, if honest sexual intercourse is (or can be) a moral good within marriage, why is it evil for those who are not married to each other? Certainly God knows that the degree of emotional love felt by unmarried persons is sometimes much stronger than that felt by many married couples. To sharpen the focus a bit more: if Jim and Jane love each other, why is it the grave matter of mortal sin for them to have sexual intercourse on the day before they marry but good for them to celebrate their marriage with honest sexual intercourse after they have married?

The answer is that when they married, they freely entered into a covenant of God's making. They solemnly promised before God and their fellow man that they would exercise caring love for each other from that time until death will separate them. They gave themselves, each to the other, without reservation. This is what makes marriage so wonderful. Each person knows his or her own sins and imperfections; each knows that the other has his or her sins and imperfections. Yet they give themselves, each to the other, in caring love, without reservation, for better and for worse, for life. They become "two in one flesh."

Within marriage, sexual relations have the potential of renewing this great act of self-giving love. With their minds and with their wills, they have irrevocably committed themselves to each other in marriage. (To emphasize what they have done in getting married, I like to use the phrase, "They have *committed* marriage.") They have united their persons and their lives spiritually. Now with their whole persons, soul and body, they have the right to express the oneness of their persons in the oneness of the full sexual union.

Two things need to be noted about marital sexual intercourse. First of all, it is a *unique* sign of their marital commitment. Of all the things they do as a married couple, this (along with its preparatory actions) is the only action that is morally right *only* for married couples. There are, indeed, many other acts that in fact they do with each other which reflect their marriage covenant—common meals, financial sharing, common living quarters, and literally hundreds of little acts of kindness, but these could also be practiced if one were living with a relative or even a very close friend. Both the Bible and the Catholic Church make it clear that sexual intercourse is intended by God to be a unique expression of love—that of marital love and commitment.

The second thing that needs to be noted is that while sexual intercourse is meant to be a unique sign of marital love, it is not always an appropriate sign of love. For example, who could call it loving behavior on the part of a husband to insist upon sexual relations when his wife is sick with the flu? (More on this below.)

The fact of unpleasant realities that may occur in any given marriage in which sexual intercourse seems far removed from the caring love of their marriage day does nothing to undermine the covenant theology of sexuality. On the contrary, it reaffirms it. To improve a poor marital relationship, a couple need to reflect on the marital meaning of sex; they need to see sexual intercourse as a physical sign of the caring, the tenderness, the intimacy they pledged at marriage. They need to consider that their physical nakedness at times of marital relations should reflect the openness and self-abandonment that they offered to each other in their marriage covenant. Married spouses understand—and some learn only through hard experience—that sexual relations can be experienced as signs of intimacy only when there is first of all a spiritual intimacy between them. Indeed, marriage is the key to understanding the mystery of human sexuality.

In summary, we have seen that God has revealed that sexual intercourse is a good act only within marriage, and we have seen that God creates a oneness out of the will of man and woman to marry which makes it good for them to express that oneness in the one-fleshness of honest sexual intercourse. What can we conclude except that God intends for their sexual union to be a unique sign, a symbol of their marriage union?

The next question which arises is this: "Once they are married, is the sex act intended to reflect the caring love the couple promised to each other?" To put it another way, "Can a husband demand sex from his wife no matter how harshly he has treated her? Does the teaching of St. Paul that a wife is to be submissive to her husband (Eph 5:22) and that she should give him his conjugal rights (1 Cor 7:3) mean that he is entitled to marital relations even if he should be drunk and abusive?"

The answer is to be found in the context of each of the passages above. St. Paul also commands that husbands are to love their wives "as Christ loved the Church and gave himself up for her" (Eph 5:25). Is that not both a beautiful and yet very forceful statement that husbands are to love their wives with a self-sacrificing love? Furthermore, in the passage of First Corinthians, Paul taught that "the husband should give to his wife her conjugal rights and likewise the wife to her husband" (1 Cor 7:3).

In the strict sense of conjugal rights that are necessary for the validity of marriage, such rights are limited to honest sexual intercourse. That is, the lack of kindness and affection do not nullify a marriage, but the refusal to engage in sexual intercourse—ever— would provide grounds for nullity.

However, in a looser sense we can say that conjugal rights extend beyond sexual intercourse. Spouses also have a right to affection from the other spouse and at a bare minimum they have a right not to be abused. When one spouse acts against these rights, his or her claim to the right to sexual intercourse is correspondingly reduced.

The point I am making is that within marriage a couple are called to keep alive the faith and the love—a caring love—they promised when they married. Perhaps the clearest statement of this continuing obligation to keep renewing their original pledge of love is found in the first and last sentences of Paul's famous discourse on marriage:

> Be subject to one another out of reverence for Christ...Let each one of you love his wife as himself, and let the wife see that she respects her husband (Eph 5:21,33).

From this combination of biblical data and personalist reflection, I believe that it is legitimate and even necessary to conclude that God intends that sexual intercourse should be at least implicitly a renewal of the marriage covenant.

At least implicitly ... The words "at least implicitly" are important. A husband and wife are not required to intend explicitly that their marital relations should be a renewal of their marriage covenant. Having this concept of marital sexuality firmly in mind can certainly give more meaning to their exercise of their marital rights, and is therefore desirable, but it is not necessary.

What is meant by the words "at least implicitly" is that the spouses, either individually or together, may not act *against* the self-giving love they promised at marriage. What is called marital rape would be an example of one spouse acting against the marriage covenant; the couple mutually agreeing to engage in spouse swapping would be an example of both spouses acting against the marriage covenant. As we shall see later, contraceptive behavior is also a mutual act against the marriage covenant.

5. The Christian teaching about love

Before applying the covenant theology of sex to specific sexual behaviors, we must ask if there is a specifically Christian teaching about love that applies to the love of husband and wife as well as to their love for their children and others.

What Jesus taught about love was a doctrine of bittersweet love. "Love your enemies and pray for those who persecute you . . ." (Mt 5:44-30). "Come to me all who labor and are heavy laden, and I will give you rest . . . My yoke is easy, and my burden light" (Mt 11:28-30). "If anyone wants to come after me, let him deny himself and take up his cross daily and follow me" (Lk 9:23). "A servant is not above his master" (Jn 13:16).

The teaching of Jesus was not limited to words. His whole life portrayed the love of God for man, and certainly the love of one spouse for the other cannot exceed the love God has for that same spouse. And what do we see in the life of Jesus that illustrates God's love for each of us? Born in humble surroundings, fasting, overcoming temptations, teaching others and being rejected, accepting his suffering, and finally his passion and death on the cross.

The point is this: there is nothing in the teaching of Jesus Christ that indicates that love is easy. In fact, everything points the other way. As we shall see, when He taught about the permanence of marriage, certainly a teaching about sexual love, His disciples understood the great difficulty implied by His teaching, and some of them wondered why a man should marry at all if he couldn't get rid of a bothersome spouse. Marriage is sweet, but the fullness of God's revelation that marriage is truly permanent adds a dimension that at times becomes bittersweet, a burden—even if a light one, a yoke—even if an easy one.

The next point is this: Is there any reason for a Christian to think that other aspects of Christ's teaching about marital love will necessarily be other than bittersweet? On what possible grounds can the Christian argue that because the teaching against marital contraception involves certain difficulties, he or she can thereby ignore it?

The conclusion is that it should not be surprising if the teaching of Jesus Christ about marital love and sex contains the same element of bittersweet that is found in His teaching about marriage itself.

II: The Usefulness of the Covenant Theology of Sex.

As noted above, Pope John Paul II has asked theologians to illustrate "ever more clearly the biblical foundations, the ethical grounds, and the personalist reasons" behind the teaching against marital contraception. Furthermore, he said, "Thus it will be possible, *in the context of an organic exposition,* to render the teaching of the Church on this fundamental question truly accessible to all people of good will" (emphasis added). I believe that "an organic exposition" means treating the morality of birth control in the context of other sexual behaviors such as fornication, adultery and sodomy.

The covenant theology of sex fulfills the requirements for a useful theology as noted by the Pope (biblical, ethical, personalist), and in the rest of this chapter I will address each of these criteria plus several others that I think are necessary for a theology to be useful today. In short, I propose to show, very briefly in most cases, that the covenant theology of sex is 1) simple, 2) biblical, 3) ethical, 4) personalist, 5) theological, and 6) ecumenical. Furthermore, it lends itself to "an organic exposition," and thus it 7) distinguishes between marital and non-marital sex and 8) provides a key for understanding not only the evil of contraception but also the evil of adultery, fornication, sodomy and other sexual behaviors condemned as objectively sinful by the Catholic moral tradition. I believe that the covenant theology of sex is also 9) realistic. It provides a terminology that avoids the sometimes austere quality of previous theological terms and also avoids the subjective mushiness and inaccuracy of much of contemporary talk about sex, love and marriage. Finally, 10) it provides both a norm and an ideal.[1]

1. Simple

Any two people who are mentally and spiritually capable of committing themselves to marriage are also capable of understanding this covenant theology of sex and marriage. In fact, if a couple either cannot or will not understand or admit the elements or beliefs involved in this concept of marriage and sex, then it is questionable whether their proposed union should be called a Christian marriage. What are these elements or beliefs?

1) God the Creator has created us, loves us and knows what is good for us.

2) God has created the human relationship of marriage and has told us that marriage lasts for a lifetime. In short, God's creative love has determined the basic rules of marriage.

3) Christian marriage is a covenant which is much more than a contract. The whole purpose of human contracts is to spell out very definite limits to what is covered, and they can be changed by mutual consent. However, a covenant entails unlimited liability. This has been traditionally stated in the marriage vows as "in sickness and in health, for richer and for poorer, and for better and for worse."

4) When you marry, you make no pledges at all about having romantic feelings toward your spouse, either always or occasionally. Rather, you are promising to exercise caring love of the kind described by St. Paul in 1 Cor 13: "Love is patient and kind..."

5) Sexual intercourse is intended by God to be a sign of your marriage commitment, your pledge of caring love for better and for worse. It symbolizes both the covenant relationship that God has created and your own personal entry into that covenant with each other and with God.

It needs to be said in connection with the fourth point that although one cannot pledge that he or she will always "feel" well-disposed to the other spouse, each does have an obligation to invite and nourish such feelings as much as is reasonably possible. Indifference is the common opposite of love within marriage, so each spouse is obliged not to be indifferent but to try to feel good about his or her spouse and to encourage such feelings in return by, for example, thoughtful anniversary and birthday gifts and by frequent compliments.

Each of the previous five points is basic for understanding Christian marriage and could be elaborated upon at length, but in their brevity they should be comprehendible by everyone capable of entering marriage.

2. Biblical

What could be more biblical than a theology of sex based upon the covenant, probably the most basic theme of the Bible? The application of the covenant theme to marriage was first developed by the prophet Hosea. Through His words, God revealed the highly personal nature of His love for His people as the love of a faithful husband for his wife. Hosea even called Israel a whore for her unfaithfulness to Yahweh. In Hosea, God used marriage to reveal something about His covenant with his people; and in Ephesians 5, Paul used the covenant of Christ and His Church to reveal something about marriage. With this sort of biblical precedent, it is certainly legitimate to search for the meaning of sexual intercourse in terms of the covenant of marriage. In short, the covenant theology of sex is based upon and is in accord with all of the biblical concepts of sex, love, covenant, and marriage. It accepts both the eroticism of the Song of Songs and the self-oblation of 1 Corinthians 13 as constitutive of married love.

Specifically, the covenant theology is biblical because it allows for an interpretation of Genesis 38:10 that sees here the sin of contraception as a sin against a covenant. As is shown in Chapter 15, "Biblical Foundations," Onan was not the only one to violate the Law of the Levirate in this specific situation, for his father and younger brother also disobeyed it by default. However, Onan engaged in the act called for by the Levirate "covenant" but contradicted it. The sin for which the sacred authors tell us he was punished was not the violation of the Levirate which he would have violated if he had merely refused to have intercourse with Tamar; rather it was his participation in the covenanted act and his contraceptive invalidation of it that was so sinful that he was punished while the other Levirate-violators in his family were not.

The covenant theology is in accord with St. Paul's self-styled concession to married people about not refusing each other except perhaps for a while by mutual agreement lest they be tempted by lack of self-control (1 Cor 7:3-6). Whether the abstinence be for prayer or more secular values, the covenant theology merely states that when they do come together again, it must be a valid renewal of the marriage covenant.

It is, of course, in accord with the further Pauline teaching in Ephesians 5 where the self-sacrificing love of Christ for His Church is held up as the model for a husband's love for his wife. The new covenant was made in the blood of Christ shed for His Church for its holiness, and this covenant theology calls for a somewhat analogous death to self in order to promote the holiness of each marriage.

The covenant theology is biblical in the sense that it calls for those values and attitudes which are specifically and habitually rejected by the world—a radical teaching on fidelity to the marriage covenant, an attitude of denial of self and trusting surrender to Christ, and an attitude toward material goods that tends to place one among the Bible's little people, the *anawim*, rather than among society's beautiful people.

Finally, the covenant theology of sex actually takes its start from all the biblical teaching about sex, a teaching which condemns all forms of intentional orgasmic sexual behavior except honest, non-contraceptive intercourse between husband and wife.

3. Ethical

Pope John Paul II has called for theologians to show "the ethical grounds" for the evil of contraception. Ethics is different from moral theology; for while moral theology takes its start from revelation, ethics limits itself solely to the use of reason. Its first principle is "Do good and avoid evil," and it seeks to demonstrate by reason the goodness or evil of certain actions.

Such an effort is best undertaken by moral philosophers, and this book makes no claims to provide any sort of in-depth ethical analysis. However, what I will do in Chapter 2, "Sex Outside Marriage," is to make use of a philosophical tool called "ordinary language analysis" to illustrate that sex is supposed to be a marriage act and that non-marital sex is wrong.

In ethical terms, the great evil of marital contraception is that it is intrinsically dishonest. It pretends to be an act of love, but it destroys the act as a symbol of the self-giving promised at marriage. Contraceptive behavior is "getting" behavior, not giving behavior, whether one or both spouses are in the "getting" mode. As such, one form of contraceptive behavior is essentially no different from another, and they may all be reduced to masturbation.

4. Personalist

The emphasis in this theology of sex is on what two persons have willed to do in entering the covenant of marriage, creating the two-in-one-fleshness revealed by God in Genesis. This theology does not in the least contradict the more physiological theologies applied to the marriage act, but its emphasis is on the freely-willed self-donation that made their desired union a marriage. That is, instead of focusing on the natural orientation of the human sexual organs or even on the anti-procreative (and therefore anti-marital) meaning of contraception, it focuses first and foremost on what each spouse did in making the commitment of marriage. In effect, it says: "Be honest with yourself. You made an unreserved gift of yourself in marriage. Don't contradict your gift of self through acts of contraception, acts of sex with serious reservation."

5. Theological

Nowhere in Scripture are to be found the words, "Sexual intercourse is intended by God to be at least implicitly a renewal of the marriage covenant." Yet, that concept is contained in Scripture. Just about every imaginable form of sexual activity is mentioned in Sacred Scripture, but the only form that is recognized as legitimate is that of marital intercourse. I think it is indisputable that God has revealed that sexual intercourse is intended to be essentially covenantal. In short, theology goes beyond the mere quotation of Scripture and attempts to put things together; when Scripture provides an answer to what is right or wrong, theology attempts to explain why.

6. Ecumenical

Any theology which proposes to be ecumenical today must be biblical and have its roots in a Tradition that at one time was accepted by those whom Protestants recognize as their spiritual ancestors. The proposed covenant theology of sex is certainly biblical, and it is also firmly rooted in a Tradition that in America, at least, was vocalized even more by Protestants than by Catholics. It is an undeniable fact of American history that in the 19th century, anti-contraceptive laws were passed by Protestant legislatures for a largely Protestant America. Looking for documentation of Protestant Church positions on birth control prior to Lambeth of 1930, I was told by Professor Paul Ramsey of Princeton that I was wasting my time trying to prove the obvious. That is, so universal was this belief that it simply would not have been the subject of Church statements any more than we would expect today a statement that stealing is immoral.

However, the memory of this historical Tradition has been lost to contemporary Christians. At every opportunity afforded, I ask groups of Catholics and Protestants how many are aware that until 1930 no Christian Church had ever accepted contraception as morally permissible. Perhaps three in 100 might know that bit of Christian history; small wonder that *Humanae Vitae* has been so widely regarded simply as a papal idiosyncrasy rather than an affirmation of a Tradition universally held by all Christian churches until 1930 and reaffirmed in one way or another by every Pope since then with the exception of the short-reigned John Paul I.

There is some reason to hope that the memory of Protestant opposition to unnatural forms of birth control will be revived. A small book published in 1989 lists 99 Protestant theologians who taught against Onanism, including actual quotations from 66 of these. Martin Luther, John Calvin, and John Wesley were strongly opposed to unnatural birth control, with Luther calling it a form of sodomy, Calvin calling it the murder of future persons, and Wesley saying it could destroy your soul. In his introduction to that section of the book, the author states: "We have found not one orthodox theologian to defend Birth Control before the 1900s. NOT ONE! On the other hand, we have found that many highly regarded Protestant theologians were enthusiastically opposed to it, all the way back to the very beginning of the Reformation."[2]

7. It can distinguish . . .

Because the belief that sexual intercourse is meant to be a renewal of the marriage covenant is based solidly on the biblical concepts of covenant, marriage, and love, it can distinguish between marital and non-marital sex. Before marriage, there is simply no covenant to renew; therefore non-marital sex pretends to be what it is not and cannot be, so it is simply dishonest sex, a lie. That holds true whether the sexual activity is the premarital sex of an engaged couple, the experimental sex of teenagers, or adultery. Whatever

18

the situation without the marriage covenant, sexual relations are intrinsically dishonest and immoral.

Such an understanding of sex is radically different from the soft calculus of much of contemporary talk about sex. For example, one high school text says: "Sexual union should always take place in the context of love—of genuine concern for both your own welfare and that of the other. Your relationship should bring happiness and growth to both of you. You will, therefore, consider the possible consequences of your words and actions, and you will not risk hurting yourself or another unnecessarily."[3]

Or again; "Rather, according to both the laws of society and the Gospel of Jesus, what is wrong or immoral is what hurts or risks hurting yourself or others unnecessarily, without sufficient reason."[4]

Examples could be multiplied both from the same high school text or others. My criticism about this way of talking about chastity is not that the author is probably trying to discourage pre-marital sex—obviously a good intention. Nor would I deny that such reasoning contains large grains of truth. The point is rather that such talk is essentially a soft calculus that does not say a firm biblical "no" to anything. It implies that the people involved will be able to calculate the possible harm to be done and will refrain from sex because of such possible consequences, but nowhere does it say that sex outside of marriage is simply a lie and an act of fornication even if the two people manage to rationalize their way around all the obstacles and think they have "sufficient reason" for taking those risks of hurting themselves or others. Such talk is an invitation to calculating and rationalizing. Given the tendency of passion once aroused to interfere with clear and reasonable thinking—even if calculus were all that was needed—this kind of "explanation" is ultimately seductive.

By ignoring the absolute prohibition on fornication as in the examples cited, modern authors erode consciousness of the sovereignty of God. As Father Richard Roach, S.J., puts it, "God's sovereignty is violated whenever we knowingly and freely break an absolute prohibition."[5]

However, the concepts that sex is meant to be a renewal of the marriage covenant and that non-marital sex is a violation of the God-created meaning of sex operate on a different plane entirely— the plane of discipleship rather than consequentialism. I agree that the unhappy consequences of non-marital sex need to be pointed out again and again, but I insist that any theology of sex and that any discussion of sex in a religious environment must go beyond the pragmatic to the biblical foundations and to the symbolic meaning of sex as a renewal of the marriage covenant.

8. Applies to all . . .

As has already been indicated, the understanding that sexual intercourse is meant to be a renewal of the marriage covenant provides a clear explanation for the evil of non-marital intercourse whether it be technically adultery or fornication, whether between lovers or with prostitutes: there is no covenant to renew. Sodomy between homosexuals is condemned on precisely the same grounds as fornication between heterosexuals: there is no valid marriage covenant to renew. The evil of bestiality should be apparent without further elaboration; and if the whole meaning of freely-willed sexual actuation is to renew at least implicitly the mutual love and faith pledged at marriage, then the evil of the essentially self-centered act of masturbation is apparent.

Granted, with the covenant theology of sex, all of this becomes very simple and deductive, but who ever said that a theology about matters that affect every man and woman had to be complicated or understandable only to those trained in philosophy and theology?

Chapter 2 applies the covenant theology more completely to non-marital sex, and Chapter 3 applies it to sex within marriage and addresses the issue of marital contraception. The sequence of Chapters 2 and 3 follows the principle of dealing first with the more known and then the less known.

9. Realistic terminology

Too much of the talk about sex within marriage uses terminology that is inaccurate or misleading; sometimes it appears to be the result of wishful thinking. For example, one priest-teacher of college theology told his students that at the instant of marital orgasm the floodgates of sanctifying grace were opened. When the students asked my opinion as a married layman, I had to say that the professor was confused between grace and sperm count.

More typical is this: "The act of sexual intercourse between two people is, in itself, beautiful and good."[6] That's misleading because as it stands it makes no distinction between marital and non-marital intercourse, nor does it address the real situation within marriage when intercourse is sometimes neither good or beautiful.

Another inaccurate, misleading statement: "...the Church understands the act of sexual intercourse to be the ultimate expression of love and fidelity between two people."[7] The author goes on to qualify that the Church means married people so in the context the flaw of not mentioning marriage is corrected. However, my first objection is to the phrase, "ultimate expression of love and fidelity." Precisely what does that mean? "Ultimate expression" is a fuzzy, imprecise phrase that may conjure up visions of ecstasy but can mean different things to different people. My second objection is that the description uses the verb "to be" in the sense of "sexual intercourse is the ultimate expression..." There is a world of difference between "meant to be" and "is."

Real life examples. Every priest, marriage counselor, and married couple with any honesty and realism can come up with real life examples that mock the notion of marital sex as good, beautiful, and the ultimate expression of love, fuzzy as it is. John has sat in front of the TV screen all Sunday afternoon completely engrossed in football. The combination of beer and provocative cheerleaders has steered his imagination towards sex. He calls into the kitchen to his wife who feels neglected and hates beer breath, "Go get yourself ready for 'making love' at half-time. Should be about another 10 minutes." Translated "Go put in your diaphragm and foam because I want relief of sexual tension instead of watching the half-time show." Love? Beauty? Ultimate expression of love and fidelity? Absurd, but too frequently that's what is being fed to young people in supposedly Christian education today.

In the fall of 1989 as I was working on this book, I received three letters in three days from women complaining about their marital situations. In each case, the husband was insisting upon complete fellatio. Sometimes it was a substitute for periodic abstinence; at other times it was in place of normal genital-genital intercourse.

In another case, a woman called to say she and her husband had been practicing "NFP"(natural family planning) for eight years, having taken instruction from a program not associated with the Couple to Couple League (CCL). All during this time they had practiced mutual masturbation instead of sexual self-control during the fertile time. Then she happened to read in CCL's book on NFP, *The Art of Natural Family Planning,* that such activity is "contrary to the Christian tradition of sexual morality which holds that deliberate ejaculation must take place only within the vagina" (70). Her phone call was not to criticize us, but simply to find out if we had a priest on staff to whom she might "go to confession" over the phone. (We don't.)

The last case I will mention was a letter from a man who responded to a fund appeal letter in which I had mentioned the difficulty of finding couples who were interested in natural family planning. He wrote to tell me that if we taught couples "NFP" as he and his wife practiced it, couples would be breaking down the doors. He then described their practices of completed oral and anal sex during the fertile time.

The point I am trying to illustrate is that too much of what passes for "marital sex" has nothing to do with authentic marital love, and some of it is nothing more than marital sodomy, the same sort of perverse activities that constitute homosexual sex. That's why any talk about marital sexuality has to distinguish between morally good and morally bad sexual activity.

Evaluate closely the statement, "Sexual intercourse is meant to be at least implicitly a renewal of the marriage covenant." Such terminology easily recognizes the difference between what sex *should be* and what it frequently *is*. The use of "meant-to-be" clearly implies a standard set by the Creator above and beyond the intentions of the participants. It carries within it the norm that sexual intercourse is intended by God as a sign of marriage, not just affection regardless of marital status.

The phrase "at least implicitly" recognizes that it is not necessary that married couples consciously tell themselves or each other, "Let us renew our marriage covenant."

The fact that the whole statement is built upon the marriage covenant provides a concrete, objective norm, and the notion that sex is meant to be a renewal of that covenant places each act of sex within the standard of the valid Christian marriage.

In my opinion, it is erroneous to say flatly, "Marital intercourse **is** a renewal of the marriage covenant." Such talk fails to distinguish among the wide variety of sexual acts within marriage. On the one hand there is sex as it should be—affectionate and non-contraceptive. On the other, there are acts of marital rape, contraception and marital sodomy. Thus, in order to have realistic terminology, it is necessary to state what God intends sex to be and to avoid making "is" statements that cover a multitude of dissimilar acts.

10. Simultaneous norm and ideal

One of the most common errors of modern discourse about sexual matters is the treatment of the norm as an ideal. The context is inevitably that the ideal may be relevant for people far advanced in sanctity but not for the common man and woman. The notion that the doctrine of marital non-contraception reaffirmed by *Humanae Vitae* is a binding norm that applies to all is either denied or disregarded. Unfortunately, once this norm of marital chastity is treated as an idealistic dream, so are all of the other norms of chastity both within marriage and outside of it. And for good reason: it is certainly easier to practice the periodic abstinence required by natural family planning than the total abstinence required by the chaste single life whether heterosexual or homosexual.

Perhaps it may be easier to retain the norm as a norm if an ideal is presented simultaneously within the same concept. At any rate, that is what the covenant theology of sex does. The **norm** is that at a minimum the act of sexual intercourse must meet three conditions:

1) The man and woman must be validly married to each other;

2) The act must not be one of marital rape;

3) The act must not be positively and intentionally closed to the transmission of life; i.e., it must be an act of non-contraceptive, non-sterilized, completed genital-genital intercourse.

The **ideal** goes beyond that and reminds each married couple that the act of marital coitus is really meant to be a renewal of the faith and caring love they pledged to each other at marriage, the more conscious and explicit this renewal, the better. The ideal sets the stage for an examination of conscience that can help each person grow in marital love. "If I'm anticipating 'making love' this evening, what is there about my day-to-day, hour-by-hour social intercourse with my spouse that reflects the caring love I pledged at marriage? Have I tried to be helpful, to lighten the burdens of my spouse? Have I done anything to make my spouse feel loved and esteemed?"

The challenge of the marriage covenant. To the extent that a married couple can answer such questions affirmatively, to that extent their acts of sexual intercourse can become more expressive of honest marital love.

Almost everyone will recognize his or her own failure in terms of the ideal, but such failures, depending upon their nature, are the matter of imperfections or venial sin and do not necessarily exclude one from the communion of the sexual embrace.

Such a theology of sex does not condemn marital coitus for the relief of sexual tension provided that it fulfills the minimum requirements of the norm. However, it is realistic and recognizes that such acts are a far cry from those acts which reflect much more explicitly the caring love of the original marriage covenant. In short, this theology of sex recognizes that it is the little things of daily and hourly social intercourse between husband and wife— taking out the garbage, cleaning up a mess, the kind word, the smile—that are the elements of "making love" in marriage; it recognizes that the act of marital coitus "makes love" pretty much in direct proportion to the effort put into the non-genital aspects of the marriage.

In my opinion, an especially beautiful attribute of the covenant theology of sex is that it provides a challenge to each married couple at every stage of their life together—young or old, fertile or infertile. The non-contraceptive aspects of the norm will pass into practical irrelevance after menopause, but the challenge of keeping their sexual intercourse a symbolic renewal of the love they pledged at marriage will pass away only when they do.

The belief that sexual intercourse is intended by God to be at least implicitly a renewal of the marriage covenant is rooted in Scripture and is based also on the personal commitment of the couple. It is a simple concept that is ecumenical and provides a key for explaining the evil of non-marital sex.

Finally, at one and the same time, it affirms the norm of marital non-contraception and provides an ideal, a never ending, marriage building challenge to each and every married couple regardless of age or fertility.

All of this leads me to hope that many will find the covenant theology of sex useful for helping couples improve their marriages as well as for defending the teaching of the Church reaffirmed by *Humanae Vitae*.

2

Sex Outside Marriage

Introduction

The introductory question to this chapter is this: "Is there an **intrinsic** link between sexual behavior and love?" I believe that any honest person, after a bit of reflection, will conclude that there can be love without sex, and sex without love, so there is no *intrinsic* connection between them. The second question then becomes, "Under what circumstances does sexual behavior represent authentic human love?" The covenant theology of sex replies, "When sex is at least implicitly a renewal of the faith and love of the original marriage covenant."

However, there is a wide range of sexual activity which is possible outside of marriage, and much of it is common today. Therefore, these activities need to be evaluated, and in this chapter I make that evaluation in two ways. First, I will show how these behaviors fail to meet the norm of the covenant theology of sex; secondly, I will show how this conclusion is supported by the way that ordinary language treats them, thus illustrating a harmony in this matter between theology and a common sense view that I believe springs from the depths of human nature despite the widespread reality of sexual sinfulness. The analysis from ordinary language doesn't really *prove* anything, but it illustrates that even common secular discourse recognizes, at least indirectly, that sexual intercourse is meant to be a marital act. Several things need to be noted before we look at the various behaviors.

1. Revelation, not philosophy. The first point to be noted is that these various non-marital behaviors are all condemned by God's revelation as contained in Sacred Scripture and interpreted by Sacred Tradition. Good moral philosophy also arrives at the same conclusions, but the starting points in theology are Sacred Scripture and Tradition.

It must also be noted that God doesn't argue with us. That means that God has not provided reasons to prove that what He reveals is true. For example, when God revealed "Thou shalt not commit adultery," He did not add "because . . ." The proper response of the creature to revelation by his Creator is faith and obedience, not argument.

2. The natural moral law and disciplinary law. What God has revealed to be right or wrong about certain forms of behavior is that way because of our very nature as human persons made in the image and likeness of God. That is, adultery isn't wrong just because God said it is; rather God told us that adultery is wrong because that's the way it is in the very order of His creation. To put it another way, what God has told us about adultery and certain other behaviors is not arbitrary. Such teaching is not just a rule that can be changed by His Church later on. His revelation about marriage and adultery is based upon and reveals something further about human nature itself.

Teaching and law about behavior which is rooted in our human nature is entirely different from disciplinary laws of the Church. The classic examples for Catholics are the fasting laws. Prior to the Second Vatican Council, the disciplinary law of the Catholic Church forbade most Catholics over the age of 14 from eating meat on Fridays. Furthermore, theologians commonly taught that the obligation not to eat meat on Friday was binding under the pain of mortal sin.

Every educated Catholic in 1965 recognized that this was purely a disciplinary law, that the sin involved in eating meat on Friday was the sin of disobedience, that eating meat on Friday was not against the very nature of being a human person. Every educated Catholic recognized the huge and unbridgeable difference between the fasting laws of the Church and those which were and are rooted in human nature, that is, the natural moral law. And every educated Catholic knew that a change in purely disciplinary laws of the Church had nothing to do with any possibility of changing teaching about the natural moral law. Unfortunately, the history of the Church around 1968 indicates that there were many poorly educated Catholics who erroneously assumed that a change in fasting laws meant that the Church could also change its teaching about love and sexuality.

3. Positive law and universal negative absolutes. In a somewhat similar vein, we have to distinguish between positive law and negative law. Positive law is a command to DO something. An example of positive law is the third commandment, "Keep holy the

Sabbath day." The positive law of the Church further specifies this by a commandment of the Church—to worship at Mass on each Sunday and Holy Day of Obligation. There are exceptions to positive law. If you are sick, you are not obliged to worship at Mass on Sunday.

However, negative law is a command NOT to do something. And when a negative law has to do with the order of creation or the natural moral law, it is universal in its application. Its commands are called **universal negative absolutes**. That means that "Thou shalt not commit adultery" applies all the time and in all places. There are no exceptions.

It should also be noted that the universal negative absolutes do not order us actually to **do** anything specific. No one who understands what God's Church is actually teaching can say that God or the Catholic Church is "always telling me what to do." To stay with the example I've been using, "Thou shalt not commit adultery" does not tell me how often I should have relations with my wife, and it does not tell me what I should do to build up marital love and affection in my marriage. Much is left to my imagination. However, it forbids me at all times and in all places from having sex with anyone other than my spouse and, of course, from activities that would probably lead to such illicit behavior.

4. The word "Love." One last reality must be touched upon before taking up the various forms of non-marital sex, and that's the word "love." If one thing has become evident in the controversy on birth control and in the entire debate on sexual ethics, it is that the word "love" has become meaningless for all practical purposes. Cardinal Suenens in his book *Love and Control*[1] recalled the story of the wise man who was asked what he would do if he had all the power in the world. The wise man answered that he would restore words to their original meanings. People commit crimes of "love"; they commit murder, theft, deceit and adultery for "love." The word "love" in a certain sense has degenerated to mean something someone may like to do because it might make him or her feel good in doing it.

In the area of sex, the sex act is frequently referred to as the act of "making love." Unfortunately, this terminology may lead some to think that love can be produced by an action and that repeated action will produce a lover. The ordinary language of common people supports traditional Christian teaching in showing the error of making any sort of automatic connection between sexual activity and love. I think it's important to understand at every level of our being that there is no intrinsic connection in practice between love and sex, even within marriage. Once we understand that, we are in a much better position to determine when sex is an authentic expression of human love.

I. Evaluation of Certain Heterosexual Actions

1. Rape

At the bottom of the moral scale of sex acts is forcible rape. This action involves the same anatomical act as that of two married persons, and it is possible that some acts of rape are conducted with less excitement and violence than some voluntary sex acts between married couples. But can people actually think that rape is expressive of love? You answer, "NO!" but I remember a magazine article describing certain underprivileged people which leads me to think otherwise.

In the case in mind, a young man raped a girl one night and then called her up the next night to ask for a date. It is not impossible that, having been brainwashed about sex being "making love," he might have thought that rape might be an acceptable way of introducing himself. Then I have read that in some sections of the Sicilian culture it is not uncommon for a young man to rape a girl in order to get her hand in marriage. Apparently the stigma of rape is so bad for the girl that she has to become the rapist's wife or she will remain single for life.

In terms of the covenant theology of sex, it is obvious that rape is immoral. First of all, in order for sexual intercourse to be a morally good act, it must be an unforced act; secondly, it must be an act between two people who have entered the marriage covenant together. However, the act of rape under discussion does not meet either criterion. Obviously, there is no marriage covenant to renew, and secondly, threat, force, and violence multiply the evil of this act.

The Christian condemnation of rape is rooted in Scripture but is stronger and more universal than the biblical condemnations. That is, the Christian condemnation of rape makes no distinctions based on the status of the person raped. In contrast, Deuteronomy 22:23-27 is concerned specifically about a woman who is betrothed, and verses 28-29 are concerned with a virgin who is not betrothed.

It may be hairsplitting, but these distinctions do not specifically mention the rape of a non-betrothed non-virgin, perhaps even a married woman, and the reason may be that these verses are concerned primarily with establishing legal punishments. The account of the rape of the concubine in Judges 19-21 is complicated by the fact that the multiple rape is compounded by murder, and the account seems to be primarily concerned with the murder and its revenge. Likewise the rape of Tamar by Ammon (2 Sam 13) is made complex by the fact that it was also incest.

Perhaps the clearest biblical indication of the universality of the evil of rape is found in Genesis 34 where the rape of Dinah is not clouded by the additional evils of incest and murder or distinctions of status. Although there is still an extraneous factor—the fact that the rape was committed by a non-Israelite against a daughter of Jacob—the account clearly teaches how the Jews regarded rape even before they received the Law of Moses (Ex 20) and the laws against many other forms of sexual immorality (e.g., Leviticus 18, Deuteronomy 22).

Catholic teaching rises above any hairsplitting distinctions that might be found in the Old Testament and clearly condemns rape under all circumstances, whether the woman is single, engaged, married, virgin or non-virgin, whether previously known to the rapist or not. In fact, as we shall see, *Humanae Vitae* condemns marital rape at the same time that it condemns marital contraception. You will not find modern treatises about the evil of rape simply because it is universally agreed that it is evil. It is difficult to imagine even the most heretical of theologians accepting rape as morally acceptable.

One might say that the teaching about rape illustrates another teaching of the Church—that God has not limited his revelation to the written text of the Bible but has likewise entrusted it to Sacred Tradition formed within the united body of the apostles and carried on and faithfully interpreted by their successors in the Church established by Christ upon Simon Peter. The teaching of the Church about rape, for example, is based upon the biblical teaching; it in no way contradicts the biblical witness but it is fuller, more complete.

The theological condemnation of rape is supported by the ordinary use of language. The very word "rape" in our ordinary language tells us that we know this is not an act of love. Our ordinary use of language also makes it clear that there is a common understanding that the evil of rape is not the force and the violence but the sexual violation of a person. This common understanding is reflected in penal codes which clearly distinguish between assault and non-sexual abuse, force and violence on the one hand, and the sexual violation of rape. I believe that this ordinary use of language and the penal codes reflect something deep in the heart of man that recognizes that sex is meant to be a marriage act, a renewal of the marriage covenant, even though such terms may be unfamiliar to most.

2. Fornication

A step up the scale is the voluntary sexual intercourse of two unmarried people. Here it is common to distinguish between the interpersonal relationship which is casual and that which is between two people who have signified their intention to become man and wife. And again, in the casual relationship it is customary to distinguish between the one in which the two people really like each other and the one in which one person is effectively paying for the use of the other. I say that these forms are a step up the scale because at least they are generally mutually voluntary.

The ordinary use of language both confirms this conclusion and makes further distinctions which can be helpful in understanding that there is absolutely no intrinsic connection between love and acts of sex.

Our ordinary use of language puts prostitution at the bottom of voluntary non-marital sex. Is prostitution an act of love? Is it made so by having one party to the act say, "I made love so many times today?" or, "It cost me ten dollars to make love last night?" I think that the accumulated wisdom of ages has been reflected in our use of the word "prostitution" for this, a word which tells us of a complete disassociation of love and sexual relations. In this particular case and in others also, it is a shame that our genteel ears have refused to let our tongues use an expression which ordinary language has developed for many instances of sexual intercourse. The simple, straight-forward, Anglo-Saxon four letter word for fornication may be considered vulgar but it does a wonderful job of communicating. It says that the act wasn't really rape, but it certainly wasn't love either.

While condemning the act of prostitution as being a violation of the order of creation, we must be wary of condemning the prostitute. What if she is a victim of white slavery, afraid for her very life to run away? What if she has concluded that this is the only possible way in which she can support her children now that her husband has

30

been killed? Fear, fear, and more fear certainly will be taken into account by our heavenly Father in His judgment of those who violate one aspect of the interpersonal order of creation because they feel driven by other violations of that same order of creation. In fact, is it not entirely possible that the sins of some prostitutes may be less than those of comfortable Christian married couples who believe they are above the teaching of twenty centuries of Christian morality and freely and knowledgeably use unnatural methods of birth control?

There can be no denying the very real affection, liking, and desire that many unmarried people feel for each other and which they try to express in sexual intercourse. Is this really to be honored by the name of "love"? Again, our ordinary language has given us the word "fornication" to describe this sort of activity. "Fornication" is undoubtedly a value word; it says something besides "sexual intercourse," and it distinguishes this sort of affective behavior from that which takes place between two people married to each other.

Should "fornication" be used to describe sexual relations between people who have openly pledged to marry each other at a definite date in the future? (In this discussion, I will limit "premarital" to those circumstances.)

It is not uncommon to see very fuzzy writing to the effect that sexual activity should be appropriate to the degree of the relationship. Written in books for teenagers, such statements are dangerous and misleading; they are open to all sorts of rationalization, for it is not at all difficult for an adolescent couple who are attracted to each other to rationalize that they are almost married and that therefore they should be able to have sex at least on special occasions, etc. Instruction based on the covenant theology of sex will easily avoid such pitfalls.

Another way of undermining Christian teaching against sex outside of marriage is to speculate that maybe St. Paul's condemnation of fornication **really** meant prostitution, and that therefore pre-marital relations are not forbidden by Sacred Scripture. But if fornication means prostitution, why do we have an ordinary language use of the two words, an ordinary person's understanding that these two words describe the sexual act in quite different circumstances? Certainly the word "prostitution" was available to St. Paul and on one occasion Paul specified prostitution (1 Cor 6:15). Another possible explanation of why he specifically condemned fornication in Romans 1 and Galatians 5 while not specifically mentioning prostitution (or why St. Jerome translated the Greek *porneia* as the Latin *fornicatio*) is that prostitution was probably admitted by all to be evil; in contrast there may have been a certain amount of pride and rationalization in fornication and in some of the other sins that he condemned, and Paul wanted to correct this. (See this subject also in Chapter 15, "Biblical Foundations.")

In my opinion, pre-marital relations deserve to be described as fornication and fall under Paul's emphatic condemnation. However, even for those who want a special category for pre-marital relations (in the restricted sense of the term), it can be pointed out that the necessity for using "pre-marital" indicates that our ordinary language distinguishes between these pre-marital sex acts and those of the same couple after they are married. There is an ordinary common sense understanding that there is something morally defective about pre-marital relations, and this is backed up by the evident concern about pre-marital relations as indicated by the number of surveys which seek to identify such behavior.

I think that it is worthwhile to spend a moment on this. Here is a couple, John and Mary. They intend to be married in September. But now it is May. They love each other. They yearn for each other. They feel the psychological need for a concrete sign of being fully accepted by the other, a felt need which may completely pass once they are married. Why should they be deprived of this moment of sexual joy just because they haven't stood before the proper witnesses and exchanged their vows?

The answer is simple: they aren't married yet. They haven't yet "covenanted" with each other for life. All that they have done is to indicate in a non-binding way that they hope and intend to enter the marriage covenant in September. They are in no way ready to express a covenantal renewal until they have first of all entered something which they can then renew.

If they are ready to covenant and want to express their love in the sexual union, then they should immediately advance the date. It is a cruel misuse of terms to say that this couple is already "married" for if there is one thing which is common knowledge among ordinary folk, it is that you are free to back out anytime before you say "I do." It is the common understanding of mankind that the obligations of marital fidelity do not begin until the couple have formally married each other. By the same token, the right or privilege of expressing love in the sexual union does not begin until this couple has entered into the marriage covenant.

If that seems arbitrary, consider this analogy which I read someplace but have forgotten the source. A married couple was discussing these matters with a priest who seemed to be a bit confused. So the husband asked him: "Father, could a man celebrate Mass before he was ordained a priest, like maybe just the night before?" "Of course not." "Well, Father, it's the same with marriage. You couldn't celebrate Mass until you received your sacrament; we couldn't celebrate marriage without our sacrament."

I think there's a lot in that simple comparison. For a man to attempt to celebrate Mass before he has received the Sacrament of Holy Orders would be high fraud, probably sacrilege. It would be intrinsically dishonest and therefore certainly sinful. For a man and woman to attempt to celebrate their love in sexual union before they marry—and in the case of Christians, thus receive the Sacrament of Matrimony—is also intrinsically dishonest and therefore sinful. The fact that both the future priest and the future married couple may have a strong desire to perform those acts proper for a priest and a married couple respectively says nothing at all about the morality of their doing them. In both cases a change in their very **being** must take place before they may validly perform such acts.

3. Adultery

"Thou shalt not commit adultery" (Ex 20:14). "You have heard that it was said, 'Thou shalt not commit adultery.' But I say to you that everyone who looks at a woman with lustful intention has already committed adultery with her in his heart" (Mt 5:27-28).

As the sexual revolution became institutionalized and many who purported to be theologians became seduced by its initial allure, the old sin of adultery began getting a new look in the Sixties and Seventies. Imagination went wild and adultery was seen by some as not just being unfaithful but as something positive, a love-refreshing relation which makes persons better able to cope with the problems of their individual marriages and careers. Episcopalian Bishop James A. Pike[2] drew the example of a striving politician who was receiving one setback after another at a convention. A woman at the convention begins to work for him, offers to help in any way and then offers herself. (She has become unhappy with circumstances in her own marriage.) They bed down together. He rises psychologically recharged to fight the battle for good politics; she leaves with a new determination to make her own marriage go on. Neither other partner will ever know or will ever be "hurt"; it seems that nothing but good has come of it. Therefore, shouldn't we realize that "Thou shalt not commit adultery" should be modified with "most of the time" or "except under extenuating circumstances"? If such rationalizing sounds as if it comes from the same source which "tricked" Eve in the Garden of Eden, it should not be surprising.

The approach of dissenters working in Catholic theology has been more guarded. They have not been anxious to tell the Catholic world that they dissented not only on birth control but also on adultery. Instead, they developed principles for making decisions that undermined not only traditional Christian teaching on birth control but also every other area of moral behavior. It is not that the dissenting theologians do not know that their principles cannot say a firm "no" to any imaginable behavior. Far from it!! Sometimes they give tacit assent when others point these things out, and sometimes they openly admit it.

For example, in 1971 I wrote an article that appeared in a major theological journal read by all the dissenters, and I showed that the decision-making principles of Charles Curran could allow spouse-swapping.[3] No one challenged it. No one said I was creating a straw man. In fact, three years later, Father Thomas Dubay wrote in the same journal that my challenge to dissent was still awaiting a response![4]

An example of openly admitting that their principles of dissent cannot say a firm "no" to any imaginable behavior is found in a 1977 book written by a committee of the Catholic Theological Society of America, a book which well represented the thinking of dissenters. It departed from regarding universal negative absolutes as binding and instead provided a soft and subjective criterion: *"Wholesome human sexuality is that which fosters a creative growth toward integration"* (emphasis in original).[5] It discussed both ordinary adultery and spouse-swapping and could not say a firm and universal "no" to either. It frowned on such activity but remained open to the possibility that social sciences might show that somehow some people derived some pragmatic benefit from it; and thus all it could conclude about adultery and spouse-swapping is this: "Thus, while remaining open to further evidence from the empirical sciences, we would urge the greatest caution in all such matters, lest they compromise the growth and integration so necessary in all human activity."[6]

That is utter nonsense, but that is what has been passing for "mainline" moral theology in the Catholic Church in the United States and probably the rest of the West since *Humanae Vitae*. Catholic teaching against adultery of every form remains the negative moral absolute of Sacred Scripture and Sacred Tradition:

"Thou shalt not commit adultery—under any circumstances." However, the "dissenting" theologians have proved willing to compromise universal Christian teaching against adultery, fornication, homosexual behavior, incest, and even bestiality in order to find a way to compromise the pre-1930 universal Christian teaching against marital contraception.

A problem with the traditional explanation of the evil of adultery is that it centers upon the injustice of adultery and how it goes against the purposes of marriage, namely, the building of the marriage bond and the good of children. However, such argumentation, though true, leaves itself open to the effort to rationalize that any particular act of physical adultery shouldn't really be called adultery because there was no apparent injustice (in the case of mutual consent) or that this act of adultery caused no hurt and actually may have "helped" the respective marriages. Any explanation of the evil of adultery which focuses upon the hurt to the innocent party is open to the rationalization that if apparently nobody gets hurt, then so what? Hasn't the general purpose of the commandment been observed? In short, there are serious problems with a theology that is *de facto* consequentialist, i.e., which attempts to explain an evil solely or primarily in terms of its consequences, particularly when the subject is the morality of relatively private acts.

Thus, we must look further. Why did Jesus tell us that even the adulterous intention was already the sin of adultery? Who was hurt by it? Only the one person involved who was injuring himself by his personal unchastity. The adulterous intention is not wrong simply because Jesus told us it was; rather He told us it is wrong because it **is** wrong independently of His words. An ethic of "so long as nobody else gets hurt" cannot be reconciled with Scripture.

The theological supporters of the sexual revolution ask us to leave universal negatives and treat adultery in terms of apparent consequences. If the two people in Bishop Pike's fiction about adultery gave each other a psychological boost and therefore "helped" each other, should we not admit that this was loving, helpful behavior? Should we not say then that this was not "adultery", a negative value description, but rather an act of authentic human love? Should we not admit that here we have a wonderful example of modern emancipation from a rigid archaic code in favor of modern man who is self-determining and who must create his own life and values as he evolves and progresses? Certainly the adjectival approach (the use of such sympathy-evoking words and phrases such as emancipation, archaic code, modern, self-determining, evolution, and progress) paves the way for a new interpretation of the commandment. However, the Christian must look at problems and solutions from within the context of salvation history. Here he finds that the important thing is the covenant relationship between God and his people. He finds in Hosea that the people's practice of idolatry is not called simply "idolatry" but is called adultery— because they have strayed from their covenant relationship; they have entered into other relationships which they considered more immediate and more helpful.

The case for adultery can be argued on all the personalist bases that are put forward for contraception. An outside affair might help avoid the greater evil of the marriage breaking up. An outside affair might aid in the personality development of the one; the two people who are not married to each other may genuinely love each other, may be willing to do anything for each other; why should they be restrained by a code kept alive in the Catholic Church for almost 2,000 years? Why should they be stunted?

My answer is twofold.

1. The easiest way to see the evil of adultery is to view it in the light of the covenant theology of sex. From an analysis of the overall teaching of Scripture about sex and from an analysis of the personal commitment involved in committing marriage, we have concluded that God intends that sexual intercourse should be at least implicitly a renewal of the marriage covenant. Obviously in the act of adultery there is no marriage covenant to renew. Therefore acts of adultery are essentially and intrinsically dishonest and evil.

Because adultery as defined by Jesus is so common today, its evil is commonly ignored or simply not realized. Therefore it needs to be affirmed and reaffirmed that the primary evil of adultery is that it violates God's covenant with mankind. In the original covenant of creation, we read: "Therefore a man leaves his father and his mother and cleaves to his wife, and they become one flesh" (Gen 2:24). "One flesh" does not refer just to the physical unity of sexual intercourse but primarily to the unity of their persons as husband and wife, a unity so close and unbreakable that St. Paul compares it to the unity of Christ and his Church (Eph 5:32). Yes, there are unhappy consequences to adultery, but the primary evil of adultery is not to be found in those consequences but in the violation of the original creation covenant and in the violation of the vows made to each other and before God when the couple married.

The same thing can be said about **fornication**. What makes adultery worse than fornication is what moral theology has traditionally focused on—the injustice to the innocent party and the breaking of one's solemn promise of fidelity. These are not just felt consequences. The injustice to the innocent party remains an injustice, and the breaking of one's solemn promise is an evil even if the innocent party remains ignorant and therefore does not feel the offense.

2. The ordinary use of language once again confirms the theological conclusion. Our ordinary use of language sharply differentiates sexual relations between lovers who are married to each other and between lovers who are married to someone else. I believe a good case can be made for the fact that although prostitution is adultery when at least one party is married, the word "adultery" is ordinarily used to describe "non-commercial" sexual relations; it carries in ordinary language the connotation of personal affection and desire. I think that adultery is more than just a seeking of relief; relief from sexual tension can be obtained through the evil of masturbation. I am quite sure that generally adultery is more than just a physical relationship, that it usually is a personal relationship as well. Therefore I think that the common ordinary use of language has already taken into account the personalist reasons that can be argued and has given to these interpersonal sexual relations the dishonorable term, "adultery."

4. More Socially Accepted Forms of Illicit Sex

In terms of the covenant theology of sex, every form of non-marital sex is objectively evil because there is no marriage covenant to renew. To repeat, based on biblical data, this theology asserts that God intends that sexual intercourse should be a marriage act, a bodily celebration of the self-giving love pledged at marriage, at least implicitly a renewal of the marriage covenant. Therefore where there is no marriage covenant, acts of sexual intercourse are intrinsically evil.

That includes not only the obvious cases of prostitution and fornication and adultery but also various forms of behavior that are now so common they have gained a certain acceptance in the West.

Mistressing usually involves adultery and is frequently just a form of long-range prostitution in which a man provides financial support in return for sex.

Living together as sexual partners without marriage remains a case of living in the sin of fornication or adultery.

Contractual non-marriages. The covenant theology of sex explains why certain forms of legal marriages are neither the natural covenant of marriage nor the Christian sacrament of matrimony. In some cases, the sexual partners specifically disavow making a marriage covenant. Instead, they write a marriage contract which includes provisions for divorce if certain conditions should occur. That is specifically contrary to the unlimited commitment of the marriage covenant. As a result the individuals never "commit marriage," their relationship is really nothing more than a legalized form of fornication or prostitution, and their sexual relations are objectively immoral because they are not and cannot be a renewal of a marriage covenant.

Invalid marriages. Another form of invalid sex occurs between couples engaged in serial polygamy—divorce after a valid, sacramental marriage and subsequent "remarriage." This is what Jesus called "adultery"; see adultery in Chapter 15. When a couple enter the Christian covenant of marriage, a change in their very **being** occurs. They are marked before God as married to each other for life. The relationship-in-being cannot be broken. So even if they obtain a civil divorce from each other, the spiritual covenant of marriage remains, and they cannot enter a second true marriage covenant. If such persons enter a second civil marriage, their sexual relations with that second person cannot be a renewal of a valid marriage covenant and are therefore objectively immoral.

II. Evaluation of Other Sexual Behaviors

A Christian theology of human sexuality must be able to explain the evil of various actions that have traditionally been called sexual perversities. Such matters are usually not discussed in polite dinner conversations, but they have long been the subject of investigation by moralists and sexologists as well. The most famous of the latter was, of course, Sigmund Freud, though he was also much more than that. Reference to him will be useful for three reasons: 1) He openly advances a theoretical criterion by which sexual activity can be evaluated. 2) It may prove psychologically helpful for many to realize that one need not be a Roman Catholic to conclude that those forms of sexual activity which positively exclude the possibility of reproduction are perverse. 3) His testimony helps to answer the objection that only Catholics (and Orthodox and some Protestants) see anything wrong with contraception.

The following quotations are from a series of lectures given by Freud in Vienna during the year 1917-1918.[7]

Our duty is to account satisfactorily in theory for the existence of all the perversions described and to explain their relation to normal sexuality, so called.

Such aberrations from the sexual aim, such erratic relationships to the sexual object, have been manifested since the beginning of time through every age of which we have knowledge, in every race from the most primitive to the most highly civilized, and at times have succeeded in attaining to toleration and general prevalance (269).

Perverted sexuality is nothing else but infantile sexuality, magnified and separated into its component parts (272).

For if a child has a sexual life at all, it must be of a perverted order, since apart from a few obscure indications he is lacking in all that transforms sexuality into the reproductive function. Moreover, it is a characteristic common to all the perversions that in them reproduction as an aim is put aside. **This is actually the criterion by which we judge whether a sexual activity is perverse—if it departs from reproduction in its aims and pursues the attainment of gratification independently**. You will understand therefore that the gulf and turning point in the development of the sexual life lies at the point of its subordination to the purposes of reproduction. Everything that occurs before this conversion takes place, and everything which refuses to conform to it and serves the pursuit of gratification alone is called by the unhonored title of "perversion" and as such is despised (277; emphasis added).

Obviously Freud is condemning all those forms of sexual activity that do not result in human heterosexual copulation using the respective reproductive organs. He does not specifically mention contraception nor does he mention anal or oral copulation either. He contents himself with one criterion, the departure from reproduction in its aims and the pursuit of the attainment of gratification independently. Contraception was certainly practiced in Europe when Freud spoke; he could not have helped but know about it; yet he did not exclude it from his condemnation of perverse behavior.

Freud was certainly not a Christian moralist as is evident from his dismissal of conventional morality. Yet he saw that the reproductive purpose was so essential to human sexuality that he made its exclusion the criterion for evaluation of sexual perversion. On this point, Freud provides an example of natural moral law philosophy that is very much in accord with the work of solid Christian philosophers. He also provides an excellent testimony to educated thinking about sex only thirteen years before the Church of England accepted the revolutionary concept that it was no longer perverse to pursue gratification while consciously seeking to destroy the naturally reproductive purpose of marital intercourse.

The covenant theology of sex also finds to be immoral those actions which fall under Freud's classification of perversion.

1. Masturbation

Masturbation is condemned by the covenant theology of sex because it violates what is meant to be an interpersonal renewal of the covenant. Masturbation is a solitary act and has nothing to do with a renewal of the marriage covenant. Furthermore, that form of masturbation which some moralists want to say is not the human act of masturbation but the human act of obtaining semen for fertility analysis is also rejected by the covenant theology of sex. This theology removes sexual activity from the sole realm of a person's intention and asks if the activity is an interpersonal renewal of the marriage covenant. Masturbation, even for semen to be used to foster fertility, is still the deliberate action of a human being who has de-personalized, de-humanized sexual activity which is meant to be solely an interpersonal expression of the marriage covenant. It is no less against the order of creation than is artificial insemination. Both take an action meant to be interpersonal and make it only biological—despite any and all good intentions. Sexual activity plays such an important role in the life of man that any deliberate sexual stimulation, and especially that culminating in orgasm, is a significant human act to be considered in itself and not just as part of a larger totality.

It should be noted that on 29 December 1975 the Sacred Congregation for the Doctrine of the Faith reaffirmed traditional Catholic teaching against masturbation;[8] and on 22 February 1987, the same congregation reaffirmed traditional Catholic teaching against artificial insemination of all sorts, whether the older and simpler transfer of a husband's semen to the wife's uterus or fallopian tubes; or the newer technology of *in vitro* fertilization and embryo transport.[9]

2. Homosexual sex

Homosexual sex is definitely interpersonal activity. Some homosexuals "marry" and tend to remain "faithful" to each other, are not promiscuous, and consider themselves to be living a "higher life," one which does not burden the world with more mouths to feed. Some would say that they do not consider their behavior as "selfish" nor do they consider that they are doing something which is "un-natural" for them. They may regard normal heterosexual activity as "un-natural" for themselves.

Knowledge of how many active homosexuals live and how their promiscuity may involve dozens or even hundreds of different contacts in a single year must fill a Christian with both disgust and pity. On the other hand, the person with homosexual tendencies who remains chaste deserves admiration and support. Back in the mid-Sixties a person like this called me on the phone to ask if I did any counseling. We got talking and he said he was what people called "a queer." He wasn't giving in to his tendencies; he was going to Mass and receiving the sacraments regularly, but he felt com-pletely left out of society. The whole society, even Church groups, seemed oriented to the couple—already existing or matchmaking. Where was there a place for him who had no interest in matchmak-ing but did need honest companionship? My sympathies extend to people such as this young man in a way that they do not to the contraceptive couple—even that couple whose family situation calls for heroism of a sort. The married couple—even if living as brother and sister—still have each other, and that was supposed to mean a lot before they got married. They may feel constrained not to have a sexual union, and they may find this extremely difficult—but at least they have a union of mind and heart. They have the psycho-logical fulfillment of knowing that they are fully accepted by the other, loved by the other, and are being helped by the other on the path of salvation.

The person with homosexual tendencies who refuses to become a practicing homosexual frequently has no one. His can be the loneliest life of all, and my heart aches for those unknown homo-sexuals who are bravely fighting a terrific battle, alone except for their confessor and their Faith. I have great empathy, too, for heterosexual men and women who would like to marry but haven't found the suitable mate. Their loneliness can be desolate, but the chaste homosexual's loneliness is worse. As the very experienced counselor, Fr. John F. Harvey, puts it, "The heterosexual can talk to people about his situation and gain a sympthetic ear, but the homosexual person dares not talk to ordinary people about his situation. This inability to share his feelings with others makes the loneliness of the homosexual more intense and increases the temptation [to engage in homosexual behavior]."[10]

The good news for homosexuals is that they can now find support for chaste living in **Courage,** an organization founded by Father Harvey in 1980.[11]

But what about the interpersonal practice of homosexual acts? Where does it stand in a theology which works from a personalist and sacramental starting point? If the theology was based solely on personal intentions of affection and commitment, it would seem that a homosexual "marriage," if such really ever occurred, would be a valid covenant and homosexual relations would be a valid renewal of that covenant.

However, the covenant theology of sexuality is based first and foremost on the free and personal agreement to enter not just a covenant of the couple's own making, but the covenant of marriage which is a God-given relationship. It is a relationship which has an order intended by the Creator, a structure which is not dependent solely upon the intentions of the two people.

The question then arises, "How can you be sure that this structure, this order of Creation, does not include homosexual marriages?" As will be explained more fully in Chapters 5 and 6 dealing with conscience, we are always somewhat limited regarding "proofs" in any area of human life including sexuality. When dealing with human behavior, we never get the sort of mathematical proof that we can have about the statement "sixteen divided by eight equals two." In human behavior we can strive only for moral certitude when we work from reason alone. This is the kind of certitude we have for making all the big decisions in life, such as deciding that you love this particular person and want to marry. As an example, try this: Imagine you are talking with a skeptic who says he doesn't think you really love your spouse or your mother. Try to prove it to him. If the skeptic has any sort of imagination at all, he will be able to answer anything you advance. Finally, you will be driven to conclude that he is just being absurd to deny all the practical evidence, but this still doesn't amount to mathematical certitude. What you have arrived at, however, is a moral certitude that you love your spouse or your mother, etc. I believe you can arrive at moral certitude about the evil of homosexual actions based upon human considerations, and I think that moral certitude is raised to the levels of the certitude of faith by the constant teaching of the ordinary magisterium of the Church.

In answering that an interpersonal relationship of fidelity, care, and affection between two homosexuals cannot be the structure of marriage, I would point first of all to the common consent of mankind that marriage takes place only between people of the opposite sex. I think we can say without fear of contradiction that homosexuality has always been regarded as an abnormality, no matter how widely practiced.

Second, I would enlist the service of Freud who taught, as we have seen, that the criterion for judging the perversity of a sexual act was whether or not it departed from reproduction in its aims and purposes. As some New York homosexuals argued in the mid-Sixties, their way of life certainly is one answer to population problems. It will never be reproductive, and so, according to Freud, it is perverse.

Third, I would call attention to the long history of a natural moral law tradition which has pointed out very well that man's and woman's sexual organs complement each other; one is made for the other; and only through heterosexual activity can reproduction occur. Even various forms of artificial fertilization require hetero-sexual activities, although depersonalized and immoral. The sexual power is oriented to reproduction at all levels of life. The fact that man can use his sexual power just for personal enjoyment to the positive exclusion of any possibility of reproduction is a sociological fact but still does not deny the natural, normative orientation of sexual activity towards reproduction. It is God, not the Pope, who has joined the unitive and procreative aspects of sexual intercourse.

I think it is worthwhile to note that the covenant theology of sex does not contradict the natural moral law tradition which has been biologically oriented. At times it is necessary to look at the physiology of man, for man is not just spirit and intentions but matter and physiology as well. I think it is an advantage of this covenant theology that it can still make use of the natural law tradition. The covenant theology does not exclude but rather takes into itself the values and many of the arguments of the natural moral law tradition. I consider it a higher-level explanation because it can answer more problems in a more completely human way, but it does not simply do away with the tradition of the past as somehow irrelevant.

Fourth, there is the Judeo-Christian tradition contained in the Scriptures condemning homosexuality. For many Christians and

Jews, this is the most powerful argument. However, I refrain from depending on it exclusively because any argument based on Scripture may be attacked by the simple method of interpretation. Now, everyone who knows anything about the interpretation of Sacred Scripture knows that Scripture must be interpreted within the proper contexts, and the most important context is the entirety of biblical and oral Tradition. There is utterly no doubt that the meaning of sexuality given throughout the entirety of Scripture and Tradition is that the sexual act is a marriage act between man and woman for the sake of family and children.

Nevertheless, proponents of various sexual deviations persist in trying to undermine the overall biblical teaching on sexuality by manipulating certain texts as is indicated further in Chapter 15. The Lord Jesus knew this would happen, and that is why He directly founded his living Church with the promised guidance of the Holy Spirit, and it is through His Church that we have the Sacred Scriptures. Thus, a Scripture passage really gets its teeth only from the use of it by the Church in its teaching. In this latter case we can rely on our faith that the Holy Spirit, the guiding author of Scripture, also guides the Church in its ordinary teaching as well as in its extraordinary solemn definitions whether by Pope and Council together or by the Pope alone.

In this light, two Vatican teachings take on crucial importance. In 1975, Pope Paul VI ordered the publication of the above-mentioned *Declaration on Certain Questions Concerning Sexual Ethics* which had this to say, among other things, about homosexual behavior:

> For according to the objective moral order, homosexual relations are acts which lack an essential and indispensable finality. In Sacred Scripture they are condemned as a serious depravity and even presented as the sad consequence of rejecting God. (See Rom 1:24-27; 1 Cor 6:10; 1 Tim 1:10.) This judgment of Scripture does not of course permit us to conclude that all those who suffer from this anomaly are personally responsible for it, but it does attest to the fact that homosexual acts are intrinsically disordered and can in no case be approved of (n.8).

In 1986, Pope John Paul II ordered the publication of the second document, *On the Pastoral Care of Homosexual Persons*[12] which responded to efforts by homosexual advocates to undermine the forceful witness of Sacred Scripture. Quoting Vatican II it noted:

> It is clear, therefore, that in the supremely wise arrangement of God, Sacred Tradition, Sacred Scripture, and the Magisterium of the Church are so connected and associated that one of them cannot stand without the

others. Working together, each in its own way under the action of the one Holy Spirit, they all contribute effectively to the salvation of souls (*Dei Verbum,* n.10).

The Vatican document noted that although there was "remarkable diversity" between the times of the Old Testament and New Testament condemnations of homosexual behavior,

There is nevertheless a clear consistency with the Scriptures themselves on the moral issue of homosexual behavior. The Church's doctrine regarding this issue is thus based, not on isolated phrases for facile theological argument, but on the solid foundation of a constant biblical testimony (n.5).

Regarding specific texts, the Vatican document notes the overall plan for sex in the Genesis creation accounts, and its being obscured by sin in Genesis 3. About the Sodom account in Genesis 19:1-11, it notes, "There can be no doubt of the moral judgment made there against homosexual relations. In Leviticus 18-22 and 20:13, . . . the author excludes from the People of God those who behave in a homosexual fashion" (n.6). In 1 Corinthians 6:9, St. Paul "lists those who behave in a homosexual fashion among those who shall not enter the kingdom of God" (n.6), and in Romans 1:18-32 "Paul is at a loss to find a clearer example of this [disharmony between God and his creatures] than homosexual relations. Finally 1 Timothy 1, in full continuity with the biblical position, singles out those who spread wrong doctrine and in v.10 explicitly names as sinners those who engage in homosexual acts" (n.6).

The teaching of the Catholic Church, based firmly on Sacred Scripture and Sacred Tradition makes it clear that homosexual acts are intrinsically evil. The covenant theology of sex finds this evil to be essentially the same as that of fornication and adultery—the acts fail completely to be in any way a marriage act, an act that at least implicitly renews the original commitment and self-giving love of the marriage covenant.

The teaching of the Church and the covenant theology of sex are confirmed in their condemnation of homosexual acts by the analysis of even some of the abusive use of ordinary language in referring to persons who practice homosexual behavior. In alphabetical order, bugger, fag, queer and sodomite are words commonly used to describe those who engage in homosexual acts. Unfortunately, these words are sometimes (and quite hypocritically) used by heterosexually immoral persons, who may be engaged in identical perversities, to ridicule chaste homosexual persons or even certain persons with no homosexual orientation whatsoever. In contrast, the self-labeling of themselves as "gay" by active homosexuals has practically eliminated that word from normal discourse. For example, someone writing in the last three decades of the twentieth century simply could not say about a fun-filled normal parish picnic that "a gay time was had by all" without being accused of, at best, a poor choice of words.

I believe that deep within the human heart there is a basic recognition that sex is meant to be a marriage act ordered toward the creation of family. While the Church—and most humane-minded people—have great toleration of occasional weakness, people generally come to have disgust for both the heterosexual and the homosexual who pursue sex for the sake of sex; and since homosexual acts are always non-marital and sterile, just sex for the sake of sex, Freud captured well the overwhelming recognition of mankind that such acts are always perverse. This disgust is reflected by the widespread—I suspect universal—use of pejorative words to describe active homosexuals.

3. Heterosexual Oral and Anal Intercourse

It is difficult to write about oral and anal intercourse. I suspect that some readers will not have known previously that people, especially married people, even did such things. Unfortunately, some people do.

When I wrote the forerunner to this book in late 1968, this particular perversity was, for the most part, written about only in manuals of moral theology. By 1989, it was being written about—and somewhat frequently—in the daily newspapers. These are, of course, the types of actions done also by active homosexuals and are equally evil when done by heterosexuals.

Some definitions and an important distinction need to be made. Fellatio refers to the contact of a woman's mouth and a man's penis; cunnilingus refers to the contact of his mouth or tongue and her vagina. If these activities are done strictly as foreplay, they can be called foreplay fellatio and foreplay cunnilingus; if they are carried to the point of orgasm apart from genital-genital intercourse, they can be called complete fellatio and complete cunnilingus. Genital-genital relations refers to normal sexual intercourse with ejaculation in the vagina.

Foreplay fellatio/cunnilingus is not condemned as foreplay to completed genital-genital marital relations if it is esthetically acceptable to both spouses. However, it must never be forced upon an unwilling spouse. A health factor must also be considered. The Herpes I virus (the cause of cold sores) can be transmitted in this way even though the transmitter may not be aware of any cold sores. The real danger of this is that Herpes I, as well as Herpes II, can become a vaginal infection; and it is possible, even though infrequent, to transmit it to a baby during a vaginal birth. As a physician told me, it used to be that if it was a mouth sore, it was Herpes I, and if it was genital, it was Herpes II. But with the increase in oral-genital contact, everything's mixed up today.

Also to be distinguished is a wife's orgasm either before or after her husband's ejaculation. If she experiences this as part of foreplay, there is no moral problem; if he assists her by way of manual-clitoral stimulation to achieve orgasm after his, there is not only not a moral problem, but it may be an act of marital virtue to assist her toward relief and full satisfaction. That is all considered to be part of the one moral act of marital relations.

However, bringing each other to orgasm completely apart from completed genital-genital intercourse is mutual masturbation and falls under the same condemnation as solitary masturbation.

Completed anal intercourse (i.e. with ejaculation) is condemned, and vaginal intercourse immediately after anal penetration (incomplete foreplay) would be so unsanitary that it is difficult to imagine any possibly moral use of anal copulation.

Thus from a moralist's perspective, the traditional moral question has to do with completed fellatio, completed cunnilingus, or anal sex in which either male or female orgasm occurs apart from completed genital-genital relations. Traditional Catholic theology on these matters has called them perversities and has been so universal that even those on the papal birth control commission who tried to justify using contraception felt obliged to condemn these forms of sexual activity. (More on this subject in Chapter 13, "A Critique . . . ".)

That is, the minority report of the papal birth control commission pointed out that the majority position was open to the practice of anal and oral copulation. The majority never really answered the objection in an adequate way but only with a gratuitous assertion that they condemned these forms of sexual activity and that, in these acts, neither the dignity of love nor the dignity of the spouses was preserved. This is basically an argument from their own authority and personal preferences; no reasons are given to explain on what grounds they based their condemnation.

I mentioned this one day to a priest who had subscribed to the contraception argument. His answer was quite frank: maybe we should just stop worrying about such things and say that within marriage "anything goes."

The brutal fact of the matter is that a theory of sex which is a *de facto* theory of personal intentionalism simply has no answer to either homosexual acts or anal/oral copulation. If the important criterion of the sexual act is the expression of "personal love" and this particular couple feels that they can best express their personal affective love, their willingness to give of each to the other through oral or anal copulation, on what basis can this behavior be condemned? On a radical personalist basis, is it not really true that "anything goes?" The couple are not consciously being selfish, they are not consciously exploiting each other, they are just being their naturally-loving personal selves, contributing to the widening experience and development of each other. If there were a taboo on oral and anal copulation, wouldn't this interfere with the natural spontaneity of sexual expression, an interference so criticized by some of the personalist advocates of contraception?

The covenant theology of sex has a strong personalist origin but escapes the weaknesses of radical personalism, i.e., *de facto* intentionalism, because it stresses the covenant of marriage. To be sure, husband and wife personally and freely will to enter the covenant of marriage, but it is a covenant of God's design, not theirs. In marriage they pledge a total self-giving love, and sexual intercourse is intended by God to symbolize that self-giving love.

More will be said about this in the next chapter dealing with birth control within marriage; for the present, it suffices to note that mutual masturbation and completed oral/anal copulation have no symbol of self-giving. They are acts of lust, not marital love, and it may be that Pope John Paul II had these and other unnatural forms of sex in mind when he warned against viewing one's spouse as an object of lust.[13]

Furthermore, since the covenant theology does not exclude but rather subsumes the natural moral law tradition, it can argue along the Freudian line that sexual behavior is perverse to the extent that it departs from reproduction in its aims and purposes. As a minimal interpretation of Freud, it is clear that he regards as perverse all mutual sex activity which is not at least mutually genital. I agree. The sex organs are made for each other; they are organs of reproduction as well as of marital love; to use them as pleasure organs while positively excluding the reproductive aspect through oral-anal copulation is a violation of the interpersonal order of the created covenant.

The Christian tradition and the covenant theology are supported by the analysis of ordinary language. Complete fellatio and cunnilingus are commonly not spoken of at all in a direct manner in ordinary discourse but are referred to as kinky sex, and, judging from things I have seen on television, there seems to be a widespread assumption that kinky sex is something a man doesn't do with his wife but with a prostitute. This assumption is reinforced by the folk-talk quoted by a famous baseball player upon his divorce, in which he put all the blame on himself: "What a man wants in a wife is a lady in the parlor, a gourmet in the kitchen, and a whore in the bedroom." The latter phrase puts in very ordinary language the traditional view of the wife who willingly goes along with kinky sex.

In all of the instances we have looked at, we have seen sexuality in action. In each instance, I have tried to show that there is a disassociation between sexuality and authentic human love. Because all of these actions go at times under the label of "making love," I have tried to show that in our ordinary language, mankind has traditionally distinguished between sexuality and love by assigning the negative-value, non-love words of rape, prostitution, fornication, pre-marital sex, adultery and kinky sex to these forms of sexual behavior. Homosexual behavior has traditionally been called perverse, and those acting it out have incurred a list of pejorative terms. It should be self-evident by this time that there is no intrinsic link in practice between sexual behavior and love and that this is both taught in Sacred Scripture and recognized in ordinary language.

3

Birth Control and the Marriage Covenant

Chapter 1 developed the covenant theology of sex; Chapter 2 applied that theology to non-marital sex, for the most part. This chapter applies the covenant theology of sex to birth control within marriage.

The questions this chapter seeks to answer are these: *Within marriage,* is there an **intrinsic** connection between sex and love? That is, within marriage, are sexual relations automatically or necessarily expressive of authentic married love? Or are there circumstances or conditions that must be fulfilled for sexual relations to be an authentic expression of married love according to God's order of creation? And if so, what are those conditions?

I believe that it takes only a moment's reflection to conclude that there is no automatic connection between sex and love even within marriage. In just a few pages, I will discuss marital rape whose reality makes it clear that sex is not automatically an expression of authentic love within marriage.

However, the basic concern of this book is marital contraception, and the basic argument of this chapter is that acts of marital contraception contradict the marriage covenant and are therefore immoral. For those who like to have things spelled out in a syllogism, the argument looks like this:

Major premise: All marital actions which contradict the marriage covenant are immoral.

Minor premise: Using unnatural forms of birth control within marriage contradicts the marriage covenant.

Conclusion: Therefore, using unnatural forms of birth control within marriage is immoral.

I am not going to argue further in support of the major premise. Such actions would include adultery and incest by married persons; they would also include non-sexual actions such as beating one's spouse. For the purposes of this chapter, I am assuming that the major premise is accepted as proved or as self-evident, at least to believing Christians. Thus, I will confine my efforts in this chapter to the issue of sexual acts within marriage which have the potential to renew or affirm the marriage covenant on the one hand, or contradict it on the other.

Marital Rape

While marital contraception is the primary subject of this chapter, I want to treat first of all the subject of marital rape.[1] The argument is identical in form to that dealing with marital contraception: just substitute "marital rape" for "unnatural forms of birth control" in the minor premise and conclusion in the above syllogism.

Pope Paul VI taught as follows in his encyclical *Humanae Vitae:*

"It is in fact justly observed that a conjugal act imposed upon one's partner without regard for his or her conditions and legitimate desires is not a true act of love, and therefore denies a requirement of the right moral order in the relations between husband and wife" (sentence 1, n.13).

Any discussion of the requirements and abuses of "the right moral order in the relations between husband and wife" must be carried on in the context of the teaching of two Pauls, St. Paul and Paul VI, for St. Paul wrote thusly:

"Now concerning the matters about which you wrote. It is well for a man not to touch a woman. But because of the temptation to immorality, each man should have his own wife and each woman her own husband. The husband should give to his wife her conjugal rights, and likewise the wife to her husband. For the wife does not rule over her own body, but the husband does; likewise the husband does not rule over his own body, but the wife does. Do not refuse one another except perhaps by agreement for a season, that you may devote yourselves to prayer; but then come together again, lest Satan tempt you through lack of self-control. I say this by way of concession, not of command. I wish that all were as I myself am. But each has his own special gift from God, one of one kind and one of another" (1 Cor 7:1-7).

Pope Paul VI was certainly aware of the above teaching which has played such a big part in Catholic teaching about marriage, but he was also aware that men and women are sinners and can and have abused sexual rights within marriage. He must also have been aware that this abuse was becoming so common that the term "marital rape" was being used to describe it.

The passage from 1 Corinthians 7 must also be taken in context. The Corinthian converts were appalled by their sinful past which was so bad that Corinth was reputed as the sin city of the Mediterranean. Now converted to Christ, they had written to ask if **all** sex was immoral, if even husbands and wives sinned by having sexual relations. One can easily imagine new converts having exaggerated ideas about marital purity and refusing to have anything to do with sex, thinking all sex was evil. Or one can imagine a spouse unilaterally deciding that even though marital sex wasn't evil, he or she would still abstain permanently as penance for past sins. It is in that context that this passage must be understood.

It must also be understood in the wider context of St. Paul's teaching in the same letter about love (chapter 13), and his condemnation of adultery and drunkenness (chapter 6:9-10), plus his teaching about sacrificial marital love in Ephesians 5:21-33.

In the proper context, there is absolutely nothing to suggest that St. Paul is teaching that a wife must submit to her husband if he is drunk, is physically or emotionally abusive, or if she is really sick. These would be the sorts of things that Pope Paul VI had in mind when teaching that forcing intercourse upon one's spouse "without regard for his or her conditions and legitimate desires is not a true act of love, and therefore denies a requirement of the moral order in the relations between husband and wife." In short, marital sex can at times rightly be called marital rape, and marital rape is immoral.

As an aside, it can be noted that St. Paul is clearly teaching that the relief of sexual tension is a legitimate reason for honest marital relations. Just as clearly, he teaches that one spouse may not unilaterally deny the other spouse's legitimate request for marital relations for insufficient or trivial reasons ("I don't want to get my hair messed up") or false spirituality ("I'm getting more spiritual so I'm not interested in having sex more than once a month"). I think we can also infer St. Paul would strongly condemn using sex as a bargaining chip to attain some goal completely unrelated to their marriage relationship ("So I can buy myself that new coat—which I really don't need").

The point of all this is that even within marriage sexual intercourse is not necessarily a morally good act. To be a morally good act, marital intercourse must fulfill certain objective criteria. If it fails to do so, as in the case of marital rape, it is "not a true act of love," it "denies a requirement of the right moral order," and it is therefore immoral.

If you grant that marital rape is wrong because of those reasons, then you must admit the possibility that other actions can also disfigure marital relations and make them objectively immoral, and that's precisely what's behind the meaning of the immediately following two sentences in *Humanae Vitae.*

Hence, one who reflects carefully must also recognize that an act of mutual love that prejudices the capacity to transmit life that God the Creator, according to particular laws, inserted therein, is in contradiction with the design constitutive of marriage, and with the will of the Author of life. Those who make use of this divine gift while destroying, even if only partially, its significance and its finality, act contrary to the nature of both man and woman and of their most intimate relationship, and therefore contradict also the plan of God and his will (sentences 2 and 3, n. 13).

The covenant theology of sex readily explains the evil of marital rape. To the extent that the sexual relations between husband and wife are a *de facto* denial of the love, care, tenderness, faith, hope, risk and self-denial of the marriage covenant, to that extent they are non-authentic and even invalid. Marital relations that are *opposed* to marital love are objectively sinful even though perhaps not defective from a biological point of view.

The analysis of ordinary language confirms the teaching of the Church and the covenant theology of sex. In fact, some radical feminists who seem farthest from the Church have been the most vocal in labeling abusive marital sex with the pejorative term "marital rape." Probably no other term connotes more clearly a complete disassociation between sex and love within marriage.

Marital Contraception

In applying the covenant theology of sex to the issue of birth control within marriage, I will follow this sequence or series of questions:

1. What makes a couple married?
2. What is the role of sex within marriage?
3. How is contraceptive behavior to be evaluated in terms of the marriage covenant?
4. How is modern natural family planning to be evaluated in

terms of the marriage covenant?

5. How does the covenant theology of sex correspond with the teaching of the Roman Catholic Church?

Lastly, I will address two questions that keep cropping up among those who accept the Christian teaching against unnatural forms of birth control:

6. Is natural family planning morally permissible or ought couples just let the babies come as they may?

7. Do couples have a contraceptive mentality if they use natural methods to limit their family in a selfish way?

By way of review, it is proper to reaffirm that the criterion for evaluating sexual activity is not just physical; it is not just spiritual or intentional; it is sacramental which means that the criterion is truly human. It entails that wonderful inseparable union of sign and reality, matter and spirit, interpersonal relations with each other and with the Creator, human self-determination and fulfillment of the order created by God. The criterion for evaluating sexual activity is the marriage covenant itself. Sexual activity which renews the marriage covenant is morally good; sexual activity which goes against or does not renew, at least implicitly, the marriage covenant is morally evil.

1. What makes a couple married?

A man and woman marry when they publicly promise to love each other without reservation as long as they both live. The term "love" here has nothing to do with great emotional feelings; it means caring love and fidelity even under the most trying circumstances, for better and for worse. In essence, the man and the woman make a total unreserved gift of self to each other for life, and that's what makes them husband and wife. To put it in biblical terms, they willingly enter God's covenant of marriage by making a permanent gift of self to each other.

The marriage of two Christians is the sacrament of matrimony because through baptism Christians are "marked" as belonging in a special way to Christ. Thus in Christian marriage there is the union of one Christ-bearer to another Christ-bearer. The words they utter are a sacrament, for though they are physical words they create a spiritual bond in Christ, a new relationship between this

54

man and this woman. As sacramental, the promises signify what God is accomplishing in uniting this couple.

The covenant relationship is not just of their own making. It has a God-given structure; it is a relationship co-created both by God and by the husband and wife. The man and woman must freely enter this relationship; they must make the God-intended relationship their own or there is no real covenant but just a meaningless and hypocritical ceremony. By the same token, they do not make their own unique covenant without reference to the structure intended by God. If, for example, they agreed in all sincerity that if they were to lose mutual love and affection for each other sometime in the future, they would feel free to find other mates, there simply would be no covenant of marriage. It might be a commonly accepted social custom, it might be more accurately called a state of respectable mistressing or fornication; it simply is not a marriage. God does not marry two people unless they want it; the two people cannot marry unless they are willing to enter into the relationship that God has intended.

• **The marriage covenant.** What does this covenant entail? The contraception controversy thus far has highlighted two aspects of the marriage covenant: the willingness to help each other to grow in love and the willingness to let love produce life—which in turn calls for more love from the married couple. I would like to draw attention again to the specific conditions under which the couple marry. They promise each other that they marry each other with all that is entailed in the marriage covenant **without reservation**: specifically—for richer and for poorer, in sickness and in health, for better and for worse as long as they are both still living. Needless to say, both persons are probably hoping that everything works out for better, healthier and richer. Nevertheless, it is their willingness to give of each other without serious reservation that makes the marriage. It is their willingness to accept each other, to remain faithful to each other, and to be still loving to the other under difficult and even disastrous circumstances, and to do this until they are separated by death that makes their union a marriage. It is these qualities that make their union an authentic permanent love-union and not just a socially and economically acceptable liaison or long-term affair.

• **The purpose and purposes of marriage.** The overriding

purpose of marriage is the mutual holiness of husband and wife. In effect, they covenant to help each other on the path that leads to salvation. Thus, in *Gaudium et Spes,* Vatican II labels its introductory section on marriage "The Sanctity of Marriage and the Family" (n.48). Of course, this can be said of all human relationships: in every relationship, each person should help the other to get to heaven. But within marriage and the family, there are unique relationships that arise from the marriage covenant and from birth, and thus the purpose of helping each other to possess the salvation won by Jesus Christ takes on an overriding importance for husband and wife in their relationships with each other and with their children.

Within the context of growth in holiness, the Second Vatican Council taught about two other purposes of marriage—

1) the development of their married love and

2) the procreation and education of children.

1) Interestingly, in its section titled "Conjugal Love" (n.49) the Vatican II document only **indirectly** states that the development of marital love is one of the purposes of marriage. Perhaps this is due to the ease with which such a statement can be misunderstood in an age in which the word "love" has no single meaning. Thus, section 49 of *Gaudium at Spes* teaches this purpose of marriage only indirectly:

> The biblical Word of God several times urges the betrothed and the married to nourish and develop their wedlock by pure conjugal love and undivided affection.

> This love is an eminently human one since it is directed from one person to another through an affection of the will.

> Such love, merging the human with the divine, leads the spouses to a free and mutual gift of themselves . . . Such love pervades the whole of their lives. Indeed, by its generous activity it grows better and grows greater. Therefore it far excels mere erotic inclination, which, selfishly pursued, soon enough fades wretchedly away.

> This love is uniquely expressed and perfected through the marital act. The actions within marriage by which the couple are united intimately and chastely are noble and worthy ones. Expressed in a manner which is truly human, these actions signify and promote that mutual self-giving by which spouses enrich each other with a joyful and a thankful will.

2) By contrast, section 50, titled "The Fruitfulness of Marriage" **directly** teaches the procreative purpose of marriage.

Marriage and conjugal love are by their nature ordained toward the begetting and educating of children. Children are really the supreme gift of marriage and contribute very substantially to the welfare of their parents.

Hence, while not making the other purposes of matrimony of less account, the true practice of conjugal love, and the whole meaning of the family life which results from it have this aim: that the couple be ready with stout hearts to cooperate with the love of the Creator and the Savior, who through them will enlarge and enrich his own family day by day.

Parents should regard as their proper mission the task of transmitting human life and educating those to whom it has been transmitted.

Then, after reviewing various factors that enter into the size-of-family decision and praising in a special way those parents who "with a gallant heart undertake to bring up suitably even a relatively large family," section 50 concludes with a paragraph that comes the closest of the entire document to teaching directly the "mutual love" purpose of marriage—and even then it is in the context of affirming indissolubility in the face of infertility:

Marriage to be sure is not instituted solely for procreation. Rather, its very nature as an unbreakable compact between persons, and the welfare of the children, both demand that the mutual love of the spouses, too, be embodied in a rightly ordered manner, that it grow and ripen. Therefore, marriage persists as a whole manner and communion of life, and maintains its value and indissolubility, even when offspring are lacking— despite, rather often, the very intense desire of the couple.

2. What is the role of sex within marriage?

The role of sex within marriage is to foster the purposes of marriage itself—the development of the marriage bond and the procreation and education of children. It is to be a symbol of the mutual commitment of the spouses, a renewal of their marriage covenant, at least implicitly.

Because they have now entered into a marriage relationship, a mutual personal commitment of lifelong love without reservation, the married couple are now free to express that union sacramentally in the sexual union. The sex-union now becomes a physical way of expressing their marriage covenant. The sex-union now says, "We are together; we are committed to each other; we are to love each other and we hope we **do** love each other without reservation, for better and for worse, whatever that may entail. The two-in-one-flesh-ness of our physical intimacy is a symbol of the two-become-one-ness of the permanent commitment we have made in marriage. Amen."

The sexual union under these circumstances is morally good because it is the renewal of the marriage covenant; it has become something more than physical; it has become sacramental, an outward expression of the interpersonal and God-made covenant of marriage.

3. How is contraceptive behavior to be evaluated in terms of the marriage covenant?

In making the commitment of marriage, the couple give themselves to each other for better and for worse without reservation. Sexual intercourse becomes the symbol of that initial unreserved gift of self to the other, a gift that must be carried out in the day to day living of their marriage. However, **the essence of contraceptive behavior* is that it is sex with serious reservation.** The symbol of total self-giving is contradicted by contraception, and, *de facto,* there is lacking the unreserved gift of self.

Because it contradicts the marriage covenant, marital contraception must be evaluated as evil.

---

*Contraceptive behavior, biologically speaking, is designed to achieve male ejaculation and/or female orgasm in such a way that sperm and ova are prevented from arriving at their natural union. Such behavior includes the use of condoms, diaphragms, foams, and any other physical or chemical barriers; it includes birth control drugs (the "Pill" and implants) and devices (the intrauterine device—IUD) which may accomplish their birth control purposes in several ways including early abortion; and it also includes behaviors such as withdrawal and ejaculation outside the vagina, masturbation whether mutual or solitary, completed fellatio or completed cunnilingus or anal copulation. It also includes intercourse which has been preceded by deliberate sterilization such as vasectomy, tubal ligation, or a hysterectomy done for birth control purposes. See chapter 9, "Practical Pastoral Policies," which discusses the possible moral licitness of post-sterilization marital relations during the infertile times. Thus, morally speaking, all contraceptive behavior is contrary to the divinely intended meaning of sexual intercourse as the complete marital embrace not closed to the transmission of life.

An analysis from the perspective of intentions yields the same conclusions. Any analysis of the reasons put forth for the practice of contraception find them summarized as fear of consequences of ill health, fear of economic disadvantages, or fear of a number of things which can be called worse rather than better. Contraception is both a sign of refusal to run the risk of such consequences of the marital act and the means of positively separating the unitive and procreative aspects of that marital act. By their use of contraception, a married couple do not renew the marriage covenant in their marital relations. They positively exclude in such relations all of the trust elements of the marriage covenant, those elements which require that they put their faith and their life-together in the hands of God. Such anti-covenant sex is invalid as a renewal of their marriage covenant.

Anyone who knows anything about the Catholic theology of marriage would call "invalid and therefore immoral" a marriage in which the man and woman said "We take each other for better and for richer and for health BUT NOT in sickness or poverty or for worse." The same evaluation has to be made about marital relations marred by contraceptive behavior because sex is supposed to be a symbol of the honest and full marriage commitment, a renewal, at least implicitly, of a true marriage covenant.

A third way of stating the argument is from the perspective of honesty. Adultery and fornication are intrinsically dishonest. In these sins, the couple take an act intended to be a symbol of married love and distort it. Whatever they want to call it, they know it is not a sign of permanent committed love.

Contraceptive behavior makes marital relations intrinsically dishonest. The couple may pretend their act is a symbol of self-giving love, but in their inner hearts, if they think about it, they know that the essence of their behavior is a denial of the unreserved gift of self that made them married. Such intrinsically dishonest behavior is objectively immoral.

4. How is modern natural family planning to be evaluated in terms of the marriage covenant?

By "modern natural family planning" (NFP) I mean the effort to achieve or avoid pregnancy through an informed awareness of the fertile and infertile times of the wife's fertility-menstrual cycles. There's no moral question about using NFP to achieve pregnancy, but the statement is sometimes made that couples using NFP are acting for the same purposes as couples using contraceptive behaviors and that therefore the two behaviors are morally the same. Some use this line of argument to justify contraception; others use it to condemn the use of NFP.

Pope Paul VI specifically addressed this question in *Humanae Vitae:*

If then, there are serious motives for spacing births, motives deriving from the physical or psychological condition of husband or wife, or from external circumstances, the Church teaches that it is then permissible to take into account the natural rhythms immanent in the generative functions and to make use of marriage during the infertile times only, and in this way to regulate births without offending the moral principles that we have just recalled.

The Church is consistent when she considers recourse to the infertile times to be permissible, while condemning as being always wrong the use of means directly contrary to fertilization, even if such use is inspired by reasons that can appear upright and serious. In reality, there is an essential difference between the two cases. In the first case, the husband and wife legitimately avail themselves of a natural condition; in the second case, they impede the working of natural processes. It is true that in both cases the married couples agree in positively willing to avoid children for plausible reasons, seeking to be certain that offspring will not result; but it is likewise true that only in the first case do they prove able to abstain from the use of marriage during the fertile times, when for proper motives procreation is not desirable, then making use of it during the infertile times to manifest affection and to safeguard mutual fidelity. By so doing, they give proof of a love that is truly and fully virtuous (n.16).

Pope John Paul II has also responded in *Familiaris Consortio* to the suggestion that there is no real moral difference between using contraception and using natural family planning, as follows. (A more complete text in found in Chapter 16.)

Theological reflection is able to perceive and is called to study further the difference, both anthropological and moral, between contraception and recourse to the rhythm of the cycle: it is a difference which is much wider and deeper than is usually thought, one which involves in the final analysis two irreconcilable concepts of the human person and of human sexuality (n.32).

For clarity, two points should be noted. First of all, **the end does not homogenize the means**; that is, the same end or purpose does not make morally the same all the various means to achieve that goal. Everyone recognizes this when it comes to comparing the means to arrive at the goal of owning a nice house. No serious person would say that the same goal would make selling illegal drugs and working hard as a plumber morally the same just because both were aimed at buying a nice house. The same applies to family spacing or limitation. Assuming there is a sufficiently serious reason for such family planning, the common goal does not render morally the same the evil action of marital contraception and the morally indifferent practice of periodic abstinence. Other illustrative examples of the principle are provided in the section of Chapter 13 dealing with "The Principle of the Total Human Act."

Secondly, there is a huge difference—can we call it an infinite difference?—between DOING and NOT DOING. The couple who engage in contraceptive behavior DO certain things that bring about ejaculation/orgasm and *are* acting to prevent the natural possibility of co-creating a new human person and/or allowing that person to develop.

Such contraceptive action can be either simultaneous with intercourse (as with barrier contraceptives) or actions taken before intercourse (as in the case of physical or chemical sterilization) or actions taken after intercourse (as with a douche). Morally, all such actions are contraceptive (or abortifacient), and all such actions are condemned by *Humanae Vitae* (n.14).

On the other hand, the couple using NFP to avoid pregnancy, simply are NOT DOING intercourse during the fertile time. When they DO intercourse, they do NOT ACT to prevent the natural consequences of their mutual actions. They have a firmly based hope that their actions will not bring them the responsibilities of another child to care for, but they are NOT acting to prevent their intercourse from co-creating a child. Their intercourse remains symbolic of their marriage covenant for they have done nothing to act against it. Believing that they have a sufficiently serious reason not to become pregnant at this time, they have simply chosen not to affirm their covenant in sexual intercourse during the naturally fertile time.

The following comparison between pre-marital considerations and natural family planning may make this difference more clear.

• **Pre marital considerations.** In preparing for marriage, the love of most men and women is tempered or guided by some practicality and even fear. The typical man and woman will avoid selecting a mate who is ill. This may be completely unconscious, for the healthy person's dating pattern may automatically preclude getting to know an unhealthy person very well. The real test would come only if one party to a future marriage were suddenly stricken with a debilitating life-long disease. For example, what if the prospective groom suffered an accident and head injuries that would make it impossible for him ever to earn a living? Or what if the prospective bride were struck with a crippling disease that would not only make it impossible for her to care for children but even precluded the possibility of sexual relations? Would the remaining healthy prospective bride or groom be unloving not to enter marriage with the one who had met such a disaster? I, for one, could not judge non-marriage to be a sign of non-love in this case. I feel that in such heart-rending cases greater love may be shown by tender care and solicitude given without the bond of marriage than by entering a whole way of life under such circumstances. At any rate, before marriage, neither party has pledged life-long fidelity to the other, and both the one stricken and the one left healthy are free to break off the wedding plans.

Likewise, most people entering marriage give some attention to the economics of life together. "Will I be able to support a family without finishing my education? . . . Will I ever be able to support her with her background of having had everything she ever wanted and never having had to work for a cent? . . . Will he be able to support me and our children or will I have to be working all our married life? . . . Tom is studying to be a doctor, Jim wants to teach in high school. Richard is the most fun of all to be with but he lives only for today— has no ambition at all." I am not suggesting that many people make marital decisions based just on dollars and cents; I do think that consciously or unconsciously such matters do influence the marital selection process to some degree in a great number of cases. Finally, I think it is fair to say that the whole selection process is based on the hopes of maximizing the "for better" and minimizing the risk of "for worse" in marriage. That people do this is not unloving; it is to recognize that in marriage the couple will want as many things in their favor as possible, that love is more than mutual attraction to each other's face and figure. I think it is fair to say that most people do try to minimize the risk through various selection techniques before they enter into marriage.

Furthermore, many couples and individuals, recognizing the difficulties of married life, try to reduce the risks not only through the selection process but also by postponement of marriage until they are able to accept the full responsibilities of marriage. This is not being inhuman or cold and calculating although it does involve the destruction of marriage seen as an idol to be worshipped or as the panacea of everyone's personal problems. It is simply the recognition that the covenant of marriage involves far more than the expresson of affective love and doing things together. It involves a recognition that it is sometimes good and even necessary to postpone the full union of the marital embrace in order to secure some of the other goods associated with responsible marriage. Couples such as these try to minimize the risks in marriage in a responsible way without negating in any way the risk inherent in the faith commitment of marriage itself. Having attempted to be prudent in their planning and timing, they still enter into marriage knowing that the best laid plans of men often go astray and that their commitment is not based on their plans but exists rather in spite of the fact that their plans and hopes may fail.

Some couples may find that their socio-economic-educational backgrounds make it possible to eliminate almost completely the external risks to which any marriage is liable. Others may not even care about such matters; or if they do, they are unable to do as much as they would like about them. I would be the last one in the world to say that the marriage of a young couple who marry without any savings, income, education or job prospects but only a strong love for each other is any more—(or any less)—of a valid marriage than that of the couple which has such factors as material advantages. The point is that when the people of either type of couple marry, they do so without reservation and recognize that any plans are subordinate to their marriage covenant.

To attempt to reduce the risks of marriage before entering into it is one thing. It would be something of an entirely different nature if the couple together (or either one separately) were to exclude positively the risk itself of marriage. For example, if a couple before marriage agreed that in the case of a crippling or debilitating sickness after marriage they would be "free agents" once again, or if they agreed to stick together as long as everything was working out satisfactorily but that they would be free agents once again if the union didn't work out—such a couple simply wouldn't be married no matter how grandiose the ceremony even if it were presided over by the Pope himself. To the outside world, it may look like a marriage but it is not; it is only an agreement to co-habitate as long as the sun is shining, the roses are blooming, and the jasmine is filling the bedroom with perfume.

• **Natural family planning.** By comparison, the couple who practice NFP are like the couple who attempt to reduce the external risks of marriage by the postponement of a marriage date until various conditions are more satisfactory. The couple practicing periodic continence are likewise trying to reduce the risk of the problems that they see associated with a pregnancy at this time by postponing the full sexual union as an expression of their love. They do not love each other less during the time of continence—any more so than they loved each other less during a chaste courtship. During the time of periodic continence they will have to show affection and love for each other in a manner akin to their chaste behavior before marriage. When they do choose to express their love and affection in the marital sex-union, they are hopeful that the consequences will be the same as they hoped for in their initial marriage covenant "for richer, in health, for better." They are hopeful that a pregnancy which they think will bring conditions of "for poorer, in sickness, for worse" will not occur. Nevertheless, by the fact that they are still only hopeful and have not positively excluded the possibility of pregnancy, they still enter into a valid renewal of their original marriage covenant. There is still the risk of faith, the implicit affirmation of covenant love, the trust of putting their lives in the hands of the Father-Creator.

In summary, what renders a "marriage" null and void is not prior planning but the absolutizing of the elements of "for better" to the positive exclusion of those elements considered to be "for worse." Similarly, what renders the marriage act invalid and therefore immoral is not the planning of when to have children and how many but rather the absolutizing of those plans through recourse to contraceptive behaviors, the effort to positively exclude the possibility of "for worse" from the marital embrace.

Both the original covenant and the sacramental renewal of it may be postponed. However, once the respective actions are no longer postponed but are realized, then the couple must not close their actions to the consequences that may follow.

5. How does the covenant theology of sex correspond with the teaching of the Roman Catholic Church?

The Catholic Church has not adopted any particular theology of sexuality as its own, not even the "theology of the body" developed by Pope John Paul II. The actual teaching of the Church regarding sexuality can be summarized in a few statements, just as the basics

of the natural moral law are summarized in the Ten Commandments. Such a summary would look something like this:

1. Husbands, love and respect your wives as Christ loved the
Church and gave himself up for her.

2. Wives, love and be subject to your husbands as the Church
is subject to the Lord.

3. If you marry, thou shalt marry for life.

4. If you marry, thou shalt be generous in having children in
accordance with your circumstances.

5. Thou shalt educate thy children in the way of the Lord.

6. Thou shalt not commit adultery.

7. Thou shalt not divorce and remarry.

8. Thou shalt not fornicate.

9. Thou shalt not commit homosexual acts.

10. Thou shalt not close the marriage act to the transmission of
life.

11. Thou shalt not seek venereal pleasure outside of marriage.

12. Thou shalt not seek orgasm outside the marriage act.

13. Thou shalt not look at others with lustful intention.

14. Thou shalt not tempt others to lust after you through dress,
word or action.

While the contents of this book have not dealt with each of these
points, the covenant theology of sex supports the entirety of Catholic
teaching regarding sexuality.

If I understand correctly the "theology of the body" developed by
Pope John Paul II, the covenant theology of sex is very similar. The
starting points are different. The theology of the body starts with
an analysis of the human body, the meaning inherent in the physical
act of sexual intercourse, and it concludes that sexual relations are
a nuptial act. The covenant theology of sex starts with the observation that Sacred Scripture and even other sources regard sexual
relations as having their full and proper meaning only within
marriage. Then it analyzes what makes a couple married and
concludes that sexual intercourse is intended by God to be a true

marriage act, a renewal of the original marriage covenant.

From that point on, it appears to me that the application of the "theology of the body" and the covenant theology of sex would be identical. However, I leave it to scholars who are interested in both approaches to determine such likenesses or any dissimilarities.

The phrasing of the covenant theology of sex is advantageous for instruction: "Sexual intercourse is intended by God to be a renewal of the marriage covenant, at least implicitly." Almost every couple is capable of understanding that God intends that 1) sex is supposed to be a marriage act and 2) that it's supposed to reflect their original "for better or for worse" marriage commitment, and 3) that their sexual relations should never be opposed to their original marital vows.

6. Is natural family planning morally permissible or ought couples just let the babies come as they may?

It may seem to some readers that this is a purely academic question but not a real one. Writing this in 1990, I wish to assure readers that at this point in history it is still a very real question. In the past year, I can recall receiving at least four letters telling me that the writers would no longer support the Couple to Couple League for natural family planning because they had decided to let the babies come according to God's providence. In 1985 a Protestant writer condemned the whole notion of family planning and placed NFP in the same category as contraception. And just a few days before writing this, I received a four-page single-spaced typewritten letter from a Catholic gentleman trying to prove that Catholic teaching which allows natural family planning is erroneous.

I call these people the **providentialists,** and while their number may be small, especially when compared with the vast number of contraceptionists, they are sincere, and they illustrate that the actual teaching of the Roman Catholic Church is truly the **via media,** the middle way.

The providentialists have a point. Sacred Scripture encourages married couples to have children. The "first commandment" of the Bible is still in effect: "Be fruitful and multiply, and fill the earth and subdue it" (Gen 1:28). Toward the end of the New Testament we read: "Woman will be saved through bearing children, if she continues in faith and love and holiness, with modesty"(1 Tim 2:15). Thus it is no exaggeration to say that from front to back, the Bible calls for married couples to have children.

66

Second, for centuries Catholic theology taught that the primary purpose of marriage was the procreation and education of children, and that the development of the unitive aspects of marriage was secondary. Again, certain quotations from writers of the past, even saints, make it appear that they forgot St. Paul's candid acceptance of marital relations for relief of sexual tension; at first glance their statements appear to label as venially sinful any marital intercourse not consciously seeking pregnancy.*

Third, as we have seen, even the teaching of Vatican II, though avoiding the primary-secondary terminology, laid a much heavier emphasis on the procreative dimension than on the unitive aspects of marriage and marital intercourse (*Gaudium et Spes* 47-53, especially n.50).

On the other hand, there is a reality known as Christian prudence. It is not the same as worldly prudence which calculates everything according to materialistic standards of money, health, and psycho-physical well-being. Christian prudence does not ignore any of these needs and realities, but it keeps them in place; it remembers that life is lived in the shadow of the cross on which the Savior of the world hung and died.

Catholic teaching rejects both the notion that human reason is totally depraved because of Original Sin and the opposite notion that my every thought is what God wants it to be. Rather, while recognizing our weaknesses and our tendencies to rationalize whatever seems convenient or pleasurable, it holds that under the influence of divine grace and aided by the teaching of the Church, we can use human reason to make right decisions. To repeat, there is a reality known as truly Christian prudence.

Thus, from the beginning of modern papal teaching on birth control, the Church has recognized the licitness of using natural family planning in the face of serious reasons to avoid pregnancy. Such teaching begins with *Casti Connubii,* the encyclical of Pope Pius XI which responded to the break away from the Christian

---

* Such quotations must be taken in context. First of all, in antiquity, the only way known to avoid pregnancy was either total abstinence or immoral behavior such as Onanism, including barrier methods. So any moral discourse about sexual intercourse had to emphasize the procreative aspect. Second, such quotations reflect the antiquity of the birth control issue. And lastly, individual quotations, even from saints, do not constitute the full teaching of the Roman Catholic Church.

Tradition by the Church of England in 1930.

Nor are those considered as acting against nature who in the married state use their right in the proper manner, although on account of natural reasons either of time or of certain defects, new life cannot be brought forth. For in matrimony as well as in the use of matrimonial rights there are also secondary ends, such as mutual aid, the cultivating of mutual love, and the quieting of concupiscence which husband and wife are not forbidden to consider so long as they are subordinated to the primary end and so long as the intrinsic nature of the act is preserved (Section IV, para.7).

Note the phrase: "although on account of natural reasons either of time or of certain defects . . . " The most obvious meanings of this are the time past menopause, the times of pregnancy and postpartum infertility, and the defects of female or male involuntary sterility. The physiological discoveries about the time of ovulation which are the bases for natural family planning occurred just a few years before 1930, and the formulation of the first form of natural family planning called "rhythm" or "calendar rhythm" was even closer to 1930. Since, Pius XI did not use the term "rhythms of fertility" used by Paul VI in *Humanae Vitae* (n.11), it is sometimes questioned whether Pius XI was approving of systematic recourse to the infertile times to avoid pregnancy when he wrote this.

However, three things support the position that natural family planning is explicitly accepted by *Casti Connubii*. First of all, there had been medical speculation about an infertile time of the cycle since 1840, and this had raised questions about having relations only during the infertile time to avoid pregnancy. The questions reached the Vatican, and the Vatican response in 1880 allowed the moral principle of periodic abstinence. Thus, despite the inaccuracy of the medical speculations (they guessed the infertile time was about mid-cycle, actually the most fertile time), the Vatican had approved the principle of natural family planning 50 years before it became a practical possibility, and this background was certainly known to Pope Pius XI. Second, the Vatican is a great listening post. It is almost unthinkable that word about the new discoveries in Austria and Japan had not reached Rome, the papal advisors, and the Pope. Third, as calendar rhythm became well known in the 1930s, the Pope never said anything against it.

On 19 October 1951 Pope Pius XII reaffirmed the validity of using natural family planning to avoid pregnancy in an address to Italian midwives, and the Second Vatican Council explicitly recognized the role of Christian prudence in making decisions about family size *(Gaudium et Spes,* n.50; see chapter 16 for full documentation).

Gaudium et Spes was dated 7 December 1965, and approximately two and one-half years later, 25 July 1968, Pope Paul VI issued *Humanae Vitae,* his definitive reaffirmation of the traditional teaching against marital contraception. As has already been noted, he explicitly allowed natural family planning.

Pope John Paul II has made teaching against marital contraception the primary teaching effort of the first ten years of his pontificate, 1978-1988. He has also done more to promote the knowledge of natural family planning than any previous Pope.

In his teaching document, *Familiaris Consortio,* the Pope contrasts recourse to natural family planning with contraception. Contraceptive couples

> act as "arbiters" of the divine plan and they "manipulate" and degrade human sexuality—and with it themselves and married partners—by altering its value of "total" self-giving. Thus the innate language that expresses the total reciprocal self-giving of husband and wife is overlaid, through contraception, by an objectively contradictory language, namely, that of not giving oneself totally to the other (n.32).

The couple who use NFP act in an entirely different way.

> When, instead, by means of recourse to periods of infertility, the couple respect the inseparable connection between the unitive and procreative meanings of human sexuality, they are acting as "ministers" of God's plan and they "benefit from" their sexuality according to the original dynamism of "total" self-giving without manipulation or alteration (n.32).

The Holy Father then goes on to note that the difference between using contraception and natural family planning "is much wider and deeper than is usually thought, one which involves in the final analysis two irreconcilable concepts of the human person and of human sexuality" (n.32).

Having reaffirmed the traditional teaching, John Paul II talks about the help the Church provides for couples experiencing difficulties. In addition to the necessary spiritual virtues and the sacraments he notes that

> the necessary conditions [for understanding and living the moral teaching] also include knowledge of the bodily aspect and the body's rhythms of fertility. Accordingly, **every effort must be made to render**

such knowledge accessible to all married people and also to young adults before marriage, through clear, timely and serious instruction and education given by married couples, doctors and experts (emphasis added).

Thoroughly aware that knowledge is not virtue, he continues:

Knowledge must then lead to education in self-control: hence the absolute necessity for the virtue of chastity and for permanent education in it (n.33).

Furthermore the Church has to help.

With regard to the question of lawful birth regulation, the ecclesial community at the present time must take on the task of instilling conviction and offering practical help to those who wish to live out their parenthood in a truly responsible way . . . This implies a broader, more decisive and more systematic effort to make the natural methods of regulating fertility known, respected and applied (n.35).

This is not the place to provide a complete compendium of all that Pope John Paul II has said about natural family planning. The above statements ranging from Pope Pius XI in 1930 to John Paul II provide ample evidence that the Roman Catholic Church condemns using unnatural means of birth control and accepts the use of natural family planning when a couple has serious reason to avoid pregnancy. It urges that **all** couples should **learn** NFP so they can use the information if and when they need it.

7. Do couples have a contraceptive mentality if they use natural methods to limit their family in a selfish way?

In my opinion, no. That's a very limited response to a very limited question, and I will re-phrase the question below. However, I think it is wrong and demeaning to speak of couples who use NFP in a selfish way as having a contraceptive mentality.

Note that "contraceptive mentality" is ambiguous; it means different things to different people. I think the Pope deliberately avoided that phrase when he warned against using NFP to fulfill a "decision to be closed to life which would be substantially the same as that which inspires the decision to use contraceptives."[2] (More on that below.)

Secondly, there's an old Latin saying, "agere sequitur esse"—

"action follows being." In the current context, I interpret it to mean that if you have a contraceptive mentality, you're going to engage in contraceptive behavior. Couples who practice chaste natural family planning for selfish reasons may be sinning against the purposes of marriage or even justice, but they are not committing the sin of engaging in contraceptive behavior. Therefore they do not have a contraceptive mentality.

In saying this, I am trying to keep a narrow meaning for the terms "contraception," and "contraceptive mentality." In my opinion "contraception" should be limited to physiologically contraceptive behaviors.

In this, I grant that there may be many who do not personally use contraceptives who still have a true contraceptive mentality. They may be so anti-baby and anti-people that they've never married or engaged in heterosexual relations, but they expect or even demand that those who do have sex with the opposite sex use contraception. I.e., if they had normal sex, they would put their mentality into action and use contraceptives or abortifacients.

If we start labeling non-physical actions such as the intention not to have babies by not having sexual relations a "contraceptive mentality," I think a necessary focus or sharpness is lost. For example, what if a single person stays unmarried and chaste because he or she fears the prospect of raising children? Or what if priestly celibacy were optional, say after five years of celibate priestly service, and a particular priest decided to remain celibate for fear of raising children? That is, what if his experience with the problems of families convinced him to remain celibate, in which case his decision would be based less on pure devotion to the Lord and more on a fear of taking on the responsibilities of family life? Should such a person be considered to have a contraceptive mentality? I think not. To prevent the application of the term "contraceptive mentality" to those who are unmarried and whose behavior, including their thinking, is chaste, I think it is necessary to limit the term to those who engage—or would engage—in contraceptive behavior to prevent their sexual actions from causing pregnancy.

The question about the proper or improper use of NFP needs to be asked in a different way. "Can couples use natural family planning wrongly?"

Yes. I cannot think of any gift of God which adults are not capable of using wrongly. Certainly that's true of sex itself, and just as certainly it must be true about NFP.

The most obvious wrongful use of NFP would be its use to avoid having any children whatsoever unless there is an extremely serious reason. The Catholic theologian or writer cannot safely ignore the 1948 teaching of Pope Pius XII that it could be morally permissible to use NFP to avoid having children for the entire duration of the marriage in the face of a most serious reason. However, the emphasis here would have to be on having a most serious reason, something such as the wife's life being truly threatened by pregnancy.

If a newlywed couple intended to use NFP to avoid all children throughout their marriage for less than a most serious reason, it is possible their marriage would be null and void, for they would appear to be acting against one of the root purposes of marriage— the procreation and education of children.

Another wrongful use of NFP would be its use to limit the family size very severely for no good reason whatsoever—just convenience.

As you move from the very obvious misuse of NFP, it becomes impossible to make judgments without being judgmental. However, several principles can be enunciated.

1) Christian married couples are called to be generous in the service of life. That is simply the whole tenor of the biblical-historical tradition on marriage.

2) Christian married couples are called to trust God, to trust that if they are generous, He truly will provide. In my opinion, such trust is one of the most difficult aspects of being Christian in the age of technology.

3) The procreative purpose of marriage is not satisfied just by having babies; the procreative purpose is always stated as the "procreation and education of children."

Education means primarily bringing up your children in the way of the Lord so that they can have their hearts and minds focused on the great truth of life that God made them to know, love and serve Him in this life in order to be with Him for all eternity in the next life. Of course, education today also includes the normal secular subjects as well as religion, but no couple should feel obliged to limit the size of their family so that they will be assured of being able to afford to put all their children through college. How unhappy have become so many parents who did so, only to have their children not want a college education or simply waste everybody's time and money in acquiring one!

72

I want to conclude this chapter with several quotations. We have already seen part of the first one from Vatican II.

They [the parents] will thoughtfully take into account both their own welfare and that of their children, those already born and those which may be foreseen. For this accounting they will reckon with both the material and the spiritual conditions of the times as well as of their state in life. Finally, they will consult the interests of the family group, of temporal society, and of the Church herself.

Thus, trusting in divine Providence and refining the spirit of sacrifice, married Christians glorify the Creator and strive toward fulfillment in Christ when, with a generous human and Christian sense of responsibility, they acquit themselves of the duty to procreate. Among the couples who fulfill their God-given task in this way, those merit special mention who with wise and common deliberation, and with a gallant heart, undertake to bring up suitably even a relatively large family (*Gaudium et Spes,* n.50).

The second quotation comes from the homily given by Pope John Paul II at Mass on the Washington Mall in his first visit to the United States on 7 October 1979, and I call particular attention to the next-to-last paragraph in the following quotation.

Human life is precious because it is the gift of a God whose love is infinite; and when God gives life, it is for ever. Life is also precious because it is the expression and the fruit of love. This is why life should spring up within the setting of marriage, and why marriage and the parents' love for one another should be marked by generosity in self-giving. The great danger for family life, in the midst of any society whose idols are pleasure, comfort and independence, lies in the fact that people close their hearts and become selfish. The fear of making permanent commitments can change the mutual love of husband and wife into two loves of self—two loves existing side by side, until they end in separation.

In the sacrament of marriage, a man and a woman—who at Baptism became members of Christ and hence have the duty of manifesting Christ's attitudes in their lives—are assured of the help they need to develop their love in a faithful and indissoluble union, and to respond with generosity to the gift of parenthood. As the Second Vatican Council declared: Through this sacrament, Christ himself becomes present in the life of the married couple and accompanies them, so that they may love each other and their children, just as Christ loved his Church by giving himself up for her (cf. *Gaudium et Spes,* 48; cf. Eph 5:25).

In order that Christian marriage may favor the total good and development of the married couple, it must be inspired by the Gospel, and thus be open to new life—new life to be given and accepted generously. The couple is also called to create a family atmosphere in which children can be happy, and lead full and worthy human and Christian lives.

To maintain a joyful family requires much from both the parents and the children. Each member of the family has to become, in a special way, the servant of the others and share their burdens (cf. Gal 6:2; Phil 2:2). Each one must show concern, not only for his or her own life, but also for the lives of the other members of the family: their needs, their hopes, their ideals.

Decisions about the number of children and the sacrifices to be made for them must not be taken only with a view to adding to comfort and preserving a peaceful existence. Reflecting upon this matter before God, with the graces drawn from the Sacrament, and guided by the teaching of the Church, parents will remind themselves that it is certainly less serious to deny their children certain comforts or material advantages than to deprive them of the presence of brothers and sisters, who could help them to grow in humanity and to realize the beauty of life at all its ages and in all its variety.

If parents fully realized the demands and the opportunities that this great sacrament brings, they could not fail to join in Mary's hymn to the author of life—to God—who has made them his chosen fellow-workers.

On 14 December 1990, Pope John Paul II reaffirmed the two-fold reality of generosity and prudence. In an address to a group of natural family planning teachers, he noted first of all the role of Christian prudence. Calling married couples to a "sense of responsibility for love and for life," the Pope noted that

God the Creator invites the spouses not to be passive operators, but rather "cooperators or almost interpreters" of His plan (*Gaudium et Spes*, n. 50). In fact, they are called, out of respect for the objective moral order established by God, to an obligatory *discernment of the indications of God's will concerning their family*. Thus, in relationship to physical, economic, psychological and social conditions, responsible parenthood will be able to be expressed "either by the deliberate and generous decision to raise a large family, or by the decision, made for serious moral reasons and with due respect for the moral law, to avoid for the time being, or even for an indeterminate period, another birth" (*Humanae Vitae*, n. 10).[3]

Then he taught that morality must be integrated into instruction about NFP. Noting that there is an "intrinsic connection" between the science of NFP and morality, he said that education about moral virtue "is a part of the complete integral training of teachers and of couples, and, in it, it should be clear that what is of concern here is more than just simple 'instruction' divorced from the moral values proper to teaching people about love."

He then immediately applied this to the generosity question:

In short, it [teaching moral principles] allows people to see that it is not possible to practice natural methods as a "licit" variation of the decision to be closed to life, which would be substantially the same as that which inspires the decision to use contraceptives: only if there is a basic openness to fatherhood and motherhood, understood as collaboration with the Creator, does the use of natural means become an integrating part of the responsibility for love and life.[4]

In summary, to those whose say that the use of NFP shows a lack of trust in Divine Providence (and some do say that), the Pope said that couples are called "to an obligatory discernment of God's will concerning their family." That is, they are called to develop and to use the virtue of true Christian prudence. To those who treat NFP as just another form of birth control, the Pope emphasized that the use of NFP is responsible "only if there is a basic openness to fatherhood and motherhood. . ."

In my opinion, these quotations reflect both sides of the family size decision—the recognition of the role of Christian prudence and the call to generosity in the service of life. I would add that discerning God's call to generosity, collaboration, and prudence is frequently the most difficult aspect of natural family planning.

4

Holy Communion: Eucharistic and Marital

Introduction

The substance of this chapter first appeared as an article in *Ave Maria*, 25 February 1967.[1] It was the first piece I wrote about the birth control issue, and I clearly remember what prompted me to write. I was living in Santa Clara and on a winter Saturday (early in 1966, I think) I attended a workshop on the birth control issue held in a church hall somewhere up the peninsula, probably Palo Alto. The speaker was Michael Novak who was then teaching at Stanford; he was also making a name for himself as the leading lay spokesman for those who thought the Church could and should change its teaching to allow contraception, and he held true to form in that workshop. I can't recall what he said, but I can remember my reaction. I thought his case specious, and I was angry—not just mad, but angry—and I was determined to respond. Considering the contents of what I wrote, I suspect that Novak had been using the very soft love-talk that has been traditionally used by dissenters from authentic Christian teaching on love and sexuality. So I responded by drawing a five-fold analogy between the conditions necessary for a worthy reception of the Eucharist and a worthy event of sexual intercourse. In short, Christian love is tough love, both Eucharistic and marital.

What still amazes me is the ease and speed with which I wrote that original article. I made a few handwritten notes on a half piece of paper, probably the five points of the analogy, and then started typing—the rest of Saturday afternoon and most of Sunday. I showed it to a couple of theologians the next summer, made just a few changes, and sent it off to *Ave Maria*.

I wish I could write with equal ease today! A healthy anger was my great aid at the time, but as error and evil have become ever so much more widespread and commonplace, it is correspondingly more difficult to get charged up by a healthy anger that moves one from inertia to action.

A personal note: There have been very few rewards or satisfactions in more than 25 years of defending what has been the most unpopular teaching of Christ's Church during this time, but there have been at least a few. The *Ave Maria* article drew some letters pro and con. The only one I remember accused me of blasphemy for daring to associate the Eucharistic and the sexual communions, so it was satisfying to see the Holy Father make the same association on 25 September 1982 to an organization that planned to study marriage in the light of the Sacrament of the Eucharist.[2]

It was also gratifying to learn that Michael Novak as the publisher of *Crisis* recanted his dissent in his editorial for June, 1989.[3]

What follows is the original article except for a few minor changes for clarity.

* * *

With an increasing emphasis being given to the personalist values of sexual intercourse in marriage, additional light can be gained from comparing the marriage act with another very personal type of intercourse, that of the encounter with Christ in the reception of Holy Communion. Both communions take place within the context of communities that are creations of God—the Church and matrimony, and these communities are so closely linked that St. Paul explains the community of marriage in terms of the Church (Eph. 5:21-33). Both are meant to be truly personal communions; both are meant to be a simultaneous giving and receiving; both are meant to lead men and women to lives of holiness.

Everyone is agreed today that of itself the act of sexual intercourse is a good and that in marriage it can be a means of expressing married love and be conducive to true Christian holiness. In marriage it is meant to be a true communion of persons whose bodily actions represent the communion of the total persons. Because this communion is likewise meant to lead the couple to holiness, it can very aptly be called a holy communion.

Result of sacraments

There are a number of marked similarities between these two communions—Eucharistic and matrimonial. First of all, they are both the result of sacraments given us by Christ for our salvation. If it isn't just word-picking, I think we usually refer to the sacrament of the Body and Blood of Our Lord as the "Holy Eucharist" as He becomes present to us through the consecration. Then when the faithful actually receive Him in the sacrament, we usually refer to this reception as "Holy Communion." The sacrament of Matrimony is likewise a sacrament establishing a new and sacred union between husband and wife and making it morally good to express this union in the communion of sexual intercourse.

Sacrificial offerings

Secondly, both of these communions come about as a result of a sacrificial offering. In the case of Holy Communion we have the offering of Christ to His Father, an offering at the Last Supper which looked forward to and included the fullness of giving in His death on the cross the next day. "This is my body which is given up for you" (Luke 22:19). In the case of the holy communion of matrimony we likewise have a delivering of the bodies of husband and wife to each other. As they confer the sacrament upon each other, they deliver themselves to each other without respect to circumstances, i.e., for poorer, sickness and worse as well as for richer, health and better. This is an explicit and formal recognition that in the giving of themselves to each other they are making a sacrifice.

Here we can use the word sacrifice in its common connotation of enduring difficulty or of giving up something, or we can look upon it in its etymological meaning of making holy. Perhaps the best way to take it here is that husband and wife will each grow in holiness according to the measure in which they give of self in trying to build up the other person. St. Paul is explicit in his instruction to the husband to sanctify his wife as Christ gave of Himself to sanctify the Church. The current emphasis on reform in the Church is an embodiment of the Church's belief that she must always seek to be ever faithful and true to her head and savior, Christ. Likewise are wives instructed in this spirit of obedience to a loving spouse who does not selfishly seek his own benefit but rather that of their mutual union. It is, then, this sacramental offering of self to each other, this true sacrificial offering, that makes morally good and humanly meaningful their subsequent communion in sexual intercourse.

78

Bodily gift of self

A third similarity is found in the expression of love through a bodily giving of self. Christ's love for men was incarnate and anything but angelistic: throughout His public life we see Him performing bodily good works among men as well as the spiritual healing of forgiving sins. Did this cost Him something? Certainly His weariness at Jacob's well shows His personal human expense. However, the example that Christ called our attention to was His giving up of His life in order to save men and in order to establish once again a union between God and men: "Greater love than this no man has, that he lay down his life for his friends" (John 15:13). This is also the example to which St. Paul points in his marriage discourse in which he directs husbands, "Husbands, love your wives as Christ loved the Church and delivered Himself up for her in order that He might sanctify her. . . " (Eph. 5:25-26).

In the act of sexual intercourse in marriage we likewise have the possibility of a bodily expression of love which represents a real giving of self in order to increase the union between husband and wife. This possibility is not realized in every act of sexual intercourse, even that which is morally permissible in marriage. Of itself, looked at on the lowest level, it is simply a union of two bodies. As to the human value of this union, we will have an unfortunately large range . . . the gross outrage of rape, the commercial use of prostitution, adultery and fornication (in both of which the level of affection can be very high while still lacking utterly the total meaning of human love) and the various meanings of sexual intercourse within marriage. For within marriage, there is still a range of human significance of the sexual union sometimes paralleling those outside of marriage: the act which is little more than an act of legalized rape in which there is no affection, to say nothing of love; the acts which positively exclude a real acceptance of the other person in the sense of accepting further responsibility for that person or any other person; acts which embody total acceptance of the other person and of the responsibilities which their mutual love entails; and finally that act which, as a real embodiment of their mutual self-giving love, consciously seeks to personify this love in a third person, as the communitarian love of the Father and the Son is personified in the third person of the Holy Spirit.

At this highest level, we have a love which seeks to love in the image and likeness of God, to be freely creative, a love which is

Christian for it incarnates itself, not shrinking from the self-sacrifice which will undoubtedly follow from this "incarnation," this expression of their love through a bodily giving of self. What must be understood in all of this is that the marital act is meant to be the bodily expression of the personal love between the two persons, an expression of their union with each other through a mutual giving of self.

Covenant renewal

The mutual self-giving in the communion of intercourse can be seen likewise in a fourth similarity between it and Holy Communion, the aspect of the covenant. In the Eucharistic sacrifice of the Mass, the New Covenant is constantly renewed. The person who worships devoutly at Mass and receives Holy Communion worthily is at least implicitly renewing on his part the covenant which Jesus established at the Last Supper. On the part of Christ there is no need for renewal of this covenant because as God's Son His sacrifice was perfect, and God's love as expressed in this covenant remains constant. However, on the part of man, who is constantly changing—growing closer to God or growing away from him—there is the constant need to renew our covenant, our pledge of fidelity to the Father in and through the Son and with the help of the Holy Spirit. When the worthy communicant receives the Body of Christ and says "Amen," he is in effect also saying, "I'm with you, too, all the way. If any sacrifice is demanded of me in order to be faithful to you, I am ready and willing to make it with your help."

Sexual intercourse in marriage should likewise be a renewal of the covenant the couple first made as they exchanged their promises to be faithful to each other under all circumstances. When they commune with each other in this way, they can once again renew their pledge, their covenant, to take each other completely, regardless of the consequences, be they wealth and health or poorness and sickness. Thus, sexual intercourse which is at least an implicit renewal of the marriage covenant is likewise a simultaneous giving and receiving, just as is the Holy Communion of the Eucharist.

Not every person who receives Holy Communion has these thoughts on his mind, nor is it necessary that the couples be thinking in these terms. Both of these are actions, and certain actions have a meaning in themselves and retain this meaning at the subjective level unless the human persons involved directly contradict it. For example, for the communicant's reception of the

Eucharist to be a Holy Communion, he must fulfill certain conditions at least negatively, lest what is meant to be a means of holiness for him becomes in fact a means of condemnation. He must be in the state of sanctifying grace, a friend of God, and have at the least nothing in his life which marks him as unwilling to give himself to God in any serious matter. To be opposed to God in any serious matter is to expel God from one's heart, to lose the state of sanctifying grace. The more open to God that he is, the more he will receive in Holy Communion, but at the bare minimum he cannot have any deliberate obstacles to a true communion with God, a true willingness to give himself all the way to God in any serious matter.

For the communion of sexual intercourse to be a true renewal of the covenant, and therefore a true means of growing in holiness for each other, it likewise must fulfill those conditions laid down at the time of the first covenant of their wedding day. If it is to be a truly meaningful and personal encounter with all the connotations of meetings between persons and not just bodies, if it is to be a simultaneous giving and taking, then it must involve that mutual pledge of giving to each other and acceptance of the other in this act without regard for the consequences. As with the reception of the Holy Eucharist, at the bare minimum, there can be no deliberate obstacles to this giving and receiving, lest what is meant to be a holy communion of spouses be turned into something considerably less than sacred and even sacrilegious.

A current emphasis in the theology of Holy Communion is on the disposition of the person receiving the sacrament. While not negating the minimum requirements for a valid reception of the Eucharist, increasing stress is laid upon the fact that the growth in holiness of the person, which is the intended effect of the sacrament, is not something which Christ will automatically produce even though he is infallibly present to the person in the sacrament. It is clear that His historic presence during His public life did not automatically create a state of holiness within those about Him—witness Judas, for example. Likewise today, although the grace of Christ is infinite, personal growth in grace depends not just upon the physical reception of the sacraments, but also upon the degree to which the person has responded to the actual grace of God in opening his heart to God and neighbor. And this is far from a sweet and pietistic desire to want to receive Jesus in one's heart. The Eucharist was given us at the Last Supper in order to strengthen and nourish us to keep another gift of the Last Supper: the commandment to love one another as Christ loved us.

It would be a shame if today, during a time of development in the theology of marriage, undue emphasis were placed on either a merely valid sexual marital act or on purely subjective considerations, for this would run counter to the well-balanced emphasis now taking place in the other areas of sacramental theology.

The aspect of covenant helps to maintain a balance between the subjective and the objective elements by calling to mind that objectively, the act itself must be free from deliberate and positive exclusion of its natural effects or purposes, just as the original marriage covenant or contract. It also calls to mind that subjectively, the more the act is a renewal of the love that called forth the original marriage promises, the more holy a communion it becomes.

The aspect of covenant also offers an answer to one of the perennial mysteries of married love: How can an act which both parties enjoy so much, out of which each person can gain so much personal satisfaction at the sensual, psychological and deepest levels of being—how can such an act be at the same time one of self-giving love? How if the persons are "getting" so much can they at the same time be giving of themselves? It should be noted first of all that many mature married people undoubtedly find great satisfaction from the fact that they have contributed to the pleasure of the other. In such cases, it seems that the communion of intercourse is a culmination of the real communion of their lives.

But even deeper than that, it is because their act is a renewal of their marriage covenant that they engage in a simultaneous giving and receiving. As the couple start out upon marriage, it is precisely because they have given of themselves without reservations to the other that they can now receive the beloved. And throughout their married life, it will be precisely because they have each given of themselves, even denied themselves, on behalf of the other that they will reach that state of personal development which is the immediate goal of human life, a state of true inner freedom in regard both to oneself and to other things, a freedom which frees the person for unselfish service towards God and neighbor.

Thus, just as the truly Holy Communion with Christ in the Eucharist is the result of complete openness to all that the covenant with Him demands, likewise the truly holy communion of marital intercourse is that which is truly a renewal of the marriage covenant, open to all the demands of Christian marriage, an acceptance of each other and the consequences without reservation.

Sealing of the covenant

A fifth similarity can be urged by looking at the way in which the covenant is sealed. The New Covenant made by Christ is sealed in His own blood the next day on Calvary. On His part there was a complete giving of self, an act of complete obedience, a perfect compliance with the will of the Father without regard to His own inconvenience and suffering. The matrimonial covenant is sealed by sexual intercourse which, if it symbolizes anything, symbolizes a complete mutual giving of self and acceptance of the other. In this aspect of the seal of the covenant we can see the full force of the marriage discourse of St. Paul's letter to the Ephesians. Wives are to be subject to a loving husband. Husbands are to love their wives in the same way that Christ loved the Church: He gave up His life to sanctify the Church. Likewise, the husband should not be seeking his own benefit but must be willing to sacrifice, to achieve a higher union with his spouse, through the giving of himself. In marriage as in all other phases of life, the words of Christ have new bearing: "He who seeks his life will lose it; he who loses his life for My sake will gain it."

The covenant of marriage is to sacramentalize the covenant of Christ with His Church. That is, it is to be the same reality only under difference appearances. The New Covenant was sealed by the death of him who in this way sanctified the Church, His Body. The covenant of Matrimony must be sealed likewise by the death to self in order to help the spouse, now joined in a unique oneness, to attain a life of holiness.

Conditions for validity

The similarities of these two types of personal communions is likewise helpful in reaching conclusions about the conditions for a truly valid encounter in the marital communion. For the worthy reception of the Eucharist, for a Holy Communion, the communicant at the minimum must be free from mortal sin. And what does this mean? It means that he must not be set against the covenant, that he must not be opposed to any sacrifice that might be demanded from him in order to remain true to his covenant with his Savior. For the communion of sexual intercourse to be a means of holiness or, at the least, not a means of unholiness, the spouses must likewise be free from any obstacles that will deny the covenant that they have made before God. If they have taken each other for better or for worse, their renewal of their marriage covenant must likewise be for better or for worse. Just as when they pledged to give themselves and to receive the other regardless of the consequences, so also must their subsequent communion in the marriage act be free from any denial of this covenant.

In the reception of the Holy Eucharist, it is not enough to be "generally" turned toward God. A person in a state of sin may not look back to last year (when faced with fewer temptations he was not in a state of sin) and receive the Eucharist on the basis of last year's state. His present state is all-important. Nor may he look forward to the unknown future and, under an intention to leave the state of sin sometime in the future when conditions are less pressing, receive the Eucharist in his present state of sin. The worthiness of his Communion depends upon his present state of soul, his present willingness to give of himself in following Christ. In other words, he may not play a percentage morality and state that since most of the time he is open to the sacrifice required by Christian life, he may therefore worthily receive Communion at any time even though he be temporarily alienated from God and unwilling to live the life of love as his circumstances demand it. What he must avoid in this particular example is the false application of what might be called a principle of totality.

One of the current [mid-1960s] questions concerning marriage and sexual intercourse is whether it is not sufficient to have the marriage as a whole open to the service of life but permissible to exclude positively that openness to life in the expression of mutual love in sexual intercourse. It renews again the conflict between the purposes of marriage—procreation and mutual development. Or to state it positively, would it not be permissible to positively preclude the possibility of conception through direct contraception? According to some, a principle of totality, under which the marriage as a whole is open and generous in the service of life, would be sufficient; but it would not be necessary for each and every act of married sexual love to reflect that openness even in a minimal way, i.e., at least open to the remote possibility though not intending procreation.

Personally, I find the approach very attractive, especially when I imagine some family burdened by a severe health problem on the part of the woman which makes pregnancy extremely dangerous, and whose openness to the service of life is witnessed by the adoption of other children. Because of these hardships, it is all the more important that the question be clearly answered: Is marriage itself and the overall generosity and openness to life the only sacred reality involved, or is the act of married sexual intercourse something sacred of itself—something whose sacred character must be respected in every instance regardless of circumstances? Or to put the question in terms of today's ethical theories, is the sacred character of the married sexual act something absolute or is it conditioned by the situation of the married couple?

Conclusion

It is the task of anyone who hopes to shed light on a problem not to construct a theory to support his sympathies but rather to show by reason, example and analogy the inner unity of the entire Christian faith. Thus it is that this analogy between the Holy Communion of the Eucharist and the holy communion of married intercourse must reach its conclusion, namely, that in order for marital sexual intercourse to be a valid expression of marital love and thus a means toward growth in holiness, it must at least be free from abortive, sterilizing and contraceptive impediments to the transmission of life.

The comparison has been made that the two communions are similar because they are both the results of sacraments, both the result of sacrificial love, both an expression of bodily love, both a renewal of the covenant, both covenants sealed with a death to self. Because of this, just as each reception of the Eucharist is in itself a sacred reality signifying complete acceptance of the covenant, likewise each act of married sexual love is a sacred reality. It entails a renewal of the marriage covenant, an acceptance of each other regardless of the circumstances, even if this renewal should lead to sickness or to poorness or even to death itself. That degree of self-giving is certainly going to require a supernatural faith, a deep and abiding realization that only he who loses his life for the sake of Christ will find, and that he who seeks his life will lose it.

The Christian must come to realize that it is only through a constant, ever-increasing gift of himself to God and neighbor that he can arrive at the true development of himself. The married couple must come to realize that their desire to increase their mutual love and self-development can be fulfilled only through the self-giving which they signified through their exchange of marriage promises.

In this manner, with every act of intercourse a renewal of the marriage covenant in which they pledged undying fidelity to each other regardless of the situation, the married couple enter into a truly holy communion, a true source of grace and the occasion of the fullness of married love.

Part II

Conscience

5

Fundamentals about Conscience

The importance of having correct **ideas** about conscience *and* a **correct** conscience cannot be overestimated. It is literally a matter of life and death importance. Adolf Eichmann, the director of Hitler's mass murder campaign against Jews and others whom Hitler deemed undesirable, provided the classic statement to show this importance when he argued in his defense: "I was following my conscience."

On the other hand, Dr. Bernard Nathanson stopped being one of the chief abortionists in the United States because he could no longer live with his conscience. A whole organization called Women Exploited by Abortion came into being to provide a voice for women who have had abortions but whose consciences led them to reject their past behavior and to witness against it.

There's a lot of planned confusion in some talk about conscience. You may hear about the "supremacy of conscience" and the need to "respect the consciences of others." There is a grain of truth in such phrases, but what about the person who collects door-to-door for a charity—but then keeps it all for himself, and, when apprehended says he was just following his conscience? Examples could be multiplied to illustrate the need for clarity about conscience.

The Meaning of Conscience

Etymologically, the word conscience comes from two Latin words—*cum* (with) and *scientia* (knowledge)—thus meaning "with knowledge." You can say that a judgment of conscience is a judgment made with knowledge; but while that's true, it's not very helpful except to raise further questions about the sources and the truth of that knowledge.

What conscience isn't

However, this very basic understanding of conscience—a judgment made with knowledge—enables us to realize that conscience is **not a feeling** though you may feel bad after going against your conscience—at least at first.

Also, conscience is **not simply an inner voice** in the sense of some sort of organ or direct communication from God. However, I do not want to rule out all intuitive knowledge. I think many people are gifted with the intuitive knowledge that certain actions are wrong, but as I and, I am sure, countless others have discovered, it is extremely easy to rationalize away the promptings of a conscience based upon intuitive knowledge, especially as a young person. "If this were *really* wrong, my parents or teachers would have told me; but they haven't (of course, I haven't asked); so it must be okay . . ." Furthermore, as I have listened to individuals and heard of whole primitive cultures which have at least initially rejected unnatural means of birth control, I remain convinced about the reality of intuitive knowledge in this area; but the pressures of contraceptive propaganda illustrate the need for a more certain and concrete form of knowledge which I will discuss later.

In saying that conscience is not simply an inner voice in the sense of a direct communication from God, I do not want to rule out the role of the Holy Spirit in communicating with an individual person. Whenever you pray for guidance as to whether you should do this good thing or that good thing, you are asking for that sort of divine communication. Examples abound: the single person should pray for guidance concerning a vocation to marriage, the priesthood, or religious life. The unwed pregnant mother should pray for guidance as to whether she should raise the child herself or give her baby up for adoption. Parents should pray for guidance as to whether to seek another pregnancy.

What I am ruling out is the appeal to conscience as some sort of direct divine communication which exempts the person from the Commandments or other binding obligations. The single person shouldn't pray for *guidance* as to whether he or she should follow a career of prostitution. The well-instructed Catholic unwed expectant mother shouldn't need to pray for *guidance* about abortion. Spouses shouldn't need to pray for *guidance* about entering a spouse-swapping arrangement. In all of these cases, God has made it abundantly clear what is immoral; and it's wrong to pretend He hasn't given us that guidance. In all of these cases the prayer must be for the *strength* to keep the Commandments. Knowledge is not virtue; we absolutely need the grace of God to keep the Commandments, and we also need to pray for that grace.

What conscience is

Catholic theology used the word "conscience" in three complementary ways: **capacity, knowledge,** and **practical judgment.**

Capacity. Vatican II teaches that "Conscience is man's most secret core, and his sanctuary. There he is alone with God whose voice echoes in his depths" *(Gaudium et Spes* 16). Pope John Paul II used that quotation and noted: "Conscience, in fact, is the 'place' where man is illuminated by a light which does not come to him from his created and always fallible reason, but from the very Wisdom of the Word in whom all things were created."[1]

Terms such as "secret core," "his sanctuary," and "the place" indicate that the subject is man's capacity to form judgments about right and wrong.

Knowledge. The above quotation from the Pope (which is repeated in the next chapter in the fuller context of a papal address to theologians) also points at God's role in enlightening the human conscience, and that's what we've called the knowledge element of conscience. Discourse about the formation of conscience also indicates the knowledge aspect of conscience.

Practical judgment. However, conscience is more than knowledge. Human persons cannot live in an ivory tower of knowledge alone. We have to bring that knowledge to bear upon matters that demand a decision such as: I will take an answer from my fellow student's exam or I will not look. I will let the baby live or I will not. I will or will not enter the seminary. We will or will not attempt to enlarge our family.

That's why Catholic moral theology teaches that **conscience is a practical judgment that I must do this good or avoid that evil**.

As a *practical* judgment, it is not just an intellectual matter; rather it is a practical decision that "this is good and I must do it" or "this is evil and I must avoid it."

As a *judgment,* it is based on the knowledge you have about the good or evil of a proposed action.

Correct and erroneous conscience

You can have a correct or erroneous conscience depending upon the value of the knowledge on which you base your judgment. Who are we to say that Eichmann was lying when he said he was following his conscience? But you want to scream, "Your conscience was all wrong!" Maybe Eichmann actually came to believe the Hitler line about an Aryan super-race. If so, he had an erroneous conscience, and you rightly want to say, "But that's no excuse. You had an **obligation** to form a **correct** conscience."

Some people like to talk about an "informed" conscience, but that's not helpful until you supply the adjectives "rightly" or "incorrectly"; and that brings you back to the standard terms—correct and erroneous conscience.

Objective and subjective elements

Objective refers to the action you are considering in its objective moral reality. The action will be right or wrong in objective reality regardless of how you or anyone else judge it. For instance, in the order of objective moral reality, it is either wrong or not wrong to kill an unborn baby. It can't be both. For your judgment to be correct, it must conform to the objective reality about the morality of such an act. Otherwise your judgment of conscience is in error.

Subjective elements refer to the person who makes the judgments of conscience. It refers to some elements known only to God such as whether the person incurs the **guilt of sin** for doing what is objectively a wrongful action. If the person says, "I know now that what I did was, in objective reality, an evil thing, but I didn't know at the time it was wrong," that person would have to ask himself, "But was my ignorance *vincible* or *invincible?*"

•**Vincible ignorance** is ignorance you can and should overcome with the means at your disposal. There is a saying in American law that "ignorance of the law excuses no one." In terms of moral guilt or innocence, that phrase applies only to vincible ignorance because as human beings we are obliged to make a reasonable effort to find out the truth which can be found. Vincible ignorance means that a person had at least *some clue* that an action might be morally wrong in objective reality but did not take reasonable steps to follow up on that clue. The same would hold true if he had *some* clue that a certain action might be morally obligatory in objective reality.

• **Invincible ignorance** refers to ignorance that a person in her or his circumstances cannot be expected to overcome. The person simply has *no clue* that a certain action or a way of life is, in objective reality, morally obligatory for its performance (if it is a good act) or its avoidance (if it is a bad act). A person with utterly no contact with Christianity cannot overcome his ignorance about Christ.

• **Certain** and **doubtful** refer to subjective states of the person. If you are *certain* about the morality of some action, you *may* or you *must* follow your conscience depending upon the type of action. For example, if you are certain it is wrong to donate infected blood to a blood bank and you are certain you have infected blood, then you *must* follow your conscience and not give blood. On the other hand, if you are certain that it is not wrong to donate healthy blood and you have healthy blood, then you *may* or *should* donate your blood.

To be "certain" means that you are convinced by reasons that make sense to you here and now. It does not mean that you can absolutely rule out at least a slim possibility that you might be making a mistake about the moral right or wrong of the action you are now considering. For example, let's take an action that's not burdened with the grave matter of mortal sin. Mr. Smith discovers mud all over the floor by the back door. He sees Johnny, his third grade son, and his friends playing in the yard, mud all over their shoes. So he deduces that it was Johnny and his friends. He confronts Johnny who denies responsibility. But Mr. Smith knows that lately Johnny has been telling lies whenever he gets caught disobeying one of the house rules. So he administers a discipline of having Johnny write 100 times, "I must always tell the truth." That night he learns that his wife was the mud-tracker. At the time he was certain enough to take the sort of action he did; he had the kind of certainty that parents need for managing a home and administering discipline for actions of which they are not a direct eye-witness. He may apologize to Johnny; he may feel good that he confined the discipline to a non-corporal punishment; but he can also tell himself that he did the best he could with the information that was available to him at the time including his conviction that discipline for young children should be administered promptly.

If you are *doubtful* about the morality of some action, you shouldn't act, but instead you should get advice and clarify your conscience. The wisdom of the axiom "you should not act on a doubtful conscience" is easily seen in the common example about the hunter who hears a lot of noise in the bushes but isn't certain if it's an animal or a fellow hunter. That happened to me the only time I ever went deer hunting—after struggling up a steep, brushy knoll on all fours I raised my head and looked into my friend's rifle barrel! Fortunately, he clarified his doubtful knowledge by waiting. As I wrote at the beginning of this chapter, conscience decisions can literally be matters of life or death.

The Obligation to Follow Your Conscience

The obligation to follow your conscience is fundamental to being human for it is simply another way of saying we must do good and avoid evil. It is such a basic principle that you simply can't talk about morality with someone who would say that he was not obliged to follow his conscience, that he was not obliged to do good and to avoid what he knows is evil. Germain Grisez has said it well:

> The duty to follow one's conscience is neither one specific responsibility among others nor a supreme responsibility which perhaps could conflict with and nullify others. For no matter what in particular one ought to do, one ought to follow one's conscience. That is so because the duty to follow conscience is reducible to the duty to do what is morally good.[2]

Grisez notes that the statement, "One ought to do what is morally good" is "true by definition," and as such doesn't call for discussion. However, he says it can still be "interesting and informative to say: 'One ought to follow one's judgment of conscience' " *because it implies that "[you] ought to follow [your] judgment of conscience in the face of a temptation not to do so"* (emphasis added).

The difference between "may," "should," and "must"

All three of these words are used in talk about conscience.

You *may* follow your conscience.

You *must* follow your conscience.

You *should* do this or avoid that.

The difference between *may* and *must* stems from both the 1) nature of the action and 2) the certainty of the knowledge you can attain.

The nature of the action. Negative obligations can be universal and absolute so that there are no exceptions. Such prohibitions are called **universal negative absolutes,** and the Church's teaching against abortion and marital contraception are examples of such universal negative absolutes. "Thou shalt never directly kill an unborn baby." "Thou shalt never engage in marital contraception." At the level of the properly formed Catholic conscience, such teaching becomes "I must never abort a baby; I must never use or recommend marital contraception." At the level of responding to here and now temptation, the person with a properly formed conscience will make the practical judgment of conscience: "I must not abort *this* baby; I must not give in to *this* temptation to use or recommend marital contraception." The strength of "must" here means that what is forbidden is the grave matter of mortal sin.

Having rejected unnatural methods of birth control, you still have other decisions. Must you let the babies come as they may or may you use natural methods of family planning? You search for Catholic teaching and you find out that the Church teaches that marriage is for family, that married couples are called to be generous in the service of life, but that no specific numbers of children are given; you discover that you would need an *extremely* serious reason to choose not to have *any* children, and that you need a *sufficiently* serious (even though not "extremely serious") reason to postpone pregnancy and/or limit your family size. Furthermore, although I am not aware of any specific teaching on the matter of temporary spacing, I think you can draw a proportion between the duration of the spacing intended and the seriousness of the reason required. It would not require much of a reason to decide upon two year spacing between babies because that appears to be a very natural norm with fully natural or ecological breastfeeding. On the other hand, I think that to decide on four year spacing would require sufficient "physical or psychological conditions of husband and wife or . . . external conditions" (*Humanae Vitae*, n.16).

Forced with a "family planning" decision, you may judge that here and now you have sufficient human resources to take care of another baby and the family you already have. You *may* or even *should* choose to let the babies come as they may. On the other hand, you may have sufficient reason to judge that you *may* or

94

should choose to postpone pregnancy through natural family planning.

As an example of the latter case, let us imagine that you have had four babies in the first five years of your marriage, the wife is exhausted, you are just barely able to pay your bills, etc. You reach the conclusion that you have very serious reasons for postponing pregnancy and that you *should* practice natural family planning. In fact, your "should" is so strong that you feel it is a "must." I use the term "should" here because if you do not practice NFP but instead both mutually and freely agree to allow more babies to come as they will, you are not entering the area of the grave matter of mortal sin.

"Should" works the other way too. Let us imagine that you have four or five children, well spaced out, no big problems, and you are still in your mid-to-late thirties. You feel drawn to have another baby, you can't really think of a serious reason not to, but you're fearful. All the "what ifs" start bothering you. What if the next baby isn't healthy and requires all sorts of care? What if the husband loses his job? etc. What if after seeking counsel you think you should but you're afraid? That sort of "should" is also not the "must" whose violation necessarily involves the grave matter of serious sin. Furthermore, as a perceived positive obligation, it does not have the universality of a universal negative absolute.

These cases of "should" illustrate the need for a prayerful dialogue with God concerning matters that go beyond the clear universal negative absolutes of the Church's moral teaching.

A good counselor might affirm to the first couple the Church's teaching that parenthood involves caring for and educating one's children, not simply begetting them. To the second couple he might affirm the Church's teaching about generosity in the service of life and the need for prayer to have more trust in God. But he should encourage both couples to seek from God what *He* wants. God may be calling one couple to further develop sexual self-control and non-genital marital courtship. The Lord may be calling another couple to an extra measure of trust and generosity. However, these are conclusions that cannot be arrived at by a third party counselor; they need to be the result of prayer.

The certainty of your knowledge. If in your search for the truth you discover that the Church has clear and specific teaching on the subject of concern, then you have certain knowledge and are obliged to form your conscience accordingly. On the other hand, on some matters you may find that there is an absence of clear and specific teaching and that competent theologians, faithful to the whole official teaching of the Church, are, in fact, divided into two or more schools of thought on the matter. Or the teaching may be clear, but there are differences about its application to concrete cases. In the absence of clear and authoritative teaching on the part of the magisterium, you may—indeed, must—form your conscience according to the line of reasoning that seems best to you. This is what is known as the theological theory of probabilism. Such a theory doesn't say you can do anything that comes to mind; rather it is intended to offer you more than one well-considered opinion to assist the formation of your conscience.

Note well: the theory of probabilism does not apply to the birth control issue because the Church has clear and authoritative teaching against all forms of marital contraception. In the years 1964-1967, some theologians were arguing that the teaching was no longer certain and that therefore probabilism could be applied. However, the issuance of *Humanae Vitae* eliminated all such theorizing and wishful thinking. Even those who believe the teaching is wrong have to admit that it is clear and authoritative.

The Obligation to Form Your Conscience Correctly

Since we have the obligation to make and to follow the judgment of conscience, we also are obliged to make sure that our judgments are correct. We have the right and the duty to do what is right; we also have the right and a duty to find out what is the right thing to do. Another way of saying this is that as human persons we have a fundamental obligation to live according to the truth, and that means we have a fundamental obligation to seek the truth.

Those statements are so obvious and fundamental no thinking person of good will can deny them. What is controversial in our day is this: where do you find out what is the right thing to do? When there are differences in teaching, when the pop columnists in a secular culture say one thing and the Catholic Church teaches something else, who should I believe teaches the truth about the way that leads to eternal life?

I believe that God has given us a firm and certain way to know what is morally right and wrong. Jesus Christ taught, "I am the way and the truth and the life" (Jn 14:6), and He established a historical and visible Church upon Simon, whose name He changed to Peter or Rock, in order to keep His teaching alive and available for all men of all times. Therefore I believe that the correct conscience is the one which is conformed to the formal teaching of the Roman Catholic Church. The reasons for that statement of faith and the reasons I believe there is no other easily accessible source of the full truth about moral right and wrong are spelled out in the next chapter.

6

Forming a Correct Conscience

The truth question is at the core of any discussion about birth control. If it is true that it is objectively immoral for a married couple to use unnatural means of birth control, then everyone is morally obliged to avoid such behavior, for every human being is called by God to live according to the truth. If it is not true, then the Catholic Church is guilty of teaching false doctrine despite the efforts of critics to correct her.

The primary question about a teaching is, "Is it true?" However, the truth about some moral matters is not immediately self-evident or easily arrived at by unaided human reason. Then the real questions become, "How can I **know** if a particular teaching is true?" and **"Whom** shall I believe?" Or the questions can be combined: "How can I know if Catholic teaching about birth control is true?"

That is what this chapter is all about.

First, however, let me give you a brief map of this chapter. It is divided into two major parts, "Coming to know the truth" and "Applying *Lumen Gentium* 25 to *Humanae Vitae*." Within the first part, the first section deals with principles of knowledge and the second section deals with various ways in which the Catholic Church teaches. The second major part of the chapter applies the "certain knowledge" criterion of Vatican II to the birth control issue.

I. Coming to Know the Truth

A. Principles of Certitude

1. What is truth?

The question of Pilate to Jesus, "What is truth?" (John 18:38) is still with us today. When we speak about truth in the context of a

98

statement, we mean that the statement is true if it corresponds to reality. The Latin phrase used for centuries is that truth is "adequatio rei et intellectus," an equation or equality between the thing (rei) and my understanding of it (intellectus).

The truth about some forms of reality is so easy to arrive at that we scarcely think about it. "Two plus two equals four" is a statement about one form of reality, mathematics. You are certain that "$2 + 2 = 4$" is a true statement, i.e., that it accurately describes reality, and your certainty in such matters is called mathematical certitude. However, mathematical certitude exists only in the field of mathematics; it doesn't exist in the area of real life decision making.

2. Moral certitude

Most of the important decisions you make are based on moral certitude. I find it the hardest kind of certainty to describe, so I'll start by saying what it isn't.

It isn't mathematical certitude, for that exists only about numbers and, to a certain degree, about things that can be scientifically observed and quantified.

And it isn't the certainty of faith which comes from God's revelation. Example: the orthodox Christian belief in the Trinity.

Rather, it's the kind of certainty that's ultimately involved with faith in people. When you cross a bridge, you normally have moral certitude that it won't collapse under you, and that boils down to your making an act of faith in the designers and builders of the bridge and the people who are supposed to make periodic inspections. Normally, you don't even think about all the acts of faith you make in your fellow human beings as you trust them to stay in the proper lanes as you and they drive down the streets, stop for stop-signs at intersections, etc., but you are constantly making at least implicit acts of faith so that you have moral certitude that you can safely drive the streets, etc.

The relationship between your act of faith in someone else and the corresponding moral certitude is more clear when you are dealing directly with other people on a one to one basis. Let's look at some examples.

• **The home front.** "Dad, can I have the car to go to the ball game? I'll come right home afterwards."

If dad says okay, he's making three acts of faith: 1) that his child can drive safely, 2) that his child will actually go to and stay at the ball game and 3) that his child will come directly home from the game as soon as he leaves it.

Again, "Mom and dad, I want to go hear *Satan's Sexy Six* rock band this Friday night. Don't worry about their name. It's just a big put-on; they are really harmless as a church choir."

I suggest that parents would be more than justified in refusing to believe their teen-ager on that one. It's not that you as a parent want to accuse your child of lying, but you may well think that your child is deceived. You've read an article or book about rock bands and music, and you figure that anyone who labels themselves that way has to be mighty suspect. You don't have mathematical certainty, but you think it's highly probable that your child has been deceived. Then you go even further. You reflect that if it is not a Satanic sexually oriented rock group, then it is definitely using a misleading name, and you're certain that such misleading is false advertising. On either count, you don't want your family to support it; you have the moral certainty to make the practical decision, "No, you're not going to such a concert."

• **The jury.** An extremely clear example of the relationship between acts of faith and moral certainty is found in the courtroom. A man accused of a crime denies his guilt. Whom does the jury believe—him or the prosecutor? Is the accused believable? Are the witnesses believable? In the American system, the jurors are instructed that they must arrive at a moral certainty that the person is guilty. Otherwise, they have to declare him not proven guilty. They are not required to arrive at mathematical certainty, but at certainty beyond reasonable doubt.

3. Motives of credibility

In all these cases, your decision to believe somebody depends upon that person's believableness, and that's what we mean by "motives of credibility." Again, many of your decisions that involve acts of faith in other people are such that you hardly think about "motives of credibility" in so many words, but you are, in fact, basing your decisions on your sizing up the believability of the other person.

• **The home front.** If your son who asks for the car has a track record of doing what he promises to do, he is believable when he says he will be home right after the game. On the other hand if his "on-time" record has been spotty and has been getting worse, his credibility has been damaged. You are perplexed. You no longer have any solid reasons for believing him except a sort of blind or anxious hope. If you let him have the car, you have no moral certainty he'll be home on time. Rather, a decision to let him have the car would be based on wishful thinking, and such decisions frequently result in anxiety and self-recrimination—"I knew I shouldn't have let him have it; I could kick myself for being so stupid."

• **The jury.** If you are in the jury, you may listen to "expert witnesses" testify about certain matters including the psychological state of the accused. No effort will be spared in trying to convince you that such expert witnesses are truly knowledgeable and therefore believable in their fields of expertise. However, what if you hear two expert witnesses give contradictory testimony? Wouldn't you be perplexed? Wouldn't you want to know more about each of the alleged expert witnesses?

For example, imagine that you are on the jury for a man accused of murder. Let us say that there is no question of fact: everyone, including the defense, is agreed that he did kill the other person. However, the defense is pleading a form of temporary insanity, and a psychiatrist for the defense has just given a very convincing testimony that the accused at the time was absolutely incapable of the sort of reasoning and pre-meditation required for the crime of murder. On the other hand, a psychiatrist for the prosecution has contended that the accused was capable of the reflection required for the crime of murder. Now you're truly perplexed. Let us imagine further that the judge instructs you that if you are truly perplexed, you have to declare the accused "not guilty" of pre-meditated murder but that you may find him guilty of some lesser offense such as manslaughter that does not require pre-meditation.

However, let us further imagine that the prosecuting attorney forced the defense psychiatrist to admit that he didn't believe in free will but was an absolute determinist. In other words, the defense psychiatrist believed that what you do is absolutely determined, not just influenced, by your background; he believed that you and everybody else on the jury would do exactly the same thing if you came from the defendant's background; so he believed that any pre-meditation was nonsense since the thoughts were pre-determined anyway. Therefore, because of these beliefs or opinions, he could say that **any** accused was incapable of the pre-meditation required for any degree of crime requiring reflection and free will.

Would you really believe someone who believed that neither you nor the accused had free will, that even your decision as jurors was pre-determined? I hope you would find such an "expert witness" simply unbelievable because of his unrealistic opinion about that which separates men from beasts, namely, their spiritual powers of intellect and free will.

(The fact that a particular psychiatrist proved to be unbelievable doesn't settle the question about the accused. You might still be perplexed and in need of testimony from a *believable* expert for the defense; you certainly couldn't vote "guilty" of a capital offense if you remained perplexed.)

4. Birth control, truth, and credibility

You, the individual person, are like a one-person jury when it comes to birth control. In other words, whom are you going to believe?

Let us imagine, for the sake of illustration, that you are trying to look at the whole birth control issue with an open heart and mind. Let us further imagine that you are a Christian who believes fully in God, in Christ as the God-man, and in the Holy Spirit's continued guidance of the Church, however you mean church, and that you don't have any strong denominational affiliation. You know you are reasonably intelligent because you were a B student in high school and college. You begin your search for the truth.

• **Philosophy.** First of all, you begin with what philosophy has to say about birth control. You are immediately impressed by the fact that there are different schools of thought among philosophers regarding very basic fundamentals such as the use of free will; then you find that even among those who believe in God and free will, there are still differences about sexual morality including birth control; finally, you find that even among those who agree that it is wrong to use unnatural forms of birth control, there are differences as to *why* it is wrong. Pausing a bit, you tell yourself, "There's got to be a better way!" You aren't denying that human reason unaided by divine revelation can arrive at the truth of important moral matters, but you figure that God must have given common men and women an ordinary and certain way to know moral right and wrong because more than 99.99% of the human race could never undertake such a study of ethics.

However, your brief encounter with philosophy has enabled you to make one logically 100% certain conclusion: **the morality of using unnatural methods of birth control is not self-evident.** If it were, all the philosophers would agree, but that is obviously not the case.

You have also arrived at a second very certain conclusion, namely, that God, if He wanted people to have certain knowledge about birth control, must have given us some other way to know. Along the way of your philosophical inquiry you learned about three ways of knowing—reasoning, intuition, and faith. You have just put aside philosophic reasoning as the way God expects mankind in general to arrive at the truth about love and sexuality, and a moment's further reflection dismisses intuition as well. It's not that you doubt the reality of intuitive knowledge; rather, you quickly realize that there is such a multitude of contradictory thought about birth control that it would hardly be fair to try to make the God of Truth responsible for such contradictions.

Therefore you are left with the possibility that God has chosen knowledge-through-faith as the way to know for certain what God expects of us regarding birth control; or, to put it a bit more philosophically, to know for certain what is the truth about love, sex, and birth control.

• **Religion.** Notice what has happened. When you recognized that the answer to the moral question of birth control was not self-evident, and when the reasoning of the philosophers didn't make the answer almost self-evident or at least easily conclusive to you, you turned to religion for the answer. In effect, you are saying, "Since it's not self-evident or easily arrived at by unaided human reason, **who can I believe** has the true answer to the birth control question?

As a believing Christian, you believe that Jesus Christ is "the way and the truth and the life" (John 14:6), so you inquire what the various churches teach. You soon realize that the teaching that it is immoral to use unnatural methods of birth control was unanimous among all the Christian churches up until 14 August 1930. At that point in history, the Church of England accepted the use of unnatural means of birth control as morally permissible. Very shortly thereafter (31 December 1930), the Roman Catholic Church through Pope Pius XI strongly reaffirmed the traditional teaching against unnatural forms of birth control. You also come to realize that almost all the Protestant churches have, in the ensuing years, accepted unnatural means of birth control as morally acceptable. Faced with contradictory teachings by different churches, you are perplexed. Whom should you believe?

You are very much in the same predicament as the juror after hearing contradictory testimony. So you ask, "Where do I find the proper motives of credibility?" Rather than go into an examination of the "truth claims" of each church, you hope that you will find something similar to the free will issue with the psychiatrists. To your surprise, perhaps, you find that all the mainline Protestant Churches in the United States which accepted contraception have also accepted killing unborn babies as morally acceptable. You recognize this issue as being as close to self-evident as you can hope to see in a moral question, and you conclude that the mainline Protestant Churches are 100% wrong on abortion. You further conclude that if they are so wrong on something so evident as killing unborn children, they offer you no motives of credibility for believing they are right about the less obvious but closely related issue of birth control.

Your examination of the evangelical and fundamentalist churches reveals a much greater unanimity about the evil of abortion but a very mixed situation on birth control. It seems to vary almost from one local congregation or minister to another with a few rejecting even the use of natural family planning, others sharing Catholic belief, but many accepting any imaginable form of non-abortifacient contraceptive behavior, perhaps even marital sodomy. You conclude that such variation does not provide you with the motives of credibility you are looking for.

You are led to a closer examination of the motives of credibility of the Roman Catholic Church. You come to realize that the birth control issue is not a new one but has arisen in various centuries and in various ways. The answer of the Catholic Church has always been a universal negative to unnatural means of birth control. You come to understand all the pressures that were put upon Pope Paul VI to accept contraception in the 1960s, and you recognize that he spoke prophetically in *Humanae Vitae,* his 1968 reaffirmation of the traditional teaching against unnatural forms of birth control.

You also come to realize that there is tremendous division within the Catholic Church about birth control; surveys show that in Western Countries the majority of married Catholics in their fertile years use unnatural forms of birth control, and it appears that a majority of their priests see nothing wrong with it. However, you also notice that Pope John Paul II has been even more emphatic about the truth of the teaching of *Humanae Vitae* than was its author, Pope Paul VI. He is steady like a rock. He will not conform the teaching of the Church to the practices of the people. Rather he keeps insisting that the teaching reaffirmed by *Humanae Vitae* is **true** and that therefore it cannot be changed; what must change is the practice of people who need to conform their lives to the truth.

Gradually and with prayer it dawns on you that the Roman Catholic Church alone offers you sufficient motives of credibility. Only the Catholic Church offers you the history, the consistency of teaching, and the forthright affirmation of this teaching as true, despite all opposition. You finally conclude that she alone is God's "expert witness" whose teaching can clarify the perplexed conscience. You have come to believe in her as the conveyor of God's truth about love; it remains only to ascertain precisely what she teaches about this important area of married life.

The above is not intended to be any sort of complete statement of reasons for faith in the Catholic Church as God's unique instrument for the salvation of mankind. For Catholics, it is simply a review of what is implicit in their faith already. For agnostics, it may be helpful to understand that something like this was responsible for the conversion of Malcolm Muggeridge from agnosticism to entry into the Catholic Church; and Dr. Herbert Ratner has noted that it was the unique role of the Roman Catholic Church in upholding the teaching against contraception in the 1930s which was the impetus of his conversion from Judaism to Catholicism. Some Protestants may find solace in the fact that Protestant Christianity retained the traditional teaching against contraception from the Reformation to 1930; others may find the acceptances of unnatural forms of birth control and then abortion a challenge and an impetus to examine the full truth claims of the Catholic Church.

My whole point in this exercise is to point out that if the truth about some moral matter of great importance is not self-evident or easily arrived at by unaided human reason, then, in all honesty, you have to admit that you have to turn to someone else for that truth, and that's what we mean by faith. And, finally, before you believe someone else about something very important, you ought to examine the reasons for believing that person or corporate person (church), and that's what is meant by examining the motives of credibility.

I have completely omitted the option of believing yourself—listening to your own opinions—because I have assumed that if you've read this far, you are conscientious enough to be wary of your own initial opinions and rationalizations especially in matters of sexuality where self-interest runs so high. I assume that your knowledge of your own sins and weakness leads you to recognize that you must look for the truth outside of yourself, that you must look to God's revelation.

B. How the Catholic Church Teaches

Once you arrive at the conclusion that only the Roman Catholic Church offers you sufficient grounds for believing that she is God's "expert witness" about marital love and sexuality, you determine to find out precisely what it teaches about birth control. However, you quickly find out that there is within the Catholic Church a debate as to whether the teaching against marital contraception is taught "infallibly." In other words, you find yourself confronted with two questions: one of fact, and the other of certainty. Thus I must sidetrack you with a brief review of **how** the Church teaches. What has happened is this: We started with the question, "How can you **know** if the Church's teaching on birth control is true?" Now we have slightly modified that question as follows: "How can you **be certain** that the Church's teaching on birth control is true?" Of course, "to be certain" is the same as "to know with certainty," but it's a less awkward way of saying it.

Degrees of certainty

There are some matters on which thoroughly orthodox Catholic theologians disagree; their reasoned opinions on such matters after some debate may reach the status of a **probable opinion**. The currently operating theory in the Church holds that when you are perplexed about an issue on which there are different probable opinions, you are free to follow the reasoning that appears most convincing to you. However, probable opinions operate only in the absence of official and certain teaching on the matter; birth control is not an issue in which the probabilism theory can be applied.

On some other matters, there is universal agreement among orthodox theologians, and such teaching is called **theologically**

certain. It is not yet called "infallible," but it provides you with the clear certainty you need for informing your conscience and making practical decisions.

At the top of the scale are the teachings which are **infallibly** taught by the Church, and these are called *de fide*, "of divine faith," i.e., to be believed as revealed by God directly through the prophets, Christ, and/or the Apostles or through the order of creation and clarified by the Church. When the Church teaches something infallibly, she is saying that the authority of God Himself is behind this teaching and that therefore there is no possibility whatsoever that it is in error. That does not mean that the formulation of that teaching can never be improved or clarified, but it absolutely excludes that a contradictory teaching could be true.

Ways of teaching infallibly

You're not done yet. Teachings can be taught infallibly in three different ways. Doctrine can be known to be taught infallibly by 1) an ecumenical council of the Church teaching in a solemn definition, 2) by the Pope teaching *ex cathedra,* and 3) by the universal ordinary magisterium of the Church.

1. An example of **an ecumenical council** teaching infallibly would be the formulation of the Nicene Creed by the Council of Nicea in 325. An arch-priest named Arius had started to teach that Jesus Christ was not *really* God, not the same substance (*homo-ousios*) as the Father but only very much *like* God (*homoi-ousios*). The bishops of the Church gathered together at Nicea and declared that Jesus was "of the same substance" (*homo-ousios*) as the Father, true God of true God.

They did not then issue a statement saying, "We have infallibly defined the dogma of the divinity of Christ." No, such terminology was not yet developed. However, they were conscious of making a definitive teaching as true and to be held by all as true, and later theologians would point to this as an example of an ecumenical council teaching infallibly.

(Note the similarity of the two prefixes homo—same and homoi—similar. In Greek, the difference in spelling amounted to the Greek letter for "i"—"iota." In this case, one iota characterized the infinite difference between being God and not being God.)

2. **Papal infallibility** was solemnly defined in 1870 by the first Vatican Council: "The Roman Pontiff, when he speaks *ex cathedra,*

that is, when, acting in the office of shepherd and teacher of all Christians, he defines, by virtue of his supreme apostolic authority, doctrine concerning faith or morals to be held by the universal Church, possesses through the divine assistance promised to him in the person of St. Peter, the infallibility with which the divine Redeemer willed His Church to be endowed in defining doctrine concerning faith and morals; and that such definitions of the Roman Pontiff are therefore irreformable because of their nature, but not because of the agreement of the Church."[1]

The prime examples of papal *ex cathedra* teaching are the papal definitions of the Immaculate Conception (1854) and the Assumption of Mary (1950). It is debated whether the teaching of Pius XI in *Casti Connubii* was such a teaching, but more about that later.

3. The **universal ordinary magisterium** of the Church is the ordinary way in which the Church teaches infallibly about morality. The Code of Canon Law teaches that "the College of Bishops also possesses infallibility in its teaching . . . when the Bishops, dispersed throughout the world but maintaining the bond of union among themselves and with the successor of Peter, together with the same Roman Pontiff authentically teach matters of faith or morals, and are agreed that a particular teaching is definitively to be held. No doctrine is understood to be infallibly defined unless this is manifestly demonstrated."[2]

The teaching of the universal ordinary magisterium on morality is generally less solemn because for the most part there have been no really serious challenges. For example, up until recently no one who called himself a Catholic theologian would have dared to say that Catholic teaching against sex outside of marriage was erroneous. Such teaching is so clear in Scripture and the interpretation has been so universal throughout the centuries that it is very unlikely that Fr. Charles Curran will gain more than a handful of allegedly Catholic theologians to declare with him that "biblical teaching that sex outside of marriage is sinful must be seen as out of date—evidence of a less sophisticated age."[3] Rather, such teaching of Fr. Curran will be seen increasingly as the fruit of what appears to be an intellectual pride of the same sort which prompted him in 1968 to declare the formal teaching of *Humanae Vitae* erroneous and to lead the dissent against it.

Vatican II, *Lumen Gentium*, 25

Because the teaching of the universal ordinary magisterium tends to be of a more general nature until provoked by a very serious challenge, it is not always as succinctly stated as you might like it to be. Furthermore, when the moral teaching of the Church is challenged, it is no small matter to **prove**, for example, that the evil of fornication is taught infallibly by the ordinary magisterium of the bishops throughout the world.

I am not suggesting in the least that it is difficult for a believing Catholic to **know** what the Church teaches about basic moral matters. Theologian Karl Rahner put it this way:

Furthermore, the Church teaches these commandments with divine authority exactly as she teaches the other "truths of the Faith", either through her "ordinary" magisterium or through an act of her "extraordinary" magisterium in *ex cathedra* definitions of the Pope or a general council. But also through her *ordinary* magisterium, that is in the normal teaching of the Faith to the faithful in schools, sermons and all the other kinds of instruction.[4]

The only point I am making is that when some moral teaching is challenged, it can be a rather massive effort to **prove** by documentation that it has been taught by all the bishops, always and everywhere.

Therefore, the Lord has given his Church a much easier way of clarifying precisely *what* the universal ordinary magisterium teaches and *how*. This is spelled in another paragraph of *Lumen Gentium* 25. The text is worth quoting in full.

Bishops, teaching in communion with the Roman Pontiff, are to be respected by all as witnesses to divine and Catholic truth. In matters of faith and morals, the bishops speak in the name of Christ and the faithful are to accept their teaching and adhere to it with a religious assent of soul. This religious submission of will and of mind must be shown in a special way to the authentic teaching authority of the Roman Pontiff, even when he is not speaking *ex cathedra*. That is, it must be shown in such a way that his supreme magisterium is acknowledged with reverence, the judgments made by him are sincerely adhered to, according to his manifest mind and will. His mind and will in the matter may be known chiefly either from the character of the documents, from his frequent repetition of the same doctrine, or from his manner of speaking (n.25).

What does it mean to "accept their teaching and adhere to it with a religious assent of soul"? What does it mean to give "religious submission of will and mind" ... "to the authentic teaching authority of the Roman Pontiff, even when he is not speaking *ex cathedra*"? What it means is this: **to accept as *true* what the Pope teaches when he makes it clear that what he is teaching is to be held as true.**

What sort of certainty do you have when you accept such teaching as true? It is not yet the highest kind, the certitude of faith that a doctrine is taught infallibly, but it is far more than the moral certainty you have when making day to day decisions. It also goes beyond what theologians call "theologically certain" because that phrase can refer to the logical conclusion of a syllogism or a universal consensus among orthodox theologians. Let us call it "religious certainty," the sort of certainty that renders the question, "Is it taught *de fide?*" purely academic. It's a certainty that the particular teaching is true because it is the work of the Holy Spirit.

For example, take the certainty of a Protestant who accepts the teaching against marital contraception as true. He wouldn't be accepting this teaching on the word of any church, his own included. Rather, he would be looking at the Onan account in Genesis 38 and the universal teaching of all Christian churches until 1930. Essentially, he would be saying that such a massive witness led him to believe that the Christian teaching against marital contraception must be the work of the Holy Spirit and therefore true. I don't know what else to call that except religious certainty.

II. Applying *Lumen Gentium*, 25 to *Humanae Vitae*

In the first part of this chapter, we looked at the process by which a seeker after truth can know with certainty that a moral teaching is true. In this second part, we will look at the doctrine of marital non-contraception in the light of the teaching of *Lumen Gentium,* the "Dogmatic Constitution of the Church."

According to the dogmatic teaching of Vatican II, you can have all the certainty you need for "religious submission of will and of mind" to the teaching of the Pope when he makes it clear that such teaching is to be held as true: "the judgments made by him are [to be] sincerely adhered to, according to his manifest mind and will."

How do you apply all of that to the papal teaching on birth

control? *Lumen Gentium* 25 quoted above tells us: "[The Pope's] mind and will in the matter may be known chiefly either from **the character of the documents, from his frequent repetition of the same doctrine, or from his manner of speaking.**" We are blessed with an abundance of material since 1930 when the teaching on birth control first became a matter of division between Christian churches. I think this evidence will make it clear to any fair-minded person that all the criteria of *Lumen Gentium* 25 have been amply fulfilled and we can therefore have religious certitude that the doctrine of marital non-contraception is true. In fact, Pope John Paul II has ensured that all the criteria have been fulfilled in his pontificate, lest there be any doubt. What follows are sections on each of the three criteria taught by *Lumen Gentium* 25.

1. "The character of the documents"

Not just one but three key documents have been issued by the popes since the Anglican division of 1930, and all three are clearly **teaching documents** issued specifically to clarify doubts that had arisen.

Casti Connubii was issued by Pope Pius XI on 31 December 1930 in response to doubts raised by the Lambeth Conference of the Church of England on 14 August 1930.

Humanae Vitae was issued by Pope Paul VI on 25 July 1968 in response to doubts raised initially by the operation of the Pill and magnified by a spirit of change that was widespread in the Church in the 1960s.

Familaris Consortio was issued by Pope John Paul II on 22 November 1981 in response to doubts raised by speculation as to whether the successor to Paul VI might change the teaching of *Humanae Vitae*. It may sound silly to us today, but the contraceptionists in the Church have grasped at any straw in the wind, so they speculated that perhaps a non-Italian pope, one who didn't come up through the Curia, and one who seemed to have a real feel for the people might change the teaching on birth control. The apostolic exhortation *Familaris Consortio* authoritatively put an end to all such speculation.

All three of these documents are formal, universal teaching

documents. That is, they are not just a few remarks delivered to a small pious association having a private audience with the Pope, but they are addressed to an ever increasing circle of teachers. The encyclical letter *Casti Connubii* was addressed "To Our Venerable Brethren, Patriarchs, Primates, Archbishops, Bishops and Other Local Ordinaries Enjoying Peace and Communion with the Apostolic See." In other words—to all the primary teachers in the Roman Catholic Church.

The encyclical letter *Humanae Vitae* was addressed "To the Venerable Patriarchs, Archbishops and Bishops and Other Local Ordinaries in Peace and Communion with the Apostolic See, to Priests, the Faithful and to All Men of Good Will." You cannot find a more inclusive address unless you wanted to say "and men of bad will" which would be rather superfluous since men of bad will would not listen anyway.

Familiaris Consortio is an apostolic exhortation, and as such does not begin, as a letter does, with a list of those to whom it is addressed. However, in its conclusion, its papal author includes a wide ranging list as follows:

At the end of this Apostolic Exhortation my thoughts turn with earnest solicitude:
to you, married couples,
to you, fathers and mothers of families;
to you, young men and women, the future and the hope of the Church and the world, destined to be the dynamic central nucleus of the family in the approaching third millenium;
to you, venerable and dear Brothers in the episcopate and in the priesthood; beloved sons and daughters in the religious life, souls consecrated to the Lord, who bear witness before married couples to the ultimate reality of the love of God;
to you, upright men and women, who for any reason whatever give thought to the fate of the family.
The future of humanity passes by way of the family (n. 86).

If there were nothing else to go on, the character of these three papal documents would be fully sufficient for making it certain that every Catholic must give religious assent to the universal teaching against marital contraception.

2. "His frequent repetition"

The second criterion listed by *Lumen Gentium* 25 for knowing whether the Pope is truly calling for religious submission of will and of mind to a particular teaching is "from his frequent repetition of the same doctrine."

Pope Pius XI

There was no need for Pius XI to keep repeating what he said in *Casti Connubii*. His manner of speaking (which you will see in the next section), the radical nature of the Anglican break with Tradition, the promptness of his response, and the absence of any dissent among Catholic theologians combined to make *Casti Connubii* practically undisputed until about 1960 when the Pill added a new fuel to the fires of the sexual revolution.

Pope Paul VI

It can be argued that Pope Paul VI should have repeated the doctrine of marital non-contraception he reaffirmed in *Humanae Vitae*. However, because the doctrine of *Humanae Vitae* was so unexpected by the ruling liberal theological clique, repetition was unnecessary. The loudness of the dissent only proved that the dissenters knew very well what the teaching of the Church was and is.

Pope John Paul II

The frequency with which Pope John Paul II has reaffirmed the doctrine of marital non-contraception has been amazing to everyone. It is almost as if with *Lumen Gentium* 25 in mind, he pledged to himself that he would fulfill all of its requirements so completely that no one could have the slightest doubt that he was teaching that religious assent must be given to the doctrine of marital non-contraception.

What follows are eighteen pages of quotations and commentary which demonstrate the "frequent repetition of the same doctrine" by Pope John Paul II between 1979 and 1989.

When he was elected Pope on 16 October 1978, speculation started: what would he do about *Humanae Vitae*? Not that there was any reason to speculate—when he was Archbishop of Kracow he had made natural family planning instruction a normally required part of marriage preparation! However, all such speculation was ended before the end of the first year of his pontificate. On **5 October 1979,** while visiting the United States, he spoke to the American bishops. Noting their own reaffirmation of *Humanae Vitae* in 1968, he said:

> In exalting the beauty of marriage you rightly spoke against the ideology of contraception and contraceptive acts, as did the encyclical *Humanae Vitae.* And I myself today, with the same conviction of Paul VI, ratify the teaching of his encyclical, which was put forth by my predecessor, 'by virtue of the mandate entrusted to us by Christ'."[5]

Less than a month later, on **3 November,** he reaffirmed the doctrine again while speaking to a French natural family planning group:

> There must be no deception regarding the doctrine of the Church such as it has been clearly set forth by the Magisterium, the Council, and my predecessors; I am thinking especially of Paul VI's encyclical *Humanae Vitae.*[6]

On **16 January 1980,** the Holy Father delivered the fifteenth talk in a series of sixty-two addresses on the "theology of the body" which he gave between 5 September 1979 and 6 May 1981 (the week before he was shot by Mehmet Ali Agca).[7] Though he did not directly restate the doctrine of marital non-contraception, he reaffirmed it indirectly by teaching that in order for a couple to be able to make a sincere gift of themselves they must possess true sexual freedom. Rather obviously, whether a person must exercise self-mastery is at the heart of the birth control issue.

> We mean here freedom particularly as *mastery of oneself* (self-control). From this aspect, it is indispensable *in order that man may be able to "give himself",* in order that he may become a gift, in order that (referring to the words of the Council) he will be able to "fully discover his true self" in "a sincere giving of himself".[8]

In **the fall of 1980,** an international group of bishops convened in Rome for the Synod on the Family and declared:

> This Sacred Synod, gathered together with the successor of Peter in the unity of the faith, firmly holds what has been set forth in the Second Vatican Council (cf. *Gaudium et Spes* 50) and afterward in the encyclical *Humanae Vitae,* particularly that love between husband and wife must be fully human, exclusive and open to new life (*Humanae Vitae,* 11; cf. 9,

114

12).[9]

No one can say the doctrine of marital non-contraception is just a Roman teaching; the Synod was composed of bishops from around the world.

In **February of 1981,** Pope John Paul II traveled to the Philippines, a country with a relatively high birth rate and a target for programs pushing abortion and unnatural birth control. At a sunset Mass, the Pope reaffirmed Catholic teaching on marital love and sexuality:

> The Church will never dilute or change her teaching on marriage and the family . . . On my part, I owe it to my Apostolic office to reaffirm as clearly and as strongly as possible what the Church of Christ teaches in this regard and to reiterate vigorously her rejection of artificial contraception and abortion.[10]

On Sunday, **3 May 1981,** John Paul II addressed about 20,000 people attending a somewhat inter-religious family life conference in Rome, and noted that "in the human person what is carnal and what is spiritual interpenetrate, and therefore the two great dimensions of parenthood, procreation and education, also interpenetrate." Toward the end of his talk he quoted section 51 of *Gaudium et Spes* to teach marital chastity:

> "Therefore the acts proper to conjugal life, ordered according to authentic human dignity, must be honored with the greatest reverence . . . All this is possible only if the virtue of conjugal chastity is seriously practiced."[11]

On **15 December 1981,** the Pope released a lengthy teaching document, *Familiaris Consortio,* usually rendered in English as "The Apostolic Exhortation on the Family" (and actually dated 22 November 1981). Here, within a major document which synthesized the teaching of the 1980 Roman Synod on the Family and treated many aspects of family life, John Paul II repeatedly reaffirmed *Humanae Vitae*. In section 29, he quoted Proposition 21 of the Synod (quoted above). In section 32 he referred to the teaching of Vatican II concerning the necessity of the virtue of marital chastity in order to follow the truth of the Church's teaching on birth control, and he further noted in the same section the difference between contraception and natural family planning: "It is a difference which is much wider and deeper than is usually thought, one which involves in the final analysis two irreconcilable concepts of the human person and human sexuality."

In section 33 he strongly encouraged the teaching of natural family planning in the context of education in chastity:

Accordingly, every effort must be made to render such knowledge accessible to all married people and also to young adults before marriage through clear, timely and serious instruction and education given by married couples, doctors and experts. Knowledge must then lead to education in self-control: Hence the absolute necessity for the virtue of chastity and for permanent education in it.

In section 35 he urged the whole Church to make a greater effort to teach natural family planning:

With regard to the question of lawful birth regulation, the ecclesial community at the present time must take on the task of instilling conviction and offering practical help to those who wish to live out their parenthood in a truly responsible way . . . This implies a broader, more decisive and more systematic effort to make the natural methods of regulating fertility known, respected and applied.

Familiaris Consortio by itself would fulfill the requirements of *Lumen Gentium* for making clear the "manifest mind and will" of the Pope, but it was just the beginning.

On **3 July 1982,** the Pope addressed a natural family planning conference in Rome and repeated what he had said in *Familiaris Consortio* about the Church taking on "the task of instilling conviction and offering practical help" with natural family planning (cf. n.35). But first he noted man's current state of sinfulness: "We well know that it is not easy for man to know God's will fully, and it is still less easy to carry it out because of the intrinsic limitations of the human condition and because of the grave wounds that sin has left within us."[12]

November of 1982 saw another reaffirmation in Spain where, according to the United Press International report,

Pope John Paul II laid down strict Roman Catholic laws on abortion, birth control and premarital sex to hundreds of thousands of Spaniards in the capital and then took his message to the countryside . . . The Pope's insistence on maintaining the Vatican's ban on contraception was . . .

controversial in Spain, where birth control pills are freely available and widely used by the nation's overwhelmingly Roman Catholic population.[13]

There was no letup the next year. In **March, 1983** the Pope drew American headlines reading "Pope Attacks Divorce, Abortion, Contraception in Panama Visit" as he told a Panamanian throng, "Say no to the union not sanctioned by marriage, and to divorce. Say no to contraception and no to the crime of abortion that kills innocent human beings."[14]

In late **May of 1983** the Pope addressed the first plenary assembly of the Pontifical Council for the Family and told the 20 couples from all over the world that they must defend "the inseparable relationship between conjugal love and service to life . . . It is absolutely necessary that the pastoral action of the Christian community be totally faithful to what is taught by the encyclical *Humanae Vitae* and by the apostolic constitution, *Familiaris Consortio.*"[15]

The fall saw the Pope vigorously reaffirming the teaching of *Humanae Vitae*. On **5 September 1983** he told a group of American bishops in Rome for an *ad limina* visit that the compassionate bishop "will proclaim the doctrine of *Humanae Vitae* and *Familiaris Consortio* in its full beauty, not passing over in silence the unpopular truth that artificial birth control is against God's law."[16]

On **17 September 1983** he made a statement as strong as that of Pope Pius XI in *Casti Connubii*. To a group of more than 50 priests who had participated in a seminar on responsible parenthood, Pope John Paul II made this statement:

In a word, contraception contradicts the *truth* of conjugal love. **Contraception is to be judged objectively so profoundly unlawful as never to be, for any reason, justified.** To think or to say the contrary is equal to maintaining that in human life situations may arise in which it is lawful not to recognize God as God (emphasis added).[17]

The "manner of speaking" stated by Vatican II as a way of knowing the true papal teaching could scarcely be more clear and strong. The Holy Father, speaking to other bishops, said that using unnatural forms of birth control is against God's law and that such teaching is true. Then to a group of priests who were well acquainted with the arguments to justify contraception, he taught that marital contraception can never be justified.

Let us recall again what we are doing in this section which is so filled with quotations. We are showing that Pope John Paul II has fulfilled beyond any question of a doubt the requirements of *Lumen Gentium* for making clear the doctrine to which all faithful Catholics must give "religious submission of will and mind." And in this subsection, we are showing how John Paul II has fulfilled the criterion of "frequency of repetitions," even though there is an occasional reference to his "manner of speaking." The importance of the Pope making it so clear that he has fulfilled all the requirements of *Lumen Gentium* 25 cannot be overestimated since, to jump ahead for a moment, a new Profession of Faith and Oath of Fidelity came into force 1 March 1989. It **must** be taken by bishops, priests, deacons, seminary professors of philosophy and theology, and Catholic university teachers of faith and morals in accord with Canon 833. It **may**, and in my opinion, **should** be taken by everyone involved in Catholic education and the public life of the Church. The concluding paragraph of the Profession of Faith states:

What is more, I adhere with religious submission of will and intellect to the teachings which either the Roman Pontiff or the college of bishops enunciate when they exercise the authentic magisterium even if they proclaim those teachings in an act that is not definitive.[18]

It can be expected that some will say that the teaching of marital non-contraception reaffirmed by *Casti Connubii, Humanae Vitae* and *Familiaris Consortio* is not such a teaching; however, this review makes it clear beyond a shadow of a doubt that the doctrine of marital non-contraception must be adhered to with religious assent of mind and will according to the teaching of Vatican II's *Lumen Gentium*.

The Pope stressed the urgency of doing much more to preach and teach natural family planning when he spoke to another group of American bishops on **24 September 1983.**

A special and important part of your ministry to families has to do with natural family planning. The number of couples successfully using the natural methods is constantly growing. But much more concerted effort is needed.[19]

On **9 October 1983,** officiating at the marriage of 38 couples in St. Peter's Basilica, Pope Paul II told the couples,

As spouses the Creator calls you to procreation: to responsible procreation. To assume in marriage the task of responsible parenthood means *to cooperate consciously* with the Creator's action . . . This means to discern the rhythms of human fertility and to regulate your parenthood according to these rhythms."[20]

On **24 November 1983** he spoke to a group of bishops from Puerto Rico making their *ad limina* visit to Rome.

I therefore exhort you to continue always to spread, without ambiguity and dissimulation, the Church's teachings on the subject of the family, the particularly important nucleus of civil and ecclesial society. In this respect, never fail to teach, in all their riches and to their whole extent, the teachings of my predecessor Paul VI, contained in his Encyclical *Humanae Vitae.*[21]

On **5 December 1983,** the Sacred Congregation for Catholic Education issued a document titled "Educational Guidance in Human Love." This dealt primarily with sex education, and the sections dealing with pre-marriage catechesis affirmed that the moral evils of contraception should be taught "to the young at an appropriate age."[22]

If it would be impossible to surpass the strength of the statements made in 1983, the Pope would still manage to make a unique emphasis in **1984. On March 1,** speaking to a group of priests participating in a seminar on responsible parenthood, the Holy Father emphasized that the teaching of *Humanae Vitae* expresses the **truth** of human nature. He asked, "When, in fact, is the human conscience 'reconciled', when is it deeply at peace? When it is *in the truth.* And the two documents cited above, *Humanae Vitae* and *Familiaris Consortio,* in fidelity to the Church's tradition, have taught *the truth* of conjugal love, inasmuch as it is a communion of persons." And again: "The moral norm taught by *Humanae Vitae* and *Familiaris Consortio* is the defense of the entire truth of conjugal love, since it expresses the *absolutely necessary* demands of this love."[23] (In this and subsequent quotations, all emphasis was in the original English text.)

A **bit later in March** the Pope reaffirmed the teaching against contraception and sterilization while receiving the *ad limina* visit of bishops from Costa Rica.[24] Then on **22 March 1984,** the Bishop of Rome met with the Episcopal Council and the presbyterate of the Diocese of Rome. Referring to *Humanae Vitae,* he noted that "it was certainly a prophetic voice of the Church and especially of Pope Paul VI . . . It says 'yes' to responsible motherhood and fatherhood; it says 'no' to everything that is artificial contraception. And it says 'no' decisively and clearly."[25]

In June, while speaking to two congresses on marriage, family and responsible procreation, he addressed the importance of providing the practical help of natural family planning instruction:

"The Church is extremely grateful for what you are doing . . . The teaching of natural methods is extremely vital for the human and Christian well-being of so many couples, and hence it must never be something purely technical. It must be rooted in true science and in a complete view of the human person."

He then went on to say why:

"The ultimate reason for any natural method is not simply its biological effectiveness or reliability, but its consistence with a *Christian view of sexuality* as expressive of conjugal love. For sexuality reflects the innermost being of the human person as such, and is realized in a truly human way only if it is *an integral part of the love* by which a man and woman commit themselves *totally* to one another *until death* (cf. *Familiaris Consortio,* 11).[26]

In saying this, the Holy Father was teaching that sexual intercourse is essentially a **marriage** act, an act symbolic of the covenant of love made by the couple as they entered the sacrament of marriage. Furthermore, marital relations will be truly human only insofar as they reflect the self-giving love pledged at marriage.

By this time, Pope John Paul II had said and done more than enough to fulfill the criteria of Vatican II for demonstrating his mind and will in authoritative teaching—*Familiaris Consortio,* frequent repetition, and the clear and strong words of September 5 and 17, 1983. However, in **July of 1984,** Pope John Paul II opened an unprecedented teaching effort regarding love and sexuality. On July 11, he began the first of a series of 15 speeches to uphold the teaching reaffirmed by *Humanae Vitae,* but these speeches would be different from the many affirmations he had made over the previous five years. These talks would seek to explain and uphold the truth through a "theology of the body." He had given many talks about the theology of the body before, but this series of speeches would still be unique for at least three reasons: the series was announced ahead of time, the public announcement indicated that there would be at least twelve, and the purpose—to uphold in a most public way the truth of the doctrine of what we may call "marital non-contraception"—was clearly stated. What follows does not pretend to be summary of that series of talks, but I believe it is still helpful to review at least some of the content of those talks as they unfolded between July and the end of November in order to sample or pick up the flavor of this extraordinary teaching effort. These talks are now published in a small book, *Reflections on Humanae Vitae: Conjugal Morality and Spirituality,* and subsequent parenthetical references are to page numbers in that publication.[27]

11 July 1984: The Pope opened the series of talks with a special reference to sections 11 and 12 of *Humanae Vitae* and this explanation:

The considerations I am about to make concern particularly the passage of the Encyclical *Humanae Vitae* that deals with the "two *significances* of the marriage act" and their "inseparable connection." I do not intend to present a commentary on the whole encyclical, but rather to illustrate and examine one of its passages. From the point of view of the doctrine contained in the quoted document, that passage has a central significance (2).

He concluded this first talk by noting,

"The moral norm, constantly taught by the Church in this sphere and recalled and reconfirmed by Paul VI in his Encyclical, arises from the reading of the "language of the body *in truth*" (6).

The phrase "in truth" illustrates the great concern of the Pope. As the vicar of Christ who is *the* truth, he is concerned that all men, and especially disciples of Christ, know and live the truth about love. In this first talk of the series of fifteen, John Paul II used the phrases "the truth" and "in truth" eight times in a very short document.

18 July 1984: "The Encyclical *Humanae Vitae,* therefore, contains the moral norm ... Acts in conformity with the norm are morally right, while acts contrary to it are intrinsically illicit ... This norm is in accordance with the sum total of revealed doctrine contained in biblical sources (cf. HV, n.4) ... It seems to be totally reasonable to look precisely in the 'theology of the body' for *the foundation of the truth of the norms* that concern the fundamental problematic of man as 'body': 'the two will become one flesh' (Gen 2:24) (9-10).

25 July 1984: In this speech the Holy Father taught that *Humanae Vitae* is truly pastoral, not abstract and indifferent to human conditions. "Pastoral concern means the search for the true good of man, a promotion of the values engraved in his person by God" (18).

1 August 1984: The Pope made the first of several affirmations that natural family planning should not be used selfishly. "The concept of 'responsible parenthood' contains the disposition not merely to avoid 'a further birth' but also to increase the family in accordance with the criteria of prudence" (22).

He then went on to make an indirect reference to the language of the body, noting that the relevant principle of conjugal morality is, therefore, "fidelity to the divine plan manifested in the 'intimate structure of the conjugal act' and in the 'inseparable connection of the two significances of the conjugal act,'" (23), i.e., the unitive and the procreative meanings.

8 August 1984: The Pope noted that *Humanae Vitae* recognized that couples using unnatural methods of birth control "can be motivated by 'acceptable reasons' for postponing pregnancy; however, this *does not change the moral character which is based on the very structure of the conjugal act as such*" (27). Then, he noted that "the theology of the body is not merely a theory, but rather a specific, evangelical Christian pedagogy of the body," deriving from the nature of the Gospel which "reveals man's true good, for the purpose of modeling . . . man's earthly life in the perspective of the hope of the future world" (28). This is reminiscent of the epigram of John Wesley that in all the big decisions of life, you should have one eye on heaven, the other on hell.

22 August 1984: The Pope focused on the responsibilities inherent in being a human person: "Man is precisely a person because he is master of himself and has self-control. Indeed, insofar as he is master of himself he can give himself to the other" (32-33).

Then, he noted that the very language of the body signifies both love and potential fecundity and that both "pertain to the intimate truths of the conjugal act." However, contraceptive behavior denies one aspect of this truth. "Therefore, in such a case the conjugal act, deprived of its interior truth, because artificially deprived of its procreative capacity, ceases also to be an act of love" (33).

Continuing to sharpen the focus on the true meaning of the conjugal embrace, the Holy Father noted how contraception violates the truth of self-mastery and of the reciprocal gift of each other: "Such a violation of the interior order of the conjugal union, which is rooted in the very order of the person, **constitutes the essential evil of the contraceptive act**" (34, emphasis added). In short, contraceptive behavior is intrinsically a denial of the meaning of being a person and of the marital meaning of sex. That is why it is so evil and why the Church can never change its teaching regarding such evils!

28 August 1984: The lectures of this week and the next focused upon the proper attitudes and use of natural family planning. *Humanae Vitae* "underlines that a right and lawful regulation of fertility demands above all from husband and wife a definite family and procreative attitude . . . It requires 'that they acquire and possess solid convictions about the true values of life and of the family' (HV 21)" (37). What is at stake, moreover, "is not merely a matter of a definite 'technique' but of *ethics* in the strict sense of the term as the *morality of conduct*" (38).

Thus, "in the case of a morally upright regulation of fertility effected by means of periodic continence . . . it is a case of living by the Spirit (cf. Gal 5:25)" (39). Why? The virtuous right use of natural family planning "is determined not so much by fidelity to an impersonal 'natural law' as to the Creator-Person, the Source and Lord of the order which is manifested in such a law" (40).

5 September 1984: The international press took note that in this talk the Pope noted that natural family planning can be abused:

The use of the "infertile periods" for conjugal union can be an abuse if the couple, for unworthy reasons, seeks in this way to avoid having children, thus lowering the number of births in their family below the morally correct level, [which is] established by taking into account not only the good of one's own family, and even the state of health and the means of the couple themselves, but also the good of the society to which they belong, of the Church, and even of the whole of mankind (44).

Responsible parenthood [is] in no way exclusively directed to limiting, much less excluding children; it means also the willingness to accept a larger family (44).

Finally, the Holy Father quoted *Humanae Vitae* to show that what is at issue is not just a technique, but "an attitude which is based on the integral moral maturity of the persons and at the same time completes it" (47).

3 October 1984: The Holy Father noted that in *Humanae Vitae*, "the view of married life is at every step marked by Christian realism"(53). That is, it both recognizes the difficulties of living a chaste, non-contraceptive marriage, and it also places those difficulties in the light of the narrow gate of life and the thought of eternity. Furthermore, the encyclical points out the necessity of prayer, the Eucharist, and the Sacrament of Penance. "These are the means—*infallible and indispensable*—for forming the Christian spirituality of married life and family life"(54).

10 October 1984: John Paul II squarely faced what has been deliberately avoided in most of the 25 years of the modern debate about birth control. The difficulty of the Christian Tradition against marital contraception and other abuses of sexuality "arises from the fact that the power of love is implanted in man lured by concupiscence: in human subjects love does battle with threefold concupiscence (cf. 1 Jn 2:16), in particular with the concupiscence of the flesh which distorts the truth of the 'language of the body.' And therefore love, too, is not able to be realized in the truth of the 'language of the body' except through overcoming concupiscence" (58-59).

I might add that while contraception violates the truth of the conjugal embrace, there is also another great lie today. The realities of human weakness, lust and concupiscence are widely denied, and instead every base sexual inclination is treated as normal, as something to be accommodated, not fought against as if your very life depended on your fight. The Pope's reminder of our difficulties with concupiscence was necessary and timely.

24 October 1984: With this talk, Pope John Paul II opened a series of three lectures dealing with the virtue of continence, a virtue which needs a "clear perception of the values expressed in the law and the consequent formation of firm convictions" plus the proper "disposition of the will" (62).

Whereas "concupiscence of the flesh ... makes man in a certain sense blind and insensitive to the most profound values that spring from love," (63) the virtue of continence enables a couple to practice many "manifestations of affection" (67) that build and can express their marital communion.

While the virtue of marital chastity first of all enables the couple to resist the concupiscence of the flesh, it goes beyond that to "progressively enrich the marital dialogue of the couple, purifying it, deepening it, and the same time simplifying it" (64). In other words, marital chastity helps a couple to enrich their social intercourse so that their sexual intercourse will be a fitting reflection of their marriage covenant and ongoing relationship.

31 October 1984: In this talk, the Pope made a helpful distinction between excitement and emotion.

Excitement seeks above all to be expressed in the form of sensual and corporeal pleasure; that is, it tends toward the conjugal act which (depending on the "natural cycles of fertility") includes the possibility of procreation.

Emotion, on the other hand, is a much broader response to another human being as a person even if conditioned by the femininity or masculinity of the other person. It "does not *per se* tend toward the conjugal act but limits itself to the other 'manifestations of affection'" (74).

7 November 1984: The periodic continence of natural family planning should not be thought of as a mechanical application of biological laws. What makes it truly natural is at the deeper levels of personhood wherein the person has developed the virtue of continence and the resulting freedom of self-mastery:

The virtue of continence in its mature form gradually reveals the "pure" aspect of the spousal meaning of the body. In this way, continence develops the personal communion of the man and the woman, a communion that cannot be formed and developed in the full truth of its possibilities only on the level of concupiscence" (80-81).

21 November 1984: "In the spiritual life of married couples there are at work the gifts of the Holy Spirit, especially the 'gift of piety,' that is, the gift of respect for what is a work of God"(83). This, coupled with love and chastity, enables a married couple to respect both the integrity of the conjugal act as God made it and to respect the gift of each other. From this respect for the work of God, "all the 'affectionate manifestations' which make up the fabric of remaining faithful to the union of marriage derive their true spousal meaning. This union is expressed through the conjugal act only in given circumstances, but it can and it must be manifested continually, every day, through various 'affectionate manifestations' which are determined by the capacity" of the person to do something for his or her spouse out of love without necessarily expecting something sexual in return (85).

28 November 1984: In this last talk of the series, Pope John Paul II noted that "the catechesis which I began over four years ago and which I am concluding today can be summed up under the title: 'Human love in the divine plan,' or more precisely, 'The redemption of the body and the sacramentality of marriage.' The catechesis can be divided into two parts"(89).

The first part was based on a study of Christ's words about the indissolubility of marriage, about concupiscence, and about the resurrection of the body.

The second part "was dedicated to the analysis of the sacrament based on the Letter to the Ephesians (5:22-23)" which in turn refers to the biblical beginning of marriage in Genesis 2:24.[28]

The Pope went on to note that the term "the theology of the body" was used extensively in both parts of the catechesis and that the fifteen talks dealing with *Humanae Vitae* constitute the final part of the overall catechesis dealing with the redemption of the body and the sacramentality of marriage. In short, there can be no authentic catechesis about marriage without an affirmation of the truths expressed in *Humanae Vitae* (89-96).

My incomplete files do not show any statements of Pope John Paul II dealing directly with the contraception issue during **1985**. However, on January 28, the official Vatican newspaper published an article by Archbishop Edouard Gagnon, Pro-President of the Pontifical Council for the Family, commenting upon the series of talks the Holy Father had concluded the previous November 28th. Archbishop Gagnon noted that "In the preface to the Polish translation of *Humanae Vitae* he [John Paul II when he was bishop of Krakow] wrote: 'The doctrine concerning the ethics of marriage has been transmitted and defined with precision by the authority of the Magisterium of the Church in *Humanae Vitae*. Therefore, after the promulgation of this document, it is difficult, as far as Catholics are concerned, to speak about inculpable ignorance or about error in good faith.'"

Archbishop Gagnon continued:

Today, after the Synod on the family, after the Exhortation *Familiaris Consortio*, and above all after the Pope's brilliant catecheses, there can no longer be doubts about the authoritative doctrine of the Church and about the unacceptability of dissent.[29]

10 April 1986: John Paul II has delivered some of his strongest words about sexual morality to groups of moral theologians gathered under orthodox auspices in Rome. (The heterodox or heretical theologians avoid such congresses.) His address to the participants in the International Congress of Moral Theology (7 to 12 April 1986) form an important part of that pattern. He started by noting the importance of living the truth "to which the Church is called to give witness" by quoting Matthew 7:21: "Not every man who says to me 'Lord, Lord' will enter the kingdom of heaven, but he who does the will of my Father who is in heaven."

He then noted that the "essential linkup of Truth-Goodness-Freedom has been lost to a large extent by contemporary culture. Therefore, to lead man to rediscover it is one of the particular requirements of the Church's mission today for the salvation of the world."

Noting the dangers of moral relativism he said:

Indeed, an even more serious thing has come about: man is no longer convinced that he can find salvation only in the truth. The saving power of truth is questioned. People are entrusting to freedom alone, uprooted from any objectivity, the task of deciding autonomously what is good and what is evil. In the field of theology, this relativism turns into distrust of the wisdom of God, who guides man by means of the moral law. Against the prescriptions of the moral law are opposed the so-called concrete situations, with people no longer holding, basically, that the law of God is *always* the only true good of man.

Recognizing that moral relativism is at the heart of alleged exceptions for contraception and abortion, the Pope said:

To reduce the moral quality of our actions, regarding creatures, to the attempt to improve reality in its non-ethical contents would be equivalent, in the last analysis, to destroying the very concept of morality. The first consequence, indeed, of this reduction is the denial that, in the context of those activities, there exist acts which are always and everywhere in themselves and of themselves illicit. I have already drawn attention to this point in the Apostolic Exhortation *Reconciliatio et Paenitentia* (cf. n.17). The whole tradition of the Church has lived and lives on the conviction contrary to this denial. But even human reason, without the light of Revelation, is in a position to see the grave error of this thesis.

It is the result of deep and serious presuppositions which strike at the very heart not only of Christianity, but also of *religion* as such. That there in fact exists a moral good and evil not reducible to other human goods and evils is the necessary and immediate consequence of the *truth of creation,* which is the ultimate foundation of the *very dignity* of the human person.

The Holy Father then went on to apply these principles to two pressing issues of the day:

Man bears a law written in his heart (cf. Rom 2:15 and *Dignitatis Humanae,* 3) that he does not give to himself, but which expresses the immutable demands of his personal being created by God . . . This law is not merely made up of general guidelines, whose specification is in their respective content conditioned by different and changeable historical situations. *There are moral norms that have a precise content which is immutable and unconditioned . . . for example, the norm that prohibits contraception or that which forbids the direct killing of an innocent person.* To deny the existence of norms having such a value can be done only by one who denies the existence of a *truth* about the person, of an immutable nature in man, based ultimately on the creative Wisdom which is the measure of all reality (emphasis added).

The Pope also recorded his rejection of the appeal to the numbers of Catholics who practice contraception or who say they see nothing wrong with it.

To appeal to a "faith of the Church" in order to oppose the moral Magisterium of the Church is equivalent to denying the Catholic concept of Revelation. Not only that, but one can come to violate the fundamental right of the faithful to receive the doctrine of *the Church* from those who teach theology by virtue of a canonical mission and not the opinions of theological schools.

Finally, the Pope reminded the theologians of their obligation in charity to oppose those who dissent and teach false doctrine:

The scholar of ethics today has a grave responsibility, both in the Church and in civil society.

The problems he faces are the most serious problems for man: problems on which depend not only *eternal* salvation, but often also his future on earth. The word of God uses words in this regard that we ought continually to meditate upon. Love for whoever errs must never bring about any compromise with error: error must be unmasked and judged.

The love which the Church has for man obliges her to tell man how and when his truth is being denied, his good unrecognized, his dignity violated, his worth not adequately appreciated.

In doing this, she does not simply present "ideals": rather she teaches *who* man *is,* created by God in Christ, and therefore, what his true good is. The moral law is not something extrinsic to the person: it is the very human person himself in so far as he is called *in* and *by* the creative act itself to be and to fulfill himself freely in Christ.

With humility, but with a great firmness, you have to give witness to this truth today. In recent years we have seen the growth of an ethical-theological teaching that has not lived up to this . . .[30]

5 June 1987: The Pope addressed the participants in a study conference on responsible procreation and made several very strong statements about the certainty and truth of the teaching reaffirmed by *Humanae Vitae* including this:

The Church's teaching on contraception does not belong to the category of matter open to free discussion among theologians. Teaching the contrary amounts to leading the moral consciences of spouses into error.[31]

16 September 1987: While making a tour of the United States, John Paul II addressed the bishops of the United States in Los Angeles. Referring to reports that large numbers of Catholics do not adhere to the sexuality teaching of the Church and yet appear to receive the sacraments, the Pope said,

It is sometimes claimed that dissent from the Magisterium is totally compatible with being a "good Catholic" and poses no obstacle to the reception of the sacraments. This is a grave error that challenges the teaching office of the Bishops of the United States and elsewhere.[32]

While indirect, the inference was clear: there is a basic incompatibility between rejecting the Church's teaching about the demands of love and being a "good Catholic" and receiving the sacraments.

14 March 1988: To participants in the Fourth International Conference for the Family of Europe and Africa, the Holy Father repeated the previous teaching. First, he noted that the "doctrine expounded in the encyclical *Humanae Vitae* thus constitutes the necessary defense of the dignity and truth of conjugal love." Second, he said that "It is first of all married couples themselves who are responsible for their conjugal love, in the sense that they are called

to live it in its *entire* truth." Third, he continued, the Church helps
them: "The Church assists them in this task, enlightening their
consciences and assuring them, with the sacraments, of the strength
necessary for the will to choose good and avoid evil."

However, he continued, there are problems.

Still, I cannot pass over in silence the fact that many today do not aid
married couples in this grave responsibility of theirs, but rather place
significant obstacles in their path . . .

This can also come about, with truly grave and destructive consequences, when the doctrine taught by the Encyclical is called into
question, as has sometimes happened, even on the part of some theologians and pastors of souls. This attitude, in fact, can instill doubt with
regard to a teaching which for the Church is certain; in this way it clouds
the perception of a truth which cannot be questioned. This is not a sign
of "pastoral understanding," but of *misunderstanding the true good of
persons.* Truth cannot be measured by majority opinion.[33]

On Monday, **24 October 1988,** the Holy Father addressed the
bishops from the U. S. ecclesiastical provinces of Cincinnati and
Detroit.

As we commemorate the twentieth anniversary of the "prophetic"
Encyclical *Humanae Vitae* of Paul VI, we see ever more clearly today how
relevant and positive it is.

In a world that often reduces sex to the pursuit of pleasure, and in
some cases to domination, the Church has a special mission *to place sex
in the context of conjugal love* and of generous and responsible openness
to parenthood.

We are called to provide engaged and married couples with the
fullness of the Church's teaching on human sexuality, conjugal love and
responsible parenthood. We must emphasize the sanctity of human life
as a precious gift from God that needs to be protected and fostered, while
making greater and more systematic efforts to offer instruction in the
natural methods of family planning. Natural family planning enables
couples to understand God's design for sex, and invites them to dialogue,
mutual respect, shared responsibility and self-control (cf. *Familiaris
Consortio, 32).*[34]

On Monday, **7 November 1988,** the Holy Father addressed a
meeting of the Bishop Presidents of the Commissions for the Family
of the Episcopal Conferences throughout the world; the meeting
was organized by the Pontifical Council for the Family to mark the
twentieth anniversary of *Humanae Vitae.* After noting that "it is
extremely urgent to *revive awareness of conjugal love as a gift,*" the

Pope concluded his talk by placing *Humanae Vitae* in the context of the well being of the family and society.

The future of a more human society as well, because it is inspired and sustained by a civilization of love and life, depends largely on the moral and spiritual "quality" of marriage and the family, and depends on their "holiness."

This is the supreme end of the Church's pastoral action for which we bishops have the primary responsibility. The twentieth anniversary of *Humanae Vitae* reproposes this end to all of us with the same apostolic urgency of Paul VI who concluded his Encyclical by addressing his brothers in the episcopate with these words: "We implore you to give a lead to your priests who assist you in the sacred ministry, and to the faithful of your dioceses, and to devote yourselves with all zeal and without delay to safeguarding the holiness of marriage, the better to guide married life to its full human and Christian perfection. Look upon this mission as the most important work and responsibility committed to you at the present time" (*Humanae Vitae,* n.30).[35]

Five days later, on Saturday, **12 November 1988,** Pope John Paul II addressed about 400 theologians at the Second International Congress on Moral Theology in Rome celebrating the twentieth anniversary of *Humanae Vitae.* More will be said about this document in the section dealing with the pontiff's "manner of speaking," so the following will suffice for noting it as part of his "frequency of speaking."

It [the teaching of H. V.] is not, in fact, a doctrine invented by man: it was stamped on the very nature of the human person by God the Creator's hand and confirmed by Him in Revelation. Calling it into question, therefore, is equivalent to refusing God Himself the obedience of our intelligences.[36]

Pope John Paul II was consecrated as the successor of Peter in the See of Rome on 16 October 1978. By the end of 1988, he had explicitly reaffirmed the teaching of *Casti Connubii, Humanae Vitae* and his own *Familiaris Consortio* **at least 40 times.** There is absolutely no doubt that he has fulfilled the "frequency of repetition" requirement of *Lumen Gentium* 25 for a teaching that must be accepted by all Catholics.

3. "His manner of speaking"

As we have seen, *Lumen Gentium* 25 teaches that there are

three criteria for knowing when the Pope is teaching in such a way that his teaching requires "religious submission of will and of mind." The first two criteria are "the character of the documents" and "his frequent repetition of the same doctrine." The third criterion is "from his manner of speaking." This section for the most part provides a further analysis of statements already seen, but there are some additional texts including interpretations in the official Vatican newspaper, *L'Osservatore Romano*.

Pope Pius XI

The manner of speaking of Pope Pius XI in *Casti Connubii* could scarcely have been much stronger; it may well be the single strongest statement by any Pope about a specific moral teaching. In section IV titled "Vices Opposed to Christian Marriage" he first termed marital contraception a "criminal abuse" (para. 1).

In paragraph 3 he called it a "horrible crime" and quoted St. Augustine as follows:

> Small wonder, therefore, if Holy Writ bears witness that the Divine Majesty regards with greatest detestation this horrible crime and at times has punished it with death. As St. Augustine notes, "Intercourse even with one's legitimate wife is unlawful and wicked where the conception of the offspring is prevented. Onan, the son of Juda, did this and the Lord killed him for it."

Paragraph 4 also needs to be quoted again in its entirety.

> Since, therefore, openly departing from the uninterrupted Christian tradition some recently have judged it possible solemnly to declare another doctrine regarding this question, the Catholic Church, to whom God has entrusted the defense of the integrity and purity of morals, standing erect in the midst of the moral ruin which surrounds her, in order that she may preserve the chastity of the nuptial union from being defiled by this foul stain, raises her voice in token of her divine ambassadorship and through Our mouth proclaims anew: any use whatsoever of matrimony exercised in such a way that the act is deliberately frustrated in its natural power to generate life is an offense against the law of God and of nature, and those who indulge in such are branded with the guilt of a grave sin.

The following points stand out:

1. Pope Pius XI makes an unmistakable reference to the bishops of the Church of England who had just recently permitted the use

of unnatural means of birth control. This identifies the reaffirmation of the Christian teaching against marital contraception as the primary reason for this encyclical.

2. He identifies the Catholic Church as God's special vehicle for teaching the truth about morality.

3. He specifically notes that through his words the Catholic Church is teaching because of its unique God-given role as teacher ("raises her voice in token of her divine ambassadorship").

4. He excludes any possible rationale of trying to argue that he was reaffirming the teaching only in some incomplete sense by teaching that marital contraception offends "against the law of God *and* of nature."

5. Those who practice marital contraception are sinning. When he says that they are "branded with guilt of a grave sin," he is assuming, of course, that such couples act with sufficient reflection and full consent of their wills. Thus the statement means that in the objective order, marital contraception constitutes the grave matter of mortal sin.

Pope Paul VI

In *Humanae Vitae*, Pope Paul VI first established the competency of the Church to teach "moral teaching on marriage: a teaching founded on the natural law, illuminated and enriched by divine revelation." The text continues:

No one of the faithful will want to deny that the Magisterium of the Church is competent to interpret also the natural moral law. It is, in fact, indisputable, as our predecessors have on numerous occasions declared, that Jesus Christ, when communicating to Peter and to the Apostles His divine authority and sending them to teach His commandments to all nations, constituted them guardians and authentic interpreters of the whole moral law, that is to say, not only of the law of the Gospel, but also of the natural law. For the natural law, too, is an expression of the will of God, and it likewise must be observed faithfully to attain salvation (n.4).

Then, as Pius XI had done before him, Paul VI made it clear that he was teaching in his capacity as the Pope, the chief shepherd, not just as a theologian: "We now intend, by virtue of the mandate entrusted to us by Christ, to give our reply to these grave questions" (n.6). Again, after making references to sections 49, 50 and 51 of

Gaudium et Spes, to *Casti Connubii*, and to *Mater et Magistra*, Paul VI associated himself with such teaching: "In conformity with these fundamental elements of the human and Christian vision of marriage, we must once again declare . . ." (n.14).

The rationale that Pope Paul VI had received from the papal birth control commission was called an argument from totality. Its proponents argued that individual acts of contraception would take their morality from the marriage as a whole. In Chapter 13, "A Critique . . . ," I will show the invalidity of that argument. The important point here is that in *Humanae Vitae*, the Pope specifically answered this as follows, thus eliminating any argument that he had ignored the argument.

To justify conjugal acts made intentionally infertile, one cannot invoke as valid reasons the lesser evil, or the fact that when taken together with the fertile acts already performed or to follow later, such acts would coalesce into a whole and hence would share in one and the same moral goodness . . . Consequently it is an error to think that a conjugal act which is deliberately made infertile and so is intrinsically wrong could be made right by a fertile conjugal life considered as a whole (n.14).

Section 11 contains the key sentence of the encyclical. The Pope reaffirms that this teaching is not a matter of Church discipline such as fasting laws but is the natural moral law which the Church cannot change but must faithfully teach. A footnote at the end of n.11 refers to *Casti Connubii* and to a 1951 address of Pope Pius XII in which he also reaffirmed the same teaching.

But the Church, calling men back to the observance of the norms of the natural law, as interpreted by her constant teaching, teaches that each and every marriage act (*quilibet matrimonii usus*) must remain open to the transmission of life (n.11).

Pope John Paul II

The teaching of Pope John Paul II is so copious that space does not permit any sort of complete commentary. However, several events stand out as showing that by his manner of speaking, he was showing that the teaching of marital non-contraception must be accepted by all Catholics as true and binding.

1. First of all, I repeat part of his statement to the U. S. bishops, 5 October 1979:

I myself today, with the same conviction of Paul VI, ratify the teaching of his encyclical which was put forth by my predecessor "by virtue of the mandate entrusted to us by Christ."[37]

In the first part of that statement, John Paul II clarified where he stood, and in the second part he was clearly joining Pius XI and Paul VI in stating that he was teaching this not as his personal opinion but in his capacity as the chief shepherd, the Vicar of Christ on earth.

2. The manner of his speaking to priests on 17 September 1983 is highly significant. There is no group of people in the Church who are more likely to look for exceptions to the law than priests. They have been trained in moral theology to make distinctions between positive law and negative law, how to find or make exceptions to positive law under the principle of *epikeia**, how to apply the theory of probabilism, and, in general, how to find a way out of a general obligation if one can be found in a particular case.

Thus his manner of speaking to a group of priests who had just participated in a seminar on responsible parenthood bears repeating:

When, therefore, through contraception, married couples remove from the exercise of their conjugal sexuality its potential procreative capacity, they claim a power which belongs solely to God: the power to decide *in a final analysis* the coming into existence of a human person. They assume the qualification not of being cooperators in God's creative power, but the ultimate depositaries of the source of human life. In this perspective, contraception is to be judged objectively so profoundly unlawful as never to be, for any reason justified. To think or to say the contrary

---

* Epikeia. From the Greek word for equity. "The name given in moral theology to a principle of interpretation of human laws. It means that such a law (even an ecclesiastical one) does not bind if right reason indicates that the legislator did not wish it to bind (in these particular and quite concrete circumstances), for instance if the difficulty of obeying the law here and now were disproportionate to the end which the law has in view (thus St. Thomas Aquinas, Suarez and others). —Karl Rahner and Herbert Vorgrimler, *Theological Dictionary,* Cornelius Ernst, O.P., ed., Richard Strachen, translator (New York: Herder and Herder, 1965). As indicated, epikeia applies only to human laws, not to the demands of the natural moral law.

is equal to maintaining that in human life situations may arise in which it is lawful not to recognize God as God.[38]

In other words there aren't any exceptions.

That statement stirred the opposition of the dissenters, and shortly thereafter two articles appeared in *L'Osservatore Romano* in response to the criticisms. An Italian bishop responded as follows, noting that when someone denies God the right to establish moral limits, he engages in practical atheism:

The fact remains that the words of the Holy Father lead us to dig deeply into the truth, the primary and deepest reasons which are at the base of the pontifical teaching on the subject in question: if God exists, as He does exist, and if He is the Creator of man, as He is, that is, if "at the origin of every human person there is a creative act of God", at the moment of generation, man does not operate only under God's gaze, but he cooperates with God. Along this line, contraception means that man, through his free, unilateral choice, cancels a plan which is a precise will of God: the plan of men whom God willed to create and which man vetoed.

Can this be lawful? We can understand, without justifying it (let it be understood), the act of weakness which has led a person to commit the unlawful, but we cannot understand or admit that the person claims to have acted well, since in this case he places himself above God or in God's place, which is as much as to say he "does not recognize God as God."

In the first case he enters the area where sinners are found (which in one way or another we all are) and he becomes for the Church a child to be loved more, in order to restore him to communion with God through pastoral work and the help of grace; in the second case, he sins by atheism, as in some way all of those do who place themselves in God's place, denying Him the right to establish moral limits to their actions, denying sin and affirming that man is a law until himself.

This is a serious matter, a matter which does not stop half-way, a complete matter. The Church teaches, as is its duty, the truth. And it is the truth which judges man, it is not man's habits which judge truth or which (even less) establish it. It is the immobile magnetic needle of the compass which points out the path, it is not the path which moves the magnetic needle at its pleasure. It is the truth which makes man "true," it is not man's judgment which makes the truth. These are simple things, almost childish, but they become difficult, perhaps because we are becoming unaccustomed to the truth, or because we have too many selfish reasons which impel us to deny the truth when it is uncomfortable.[39]

A professor of moral theology (Alberone College, Piacenza, Italy) commented on the criticism the Pope was receiving by recalling his words to a group of American bishops just 12 days before his strong words of September 17. On 5 September 1983 the Pope had told the bishops that the compassionate bishop "will proclaim without fear or ambiguity the many controverted truths of our age" including "the doctrine of *Humanae Vitae* and *Familiaris Consortio* in its full beauty, not passing over in silence the unpopular truth that artificial birth control is against God's law ... The bishop will be called upon over and over again to accept criticism" for such teaching. The author noted that the Pope himself had received such criticism. Then turning to the controversy raised by the address of September 17, the author noted:

Paul VI had already seen in contraception behavior which implies a *de facto* refusal on the part of the man and the woman to recognize that they are cooperators of God or "ministers of the plan established by the Creator," and the attempt to make themselves "arbiters of the sources of human life." In other words, on the objective level, contraception implies the attempt to radically exclude God as the ultimate source of personal human life in order to put in his place man and woman as "the ultimate depositaries of the source of human life," John Paul II says in his discourse.

To call such behavior lawful is, obviously, again as the Pope said, the same as "maintaining that in human life, situations may arise in which it is lawful not to recognize God as God." And he could have rightly added: "and to attempt to put oneself in his place."

The clamour which has arisen around the Pope's words appears to be a clear and significant confirmation that the "loss of the sense of sin," so widespread in countries of ancient Christian tradition, is rooted in the "loss of the sense of God." And that prevents the grasping of a true and proper practical atheism, which has subtly penetrated the hearts of those who delude themselves that they are still Christians, while they have accepted concepts and the life styles in which there is no longer room for God, but only for a puppet God to whom is paid the homage of external rites and acts, but belief in whose existence in no way affects one's individual, family or social life, now guided by criteria and principles incompatible not only with a Christian concept of life but also with a simply religious one.[40]

These articles in the official Vatican newspaper are not the formal teaching of the Church, but they are very strong statements that the Pope is not going to back off in the face of criticism, and they help to highlight the significance of the very strong manner of speaking by Pope John Paul II.

3. If there is one thing which has characterized the manner of speaking of Pope John Paul II, it is his emphasis that men and women are called to live the truth about love. This was brought out forcefully in the Pope's address (Thursday, 1 March 1984) to priests participating in a course on responsible parenthood.

When, in fact is the human conscience "reconciled," when is it deeply at peace? When it *is in truth*.

To reconcile the human conscience of married couples with the God of Truth and of Love: the human conscience of married couples is truly reconciled when they have discovered and welcomed the truth about their conjugal love.

The Holy Father then went on to point out that it is not just a merely intellectual recognition of the truth; it must be put into practice.

There exists a *real* difficulty to the reconciliation of the human consciences of married couples with the God of Truth and of Love; it is of quite another kind from the one just indicated.

Reconciliation does not occur if the married couples can *merely* perceive the truth of their conjugal love: it is necessary that by their freedom they make the truth effective and *put it into practice.* The *real* difficulty is that the *heart* of man and woman is prey to concupiscence: and concupiscence urges freedom not to consent to the authentic demands of conjugal love. It would be a very serious error to conclude from this that the Church's teaching in this matter is in itself only an "ideal" which must then be adapted, proportioned, graduated to the so-called concrete possibilities of man: according to a "balancing of the various goods in question." But what are the "concrete possibilities of man"? And of *which* man are we speaking? Of the man *dominated* by lust or of the man *redeemed by Christ*? Because this is the matter in question: the *reality* of Christ's redemption.

Christ has redeemed us! This means: he has given us the possibility of realizing *the entire* truth of our being; he has liberated our freedom from the *domination* of lust. And if the redeemed man still sins, this is not due to an imperfection of Christ's redemptive act, but to man's will not to avail himself of the grace which flows from that act. God's *command is of course proportioned* to man's capabilities: but to the capabilities of the man to whom the Holy Spirit has been given; of the man who, though he has fallen into sin, can always obtain pardon and enjoy the presence of the Holy Spirit.

The reconciliation of the human conscience of the married couple with the God of Truth and of Love is effected through the remission of sins:

through the humble recognition that we are not up to standard, so to speak, when measured against the Truth and its demands, and not through the proud reduction of the Truth and its demands to what we decide is true and good. Our freedom consists in being servants of the Truth.[41]

About six months earlier, John Paul II had linked dissent from the universal teaching of *Humanae Vitae* to a form of practical atheism. In this March 1 statement, he linked the acceptance of this teaching **to the redemption itself**. Clearly, the Pope is teaching that the doctrine of marital non-contraception is not a peripheral truth but is very close to the core of Christian belief because its acceptance or non-acceptance says so much about what you believe or do not believe about the redeeming grace of God.

4. On 10 April 1986 Pope John Paul II continued his emphasis on the radical importance of doing the truth in an address to the participants in the first International Congress on Moral Theology (Rome, 7 to 12 April).

The good of the person is in *being* the Truth and in *doing* the Truth.

Speaking of the denial that "there exist acts which are always and everywhere in themselves and of themselves illicit," he noted that such denials are "the result of deep and serious presuppositions which strike at the very *heart* not only of Christianity, but also of *religion* as such." Furthermore, "The moral law is not something extrinsic to the person: it is the very human person himself insofar as he is called *in* and *by* the creative act itself to be and to fulfill himself freely in Christ."

Finally, the Pope continued to link the birth control issue to fundamental Christian beliefs:

To appeal to a "faith of the Church" in order to oppose the moral Magisterium of the Church is **equivalent to denying the Catholic concept of Revelation**. Not only that, but one can come to violate the fundamental right of the faithful to receive the doctrine of *the Church* from those who teach theology by virtue of a canonical mission and not the opinions of theological schools.[42] (Boldface emphasis added.)

5. On 5 June 1987 the Holy Father taught that the Church's teaching on contraception is so certain that it is no longer even a matter for discussion among theologians. The context was an

address to members of a conference on responsible procreation. In the section quoted below, he acknowledges one of the greatest difficulties in promoting natural family planning, namely, priests and others who say it's not sinful to use unnatural methods of birth control.

> The difficulties you encounter are of various kinds. The first, and in a certain sense the most serious, is that even within the Christian community voices have been heard, and are still being heard, which cast doubt upon *the very truth* of the Church's teaching. This teaching has been vigorously expressed by Vatican II, by the Encyclical *Humanae Vitae,* by the Apostolic Exhortation *Familiaris Consortio* and by the recent Instruction "The Gift of Life." A grave responsibility derives from this: those who place themselves in open conflict with the law of God, authentically taught by the Church, guide spouses along a false path. **The Church's teaching on contraception does not belong to the category of matter open to free discussion among theologians**. Teaching the contrary amounts to leading the moral consciences of spouses into error.[43] (Boldface emphasis added.)

6. On 14 March 1988, the Pope repeated the same message to a similar conference. Speaking of the doctrine of *Humanae Vitae,* he called it "a teaching which belongs to the permanent patrimony of the Church's moral doctrine," and he noted the "uninterrupted continuity with which the Church has taught it." Then he repeated his teaching that the doctrine of marital non-contraception is beyond question.

> In addition, in their effort to live their conjugal love correctly, married couples can be seriously impeded by a certain hedonistic mentality widespread today, by the mass media, by ideologies and practices contrary to the gospel. This can also come about, with truly grave and destructive consequences, when the doctrine taught by the Encyclical is called into question, as has sometimes happened, even on the part of some theologians and pastors of souls. This attitude, in fact, can instill doubt with regard to a teaching which for the Church is certain; in this way it clouds the perception of a truth which cannot be questioned. This is not a sign of "pastoral understanding," but of *misunderstanding the true good of persons*. Truth cannot be measured by majority opinion.[44]

7. On 15 October 1988, John Paul II told the U. S. bishops of the State of New York that the universal ordinary magisterium is "the usual expression of the Church's infallibility."

The significance of his manner of speaking to this group of American bishops is twofold. First of all, there are some priests and perhaps some bishops who think they can avoid teaching the doctrine of *Humanae Vitae* because it has not been defined by an act of the *extraordinary* magisterium. This was a reminder that the usual way of teaching infallibly is through the universal ordinary magisterium. (See Chapter 7, "Is the teaching infallible?")

The second significance of this is that among the New York bishops was the Ordinary of Rochester who has solidly backed Rochester priest and arch-dissenter Charles E. Curran. This was a polite but obvious way of telling this bishop that he errs by his continued backing of Fr. Curran who appears to acknowledge no authority higher than his own opinions. Here's the relevant passage:

> This *magisterium* is not above the divine word but serves it with a specific *carisma veritatis certum* (*Dei Verbum*, 8), which includes the charism of infallibility, present not only in the solemn definitions of the Roman Pontiff and of Ecumenical Councils, but also in the universal ordinary magisterium (*Lumen Gentium* 25), which can truly be considered as the usual expression of the Church's infallibility.[45]

This is traditional Catholic teaching, and it was expressed this way by Karl Rahner, S.J., in a continuation of the text quoted earlier in this chapter. (See reference no.4.)

> But also through her *ordinary* magisterium, that is in the normal teaching of the Faith to the faithful in schools, sermons and all other kinds of instructions. In the nature of the case this will be the normal way in which moral norms are taught, and definitions by Pope or general council the exception; but it is binding on the faithful in conscience just as the teaching through the extraordinary magisterium is.[46]

Also of special interest in this chapter on forming a correct conscience are the following words to those New York bishops:

> Some people appeal to "freedom of conscience" to justify this way of acting. Therefore, it is necessary to clarify that it is not conscience that "freely" establishes what is right and wrong. Using a concise expression of John Henry Newman's Oxford University Sermons, we can say that conscience is "an instrument for detecting moral truth." *Conscience detects moral truth:* it interprets a norm which it does not create (cf. *Gaudium et Spes,* 16; Paul VI, General Audience, 12 February 1969).

8. **Saturday, 12 November 1988.** Just as John Paul II had

addressed some of his strongest words of 1983 to priests, so also some of his strongest words of 1988 were addressed to approximately 400 moral theologians who could fully understand the importance of what he was saying. Speaking of the doctrine of marital non-contraception, he taught its **divine origin:**

> It is not, in fact, a doctrine invented by man: it was stamped on the very nature of the human person by God the Creator's hand and confirmed by him in Revelation. Calling it into question, therefore, is equivalent to refusing God Himself the obedience of our intelligence. It is equivalent to preferring the dim light of our reason to the light of divine Wisdom, thereby falling into the darkness of error and resulting in the undermining of other fundamental principles of Christian doctrine (n.3).[47]

Then the Holy Father proceeded to teach that it is wrong to make some sort of appeal to conscience as a way to escape the obligation to form your conscience according to the truth taught by Christ through the teaching office of His Church:

> During these years, following the contestation about *"Humanae Vitae"*, the Christian doctrine on moral conscience itself has been questioned by accepting the idea of *creative* conscience of the moral norm. In this way, that bond of obedience to the holy will of the Creator, in which the very dignity of man consists, is radically broken. Conscience, in fact, is the "place" where man is illuminated by a light which does not come to him from his created and always fallible reason, but from the very Wisdom of the Word in whom all things were created. "Conscience", as Vatican II again admirably states, "is man's most secret core, and his sanctuary. There he is alone with God whose voice echoes in his depths" (*Gaudium et Spes*, 16).

> From this some consequences are drawn which are to be stressed.

> Since the *Magisterium of the Church* was created by Christ the Lord to enlighten conscience, then to appeal to that conscience precisely to contest the truth of what is taught by the Magisterium implies rejection of the Catholic concept both of the Magisterium and moral conscience. To speak about the inviolable dignity of conscience without further specification runs the risk of grave errors. There is a great difference between the person who falls into error after having used all the means at his or her disposal in the search for truth, and the situation of one who, either through simple acquiescence to the majority opinion, often deliberately created by the powers of the world, or through negligence, takes little pains to discover the truth. The clear teaching of Vatican II reminds us of this: "Yet it often happens that conscience goes astray through ignorance which it is unable to avoid, without thereby losing its dignity. This cannot be said of the man who takes little trouble to find out what is true and good,

142

or when conscience is by degrees almost blinded through the habit of committing sin" (*ibid*).

The Church's Magisterium is among the means which Christ's redeeming love has provided to avoid this danger of error. In His name it has a real teaching authority. Therefore, it cannot be said that the faithful have embarked on a diligent search for truth if they do not take into account what the Magisterium teaches, or if, by putting it on the same level as any other source of knowledge, one makes oneself judge, or if in doubt, one follows one's own opinion or that of theologians, preferring it to the sure teaching of the Magisterium (n.4).

John Paul II then reaffirmed the teaching of "no exceptions" that he had made five years earlier:

Closely connected with the theme of moral conscience is *the theme of the binding force of the moral norm taught by Humanae Vitae.*

By describing the contraceptive act as intrinsically illicit, Paul VI meant to teach that the moral norm is such that it does not admit exceptions. No personal or social circumstances could ever, can now, or will ever, render such an act lawful in itself. The existence of particular norms regarding man's way of acting in the world, which are endowed with a binding force that excludes always and in whatever situation the possibility of exceptions, is a constant teaching of Tradition and of the Church's Magisterium which cannot be called in question by the Catholic theologian (n. 5).

Theologians are accustomed to terminology about a hierarchy of truths, for example, that belief in the Blessed Trinity is more of a central core teaching of the Church than, say, its teaching about Purgatory. The theologians at this conference would be well acquainted with the efforts of various dissenters to treat the teaching of *Humanae Vitae* as peripheral, way, way down on the hierarchy of truths, having nothing to do with God Himself and not too relevant to the contemporary concern for enhancing the dignity of man. In that light, the following text is of great significance as the Pope teaches that it is not a peripheral teaching but involves **a central teaching** of Catholic faith.

Here *a central point* of Christian doctrine concerning God and man is involved. If one looks closely at what is being questioned by rejecting that teaching, one sees that *it is the very idea of the Holiness of God.* In predestining us to be holy and immaculate in his sight, he created us "in Christ Jesus for good works . . . that we should walk in them" (Eph 2:10). Those moral norms are simply the demand—from which no historical circumstance can dispense—of the Holiness of God which is shared in the *concrete,* no longer in the abstract, with the individual human person.

Furthermore, such negation *renders the Cross of Christ meaningless* (cf. 1 Cor 1:17). By becoming incarnate, the Word entered fully into our daily existence which consists of concrete human acts. By dying for our sins, he re-created us in the original holiness which must be expressed in our daily activity in the world.

Moreover, such negation implies, as a logical consequence, that there is no truth about man which is outside the course of historical evolution. To render void the Mystery of God results, as always, in rendering void the mystery of man, and the non-recognition of God's rights results, as always, in the negation of man's dignity (n.5).

In his manner of speaking, John Paul II has left no room for doubt that the doctrine of marital non-contraception reaffirmed by *Casti Connubii, Humanae Vitae,* and *Familiaris Consortio* must be believed and put into practice. He has taught:

—that to hold out for exceptions as if God's grace were not sufficient is a form of atheism (17 September 1983);

—that denying the doctrine of marital non-contraception is "equivalent to denying the Catholic concept of revelation" (10 April 1986);

—that it is a teaching whose truth is beyond discussion (5 June 1987);

—that it is a "teaching which belongs to the permanent patrimony of the Church's moral doctrine" and "a truth which cannot be questioned" (14 March 1988);

—that it is a teaching which is intrinsic to our human nature and that calling it into question "is equivalent to refusing God himself the obedience of our intelligence" (12 November 1988);

—and finally that "what is being questioned by rejecting that teaching . . . *is the very idea of the holiness of God"* (12 November 1988).

An Objection

The followers of Fathers Charles Curran and Richard McCormick, S.J., sometimes mislead or perplex the person who is seeking to form a correct conscience by trying to make it appear that the teaching Church is not united in its teaching against marital contraception; then they try to suggest that, in the face of this apparent lack of unity, Catholic believers are free to form their consciences according to the opinions of the dissenters and in contradiction to the teaching of the magisterium. The principal vehicle they use for trying to create confusion is the immediate post-*Humanae Vitae* reaction on the part of a few national groups of bishops—Canadian and European.

The first and essential thing to be noted is that no group of bishops contradicted the teaching of *Humanae Vitae;* none said that it was permissible to use contraception. The second thing to be noted is that some did say some things about conscience that were open to misinterpretation; the need for properly forming your conscience according to the teaching of the Church was not given adequate emphasis.

For example, in 1968, the Canadian Catholic Conference issued a statement that contained this sentence concerning people who had difficulty following the teachings of *Humanae Vitae*: "In accord with the accepted principles of moral theology, if these persons have tried sincerely but without success to pursue a line of conduct in keeping with the given directives, they may be safely assured that whoever honestly chooses the course which seems right to him does so in good conscience."

A more misleading statement would be hard to imagine. There are no principles of moral theology that allow a person to choose to engage in actions taught by the Church to be objectively immoral, whether such actions be adultery, contraception, fornication or sodomy. And, of course, what applies to one behavior applies to all the rest.

If a couple fail in chastity, that provides no right to call bad conduct good. Rather, *Humanae Vitae* clearly recognized human weakness and counseled couples in this way: "And if sin should still keep its hold over them, let them not be discouraged, but rather have recourse with humble perseverance to the mercy of God which is poured forth in the sacrament of Penance" (n. 25).

Whether the Canadian bishops gave their 1968 statement much prior thought is problematic, and what they actually meant is a puzzle. However, there was no doubt about its effects. It was widely interpreted to mean, "You can ignore *Humanae Vitae*; you can dissent."

Thus five years later, the Canadian Catholic bishops *de facto* admitted their 1968 statement was a pastoral disaster, and on 12

December 1973 they issued a document titled *Statement of the Formation of Conscience* which contained the following key statements:

If his [the Catholic] ultimate practical judgment to do this or avoid that does not take into full account the teaching of the Church, an account based not only on reason but on the faith dimension, he is deceiving himself in pretending that he is acting as a true Catholic must.

For a Catholic, "to follow one's conscience" is not, then, simply to act as his unguided reason dictates. "To follow one's conscience" and to remain a Catholic, one must take into account first and foremost the teaching of the magisterium. When doubt arises due to a conflict of "my" views and those of the magisterium, the presumption of truth lies on the part of the magisterium.

The bishops then quoted *Lumen Gentium* 25 about religious assent and added that the teaching of the bishops and/or the Pope "must be carefully distinguished from the teaching of individual theologians or individual priests, however intelligent or persuasive."[48]

Finally, it must be recognized that whatever possible "argument from ambiguity" which might have existed in 1968-1969 no longer exists. During the 1980s, John Paul II removed any pretext of an argument from that perspective by his clear, frequent, and emphatic teaching.

Summary

This chapter has been concerned about the formation of a correct conscience, the conscience by which you make right judgments about what you must do and what you must avoid doing. We briefly explored the need for a source of truth which can give us certain knowledge about right and wrong, and we saw that God has revealed truths not only about Himself but about man as well. The culmination of revelation was the God-man, and the Lord Jesus not only taught the truth in His earthly lifetime but also established His Church upon Peter, the rock, to continue to teach the truth about God, man, and love to all generations.

We noted various ways in which the Church teaches, and we looked closely at the teaching of Vatican II about the formation of conscience according to the teaching of the Pope. Finally, we reviewed the way in which the teaching of Pope John Paul II has fulfilled the requirements of *Lumen Gentium* 25 for a teaching requiring religious submission of will and mind.

No Pope in the history of the Church has taught more clearly and consistently, in season and out of season, about marital love and sexuality and the immorality of unnatural methods of birth control than Pope John Paul II. "His mind and will in the matter" are obvious. He has used a formal teaching document, *Familiaris Consortio*, has repeated the teaching both in Rome and in his world travels, and has used clear and very strong language. He has amply fulfilled all the requirements of Vatican II for the clear and authoritative teaching by which the believing Catholic must form his or her conscience.

There are two conclusions.

1. The person who is Catholic in any meaningful sense of that word has to recognize that God is keeping alive—even today—the unchanging truths about human love, that God is teaching these truths through the prophetic office of Peter, an office personally established by Christ. The teaching is unchanging because it is rooted in our human nature. The only thing which has changed is this: through modern natural family planning, this teaching is incomparably easier to follow than it was in 1930 or at any previous time. The first conclusion is that Catholics must give religious assent to the teaching against marital contraception and act accordingly.

2. The second conclusion is that non-Catholic Christians as well as Catholics must recognize the truth of the pre-1930 universal teaching against marital contraception. They must recognize that this is no more of a Catholic-Protestant issue than abortion. Just as in many cases they must reject their own Church's permissive stance towards abortion, so also they must reject a permissive stance towards contraception. Everyone is called to live according to the truth.

7

Is the Teaching Infallible?

Introduction

To a large extent, the subject of this chapter is academic. If you are an ordinary Catholic who simply wants to know whether the Church teaching against contraception is so firm and so certain that you are required to form your conscience accordingly, your answer (which is "yes") is found in Chapter 6. As you saw there, the believing Catholic finds all the certainty he or she needs for a certain and correct conscience from the constant teaching of the Popes since 1930. As you will recall, prior to 1930, there was no need for such specific and frequent affirmation of the teaching against marital contraception because before 1930 the teaching was part of the universal heritage of Christians. Specifically, before 14 August 1930 no Christian Church had ever said that it could be morally permissible for married couples to use unnatural forms of birth control.

The question raised in this chapter goes beyond the certainty needed for day to day living and asks, "Is the Church's teaching about birth control taught with the dogmatic note of infallibility?"

This chapter has two major parts. In the first, I show that the Church *can* teach infallibly about birth control. The second part reviews two entirely different arguments that the Church not only **can** but *de facto* **has** taught infallibly on this issue.

The first of these arguments relies upon the constancy of Christian teaching against unnatural forms of birth control, a tradition present and unbroken in all Christian churches until 1930. This argument may be even more important for non-Catholic Christians than for Catholics. They may not use the "infallible" terminology, but they cannot ignore the issue. They simply must ask themselves about the truth force of an uninterrupted teaching of nineteen centuries. Many such Christians have learned from the abortion issue that they must question the present-day teaching of their respective churches. They recognize that the *mainline* Protestant churches—and who can speak for the highly individualistic Evangelical and Pentecostal churches?—have unfortunately but almost unanimously been horribly wrong in teaching that it is permissible for Christians to kill their unborn children. Christians who recognize the evil of abortion must ask themselves, then, how they can believe their church's liberal teaching about birth control if and when it has been so wrong about the much more obvious issue of abortion. Such an examination is regularly leading Christians separated from the Catholic Church to form their consciences according to the historic and traditional teaching reaffirmed by *Casti Connubii* and *Humanae Vitae*. In fact, I have learned of Protestant couples who have had tubal ligations reversed upon becoming convinced of the truth of the traditional teaching.

The inter-denominational recognition of the truth of the historic, traditional teaching against unnatural forms of birth control can be documented. Ingrid Trobisch, a Lutheran, while not addressing theological issues, recommended only natural family planning in her well received *The Joy of Being a Woman*.[1] A Lutheran minister and his wife, Larry and Nordis Christenson, wrote of their early use of marital contraception, their discovery of NFP, and concluded that they would never return to the use of unnatural methods "even if the alternative were 21 children."[2] German Lutheran physician and theologian Siegfried Ernst has written eloquently in defense of *Humanae Vitae*, calling it a prophetic teaching and noting a contradiction between receiving the Host and taking the Pill.[3] Evangelical Mary Pride initially rejected *any* form of family planning including NFP,[4] but in her next book and in personal communication she dropped her opposition to NFP when it was used for truly serious reasons.[5] Theologically trained Charles Provan has published the findings of his research among Protestant theologians from Luther and Calvin up to 1930. Luther, by the way, regarded Onanism as sodomy, and Calvin regarded it as murder.[6] I found quite impressive Provan's list of 99 Protestant theologians who had commented against Onanism, including 66 quotations, some quite long. The distribution of these materials is bound to have a positive effect in restoring belief among Christians about the immorality of marital contraception.

In this chapter, however, I am concerned specifically with the teaching of the Roman Catholic Church, but much of what follows can be applied to the church in the sense of the community of Christian churches.

I. *Can* the Church Teach Infallibly about Birth Control?

At first sight, it may seem strange to raise the question whether or not the Church can teach infallibly about birth control considering how much the Church has said over the past centuries. One has only to leaf through John Noonan's *Contraception*[7] to realize that the Church has been teaching about this area of human behavior for some 1900 years. It may seem rather late to raise the question as to whether the Church has any unique, Spirit-led competency in this field, but the question has been raised.

More precisely stated, the question is whether or not the teaching of the Church in this area ever can be definitive and infallible or whether, by the very nature of the subject, the Church's teaching will always be fundamentally changeable and non-infallible. The latter point of view says that it is impossible for the Pope, and/or bishops in Council, to teach infallibly in this area. That is, the Church in its magisterium may have something to say in the way of human wisdom, but it has nothing to say in its unique capacity as the Body of Christ whose Head, the Lord Jesus, can continue to clarify revelation through the continued working of the Holy Spirit.[8] Somehow or other, the critics say or infer, the Spirit may lead each couple in truth, but that same Spirit cannot lead the Church to teach infallibly in this same area. It is an important question which must be answered before we can proceed to the questions about truth and the dogmatic note of infallibility.

It seems to me that if we are to answer in any decent form the question about the Church's competence to teach infallibly about contraception, we first have to have a clear understanding of what we mean by the Church and by its role as teacher. Then we can look at what is involved in contraception to see whether this falls within the scope of its jurisdiction.

A. The Church

That desirable, clear understanding of what we mean by the Church, however, has been obscured at the same time that the storm clouds of the contraception battle have been forming. Whether or not this is coincidental or whether the birth control question has actually caused confusion about the nature of the Church is beyond the scope of this book, but it is beyond question that the same years that have seen the contraception controversy have also witnessed a growing crisis of authority within the Church. I think that for the person who is interested in the Church, this crisis of authority can be interpreted as confusion about 1) what the Church is (ecclesiology) and 2) how teaching and learning are meant to take place in the Church (religious epistemology). Without entering into a lengthy investigation of the nature of the Church and current conceptions about it, I think we can look at four different elements in the Church today which receive various degrees of emphasis, an emphasis somewhat related to the personal standpoint of the individual concerned.

1. The layman. The contraception controversy has provided many a lay person with a situation without recent precedent for expressing his or her personal feelings about birth control and the teaching of the Popes. This has been encouraged by many who felt that since the laity formed the majority of the Church as the People of God, the lay voice needed to be heard. Furthermore, since the workings of the Holy Spirit were not limited to the magisterium, and since the teaching of the magisterium had been formed under different social conditions and seemed to be confused under the present social and scientific conditions, it was possible, probable, or even certain that the Holy Spirit was now to be heard through the very emphatic voice of the laity who were demanding a change in the official teaching. The tract of John Henry Cardinal Newman, "On Consulting the Faithful in Matters of Doctrine" has been referred to by those who emphasized the role of the laity in forming the Church. Newman's phrase, *consensus fidelium*, is almost a catchword in this emphasis, for if one thing seems certain in the contraception controversy, it is that there is no consensus among the Christians of Europe and North America that the traditional doctrine is true. According to this emphasis on the laity as forming the majority element in the Church, surveys that show that over 50% of the Catholics in a given area practice contraceptive birth control would indicate that the consensus of the faithful favors contraception, and this may indicate that the Holy Spirit favored it too.

However, Christ did not establish His Church as a democracy, and Cardinal Newman used the term *consensus fidelium* to describe those who held fast to the actual teaching of the Church despite the errors of theologians and many clergy. More on this in Chapter 13.

It should also be noted that much, and perhaps most, of the philosophical and theological defense of *Humanae Vitae* has come from the laity, almost entirely from the married laity, and that almost all of the leadership in the natural family planning movement consists of married laity.

2. The theologian. A second emphasis has been on the role of the theologian in the Church. It was probably the best-known fact of Catholic life, in the decade 1968-78, that the birth control commission appointed by John XXIII and continued by Paul VI ended in a divided position with the majority recommending a change in the teaching to allow contraception. (More on this in Chapter 11.) The next best-known fact of Catholic life in that decade might have been that sizable numbers of Catholic theologians and philosophers had gone on record against the papal teaching. It is not altogether clear how many of these believed that the Pope had taught wrongly, or how many merely wanted to say that, since he had not spoken in the irrevocable manner we call a *de fide, ex cathedra* pronouncement, there was still room to debate and to form one's own conscience without regarding the official doctrine as normative. At any rate, whether it was expressed in so many words, the inference was clear. How could so many learned people be wrong? How could the Pope be right in the face of this? Was not the Pope in error three times—once for not listening to his own commission, secondly for teaching an outmoded doctrine, and thirdly for being a prisoner of the Curia, officials representing only a minority of the Church's theologians? Suffice it to say two things. 1) Many theologians wholeheartedly support the magisterium; 2) the intellectual pride of a few theologians has been at the source of every heresy known to the Church.

3. Church councils. While the first emphasis noted above was on the laity and leaned on numbers, the second emphasis was on the expertise of theologians and others (although the numbers aspect is certainly there). The third makes use both of numbers and expertise but also adds a more dogmatic note. This is the appeal to a Council—a meeting of, presently, some 2,500 bishops who are supposed to have good theological advice and personal knowledge. Moreover, in addition to numbers and expertise, it is a matter of faith that when a Council sanctioned by the Pope defines a matter of faith or morals, it has been led infallibly by the Holy Spirit. In the light of the current question, the inference in the emphasis on a Council seems to be that the papal teaching should be appealed to a higher body—the Council. It is well known that this was

Luther's appeal. However, Luther is much more to be excused for this appeal than any Catholic today. Luther lived at a time of conciliarism, at a time when the shock of the Western Schism had still not worn away. We live with the heritage of Vatican I and Vatican II which leave no doubt. Neither Council leaves any room for holding that it is possible to appeal to a General Council as being above the Pope, though it is, of course, still possible to appeal a teaching not taught infallibly by the Pope to a Council-in-union-with-the-Pope in order to obtain a clarification, a definition or even a change.

The reality is that Vatican Council II deferred final decision on the birth control issue to the Pope, strongly reaffirmed the procreative dimension of marriage and marital relations, and reaffirmed *Casti Connubii* and other papal teachings against contraception by referring to them in a footnote. (See full texts of relevant sections of *Gaudium et Spes* in Chapter 16, "Documentation.") Furthermore, the 1980 Synod of the Family, composed of bishops from around the world, specifically reaffirmed the teaching of *Humanae Vitae*.

4. The Pope. The fourth emphasis has to do with the Pope himself. Until the papal encyclical reaffirmed the traditional teaching, both sides tended to make use of this emphasis. Those teaching that contraception was permissible seemed to assume that the papal authority would show that they had been right all along. Those holding to the tradition waited anxiously for the Pope to put his authority behind them showing that they had been right. However, since the Pope spoke, matters have changed somewhat. Those holding to the tradition have been reaffirmed very strongly, but if they were hoping for that tradition to be taught in the form of a solemn *ex cathedra* definition they were disappointed. Those advocating contraception were dismayed, to say the least, but they quickly rallied to point out that the Pope had not spoken *ex cathedra*. (They have been something less than quick to point out that, with the exception of the condemnation of divorce with remarriage and bigamy by the Council of Trent, no other matters of human actions have ever been taught *ex cathedra* either, nor have they been quick to point out that "freedom of conscience" in this one "undefined" area is the "freedom of conscience" that we have in all other "undefined" areas of human behavior.)

At any rate, advocates of both traditions—the one of 1,900 years and the contraceptive tradition since 1964—seem to recognize the unique role of the Pope in the Church. True, he has been severely criticized for not following the recommendations of the birth control commission (even though every informed person recognizes that the commission had absolutely no teaching authority); his teaching has been called inadequate and wrong; but the fact that such a fuss is made about *his* teaching (while little such fuss will be made about mine) is witness to the fact that there is still a belief that the Pope has a unique role in the Church and can in fact teach infallibly. To deny this formally would be to enter into formal heresy, and most theologians are avoiding this like the plague. Whether or not all or most of those who oppose the papal teaching on contraception still believe that he *could* teach infallibly in *this* area if he made his present teaching into a definition is probably known only by the Holy Spirit.

Today, then, there are these four different elements in the Church—the laity, the theologians, the bishops, and the Pope—each receiving various amounts of emphasis. All of these make up the whole Church, and exclusive emphasis on only one aspect will give a distorted picture of the whole. However, there is an order created by Christ in which the voice of one, the Pope, has a unique teaching weight and authority which the other elements do not have. After all, how can a Christian ignore the reality that Christ did single out Peter for a unique role of headship in the college of the apostles who together with him were given the responsibility of forming a new People of God?

Our understanding of each of these four elements in the Church points to the notion of a Church which is tangible and can be heard—either through a survey, a vote, or a voice. None of these elements so emphasizes the Church of the Spirit as to obscure the Church of the audible and tangible flesh. Thus when the Church teaches, it is always in a visible, tangible, and materially specific way.

B. What's Involved in "Birth Control"?

I think that it becomes clear that birth control falls within the scope of the infallible teaching authority of the Church as soon as you consider what is really involved in "birth control." After a moment's reflection, it will be obvious that teaching about birth control involves teaching about love, sex, grace, sin and change of heart, and sacrament.

154

1. Love. No one needs another book today to tell him or her that Christ gave us a law of love. If the writing and the catechizing of the Sixties through the Eighties have made one point, it has been that Jesus taught us to love one another. This is a need of every age and perhaps especially so in any age which tends to intellectualization. However the emphasis in itself doesn't answer man's needs; he wants to know the answers to two basic questions: 1) "What does Jesus mean by love?" and 2) "What does love require me to do?"

The Christian says he believes that Jesus came to reveal what love means in human form. His whole life was a revelation of what love means, and He left us with the commandment to love one another as He himself has loved us. However, even this doesn't fully satisfy, for we want to know more about love as it took place in the humanity of Christ and as it is meant to take place in our own humanity. Does the commandment of love mean that we are to have affective feelings toward our fellow man, especially towards him who has injured us or whom we fear, perhaps for very good reasons? Does it mean that unique self-giving love called *agape* in the New Testament, or does it mean the affection of friendship (*philia*), or does it mean the romantic and exciting notion of love called *eros,* despite the fact that the New Testament never uses this latter term? We know that Jesus forgave his enemies from the cross, but how did he feel towards the hypocrites and the dishonest money changers?

These are questions which are both interesting and important to the person who is serious about his relationship with Christ. I would not attempt to answer them here, for my point is rather limited. I only want to show that any specific act which is meant to express love in a human manner must fall within the scope of how Jesus, and hence his Church, teaches us to act. Certainly no one is going to challenge that sexual intercourse is meant to be such an act.

2. Sex. If sexual intercourse were merely a matter of biology or physiology, then it would be very difficult for me to see how it would come within the scope of Christian revelation. I could envisage it coming within the scope of the Church's teaching authority only insofar as everything else concerned with the body can be looked at from the point of view of the preservation of life which in turn flows from the fifth commandment. Furthermore, the reader of the Gospel will not find Jesus giving him any biology lessons.

However, Jesus does teach about sex. His teaching about

marriage and divorce was so radical that it astonished his hearers who found it so strict and such an infringement on their idea of freedom that it seemed better not to get married in the first place (Mt 19:10). In the Sermon on the Mount, a passage which in its entirety is seen frequently as a promulgation in some detail of the commandment of love, He teaches that "every one who looks at a woman lustfully has already committed adultery with her in his heart" (Mt 5:28). Even when "lustfully" has been translated (more properly, I think) as "with lustful intention," this quotation has been the source of considerable anguish to a great many men and women who have struggled and been concerned with "impure thoughts." To say that these people have frequently misunderstood the images which flit across the imagination of almost everyone who has blood in their veins and confused them with the actual desire of lust for an illicit relationship is to state a truism but still does not do away with their anguish. If Jesus had not taught this, and/or if the biblical writers had not included this, perhaps a great amount of human suffering could have been avoided. I think this is relevant to the present case in which Pope Paul VI is being criticized for the hardship that his teaching will bring to people who possibly could have had a much easier and "fuller" life if they had been permitted to go on in ignorance and "good faith."

St. Paul in Romans 1, Galatians 5 and 1 Corinthians 5, 6, and 7 is also rather obviously concerned with sexual behavior. His letters to the Romans and Galatians are sometimes called the epistles of Christian liberty, and it seems to me that Paul's concern with sexual matters in these epistles is a reflection of his great concern about what freedom means. The understatement of the year would be that St. Paul didn't think that authentic Christian freedom was achieved by following the course of passion or by doing anything that seemed to be fulfilling at the moment. The chapters in 1 Corinthians stand somewhat by themselves, but they can also be seen in the larger context of an epistle that deals with gifts of the Spirit, including the gift of overcoming universal temptations (Ch. 10) and climaxing with the gift of love and the resurrection. Thus it seems to me that Paul's teaching about sex in this letter is part of his concern with what it means to be authentically Christian and responsive to the Holy Spirit.

The more one emphasizes that sexual intercourse is meant to be an authentic expression by two persons of their mutual love—the personalist approach—the more important it is that he have an authentically Christian understanding about love. An approach to sex which is one-sidedly biological or concerned with marriage rights and duties with little talk about love would not seem, on the other hand, to require a truly Christian understanding of love.

Contraception reflects what one thinks about sex and love. Christ and the sacred authors also thought and taught about sex and love. Thus I cannot help but conclude that birth control falls within the scope of the Church's mission of preaching the gospel and applying its message of love.

3. Grace. Every time a priest teaches his people, either from the pulpit, or in the confessional, or in writing, about contraception and undermines the Church's teaching by saying that it is never a sin not to do the impossible, he is saying something about temptation, suffering and God's grace. He is saying something about his view of man in his fallen and redeemed state, his view of man who is called to share in the resurrection of Jesus and Mary by ascending Calvary with them.

Undoubtedly, the Catholic doctrine on contraception calls for great faith and willingness to walk with Christ in His earthly sojourn as well as in His resurrected glory. Living out this doctrine of Christ's Church is going to demand from many people that they really believe that "God is faithful, and He will not let you be tempted beyond your strength, but with the temptation will also provide the way of escape that you may be able to endure it" (1 Cor 10:13). To the extent that you bring in the possibility or impossibility of living out the doctrine of marital non-contraception, you are bringing in the doctrine of grace, the belief that God does provide the help that is needed to overcome temptation, to keep His commandments. It seems to me that much of the argumentation on behalf of contraception has dealt with the difficulty of couples practicing chaste natural family planning in the present sociological framework. The relationship of the doctrine of marital non-contraception to the doctrine of grace is one more reason for including it within the scope of the infallible teaching authority of the Church.

4. Sin and change of heart. The reactions to Pope Paul's encyclical included comments such as, "If contraception is sinful, well then, I guess we're just going to be sinners," and, "I'll give up the Church before I give up the pill." The quotations are not direct, but I think they fairly express the contents of some of the reactions carried in the press in the early weeks after the encyclical. Such comments say much about the willingness of people to undergo a change of heart, about their basic moral option, about what is really their god, about what they think of Christ's Church and salvation. Such comments say much more about these things than they do about contraception itself. Again the reason for including these matters is that they provide one more reason for including contraceptive birth control within the scope of the infallible teaching authority of the Church which certainly must continue to promulgate the clear teaching of Jesus about the necessity of being open to a change of heart.

5. Sacrament. Marriage is a sacrament which involves love and, normally speaking, sex. So important is marriage in our consideration of love and sex that one of the most important criteria by which we judge the moral value of sexual intercourse is the presence or absence of the marriage contract between the two people involved. This was developed more thoroughly in Part I; for the present I only wish to state that since Christ has raised marriage to the level of a sacrament, this would be one more reason for urging that contraception falls within the scope of the infallible teaching authority of his Church.

The title of this section asked, "*Can* the Church teach infallibly about birth control?" The answer to that question is an unequivocal and absolute "Yes."

Whether we look at each one of the elements in the contraception issue singly or all together, the conclusion is unavoidable: birth control is an issue which is within the competence of the Church teaching in her unique capacity as the infallible voice of Christ on earth today. It may seem that I have been belaboring the obvious, but when such an important question has been raised, it should be answered in at least a little detail. When a statement is made that puts an important area of moral behavior completely beyond the scope of the Church's unique, infallible teaching competence and authority, I think it is necessary to reply with something more than a quip that such a statement is a gratuitous assertion.

II. *Does* the Church Teach Infallibly about Birth Control?

On 15 October 1988, Pope John Paul II noted that the universal ordinary magisterium of the Church is "the usual expression of the Church's infallibility." The text is this:

This task of achieving an ever deeper understanding of the content of faith belongs to every member of the Church. But the Second Vatican Council assures us that "the task of authentically interpreting the word of God, whether written or handed down, has been entrusted exclusively to the living, teaching office of the Church" (*Dei Verbum,* 10). This magisterium is not above the divine word but serves it with a specific *carisma veritatis certum** (Dei Verbum, 8), which includes the charism of infallibility, present not only in the solemn definitions of the Roman Pontiff and of Ecumenical Councils, but also in the universal ordinary magisterium (*Lumen Gentium,* 25), which can truly be considered as the usual expression of the Church's infallibility.[9]

The reference to *Lumen Gentium* 25 deserves to be quoted in full:

Although the individual bishops do not enjoy the prerogative of infallibility, they can nevertheless proclaim Christ's doctrine infallibly. **This is so, even when they are dispersed around the world, provided that while maintaining the bond of unity among themselves and with Peter's successor, and while teaching authentically on a matter of faith or morals, they concur in a single viewpoint as the one which must be held conclusively.** This authority is even more clearly verified when, gathered together in an ecumenical council, they are teachers and judges of faith and morals for the universal Church. Their definitions must then be adhered to with the submission of faith (emphasis added).

Thus **the question becomes this:** Does the traditional teaching against marital contraception meet the requirements for being taught infallibly by the universal ordinary magisterium of the Church according to the criteria set forth by the teaching of Vatican II in *The Dogmatic Constitution on the Church (Lumen Gentium)* quoted above?

When it becomes clear that I think the answer is "yes," you

---

* *Carisma veritatis certum:* the divinely guaranteed gift of holding the truth for the sake of the Church.

might say, "In the early 1990s that's a pretty rare conviction." Well, yes and no. Yes, there is not a multitude of publications supporting that conviction; but on the other hand, there are a large number of orthodox Catholics, both scholars and ordinary educated people, who are convinced that the evidence shows that this teaching is taught infallibly by the Roman Catholic Church.

However, the crucial point is not the number of theologians who have published this conviction or the number of orthodox Catholics who share this conviction. As Professor William May put it,

> The crucial point is whether the teaching of the magisterium on contraception is infallibly proposed by the magisterium. And to determine this, one must ask whether the criteria set forth in *Lumen Gentium* for teachings infallibly proposed by the ordinary magisterium have been met in the way that the teaching on contraception is proposed. One has to look at the evidence. I think that Grisez and Ford marshalled the evidence massively to show that these criteria have been verified and no one has been able to show the contrary. Sullivan tried to do so in his book on magisterium, but Grisez subsequently showed the terrible flaws in Sullivan's work, and Sullivan never tried to answer this critique, nor has anyone else.[10]

Let's unpack the previous paragraph. The reference to Ford and Grisez is to the landmark article by Fr. John Ford, S.J., and Germain Grisez, "Contraception and the Infallibility of the Ordinary Magisterium." It has been reprinted in a book which may be more available to most readers and subsequent parenthical references are to pages in that book.[11] The mention of Fr. Francis Sullivan refers to a book in which he took issue with the Ford-Grisez thesis.[12]

What follows in this chapter is 1) a brief analysis of the argument by Ford and Grisez and 2) another brief analysis of a different sort of argument arriving at the same conclusion.

1. Ford and Grisez: infallible by reason of the universal ordinary magisterium

First of all, Ford and Grisez note that in the birth control debate "no one—so far as we know—applied the conditions for infallibility in the exercise of the ordinary magisterium to the facts of the Tradition of Catholic Teaching on contraception, and thus no one advanced the argument we are about to propose" (126).

Next they list four theological issues that they are not going to touch. The most important of these issues is whether this teaching has been divinely revealed. What they are saying is this: for the purposes of our argument, we are not going to rely upon the Onan account of Genesis 38 as a divinely revealed teaching against contraception. They don't take sides on that issue but simply prescind from it to make more clear the precise nature of their argument.

Third, they show that the infallible teaching authority of the Church extends not just to truths formally revealed but also to points which are necessary to guard and expound this deposit of faith. What this does is to prescind from the argument as to whether certain teachings of the natural moral law, e.g., that direct abortion is always murder, are matters of divine revelation or matters of the natural moral law. They quote extensively from documents referenced by Vatican II's teaching on infallibility to show that the Church's infallibility extends to matters of the natural moral law, for example, to corollaries of the Ten Commandments. Thus it extends to marital sexuality and the contraception issue. This is true whether contraception is a matter of divine revelation or only the natural moral law.

Four conditions. Having cleared the decks, so to speak, Ford and Grisez then begin their analyses of *Lumen Gentium* 25, paragraph 3.

We are now in a position to comment upon the conditions, articulated by Vatican II, under which the bishops, dispersed throughout the world, proclaim the doctrine of Christ infallibly. There are four conditions: first, that the bishops remain in communion with one another and with the Pope; second, that they teach authoritatively on a matter of faith or morals; third, that they agree in one judgment; and fourth, that they propose this judgment as one to be held definitively (145).

This is certainly not the place to paraphrase their commentary on each of these points, but two clarifications deserve emphasis.

1) The unity of the bishops with each other and with the Pope is a *moral* unity, not a mathematical unity which would be broken by one dissident vote or voice, and the authors use the events surrounding the Council of Nicea to prove this point (147-148).

2) A teaching which is taught infallibly at one point in history remains that way for the rest of history. The moral unanimity of

Pope and bishops teaching authoritatively and definitively on a point of faith or morals is not disrupted by the fact that at a later time in history some bishops may disagree. Christ gave the Church no guarantee that every bishop would always be faithful to the truth, and history has demonstrated the role of individual bishops in causing or fomenting heresy and/or schism (148-149).

   • **Universally proposed.** Ford and Grisez, like the rest of us, are spared endless historical research by the work of John T. Noonan, Jr. who summarizes his survey with a quick review of the principal figures from the third century to the twentieth and concludes:

   The teachers of the Church have taught without hesitation or variation that certain acts preventing procreation are gravely sinful. No Catholic theologian has ever taught, "Contraception is a good act." The teaching on contraception is clear and apparently fixed forever.[13]

   Noonan thought (at least when he wrote this in the years before *Humanae Vitae*) that there was still room for development which would fundamentally reverse the teaching, but such an erroneous opinion on his part does not destroy the value of the historical evidence he gathered.

   Furthermore, as Ford and Grisez point out, in the thirteen years between Noonan's book (1965) and their article (1978), the dissenters "surely would have published any evidence that the universality of the Church's teaching was interrupted by the contrary teaching of any bishop or of any other competent spokesman of Catholic thought. But no such evidence has come to light, and so there is a compelling reason to think that no such evidence exists. We conclude that the historical evidence shows that Catholic bishops dispersed throughout the world agreed in one judgment on the morality of contraception" (156-157).

   After further consideration of certain historical highlights they conclude that the first three conditions have been fulfilled:

   These considerations, we believe, make clear that the received Catholic teaching on the morality of contraception was *universally* proposed by Catholic bishops *in communion* with one another and with the successor of Peter. Bishops and Popes personally repeated the teaching in official acts, and *by their authority* they guided, supported, and endorsed the teaching by way of the seminaries in its direct application in pastoral practice (162-163, emphasis added).

162

• **To be held definitively.** Next Ford and Grisez raise this question: "But if the teaching was universal and even authoritative, was it proposed authoritatively as a point *to be held definitively?*" (163)

What does it mean to be held definitively? It doesn't mean to be held as a defined article of faith, even though some may teach it as such. Rather, "definitively" means to be taught as the only way compatible with God's order of creation and/or Christian discipleship. When the Church teaches definitively about morals, it teaches that behavior which contradicts its teaching is the grave matter of mortal sin; it teaches in a way that's obviously certain— not as an opinion of certain theologians but as the teaching of the Church. So the first point made by Ford and Grisez about this matter is especially interesting.

> We know of no evidence—and Noonan points to none—that anyone handed on the received teaching as if it were a private opinion, a merely probable judgment, or a commendable ideal which the faithful might nevertheless blamelessly choose to leave unrealized. The teaching always was proposed as a received and certain part of the obligatory moral teaching of the Church (163).

Then they note other elements that show this doctrine was taught to be held definitively: that contraceptive acts are taught to be the grave matter of mortal sin, the repetition of the teaching in the face of challenges outside the Church, and the fact that it has often been proposed as divinely revealed. They conclude by referencing the 1951 address of Pope Pius XII to Italian midwives:

> Pius XII also articulates the definitive character of the received teaching in a most emphatic way: "This teaching is as valid today as it was yesterday; and it will be the same tomorrow and always," thus applying to this point of moral teaching the unalterability that Hebrews 13:8 ascribes to Jesus Christ himself (170).

Their conclusion. Ford and Grisez conclude this section of their scholarly article with the following statement which I think deserves full quotation.

> We think the facts show as clearly as anyone could reasonably demand that the conditions articulated by Vatican II for infallibility in the exercise of the ordinary Magisterium of the bishops dispersed throughout the world have been met in the case of the Catholic Church's teaching on contraception. At least until 1962, Catholic bishops in communion with

one another and with the Pope agreed in and authoritatively proposed one judgment to be held definitively on the morality of contraception: Acts of this kind are objectively, intrinsically, and gravely evil. Since this teaching has been proposed infallibly, the controversy since 1963 takes nothing away from its objectively certain truth. It is not the received Catholic teaching on contraception which needs to be rethought. It is the assumption that this teaching could be abandoned as false which needs to be rethought (171).

Ford and Grisez then go on to raise and reply to a number of likely objections, and any serious student of the issue must read their argument in full. However, for our limited purpose, the above is sufficient. I have wanted to show only that serious theological scholars have concluded that the received teaching on contraception reaffirmed by *Humanae Vitae* is taught infallibly by the Roman Catholic Church according to the specific norms of Vatican II.

Of special interest is the fact that the Ford-Grisez argument has been practically unchallenged. The only effort to challenge it which has come to my attention consists of a few pages in a book by Fr. Francis Sullivan, S.J.[12], and responses to Fr. Sullivan have been given by Fr. Brian W. Harrison[14] and Germain Grisez[15].

As previously noted, Professor William May summarized this interchange by saying that neither Sullivan nor anyone else has successfully challenged the Ford-Grisez thesis. It appears to me that the dissenters have given the Ford-Grisez thesis the "silent treatment" lest its inherent value become widely known.

2. Lio and Harrison: infallible by reason of the wording of *Humanae Vitae*

A different and complementary approach is taken by Ermenegildo Lio, O.F.M. in his 1986 book, *Humanae Vitae e Infallibilita: il Concilio, Paolo VI e Giovanni Paolo II.*[16]

In late 1989, Fr. Lio's large book (nearly 1000 pages) had not yet been translated into English; my comments are derived from a book review by Father Brian W. Harrison,[17] a review I highly recommend to the student of this subject.

Fr. Lio's book is inaccessible to those who do not read Italian, and even if it were in English, its size and consequent cost would render it inaccessible to most readers. Fortunately, Fr. Harrison's review is sufficiently complete to convey the general line of argument, Fr. Lio's immense scholarship, and his diligent use of theological resources. My treatment here is quite summary;

references are to the Harrison review in *Fidelity*.

While Ford and Grisez argue that the moral teaching—the Tradition—reaffirmed by *Humanae Vitae* is taught infallibly because it fulfills all the requirements of Vatican II for being an infallible teaching, Fr. Lio has amassed argument after argument and document after document to maintain that article 14 of *Humanae Vitae* contains an *ex cathedra* definition of the intrinsic immorality of contraception—that is, an exercise of papal infallibility as solemnly defined by Vatican Council I in the Constitution *Pastor Aeternus* (Harrison, 44).

The Ford-Grisez and the Lio approaches are complementary. They do not contradict each other. A doctrine can certainly fulfill more than one set of requirements for being taught infallibly by God's Church.

A principal source of confusion in the birth control issue has been the assumption that in order for a Church document to be recognized as teaching infallibly, we have to "find a particularly solemn form of words (called the *modus definitorius* in Latin) employed in order to affirm that such-and-such a doctrine concerning faith or morals is revealed by God, and is a part of the Church's deposit of faith" (44).

However, Fr. Lio shows that having the words "define" or "definition" is not an essential signal of an infallible papal definition. All that is necessary is "that we have a *modus definitivus,* that is, clear evidence in the relevant documentation that the Pope is intending to hand down a certain, decisive judgment that such-and-such a point of doctrine, concerning faith or morals, is true and its contrary false. He does not have to affirm it as dogma (revealed truth) or anathematize dissidents" (44).

What makes the work of Fr. Lio so interesting and strong is that he doesn't just *assert* this broader understanding; he quotes previously unpublished documents from the Vatican archives to show that it was this broader understanding that the Fathers of the first Vatican Council had in mind when they promulgated the dogma of papal infallibility in 1870.

Working from canon 749.3 of the 1983 Code of Canon Law that "nothing is to be understood as infallibly defined unless this is manifestly the case," Fr. Lio "maintains that the relevant documents do indeed manifest very plainly Paul VI's intention of giving a decisive judgment in *Humanae Vitae,* even though he nowhere uses the word 'define' " (45).

Many casual observers of the 1968 debut of *Humanae Vitae* are aware that Msgr. F. Lambruschini presented the encyclical at the Vatican press conference and then proceeded to say that "the encyclical was *not* an infallible statement" without public reprimand (46). Is this an argument against Fr. Lio's position? Not at all. First of all, the statement was only Lambruschini's personal opinion; secondly, though he wasn't given a public reprimand, "his statements to the journalists about the 'non-infallible' nature of *Humanae Vitae* are conspicuous by their absence" from the official record of the press conference in the official Vatican newspaper (46).

Fr. Lio relates the well known confusion that existed in the mid-to-late 1960s as evidence that a decisive teaching was needed; then he shows both from prior statements of Paul VI and the actual wording of the encyclical that in *Humanae Vitae* the Pope certainly fulfilled the requirements of Vatican I for teaching infallibly.

The words introducing the formal judgment given in *Humanae Vitae* n.14 were carefully chosen: "We must therefore declare once again (*iterum debemus edicere*)."

The fact that the word *edicere*, rather than *definire* ("define"), is used here does not militate against its being an infallible definition, argues Fr. Lio: the Vatican I Fathers were not told by Bishop Gasser that there was anything sacrosanct about the *word* "define." All that is necessary is that the Pope clearly express his intention of speaking decisively and with finality on a point of doctrine, in such a way that good Catholics can be certain what the truth is (47).

And, as Fr. Lio's examination of the text of *Humanae Vitae* and preceding statements of Paul VI showed, that was most certainly done.

Fr. Harrison concludes his fine review of the Lio book with a letter of appreciation from Pope John Paul II to Fr. Lio for his book.

Personal thoughts on the infallibility issue

It is one thing for a doctrine *actually* to be taught infallibly; it is something different for such teaching to be widely recognized as such. I am convinced by the evidence marshalled by Ford, Grisez, and Lio that the doctrine is more than theologically certain; I believe with them that the doctrine is taught infallibly and therefore requires the submission of faith.

However, I also realize a practical problem. If you are a *typical* lay person or priest or seminarian (which you really aren't, or you wouldn't be reading this book), and if you should tell a typical Catholic pastor that Kippley was basing his whole case on the fact that the doctrine of marital non-contraception is taught infallibly, you would probably be greeted with anything from a snicker to a snarl. Recognizing this, I prefer to lay primary emphasis on what I think is indisputable by any informed Catholic—namely, that Pope John Paul II has amply fulfilled all the requirements of *Lumen Gentium* 25 for teaching with such certainty that his teaching against marital contraception must be accepted, at the very least, by religious submission of mind and will, i.e., accepted as true and lived accordingly. That was the task of Chapter 6.

Is there a difference between the assent of faith and "religious submission of will and mind"? (*Lumen Gentium* 25) I think there is, for the Fathers of Vatican II noted that even when the Pope isn't speaking *ex cathedra*, his teaching must be "acknowledged with reverence" and "the judgments made by him" are to be "sincerely adhered to, according to his manifest mind and will" (L. G. 25). I think the case can be made that acknowledging with reverence and sincerely adhering to his judgments is different from the full assent of faith.

The assent of faith calls for belief that God Himself is the ultimate Author of this teaching, and the only appropriate response to God as Teacher is faith.

A teaching that requires religious submission of will and mind carries with it the overwhelming presumption that it is true because it is under the general guidance of the Holy Spirit which Jesus promised to His Church at the Last Supper. If there is any dispute about the teaching, the burden of proof lies heavily upon those who would say the teaching is not true and/or binding. In the birth control controversy, the efforts of the dissenters have chiefly served to illustrate that the acceptance of marital contraception logically entails the acceptance of homosexual behavior and every other imaginable sexual act between consenting persons, i.e., the complete moral chaos of the contemporary "sexual revolution" as is shown elsewhere in this book (Part IV). Thus, far from shouldering the burden of proof, the arguments of the dissenters have served only to bolster the already overwhelming presumption that the doctrine of marital non-contraception is the work of the Holy Spirit and is therefore true.

Could the Pope make an *ex cathedra,* solemn definition regarding the immorality of marital contraception? Certainly he could, but I do not think he will. For one thing, it can be argued, as Fr. Ermenegildo Lio has done, that we already have a teaching that is infallible by reason of its wording, and that argument can be applied with equal or even greater force to the wording of *Casti Cannubii* in 1930.

Second, I think that Pope John Paul II wants to reaffirm the teaching authority of the universal ordinary magisterium, the teaching authority of the bishops in union with Rome teaching constantly on this and other issues over the centuries. He is aware that to the extent that he would solemnly define one matter of morality, certain dissident theologians would argue that since he hadn't solemnly defined something else, say the evil of fornication, then *that* issue was "up for grabs," so to speak. I think that John Paul II is well aware how dissident theologians work and therefore has avoided and will continue to avoid the solemn *ex cathedra* pronouncement.

Third, I think the Holy Father may see a distinction between the assent of faith to the ordinary magisterium and the religious submission of will and mind to the papal magisterium as indicated above. In my opinion, he has chosen to fulfill in a very obvious way the requirements for the latter because that is all that is necessary for believing Catholics to form their consciences with certainty and to act accordingly. In effect, he is leaving any academic infallibility debate to the theologians and giving the People of God precisely the firm guidance they need for making practical judgments that are in accord with the truth of human nature.

In my opinion, the year 2,000 will see more and more bishops and theologians teaching that the doctrine of marital non-contraception is infallibly taught by the Church, not necessarily by reason of a definition, but because of the insistent, consistent, and persistent teaching of the bishops doing their work as a united band of pastors scattered throughout the world and across the centuries. I think that will become a clear consensus by the fortieth or fiftieth anniversary of *Humanae Vitae.* Dissent is a blind alley, a dead-end street, a negative and un-Christian reaction which has no future.

To re-emphasize for the second or third time, at the practical level of the individual marriage, it is strictly academic whether the doctrine of *Humanae Vitae* is taught infallibly or not. The Church clearly teaches—both through the universal ordinary magisterium and through the papal magisterium that it is gravely immoral for spouses to use unnatural means of birth control. The teaching is certain and unchangeable. Catholic couples are obliged to form their consciences according to this certain teaching of the Church, and Catholic preachers, teachers and counselors are obliged to teach accordingly.

Part III

Pastoral Considerations

8

Natural Family Planning

Elsewhere in this book (especially in Chapter 13), I have illustrated the connection between accepting contraception and accepting other immoral sexual behaviors. The connection is simply undeniable at the level of logic, the "theology of dissent," and recent history. Therefore, in order to return to sexual morality in the wider sphere, it is essential to return to marital chastity, and in today's context, that entails natural family planning.

God has provided the practical help of modern natural family planning (NFP) at the same time that there has been a perceived need for conception regulation, and it must be known! Every adult, married or single, lay person, priest, seminarian and Religious should understand modern natural family planning. This does not mean that unmarried women should be charting or that priests should be able to teach the details. However, since resistance to the teaching of *Humanae Vitae* is frequently related to ignorance of modern NFP, everyone who wants to foster the practice of marital chastity should understand enough about NFP to recommend it intelligently, and every married couple should understand it even if they desire a dozen or more children.

Ecological breastfeeding

The oldest and still most widely used form of natural family planning is God's built-in plan for baby care—ecological breastfeeding. I call it "ecological" breastfeeding to distinguish it from the "cultural" breastfeeding which has little or no effect upon postponing the postpartum return of fertility. In two studies conducted by my wife and myself, we have found that mothers who followed the rules of ecological breastfeeding averaged 14.5 months of postpartum infertility.[1,2,3] More precisely, the mothers doing ecological breastfeeding averaged 14.5 months of amenorrhea (the absence of menstruation) before their first period, so in most cases they would be experiencing 15 to 16 months of postpartum infertility.

The six criteria for ecological breastfeeding are simple and approximate the sort of breastfeeding that mothers did for centuries before the advent of modern devices and customs. They are as follows:

1. No pacifiers used
2. No bottles used
3. No liquids or solids for the first five months
4. No feeding schedules other than baby's
5. Presence of night feedings
6. Presence of lying-down nursing for naps and night feedings.

These criteria ensure that the baby will nurse frequently, and it is now clear to the scientific world that it is **the frequency of suckling** around the clock that is the single most important factor in postponing the return of fertility after childbirth.[4]

In addition, there is no question that ecological breastfeeding provides not only the best nutrition but also encourages the best psychological baby care with lots of warm, physical contact between mother and baby. In the last analysis, ecological breastfeeding can be called "natural mothering," as my wife does in her book *Breastfeeding and Natural Child Spacing: How Natural Mothering Spaces Babies.*[5] Also, in her book, Sheila quotes many researchers, some of whom point out that ecological breastfeeding kept the world's population stable for eons and is still vitally necessary for both the health of mother and baby and for population stability in less developed countries.

For many couples, ecological breastfeeding will provide all the spacing they desire between babies, and the only purpose of making systematic observations would be to determine precisely when the next pregnancy occurs. However, some mothers will have an early return of fertility, and others may need more spacing. Therefore, they should understand the systematic NFP described below.

Because it is the Lord's own baby-spacing plan and because it offers so many advantages to baby and mother (and even to the rest of the family as older children learn that breasts are for nursing, not sex objects), the teaching and encouraging of ecological breastfeeding should play an important part in every natural family planning program. Unfortunately, that does not seem to be the case.

Systematic natural family planning

When most people think of natural family planning, they think of systematic NFP—periodic abstinence during the fertile time in order to avoid pregnancy. However, NFP is increasingly important for couples of marginal fertility in their efforts to achieve pregnancy. Regardless of why it is used, the basics remain the same.

This chapter is certainly not the place to explain NFP in detail; a few paragraphs are no substitute for the various books on the subject including our own, *The Art of Natural Family Planning.*[6] However, it is a simple task to describe 1) the signs of fertility and infertility that occur in the normal fertility-menstrual cycle, 2) the hormonal causes of these signs, and 3) how the signs are used.

1. The three signs. A woman's fertile time is characterized by a discharge or secretion of **cervical mucus.** This generally starts as a rather tacky substance, and by the time of maximum fertility it is generally much like raw egg white, usually producing easily noticed sensations of wetness on the outer lips of the vagina. After ovulation, it dries up and disappears. The presence of mucus is a positive sign of fertility; its subsequent disappearance is a negative sign of infertility.

At the same time, certain **physical changes in the cervix** are taking place. The cervix is the lower part of the uterus that protrudes slightly into the vagina or vaginal tract. When a woman is infertile, the cervix is generally easy to reach, the tip is firm, and the mouth of the cervix (cervical os) is closed. During her fertile time the cervix rises, the tip softens, and the os opens.

Temperature changes occur after ovulation, and a woman's waking temperature generally rises about 4/10ths of one degree Fahrenheit shortly after ovulation. A sufficiently elevated temperature pattern is a positive sign of postovulation infertility.

A fourth sign noticed by many women is a sensation, sometimes even slightly painful, in the area of one of her two ovaries around the time of ovulation; the scientific literature calls this by its German name, *mittleschmerz,* meaning "pain in the middle," i.e., about mid-cycle in the classic 28 day average cycle.

2. The hormonal causes. Two ovarian hormones cause the changes in the mucus, cervix and temperature signs. Before ovulation, rising levels of estrogen cause the cervix to secrete mucus and to undergo the three physical changes. At ovulation, an egg is released from a follicle (a container) in one of the ovaries. After ovulation, the follicle secretes the second basic female hormone, progesterone, and the progesterone causes the woman's body temperature to rise. Also, after ovulation, the estrogen level drops. The combination of decreased estrogen and increased progesterone causes the mucus to thicken and disappear and the cervix to descend, the tip to become firm again, and the os to close.

Also, the estrogen builds up the inner lining of the uterus before ovulation, and after ovulation the progesterone maintains it with a rich blood supply to prepare for possible implantation of a newly conceived baby. If conception and implantation do not occur, then the secretion of progesterone stops after about 14 days, and the inner lining of the uterus sloughs off in the process of menstruation.

3. How the signs are used. The couple who are **seeking pregnancy** will generally abstain from relations during the early part of the cycle in order to maximize sperm count. Then, when her cervical mucus shows maximum fertility, they will come together with the hopes of achieving pregnancy. They will continue to monitor her signs, for 21 days of elevated temperature provides them with a 99 percent certainty of being pregnant.

The couple who are **avoiding pregnancy** begin to abstain as soon as she notices any of the signs of fertility such as the less-fertile, tacky mucus or the opening of the cervix. (There are also more conservative rules of thumb for determining the end of pre-ovulation infertility based on her personal cycle-history, but this is not the place to explain such details.) When the mucus disappears and the temperature has been elevated for at least three days, they know they are in the time of postovulation infertility and can celebrate their marital union accordingly.

If a woman has a clear-cut five day mucus patch and the temperature rises as soon as the mucus begins drying up, there would be a minimum of seven days of abstinence. If the mucus patch is longer and/or the temperature rise is delayed, more abstinence is required; nine or ten days is fairly typical, and it usually does not exceed twelve days during normal cycles.

Methods of natural family planning

Strictly speaking, there is only one method of systematic NFP for avoiding pregnancy—periodic abstinence during the fertile time. However, the term "methods of NFP" is also used to denote different ways of determining the fertile and infertile times of the cycle.

174

1. The Sympto-Thermal Method. The method that uses all the signs in a crosschecking way is called the Sympto-Thermal Method (STM). Women are taught how to observe the cervical mucus and the physical changes in the cervix, but the cervix changes are generally taught as optional because some women may dislike making an internal observation. However, experience suggests that this is less and less common as a complaint. Women are also taught how to observe the cervical mucus both 1) at the external lips while wiping and 2) at the cervical os. Again, the internal observation is generally taught as optional. The husband is encouraged to be in charge of the thermometer and to record his wife's waking temperature. For determining the start of postovulation infertility, the positive (elevated temperature) sign crosschecks the negative (absence of mucus) for the greatest confidence and reliabililty.

In good teaching of the STM, each sign is taught well enough so that it can be used in a single-sign method if desired.

The Couple to Couple League believes in giving the individual couple the maximum freedom of choice among morally acceptable methods and thus teaches the full Sympto-Thermal Method. Long experience indicates that if a couple prefer to use only one or two of the three signs, they exercise their freedom to do so. However, if they are initially instructed only about a single sign, they do not have the knowledge-based freedom to choose a crosschecking method if they feel uneasy or are having difficulties with a single sign method.

2. The Ovulation Method. The Ovulation Method is a single sign method using only the cervical mucus, as observed only at the vulva or external lips of the vagina. Worldwide, and especially in developing countries, the most widely used form of systematic NFP is undoubtedly the Billings Ovulation Method. However, the name is somewhat of a misnomer: while the presence of cervical mucus is a positive sign of being fertile, its disappearance provides only a good presumption that ovulation has occurred. That is, there are certain situations—unusual stress is the most common—in which ovulation is delayed and the mucus disappears without ovulation occurring. Then the ovulation process resumes and ovulation occurs, generally without much advance notice from the mucus sign. In such cases, the temperature will remain low until after ovulation; and that's one of the big reasons for teaching the crosschecking STM.

3. Temperature-only methods. The post-ovulation temperature rise has been used in temperature-only and calendar-temperature methods since the 1940s, and one temperature-only system has been developed for determining the *beginning* as well as the *end* of the fertile time. While very useful in cases of scant or ambiguous mucus signs, there is little teaching of temperature-only systems today; the temperature sign is usually taught as a crosscheck on the mucus.

4. Cervix-only. Theoretically, someone could use the cervix sign by itself, but such teaching would be rare. Rather obviously, any woman making an internal observation for cervix changes can simultaneously check for cervical mucus both at the vulva and at the cervical os.

Effectiveness of natural family planning

For couples seeking pregnancy, the mucus-only and sympto-thermal methods are equally good at identifying the time of maximum fertility. However, the elevated temperature sign is unique in its ability to provide a positive sign of success in achieving pregnancy and for estimating the date of conception in irregular cycles.

For couples avoiding pregnancy, the Sympto-Thermal Method and the Temperature-only Method are more effective than the Mucus-only methods. The only American comparative study of the STM and OM showed that the STM was significantly more effective for avoiding pregnancy.[7]

With multiple studies[8] showing that the STM has a method effectiveness of 99 percent and user-effectiveness rates ranging from 85 to 99 percent, there is no reasonable doubt that the STM is as effective as any of the non-permanent and non-abortifacient methods of birth control under any conditions, and when it is used by couples of serious motivation it is in the same effectiveness ballpark with **anything** else. It has long been recognized that couples who have relations only in the time of postovulation infertility have unplanned pregnancy rates which are competitive with sexual sterilization.

The pastoral implications are clear. No matter how serious the reason to avoid pregnancy, a variation of the STM can be used. **Nothing** except complete abstinence or sexual castration (ovaries or testicles) provides 100 percent effectiveness. However, if a couple using the STM conservatively should experience a true surprise pregnancy, it would be on the order of a small miracle; and we simply must place our trust in God that He who calls life into being under such unusual circumstances will provide what is necessary for that family.

9

Practical Pastoral Policies

By "practical pastoral policies" I mean the practices and policies which can convey and support belief in the Christian Tradition reaffirmed by *Casti Connubii, Humanae Vitae* and *Familiaris Consortio.* First of all, I want to outline the problem as I see it; second, I will suggest practical ideas to alleviate it; then in the next chapter I will discuss what sort of counsel can be given to couples suffering in the hard cases.

I: The Problem

The pastoral crisis

The pastoral crisis can be summarized in one statement: in the late 1980s and early 1990s young engaged couples who want to learn natural family planning have been so rare that they constitute a miracle of grace. To see the validity of that statement, just put yourself in the shoes of any American engaged couple including Catholics. In fact, focus on the typical Catholic engaged couple, and ask yourself what there would be in their background to lead them to know and to accept Catholic teaching against using unnatural forms of birth control. The optimist says "Not much"; the pessimist says "Nothing."

The parents of our typical Catholic engaged couple have most likely used contraception and may well be sterilized. The engaged man and woman have probably never heard a word on the subject from the pulpit. If they went to Catholic high schools, and especially if they went to a so-called Catholic college, they probably were taught how to dissent without even realizing it. In their pre-marriage preparation, they were probably instructed by a con-tracepting couple. The couple who escape this contraceptive net right within the Church are indeed a moral miracle, and the situation outside the Catholic Church is even worse.The pastoral crisis is **NOT** due to the teaching of *Humanae Vitae*. After all, all that *Humanae Vitae* did was to reaffirm the teaching of *Casti*

Connubii issued 31 December 1930 which in turn simply reaffirmed the universal teaching of Christianity, which universality had just been broken by the Church of England in August of 1930. Despite the depression years, despite the imperfection of the calendar rhythm method popularized in the 1930s, and despite the large families of the 1950s, widespread acceptance of the teaching of *Casti Connubii* was still the norm in the early Sixties, and the Catholic churches were full.

To understand the real causes of the pastoral crisis, compare the 30 years from 1930-1960 with the 30 years from 1960-1990. In this latter period compared to the former, Western Catholics have generally experienced a much higher level of material prosperity, better housing, more job opportunities, better health care, and much improved old age security. The primary negative economic element in the United States has been the failure of the income tax child exemption to keep pace with inflation. In short, the economic aspects of raising children have been favorable since 1960. The practical help of natural family planning is incomparably superior and is universally available, at least through books and increasingly in face to face classes taught by trained user couples. In short, never before have Catholics had it so good; and never before in the entirety of human history has the practical help of natural family planning been so excellent and so widely available.

Despite all of these advantages, as the 1990s dawned, the NFP movement was dead in the water for lack of interest by those whom it was supposed to help, and the Catholic pews were frequently more than half-empty on Sunday mornings.

The authority crisis

The pastoral crisis is due principally to an authority crisis which is unprecedented in recent centuries. In fact, you have to go back to the times of the Reformation to find a similar crisis of authority.

Refusal to believe. Some, perhaps many, Catholics no longer believe that the magisterium of the Church is guided by the Holy Spirit in its ordinary teaching on faith and morals. It is becoming increasingly apparent that large numbers of Catholics are no longer willing to believe in the teaching authority of the Church even as exercised in *ex cathedra* definitions of either Pope or Council. In a conversation in the late 1960s, a well-educated person who described herself as searching and in touch with the feelings of the people indicated to me that dogmatic teaching as such was irrelevant. She and people like her simply were not about to accept something as true because it was taught either by the Council of Nicea or Vatican II or by any other formal means of teaching. (This of course runs counter to the explicit theologizing of those theologians who argue for a change in the teaching about contraception, but it certainly has not arisen in a vacuum.)

Lack of local ecclesial action. On the other hand, how many lay Catholics have seen bishops and priests acting as if **they** really believe the Church's teaching about love and sexuality? What they have seen for the most part is a complete lack of affirmation of *Humanae Vitae* on the part of the vast majority of their priests. In fact, if they look closely and ask a few questions, they might see that the diocesan bureaucracy has many dissenters, even in the areas of education and marriage preparation.

Others may have very solid reason to think that their bishop accepts the teaching of *Humanae Vitae,* but they wonder if he thinks contraception is serious. That is, they don't see him taking strong action to have its truths taught within his jurisdiction. They figure that if he really believed that it was the grave matter of mortal sin for people to use unnatural means of birth control, the bishop could and would do something practical about it such as at least making an entire course in chaste NFP a normal part of preparation for marriage. They might have a mental list of what they would do if they had the power of a bishop and really believed the teaching of the Church. Then when they see that nothing practical is done and that continuing dissent is allowed, they conclude that their bishop doesn't **really** believe that it's seriously sinful to use unnatural methods of birth control. And if he doesn't, they figure, why should they?

Still others may hear of a diocese in which the bishop has been doing those things that seem logical for anyone who has legitimate authority—making education in marital chastity and NFP a normal part of preparation for marriage, allowing only believers to teach in diocesan education and marriage programs, and reforming the diocesan bureaucracy. However he also sees that his own diocese is doing nothing of the sort, and he figures that this must be a conscious decision by the bishop to allow the dissenters to continue to control education and marriage preparation. He cannot see the struggle the bishop may be having; all he sees are the results. So he figures that the whole matter of marital sexuality is a non-issue in his diocese, and who is he to be more of a believer than his bishop and his priests?

Open toleration of dissent. Another key factor in the authority crisis is the open toleration of dissent by bishops. The slogan, "Use it or lose it," applies here. Bishops have the power to remove dissenting priests and educators from positions within their episcopal jurisdiction. They have the power to remove textbooks that undermine the Faith. They have the power not to approve of materials published within their jurisdiction which undermine the Faith even if they do not directly contradict it. And if they do not have direct control over the faculty at so-called Catholic colleges within their jurisdiction, they can at least clearly label colleges which teach dissent as "not a Catholic college."

However, it is questionable how well Western bishops have used their legitimate authority to foster the teaching of the Church about love, marriage and sexuality. Collectively, American bishops continued to employ Fr. Charles Curran at Catholic University of America until the Vatican finally forced his termination in 1987. Thus, for 19 years, dissenting priests, when challenged on the bankruptcy of their moral reasoning for dissent, were able to say to me, as they did, "My reasoning is the same as that of Fr. Curran who must be approved by our American bishops because they employ him to teach theology at Catholic University."

By not using their legitimate authority to stop the open dissent which cannot say a firm "No" even to the gross immorality of spouse swapping, the American bishops have lost much practical authority, especially among the dissenters. And by staffing their diocesan bureaucracies with dissenters—or allowing such staffing—many an American bishop has created grave problems for himself should he at some time get more serious about teaching the truths of *Humanae Vitae,* and such staffing certainly creates significant problems for a successor bishop who may be more serious about *Humanae Vitae.*

The full-pew policy. I suspect there has been an unspoken, unwritten but still very real policy not to be firm about *Humanae Vitae* in order not to scare people away. In other words, by not hearing anything that would disturb them, contracepting Catholics will stay in "good faith" and will keep coming to Church, and the pews will be full. By not taking action against the dissenting priests, the rectories will stay full. Lastly, perhaps by allowing moral theology acceptable to dissenters to be taught, the seminaries will be packed.

Well, the policy of silence hasn't worked. The empty pew is a phenomenon without precedent in the Catholic Church in America. There are also many empty bedrooms in rectories, and with only a handful of exceptions, seminaries have never been so empty. It's as if the emptiness of a moral theology which **de facto** accepts marital contraception and cannot say "No" even to spouse-swapping and sodomy is reflected in the emptiness of the seminaries, rectories and church pews. My question: with the benefit of hindsight, is this surprising?

Good faith and error

In addition to the problems created by the open toleration of dissent, there are other problems that affect the life and faith of the individual Catholic. The first has to do with "good faith and error."

It is axiomatic in moral theology that if you are reasonably sure that a person who is 1) doing an objective wrong, is 2) in good faith and 3) would not change if properly informed, you are not obliged to inform that person of the right way of acting. In this way, you keep him in good faith and good conscience, whereas if you tell him that his actions are objectively erroneous, you may put him in a position where he will continue to act wrongly but now in bad faith and bad conscience. It seems like a very logical theory: why put a man in a situation where he will become guilty of sin? Let him stay ignorant and blameless.

The axiom was developed as a guide for fraternal correction in cases where the harm being done was only to the person himself. For example, imagine you are the parent of a young adult whose faith is weak but who still usually participates at Sunday Mass. Imagine it's one of those weekends when a holy day of obligation falls on a Monday—such as Christmas of 1989. Imagine that you find out early in the afternoon on Sunday that this young adult simply forgot about Sunday morning Mass but was planning on attending Midnight Mass. Yet there would still be a chance to fulfill his or her Sunday obligation by attending the vigil of Christmas Mass at 4:30 Sunday afternoon. You could point this out to your adult child, but you are certain that the only effect would be a tense relationship and possible guilt on the adult child's part for not going. So this axiom enables you to avoid feeling guilty for not reminding or nagging such a child to fulfill his or her Sunday obligation in such a case.

The axiom, however, does not provide a general excuse from the obligation to instruct the errant and the ignorant, especially those for whom you have a special responsibility, nor is it an excuse from the duty to protect the common good. These are obligations in justice.

At the level of fraternal correction, there is a fine line between 1) being afraid to speak up for what is right and 2) being certain that your speaking up will have utterly no good affect and may actually have the reverse effect with regard to any particular individual. Such decisions have to be made by individual persons with regard to other individual persons.

However, it is a serious misapplication of the principle of fraternal correction to see it as an excuse for not teaching Catholic biblical doctrine about the demands of love, marriage and sexuality to Catholic congregations, under the hypothesis that the preaching of moral truth may do more harm than good, that it may make the congregation guilty but unchanged. Such refusals to preach difficult moral truths are certainly at odds with the practice of Jesus; and the thinking behind such refusals seems to make the biblical Christ either some sort of an ogre out to make people guilty or rather ignorant of the audience to which he spoke. Why did Christ lash out at the hypocrisy of the Scribes and Pharisees? Were they already in bad conscience? Considering their long standing tradition, this would be difficult to assume. Did Christ really think that they would change? Considering his recollection of the fate of the prophets, this is also difficult to assume. Thus there is at least some reason to think that they were in "good faith" and that Jesus did not really expect them to change. Perhaps He spoke for our benefit, not for theirs. If that were so, it would seem that He could have spoken in less impassioned tones. Perhaps, some might say, He never spoke out against the Scribes and the Pharisees and the biblical passages were only the product of the early Church and the evangelists who wanted to show why He was rejected and criticized. However, even though we may not have the exact words, there still must have been an event in the life of Jesus to give rise to the biblical account. Moreover, why would the *evangelists* want to show the Christ who came to *save* men making some men "guilty" by his preaching?

The more I think about it, the more clear it seems to me that Jesus spoke out against evil practices of the Scribes and Pharisees primarily because what they were doing was wrong and they needed to change. Of no little importance: they held "exemplary roles" in the Jewish religion, and thus their wrongful actions were bad not only for themselves but for the scandal created for others.

If questions can be raised about the condemnations Christ leveled at the actions of the Scribes and Pharisees of his day, they can be raised with equal validity about His teaching on sex. His words on the indissolubility of marriage were so shocking that some of the disciples said it would be better never to get married at all (if you couldn't get rid of an unsatisfactory mate). His words on lustful looks and desires have probably brought problems to millions of consciences. Why couldn't Christ have contented himself with the corporal works of mercy and left our consciences to the workings of the Holy Spirit with regard to sex?

The two-fold reality is that Jesus was fulfilling his self-imposed obligation to instruct the errant and the ignorant by teaching the truth, and that the truth is for the common good of men and women of every age and place. This is particularly true today concerning love, marriage and sexuality. The immoral use of sex and erroneous notions about love and marriage account for the feminization of poverty, the tragic breakdown of family life, and epidemic levels of sexually transmitted diseases. Does not the priest of Jesus Christ have an obligation to instruct the errant and the ignorant, and to protect and foster the common good by preaching the truth of Christ about love, marriage, and sexuality?

It seems to me that if the gospel is preached and the chips are allowed to fall where they will, we will find that the person whom we feared to change from "good faith" to "bad faith" may not go into "bad faith." He may change. Or he may just say that he doesn't believe it or that it doesn't apply to him. The human conscience has a remarkable elasticity, a remarkable ability simply not to admit as personally relevant what the person doesn't think he can achieve right now.

For the sake of the Church and its individual members, the erroneous application of the "good faith" principle of fraternal correction has to stop.

II: Practical Things to Do

The first practical thing that has to be done is at the level of ideas. Faith in the Church's teaching about the goodness of sex as God intends it and the evil of marital contraception and other sexual sins needs to be restored. After that is done, the other practical steps fall in place and will be seen as logical and sensible, but without solid theological grounding they will seem arbitrary and authoritarian.

What's the big deal?

While writing this book, I had the experience of talking about sexual behavior to four classes of seniors at a local Catholic boys' high school. The day was closed by this comment just as the last bell was about to ring: "Well, what's the big deal about using a condom?" That tied in closely with a previous question: "Do you really think someone can go to hell for using a condom?" Those simple teenage questions get to the heart of the matter, and one of the first practical things that must be done to convey and support belief in the teaching of *Humanae Vitae* is to respond to those questions.

The bottom line answer is this: using a condom mocks God, and what is more of a big deal than praising God on the one hand or mocking him on the other?[1]

How does using a condom mock God? (Of course what is said about condoms also applies to every other unnatural form of birth control.) The answer is written throughout the pages of Sacred Scripture and almost 2,000 years of the history of the Church established by Christ.

God has revealed that He is Love and that out of love He has created man and woman in His own image and likeness. That means that He gave us intelligence to know Him and wills to love Him and each other.

God gave us the gift of sex to share with us His power of procreation and as a unique way of expressing married love. God has made it clear that sex is meant to be a marriage act expressive of marital love and not deliberately closed to the transmission of life.

Everything God has revealed about love shows that love is inextricably tied up with self-giving and sacrifice. There is no such thing as free love.

God's love for man? The second person of the Blessed Trinity poured Himself out for us, took on our human nature, put up with us, and suffered and died for us. "Greater love than this no man has than that a man lay down his life for his friends" (John 15:13).

Man's love for each other? How many times did Jesus make clear the self-giving character of such love? Witness, for example, the parable of the Good Samaritan and the Last Judgment scene on the one hand, and, on the other hand, the parable of Dives and Lazarus and the parable of the two barns.

The love of spouses for each other? What could be a greater proof that the love of spouses is to be a self-giving love than the command of Ephesians 5 that husbands are to "love your wives as Christ loved the Church and gave Himself up for her" and that wives are to be subject to their husbands as to the Lord and as the Church is subject to Christ?

When a condom is used in adultery or fornication, it is a sign that such an action is intrinsically dishonest; it is a sign that such actions mock the living God who intends that sex should symbolize the self-giving love of marriage.

When a condom is used within marriage, it reflects some combination of fear and lust and/or strong contralife will. It makes it "sex with serious reservation." It contradicts the very meaning of marriage, that unreserved gift of self to the other.

In all of these cases, using a condom is a sign of a pretense of self-giving love, and so it mocks the Author of life and love and sex. And, as indicated above, what is true of a condom is true of every form of contraception. They all mock God. Those which are abortifacient such as the IUD and the Pill add grave insult to the already grave injury.

"Can a person go to hell for using condoms?" Can a person go to hell for fornicating or committing adultery or sodomy? The answer is the same in each case: of course he can because the question in each case can be rephrased: "Can a person go to hell for mocking God, for seriously misusing the gift of sex which is meant to express the gift of self within God's gift of marriage?"

Do people in fact go to hell for their sins of adultery, contraception, fornication, and sodomy? No one knows. On the one hand, the Church teaches that such behavior constitutes the "grave matter of mortal sin," but only God and the individual sinner (and sometimes only God!) can judge whether he or she gave the matter "sufficient reflection" and "full consent of the will," the other two criteria necessary for incurring the personal guilt of mortal sin.

On the other hand, the seer of Fatima, Sister Lucia, has said that a fiery vision of hell was granted to her and the other two children of the Fatima apparitions; later, the mother-in-law of Francesca, one of the Fatima children, said that it was revealed to Francesca that more people go to hell for sins of impurity than for any other reason. More basic, the Church has constantly taught that sins of impurity constitute grave matter. At the very least, there are utterly no reasons in the Christian faith for taking lightly any of the sins of sex including contraception.

The current attitude of "what's the big deal about contraception" has to be replaced by a new respect for the God-given marital meaning of sex, a deep-seated recognition that contraception makes the marriage bed one of sin. A holy fear of offending God through misusing sex and mocking him by calling sins of lust acts of love needs to be developed. If we sin through weakness, let us call our sins "sins" and confess them, but let us not fall into the even greater sin of pride—calling our sins of weakness "virtues."

This reversal of attitudes will not take place easily or overnight, but it will certainly be assisted by the following practical steps.

1. Reform Catholic education.

Questions. Is there any element within the Catholic Church more directly responsible for the lack of marital chastity than Catholic education? Can the Catholic Church in North America and Europe regain its health without reversing this situation?

Catholic education has been significantly under the control of the dissenters since the anti-*Humanae Vitae* rebellion of 1968. As early as 1972, I heard this from a college freshman: "Mr. Kippley, you're the first person I've ever heard say a good word about the Church's teaching on birth control. At the Catholic high school I attended we were taught that the theologians disagreed with the Pope and that it was okay to go with the theologians. All my friends who are getting married are going on the Pill, and they haven't the slightest idea that they are really going against the teaching of the Church." I asked the young woman where she went to school but she wouldn't tell me. "I don't want you contacting the school. And anyway, it doesn't make any difference. I've discussed this with the girls in the dorm, and they all had the same experience."

In so-called Catholic education under the control of the dissenters, students are likely to be exposed to a number of things which serve to undermine the teaching of *Humanae Vitae*, and ultimately everything else is also undermined. You cannot teach dissent from one aspect of marital chastity without having those same principles applied to every area of sexual behavior. You cannot undermine the teaching authority of the Church with regard to marital chastity without undermining it with regard to every area of morality. You cannot teach the art of disregarding the teaching of Scripture about sex without teaching the same disregard for the teaching of Scripture about the Church, the Eucharist, marriage and even Christ Himself!

The effects of dissent in education. I don't think it is really disputable that Catholic education in most North American dioceses was largely under the control of the dissenters during the Seventies and Eighties, nor do I expect much debate about the observable effects.

The situation I am closest to is the natural family planning movement. In the early 1970s there was a flurry of NFP activity. In the United States, several national organizations were established including the Couple to Couple League (CCL) established by my wife and myself in 1971, and there were a number of independent programs as well. Growth continued throughout the Seventies, but for CCL it peaked in 1980, and I think that's generally true of the rest of the NFP movement, give or take a couple years. The result is that in 1990 CCL taught less than half as many new couples as it taught in 1980—despite twice as many teachers and classes offered. When it comes to interest in NFP among couples who have been trained in Catholic schools, the silence is deafening.

The damage done by twenty years of education in dissent is evident in almost any parish except, perhaps, those serving the newest suburbs—the empty pew. In some dioceses, Sunday Mass attendance runs only at 20 to 30 percent of the Catholic population; the national average of 52% in 1989 is down substantially from 1960. And even the 52% figure is misleading. All anyone has to do to see the Catholic Church of the future in any typical parish is to mentally subtract those who completed their education before 1968. So, if you assume they completed their education by age 22, then in 1990 you would be looking only at the under-45 population. Next Sunday, mentally subtract everyone at Mass who looks 45 or over (born before 1946) and the remainder is the American Church of the future—unless authentic reform is instituted.

Catholic education in dissent is also an exercise in slow suicide. As Catholic contraceptors have half (or much less than half) the number of children their parents had, the enrollment at Catholic schools drops; then the tuition rises, thus putting Catholic education out of reach for more parents, especially those who remain faithful to Catholic teaching and have medium-size to large families.

I am not saying that the picture of a dying Catholic Church in America is due solely to Catholics using contraception. What I am saying, however, is that the principle of dissent, the principle of thinking that one's personal opinion or fancy is superior to the teaching of the Church, is anti-Christian, anti-Catholic, and, unless rapidly reversed, will reduce the Roman Catholic Church in North America to the status of a sect within the next 50 to 100 years.

What Catholic education can do. On the other hand, Catholic education can once again become a help for the salvation of both the individual person and the Church in America. The steps to reform seem obvious to me.

1) Non-believers, whether nominally Catholic or Protestant, should not be employed in Catholic schools at every level from grade schools to colleges and seminaries, especially in religion and the broad range of social studies subjects. A bishop wouldn't hire an atheist to teach a seminary course on natural theology; why should he allow those practicing unchastity, whether contraception, adultery or sodomy, to teach courses that should teach chastity and faith? An annually signed profession of faith and practice may be the only practical way of sorting out the weeds from the wheat.

2) Sex education courses should be replaced by education in chastity. This will include necessary physiology and eventually NFP instruction, but the orientation must be towards chastity. Pope John Paul II said it well in *Familiaris Consortio:*

> But the necessary conditions [for understanding and living the moral norm] also include knowledge of the bodily aspect and the body's rhythms of fertility. Accordingly, every effort must be made to render such knowledge accessible to all married people and also to young adults before marriage, through clear, timely and serious instruction and education given by married couples, doctors and experts. Knowledge must then lead to education in self-control: hence the **absolute necessity for the virtue of chastity and for permanent education in it** (n.33, emphasis added).

Of course, what applies to Catholic education applies also to that special form of adult education and formation known as prospective convert instruction. I am informed that in some parish and diocesan programs, instruction about *Humanae Vitae* is completely absent, and I've heard of one in which dissent is actively taught. Is it right that some prospective converts are being taught either directly or indirectly that it's permissible to ignore the explicit teaching of the Catholic Church about marital love and sexuality? Where this happens, is the local Church being true to her Founder and can she expect His blessings?

2. Reform the marriage preparation process.

Questions: Should preparation for Catholic marriage include and emphasize Catholic teaching about love, sex and marriage, including the teaching of *Humanae Vitae*? Is it realistic to expect contracepting couples to faithfully transmit the fullness of such teaching? If you answer in the affirmative to the first and in the negative to the second, I think what follows will make sense to you.

The time of preparation for marriage is a time of special grace. Despite the fact that many couples preparing for marriage are living in sin (or perhaps *because* of this fact), the priest is called to exercise the prophetic ministry of Christ. He must make sure engaged couples understand that Christian marriage is unbreakable; he must also make sure they understand that marriage is for family, not for mutual egoism, and that it is the grave matter of mortal sin to use unnatural methods of birth control. Furthermore, he must convey this teaching in such a way as to also convey that this is the teaching of an all-wise and loving Father whose commandments of love are for our own benefit.

In order to reform the marriage preparation process, the work of the loyal priest must be reinforced and supplemented by each part of the process. Bishops and priests must recognize that the same problems exist in marriage preparation as exist in Catholic education, so the same remedies must be applied.

1) Married couples who dissent from the teaching of *Humanae Vitae,* whether in theory or in practice, must not be allowed to participate in marriage preparation programs. A signed statement of faith and practice will prove very helpful in allowing contraceptors to find that they no longer have time for such service.

2) There must be an ironclad way of assuring that each couple understands that God Himself has created the unbreakable covenant of marriage, that the Catholic Church cannot annul a true marriage when things fall apart, and that divorce and remarriage constitute living in the sin of adultery. I say "ironclad" because it seems that in some programs, everyone thinks the subject of indissolubility is taught by someone else.

3) The basic norms of marital chastity must be taught. It is utterly amazing how many Christian couples have no idea that it is immoral to engage in masturbation, whether mutual or solitary, complete oral and anal sex, and contraceptive intercourse whether withdrawal-ejaculation, using artificial barriers, or using drugs

and other devices. CCL has a brochure that can be helpful in this regard.[2] This brochure also answers the questions about the limits of sexual behavior when the couple do not intend to conclude their activity with complete intercourse. These are questions frequently raised by couples who are abstaining during the fertile times and who desire a certain amount of physical contact within the norms of Christian chastity.

4) A brief theology of sex must be taught by priests to engaged couples so they can see the God-given meanings of marriage and sex within marriage. The concept that God intends that sex should be a renewal of their marriage covenant can be meaningful at this time in their lives.

5) Last but not least, every engaged couple must take a complete course in Natural Family Planning as part of the normal process of preparing for marriage. The course **should** teach all the signs of fertility and infertility; the course **must** teach marital chastity and generosity in the service of life.

Without such a requirement, the number of couples who start their marriages with marital chastity will remain extremely small. In 1990, experience suggests that very few couples are ready to start having children as soon as they are married, and that only two or three percent of those wanting to delay pregnancy are starting their marriages with chaste NFP. Perhaps I am wildly optimistic, but I think that if 100% of engaged couples had good pro-*Humanae Vitae* instruction from their parish priests **and** attended Catholic-oriented NFP classes such as CCL's, the number of "delaying couples" starting their marriage with chaste NFP would increase ten-fold from roughly 2.5 percent to 25 percent. Furthermore, I think that another 25 percent would come over to NFP within three years of their wedding based on their own experience—the frustration of seeking marital happiness through sexual satiation, feelings of using and being used, the unpleasantness of using unnatural methods of birth control, and the nagging of their consciences.

I think that another 15 percent to 20 percent would gradually accept marital chastity if the theme of marital chastity is preached throughout their diocese and as they gradually realize that they cannot be consistent in trying to teach chastity to their own children while refusing it for themselves.

When 50 to 75 percent of married Catholics are living lives of marital chastity and generosity in the service of life, the empty pews will once again be full. And as dioceses and seminaries resuscitate the preaching and teaching of chastity—living the truth about love—the seminaries and then the rectories will also once again be full. I am sure of it.

3. Renew preaching about love and sexuality.

Question: Can the Church's teaching about sexuality and birth control be preached from the pulpit?

The teaching of Christ in His Church about the demands of marital love must be preached in season and out of season from the pulpit. The assumption simply must be made that if adults are still showing up for Sunday Mass, they are of at least enough good faith to want to know what God expects of them. That includes preaching both the Lord's teaching about the indissolubility of marriage and the teaching of *Humanae Vitae.*

I am not suggesting that it is easy to preach about either of these truths; what is necessary for being faithful to the vocation of priesthood is rarely easy. However, it can be done, even in the mixed congregation of a typical parish.

A few years ago, I wrote a series of seven homilies based on the Last Supper.[3] Since the Mass is renewal of the Sacrifice of the Last Supper and Calvary, it is legitimate to preach about events of the Last Supper regardless of the regular Sunday readings. The idea in these homilies is to spend about 90% of the homily explaining and getting agreement about something that Jesus said or did at the Last Supper. Then the last 10% applies it to sexuality including birth control. Also, each homily refers to a CCL brochure or pamphlet that should be attached to the parish bulletin that Sunday. Further information about the homilies can be obtained from CCL and from an article which appeared in a Catholic journal in 1983.[4]

The point of all this is to illustrate that it is possible and practical to preach about these matters from the pulpit even though the subjects are sensitive. Probably the main thing a priest might get from a homily written by someone else is some ideas for his own and confidence that it **can** be done; and such preaching **must** be done.

Preaching must be accompanied by the practical help of NFP instruction—either classes or written materials. As of this writing, the only written materials I can recommend are those teaching the cross-checking Sympto-Thermal Method. The *CCL Home Study Course for Natural Family Planning* was designed specifically to assist couples who live in areas not yet serviced by CCL teachers. As an aside, I think it's appropriate to mention that the need to provide practical help to accompany the affirmation of *Humanae Vitae* was largely responsible for the formation of The Couple to Couple League. After the predecessor of this book was published in 1970, I was truly burdened by the words of Jesus, "Woe to you lawyers also because you load men with heavy burdens and don't lift a finger to help!"(Lk 11:46). I felt that by upholding *Humanae Vitae* I had gone out of my way to reaffirm what many regard as a burden, and I therefore felt obliged also to do all I could to provide the best practical help I could.

Persons interested in establishing a CCL chapter in their parish or community can contact CCL for further information. If they wish to investigate establishing an independent program, they can contact the Human Life Center.[5]

4. Catholicize pastoral counseling.

Question: How should a Catholic counsel about birth control?

When a person or a couple ask a priest or any Catholic educator about birth control, they are open to hearing the truth. If they weren't, they wouldn't be asking. What they are really asking is, "What does God really expect of us with regard to birth control?" The reason they are asking a Catholic priest or counselor is because of their belief that the Catholic Church is God's one, true church. They know what the world says about birth control, and they are asking which of the many voices they hear is the voice of God, the voice of truth.

It is irresponsible and unjust for Catholic counselors, whether priests or others,to say things that give the impression that what God expects of married couples regarding birth control is not clear—because it **is** clear.

Talk about "following your conscience" is highly misleading and utterly beside the point. The purpose of Church teaching is to enable the believer to properly form his or her conscience. Vatican II is very clear on this:

Married people should realize that in their behavior they may not simply follow their own fancy but must be ruled by conscience—and conscience ought to be conformed to the law of God in the light of the teaching authority of the Church, which is the authentic interpreter of divine law in the light of the gospel (*Gaudium et Spes,* n.50).

The incongruity of a priest or other counselor telling people to "follow their own conscience" when they ask about birth control is illustrated by estimating what his reaction would be if they were to ask about starting a spouse-swapping group or a local chapter of an organization devoted to white supremacy. A few "liberal" counselors might waffle about the spouse-swapping, but it's hard to believe that there is a single priest in the U.S.A. who wouldn't tell such people in no uncertain terms about the immorality of racism and about the Church's teaching about racial equality and justice. It's impossible to imagine the typical American priest undermining his teaching about social justice by saying it was all a matter of conscience and implying that a conscience could be rightly formed if it directly contradicted Church teaching about racial equality and justice.

Would the modern priest couch his counseling about social justice or injustice in vague terms about "the Church teaches" in such a way as to give the impression that he **had** to say such things? No, he would make it clear that he **believes** that what the Church teaches is **true** and that it is binding in the formation of the Catholic conscience.

What the socially concerned counselor—priest or anyone— needs to realize is that the single greatest cause of poverty in America is the sexual immorality that was loosed by the contraceptive-sex revolution. Such immorality is at the root of the vast, vast majority of poor family units headed by a single woman—either never married or deserted or divorced. There can be no doubt in the mind of any thinking person that the sexual revolution started with the acceptance of marital contraception, then quickly spread to the acceptance of contraceptive sex outside of marriage, then to easy divorce and repeat marriages, and finally to the mass killing of unborn children through legalizing abortion. Historical and legal documentation can be found in CCL's *Birth Control and Christian Discipleship*.[6]

The role of the counselor—priest, educator, or other counselor— is fourfold.

1) The counselor must convey the teaching reaffirmed by *Humanae Vitae* that it is always and everywhere immoral for married couples to use unnatural methods of birth control. Furthermore, the counselor must do this in a spirit of faith so that it is clear to the inquirer that the counselor believes this teaching is not just

"official" but also true. Unbelieving counselors shouldn't be counseling.

2) The counselor must help the couple understand about NFP and how to get practical help.

3) The counselor must relate the inevitable difficulties of marital chastity to the daily cross that is a necessary part of Christian discipleship.

4) The counselor must show honest compassion to those who are experiencing difficulties with marital chastity without compromising the sometimes difficult truth about the demands of love. Part of this compassion includes assisting people to develop the virtue of marital chastity through the traditional means—prayer and regular reception of the Sacraments including monthly confession, habits of self-control in eating as well as sex, good spiritual reading, and avoiding sources of temptations including the vast majority of contemporary movies and television shows.

Another part of compassion is not compromising the truth. As it was said so well by Pope Paul VI in *Humanae Vitae,* "It is an outstanding manifestation of charity towards souls to omit nothing from the saving doctrine of Christ" (n.29).

Lastly, what Pope John Paul II said about the compassionate bishop can be said of all who assist the bishop through authentic Catholic counseling.

The compassionate bishop will proclaim the incompatibility of premarital sex and homosexual activity with God's plan for human love; at the same time with all his strength he will try to assist those who are faced with difficult moral choices. With equal compassion, he will proclaim the doctrine of *Humanae Vitae* and *Familiaris Consortio* in its full beauty, not passing over in silence the unpopular truth that artificial birth control is against God's law."[7]

5. Teach moral and religious epistemology.

Question: How can an inquirer come to know the truth about love?

"Epistemology" is a $64.00 word that means "how you come to know the truth" or "how you come to knowledge." In our context, the title of this section means "Teach how you come to know the truth about moral behavior and religious belief." Why? Well, eventually the question of chastity—both marital and pre-marital—gets around to a basic question: "How can I be certain that such-and-such behavior is forbidden by God?" Whether you are a teacher trying to convey to teenagers that fornication and sodomy are immoral, or whether you are a married person asking yourself about birth control, sooner or later you have to confront and answer that question.

The Bible. The answer of some, "Look to the Bible," raises two further questions: 1) How can you be certain that the Bible is the written word of God? 2) If you believe the Bible is the inspired word of God, how can you be certain of its interpretation? Bible-only Christians say it's obvious and that they have the proper interpretation. However, as anyone can observe, they are sadly and wildly divided among themselves, especially in America where the democratic spirit has led to the establishment of hundreds of different denominations, some of which claim to have the full truth, others of which just claim to be a particular point of view or way of worshipping.

Certain fundamentalists—or Bible-believing Christians as they prefer to call themselves—claim that they interpret the Bible 100% literally, but the first thing they do is to interpret the Eucharistic accounts of John 6 and the Last Supper as purely symbolic. They do the same with the Matthew's account of Christ establishing the Church upon Simon Peter. This is not the place to reply to the many different interpretations given by Protestants—whether liberal or fundamentalist—to these passages which are right at the heart of both worship and the very being of the Church. It is sufficient to note the immense historical fact of contradictory interpretations of these vital passages, as well as many others, and such contradictions simply could not occur if Sacred Scripture were self-interpreting. God is not the author of contradiction.

Because such contradictions make it self-evident that the Scriptures are not self-interpreting, the force of the various passages which clearly condemn various forms of sexual behavior can be weakened by the Bible-only approach to Christian morality. The teenager who says mockingly, "Well, that's **your** interpretation," is only mimicking the errors of sophisticated adults—both allegedly Catholic and Protestant—whose approach to Scripture may differ but who agree in saying that the Scriptures are not really condemning—for today—what they seem to condemn.

While I greatly admire those many Christians who have been brought up in Protestant Christian faiths and who are bravely holding on to traditional Christian morality, I do not see how their appeal exclusively to a written word so differently interpreted by others can long endure the skepticism of both secular society and so-called liberal Christianity.

The Roman Catholic Church. The decline of Christian morality, with all sides interpreting Scripture to justify their position, makes it clear that Sacred Scripture needs an authoritative interpreter.

The historical fact is that God did not give us the Bible directly. Rather He first created the Church of the Old Covenant, out of which He drew the Old Testament. Jesus left us no writings. Instead He did precisely what Yahweh had done with Abram: in response to the act of faith of Simon bar Jona, He changed his name to Peter—meaning Rock (as Yahweh changed Abram's to Abraham), and founded His Church upon him. He personally founded the Church not as a democracy but as a hierarchy with Peter as the visible head, and this same basic structure remains in the Roman Catholic Church today.

Out of the Church of the apostolic era came the writings which today are called the New Testament. There were other pious writings from the apostolic era, but the Church was led by the Holy Spirit to accept some and reject others. The inevitable conclusion is that it is on the word of the Catholic Church that the writings called the New Testament are accepted as the inspired word of God.

Catholic faith for accepting the 27 books of the New Testament as Sacred Scripture rests upon the promises of Jesus at the Last Supper. Jesus promised repeatedly that He would send the Holy Spirit to lead the Apostles and their successors into the fullness of the truth. The Catholic Church believes that Jesus is keeping his word—whether it be accepting the books of the New Testament, or clarifying the natures of Christ at Nicea or teaching dogma about the Church as it did at Vatican II.

In short, when you are faced with the ultimate questions of moral knowledge and certitude, the bottom line is **God-Christ-Church-Bible.**

And whether you are teaching rebellious teenagers or inquiring adults, that also has to be the top line, or you will be lost in mindless arguments and cliches about interpretations and opinions.

6. Renew the call to perfection.

Question: Is it possible for everyone to live the teaching of *Humanae Vitae*?

Running contrary to the recent practice of not preaching difficult truths about the demands of love is the renewed emphasis on the call to perfection for all Christians. This is at the heart of the renewal of moral theology. The call to perfection, once seen as an ideal to be pursued only by professed Religious, is now seen as addressed to all who accept Christ. The laity are thus no longer regarded as capable of becoming only mediocre Christians, second class citizens in God's Church. Rather, they are seen as having co-responsibility for the mission of the Church; they are also co-responsible with the hierarchy and the Religious in answering the call of Christ to perfection; they are co-responsible for the Church's authentic expression of her faith consciousness.

Obviously the manner in which they exercise this responsibility and the call to perfection will differ among laymen and between laity and the professionally identified members of the Church—priests, bishops, and Religious.

Relevant to the debate of *non-contraception* versus *contraception* is the question of whether the stated teaching of the Church or the practice of contraception better accommodates the call to perfection. I think the refusal to practice contraception contributes to the development of a number of Christian virtues in a way that does not seem possible with the practice of contraception. More to the point, however, is the fundamental question that married couples must ask themselves: If Christ were a married man living in our circumstances, would he practice contraception? Christian teaching for 1900 years said "No." The post-Lambeth popes—Pius XI, Pius XII, John XXIII, Paul VI, and John Paul II have answered "No," and the vast majority of the national hierarchies of the world have reaffirmed the papal teaching.

The bishops and their assisting priests to whom falls the huge responsibility of leading their people to perfection have a real pastoral problem. They have to believe—really believe—that the laity are capable of answering Christ's call to perfection. The history of the promulgation of the social doctrine of the Church for the eighty years 1891-1971 suggests that many of the clergy either did not believe it or that they did not believe that the masses of the laity were ready to hear and accept it. During the Seventies and Eighties, American Church leadership tried to address numerous social issues with little grass roots support. Of course, during this time the laity were being led to believe that if they didn't like something, they could just ignore it under the guise of "following conscience."

In 1969 I wrote, "If the promulgation of the sexual doctrine of the Church is given the same kind of treatment as the social doctrine has been given for the past seventy-five years, we can expect a very prosperous and comfortable North American Church."[8]

I was wrong. I failed to see that the massive acceptance of contraception and materialism would adversely affect the Church by emptying the pews. Individual Catholics, especially nominal Catholics, may be very prosperous, but the Western Church which has become spiritually impoverished by failing, for all practical purposes, to preach the demands of Christian love, is also becoming physically impoverished. The closing of churches and schools is not a sign of health.

The answer is surely not an all-out acceptance of the social doctrine of the Church and an all-out repudiation of her sexual doctrine or vice versa. The call to perfection which our religious leaders must sound loud and clear must be based solidly on the life and teaching of Christ. In the life and doctrine of Jesus we find *both* the preaching and the living of a social doctrine which hardly condoned the personal amassing of wealth *and* a sexual doctrine that was elevated, difficult to hear, and unacceptable to many of His contemporaries.

Jesus ran no popularity contest. Nor did the prophets before him. Nor did the apostles after him. Church leaders who, for whatever reasons, avoid the difficult truths may find that they have missed a great opportunity to lead their people in answering the call of Christ to perfection. The never ending pastoral problem is the challenge of inspiring a people who are surrounded by a philosophy of materialism to realize the values and the teaching of Christ in their own lives.

7. Build a community of faith at worship.

In 1969 I wrote in this book's predecessor about providing economic help to the family which needed it, and I think that's still a good idea.[9] However, things have deteriorated in the last 20 years to the point where Roman Catholics who believe and practice what the Roman Catholic Church believes and teaches are frequently psychologically isolated in their own parishes and dioceses, and what they need is spiritual help and confirmation in faith.

In many parishes, they may get almost no affirmation of their faith at Sunday Mass. What they hear could frequently be said from the most liberal Protestant pulpit in the diocese. They may believe that the parish and high school religion programs use texts that teach heresy by omission. That is, while they don't positively contradict formal Catholic teaching, they don't support it either. The sex education or "family life" series of texts may be highly inadequate, perhaps nothing more than secular humanism with some religious-sounding labels; at worst it may involve verbal and/or pictorial pornography.

Increasingly the parents of these families are giving up on Catholic schools and turning to Catholic home education so they can fulfill their responsibilities of transmitting the Faith without being undermined by non-believing teachers and unsupportive textbooks. Despite much talk about a parish community, they feel "excommunicated" precisely because they believe and practice in accord with the teaching of the Popes.

IF responsible bishops and pastors reform Catholic education, reform the marriage preparation process, and carry out the other reforms described in this section, they will go a long way toward building a community of faith.

However, if a Catholic physician who is known to do abortions and/or sterilizations or prescribe the Pill, etc. is allowed to be a lector or distributor of Holy Communion, is not the idea of a community of faith at worship shattered?

The answer to the reform of liturgy is the same as it is for education and marriage preparation: those who do not believe the teachings of the Church should not hold exemplary roles in the life of the Church. I see no way of saying, "You can dissent on this but not on that" without encouraging the principle of dissent. I mean, are you going to say to a physician, "If you want to be up in the sanctuary, you can't do surgical abortions, but you can prescribe abortion-causing devices and drugs?" Or to Mrs. Jones, "You can't use the Pill but you can be sexually sterilized?"

Therefore, I don't see a practical alternative to this recommendation: a signed profession of Catholic faith and practice must be required of everyone holding exemplary roles in the life of the Church—distributors of Holy Communion, lectors, and members of parish and diocesan councils.

To put it another way, why not? None of us laity have any *right* to be in the sanctuary. That's a privilege. So why should those who refuse to practice sexual self-control be proclaiming the Scriptures which call for chastity? And why should those who have built their marital lives on condoms, diaphragms, pills and permanent sterilization be distributing the Body of the Lord who called for faith and a change of heart? I am not suggesting that if a married couple get carried away and masturbate on a solitary occasion that they be bound in conscience to drop from the exemplary roles. On the other hand, if they were to make masturbation during the fertile time (or the Pill, etc.) their systematic way of avoiding the demands of chaste love, then they should not feel comfortable in the exemplary roles and should withdraw. Momentary weakness is one thing; systematic unchastity is something else.

If this drastically reduces the number of distributors and lectors, so be it. The Church got along well for centuries without such "help," and perhaps some priests would feel a little more needed if they had more to do at Mass. However, the main point is this: it is a scandal and a disruption of faith to have in exemplary roles those who are known to use immoral methods of birth control. Is it not obscene that a woman may be killing her newly conceived baby with her IUD or her Pill at the same time she is reading the Word of God or saying, "The Body of Christ"? To those who say these are private sins, I say, "People talk"—sometimes very openly and loudly. Women talk about their IUDs, Pills, their tubal ligations, and their husbands' vasectomies, and men talk about their "getting fixed." It's a way of sharing their guilt and trying to get approval from friends and members of the Church. Participation in the easy but on-display liturgical roles provides another way of indirect approval for their sinful behavior. Is the Church helping individuals by giving them the opportunity for such indirect approval? Is not such approval rather a stumbling block to themselves and also to congregation members who believe that the Eucharist is meant to be a sign of unity in faith?

10

The Hard Cases

This chapter is written primarily for the priests, ministers, or counselors who openly preach the Christian teaching reaffirmed by *Humanae Vitae* and who also promote the practical help of natural family planning, and I will address them directly.

You will not promote this teaching very long before you will start to hear the hard cases. Some of the cases are hard by reason of nature, and some are self-inflicted, even if unknowingly. In other cases you will be hearing from people, almost invariably wives, who are victimized by a spouse's unchastity and sometimes compulsive sexual behavior.

Counseling Principles

Because you are most likely a sensitive person, you will be tempted to give in to false compassion, and therefore you may find it helpful to review periodically the principles of truly compassionate Christian counseling. To put it another way, as the director of the Couple to Couple League and author of items dealing with Christian sexuality, I get my share of difficult cases and honest inquiries about right and wrong. I want to share with you some of the things that encourage me to do my best to teach the truth as the Church teaches it.

Cardinal Newman's counsel

The first item is attributed to John Henry Cardinal Newman. I got it from a priest who used it in a homily, but I was unable to get further information about the source. I find it both comforting and inspirational.

I Have My Mission

God has created me to do Him some definite service. He has committed some work to me which He has not committed to another.

I have my mission.

I am a link in a chain, a bond of connection between persons. He has not created me for nothing.

I shall do good. I shall do His work. I shall be an angel of peace, a preacher of truth in my own place while not intending it if I do but keep His word. Therefore I will trust Him.

Whatever, wherever I am, I can never be thrown away.

If I am in sickness, my sickness may serve Him.

If I am in perplexity, my perplexity may serve Him.

If I am in sorrow, my sorrow may serve Him.

He does nothing in vain.

He knows what He is about.

Karl Rahner, S.J., on situation ethics

This quotation comes from Rahner's *Nature and Grace* which was published in English in 1964 when he was still thoroughly orthodox.[1] The entire quotation forms one sentence, a Rahnerian specialty.

If we Christians, when faced with a moral decision, really realized

that the world is under the Cross on which God himself hung nailed and pierced,

that obedience to God's law can also entail man's death,

that we may not do evil in order that good may come of it,

that it is an error and heresy of this eudomonic modern age to hold that the morally right thing can never lead to a tragic situation from which in this world there is no way out;

if we really realized that as Christians we must expect almost to take for granted that at some time in our life our Christianity will involve us in a situation in which we must either sacrifice everything or lose our soul, that we cannot expect always to avoid a "heroic" situation,

then there would indeed be fewer Christians who think that their situation requires a special ruling which is not so harsh as the laws proclaimed as God's laws by the Church,

then there would be fewer confessors and spiritual advisors who, for fear of telling their penitent how strict is God's law, fail in their duty and tell him instead to follow his conscience,

as if he had not asked, and done right to ask, which among all the many voices clamoring within him was the true voice of God,

as if it were not for God's Church to try and distinguish it in accordance with His law,

as if the true conscience could speak even when it had not been informed by God and the faith which comes from hearing.

The end does not justify the means

The majority report of the papal birth control commission had rationalized that acts of contraceptive intercourse could be made morally good by occurring within a marriage that had some non-contraceptive acts of intercourse. Pope Paul VI specifically rejected this hypothesis in *Humanae Vitae;* and in doing so he reiterated the moral principle that the end does not justify the means. For convenience, the passage is repeated here.

And to justify conjugal acts made intentionally infertile one cannot invoke as valid reasons the lesser evil, or the fact that when taken together with the fertile acts already performed or to follow later, such acts would coalesce into a whole and hence would share in one and the same moral goodness. In truth, if it is sometimes permissible to tolerate a lesser moral evil in order to avoid a greater evil or to promote a greater good, **it is not permissible, not even for the gravest reasons, to do evil so that good may follow therefrom.** One may not, in other words, make into the object of a positive act of the will something that is intrinsically disordered and hence unworthy of the human person, even when the intention is to safeguard or promote individual, family or social goods (emphasis added).

The end does not homogenize the means

Closely allied to the principle that the end does not justify the means is the principle that the end does not homogenize the means. That is, the same purpose does not make morally equivalent the various ways of trying to achieve that purpose. This is so self-evident to people concerning every other area of life that it is truly amazing that otherwise thinking people may actually try to justify using contraception on the basis that the Church allows NFP.

I find that I have to be very careful in pointing out the absurdity of such a position. People may later call themselves stupid for such reasoning, but they don't want you or me calling them stupid. So I find it best to get away from birth control and work with the very common example of wanting to live in a nice house. I've never met anyone, adult or youth, who would say that honest hard work and selling illegal drugs were morally the same because they both have the same purpose of buying a nice house. Once the principle is established, it can be applied to birth control.

In God we trust

This phrase which appears on American money has to be engraved in the Christian heart. In a technological age, trusting God is one of the truly difficult aspects of being Christian. When couples have a truly serious reason to avoid pregnancy, you will find that a lack of practical trust in the providence of God is frequently a major difficulty. In such situations couples need to know about the high effectiveness of modern natural family planning as indicated in another chapter; they have an equal need for reassurance and gentle reminders of their obligation to place their trust in God.

Generosity in raising children

Closely related to the principle of trusting God is the call to generosity in the service of life. You will meet many couples who have thoroughly absorbed the cultural norm of having only one or two children. They may regard having a third child as almost unthinkable despite admitting that they have no economic, health or personal-psychological reasons for not having more. They will not regard themselves as selfish; it's just that their whole way of thinking has been formed by the cultural norm of the one-or-two child family. In fact, comparing themselves with friends who have decided to remain childless, they may regard themselves as very generous in having even two children!

The teaching of NFP must take place in the context of the Christian call to generosity in the service of life, but responsible pastoral authorities cannot expect NFP teachers and/or NFP news-letters to do it all. Ministers, priests, and counselors also need to affirm this aspect of Christian married life.

You cannot decide for anybody else what generosity means in their case. The providentialists say to do nothing to interfere with procreation—including NFP, and they remind us that every baby is co-created by God who will provide the means. The culturalists say to stop at two, three would be maximum. They see nothing but problems and tell us to use everything available to keep our families very small. The Catholic position is in the middle, calling for generosity, recognizing serious reasons in some cases for more spacing and family limitation, and allowing NFP in the presence of sufficiently serious reasons.

Thus the key is to get the couple to really ask themselves if they have a truly serious reason to avoid pregnancy, whether they are really answering God's call to generosity in the service of life. A good place to start is with a reflective reading of sections 49 and 50 of Vatican II's *Gaudium et Spes*.

To be sure, the procreation and education of children mean a lot more than just having babies and sending them to the local public school which may well be a bastion of secular humanism and several other anti-Christian "isms." The real education of your children today takes time in the home, and for many it may mean total home schooling. All of that takes energy. On the other hand, education does not mean you have to pay your children's way through a private college, and many a mother has found it easier to run the household with five children than with one or two.

In short, the counseling of generosity in raising children encounters many concerns and fears. It must be tied ultimately to a religious response to God. Perhaps the best you may be able to do at first is to persuade couples not to be committed to a preset number such as two or three and to leave their future decisions up to their response to God in future circumstances.

The daily cross and Christian discipleship

The real problems of some couples are greatly magnified by an assumption that they should not have to carry the cross daily, especially a cross connected with sexuality. Not satisfying a sexual urge every day or even several times a day may be a cross for some men, especially those with a history of compulsive masturbation carried over into compulsive intercourse within marriage. The normal abstinence of NFP will be a cross for many, and when truly extended abstinence is called for, it may be a cross for almost everyone.

Therefore it seems to me that you should probably hit this problem head-on and discuss marital chastity in terms of Luke 9:23-25:

And he said to all, "If any man would come after Me, let him deny himself and take up his cross daily and follow Me. For whoever would save his life will lose it; and whoever loses his life for My sake, he will save it. For what does it profit a man if he gains the whole world and loses or forfeits himself?"

Furthermore, of the various crosses possible within family life, the cross of marital chastity and normal abstinence has to be among the easiest. Whenever I read the newspaper accounts of the tragedies afflicting various families day after day, the cross of periodic abstinence looks small by comparison.

In counseling about the cross and the price of Christian discipleship, you do not remove the difficulty but you enable your counsellee to see it in a new light and eventually to see it as an opportunity to grow in grace and as a human being. I am in no way minimizing the reality of the cross that extended abstinence sometimes is, but every suffering can become meaningful in the light of Christian discipleship. Many Christians have gained insight into the meaningfulness of suffering by reading the Jewish Victor Frankl's *Man's Search for Meaning*[2] in which he reflects on the sufferings he endured in a Nazi concentration camp.

You may also have to counsel about normal Christian practices of spirituality—personal and family prayer, self-denial, real participation at Mass, the frequent reception of the sacraments of reconciliation and the Eucharist, and spiritual reading. You may be surprised at the infrequency of prayer, self-denial, confession, and spiritual reading.

The point is this: given the effects of the Fall on human nature and given the anti-Christian, pan-sexual culture of the West, it is folly to expect the teaching of Christian chastity to be accepted by people who do not think and react with a Christian mind and heart. It's like expecting hard, sunbaked ground to soak up all the water of a cloudburst.

Pope Paul VI clearly recognized this, and both you and couples you counsel should be familiar with Part III of *Humanae Vitae*—Pastoral Directives—, especially sections 20-22. For example:

A proper practice of birth regulation requires first and foremost that a husband and wife acquire and possess solid convictions about the authentic values of life and of the family, and that they tend toward the achievement of perfect self-mastery. To dominate instinct by means of one's reason and free will undoubtedly demand asceticism in order that the affective expressions of conjugal life be according to right order. This is particularly necessary for the observance of periodic continence (n.21).

Pope John Paul II repeated much of the above quotation in *Familiaris Consortio* and introduced it this way:

Knowledge [about NFP] must then lead to education in self-control: hence the absolute necessity for the virtue of chastity and for permanent education in it. In the Christian view, chastity by no means signifies rejection of human sexuality or lack of esteem for it; rather it signifies spiritual energy capable of defending love from the perils of selfishness and aggressiveness, and able to advance it towards its full realization (n.33).

Very limited material cooperation

Moral theology frequently deals with moral pathology, and you won't counsel about marital chastity very long before you will meet the case of the unchaste husband who insists upon having contraceptive sex whenever he feels like it and threatens desertion or infidelity if he doesn't have his way.

Priests trained in traditional moral theology rely upon the principle of material cooperation to counsel the poor wife that she may allow her husband to use a condom in order to avert the greater evil of desertion or infidelity.

More will be said about this case when we look at cases, but at this stage I want to make one point: any such material cooperation should be minimal. Essentially, she is offering her vagina for his compulsive-contraceptive-masturbation, and she should not give the impression she enjoys it. In short, she should not be an active participant but rather about as passive as a corpse. His activity, after all, is objectively sinful, and sadness is appropriate.

Not Uncommon Cases

1. The already sterilized couple

Since sexual sterilization—tubal ligations and vasectomies—are so common today and are so frequently done for frivolous reasons, you can be sure that you will soon be counseling couples who have committed this objective sin once you start teaching publicly against unnatural forms of birth control. It is sometimes the easiest of the hard cases for pastoral counseling.

There are two types of sin involved in sexual sterilization. The first is one of mutilation—destroying or attempting to destroy a normal, healthy bodily organ, and that sort of sin is traditionally classified as a sin against the Fifth Commandment, "Thou shalt not kill." The second type of sin is the sin of using unnatural forms of birth control. Once a person has voluntarily had himself or herself sterilized for birth control purposes, each act of sexual intercourse is seriously stained; it objectively contradicts the meaning of the marriage act for it is a permanent way of saying, "I take you for pleasure but not for the imagined worse of pregnancy."

The problem has been complicated by much misleading counseling over the past 25 years. Many people have confessed the sin of sterilization and have not been counseled about the need to change their way of life. If truly repentant, they can be forgiven their sin of mutilation, but how can a person be forgiven now—today—for his or her future sins of contraceptively sterilized intercourse? It's impossible. And that's the dilemma of sexual sterilization which has the following elements.

1) The teaching of the Church. The teaching of the pre-1930 universal Christian tradition was summed up by Pope Pius XI in *Casti Connubii*:

> Any use whatsoever of matrimony exercised in such a way that the act is deliberately frustrated in its natural power to generate life is an offense against the law of God and of nature, and those who indulge in such are branded with guilt of a grave sin (IV, para. 4).

Thirty-eight years later, in response to questions raised by the Pill and the general erosion of personal morality in the Sixties, Pope Paul VI reaffirmed that teaching in *Humanae Vitae*:

> Each and every marriage act must remain open to the transmission of life (n.11).

In the context of the rest of the encyclical in which the Pope explicitly accepts the use of NFP for serious reasons, it is clear that "must remain open" really means "must not be deliberately closed" to the transmission of life. It is also clear that acts of deliberately sterilized intercourse are deliberately closed to the transmission of life.

2) Enjoying the fruits of sin. A second element of the sterilization dilemma is psychological or spiritual. How can a person be sorry for the sin whose fruits he enjoys? Imagine the man who thinks, "I enjoy having sex whenever we feel like it without having to be concerned about possible pregnancy. I'm glad I had the vasectomy (or my wife had a tubal ligation.)" Or the spouse who has a thought during sexual intercourse: "I am enjoying this. I couldn't be doing this if we weren't sterilized. I am enjoying the fruits of our sterilization." How can such spouses be sorry for their sins of sterilization? How can such spouses not be committing, at least objectively, the sin of contraceptive sterilized intercourse? How can a previous confession of the sin of sterilization forgive the current sin of contraceptive intercourse? And what if a spouse enjoys the fruit of their sin to the extent that he or she thinks, "I'm glad we had the sterilization!"? And, realistically, how can a spouse who is enjoying sterilized sex during the fertile time *not* be thinking in such a way except by repressing all thought? Does not such approval constitute committing the sin of sterilization all over again?

3) The possibility of doing otherwise. There are some sins whose effects are continuing despite the repentance of the sinner, but there are other sins whose effects can stop once the sinner has a change of heart. As an example of the first, if I get drunk, drive a car, maim a breadwinner whose family is then impoverished, there is not much I can do to alleviate the continuing effects of my initial sin of drunkenness. I may be in prison and unable to help support the family.

On the other hand, if I have had a vasectomy or my wife has had a tubal, we can stop the continuing effects of our sin by having a change of heart which is reflected by a change of behavior.

God does not require the impossible, but He does require us to do what is possible and necessary for right living. Therefore, if it is possible for me to change my behavior to stop future sins, I must do so.

Resolving the dilemma. There are several elements in the resolution of the sterilization dilemma. Some of these elements are necessary for everybody; others are alternatives to other elements.

1) Lasting repentance. The person who regrets having been sterilized must develop a true sorrow for a) the initial sin of sterilization and b) subsequent sins of sterilized intercourse. He (or she—but to avoid the awkward he/she I will use just "he") must move from mere wishful thinking, "I wish I hadn't done that" to a state of true sorrow and "resolve": "I am truly sorry for doing that; I would not do it again if I had that opportunity. If I had it to do over, I would stay in my normal state of fertility. I resolve to do what is necessary to undo that sin and its continuing effects."

Such repentance is required of everybody, regardless of the type of sin, and it also applies to everyone who has committed the sin of sexual sterilization.

2) The behavioral options. There are essentially three different kinds of behavior which will reflect the attitude that "if I had it to do over again, I would stay in my normal state of fertility." What is common to all three of these options is that in each case the couple decide to live **as if** they were still fertile; in other words, as if they had not been sterilized.

• **Complete abstinence.** Complete abstinence until the wife is past menopause is one option. I doubt this option will have many takers, and I do not think it is necessary, but it needs to be listed for the sake of completeness.

• **Reversal surgery plus NFP.** An ever increasing number of sterilized men and women are having surgery to undo their original surgical sterilization. This is most frequently done by persons who change their minds about having another baby, but it is also being done by persons who do it as part of their repentance.

If reversal surgery were as simple and inexpensive as vasectomies and tubal ligations, then it would be morally required for all as part of their repentance. This is the common teaching of respected moral theologians.[3] However, it is also a principle of moral theology that extraordinary burdens are not normally required as part of repentance. For example, many poor people have been seduced by public health workers into being sterilized—sometimes for no cost and sometimes even being paid to be sterilized. For such couples, the cost of reversal surgery would be a very severe burden if not simply impossible, and the reversal surgery would not be morally required. In another case, reversal surgery might constitute a grave risk to health or life because of heart conditions, reactions to anesthesia, etc. Such cases would also constitute an extraordinary burden and would eliminate the moral obligation to have reversal surgery.

However, most couples of good health and economic status will have to resolve the question of reversal surgery. My personal opinion is that there is a general moral obligation to have reversal surgery, but I would be hesitant to call it a serious obligation (i.e., the grave matter of mortal sin) provided they practice periodic abstinence as noted below. Perhaps the couple who are trying hard to do the right thing but have a general reluctance to undergo surgery might gain insight by asking this question: "If our existing family were wiped out and we wanted children, would we have reversal surgery in the effort to achieve pregnancy?"

Regardless of the reversal decision, I think the couple are obliged to abstain from relations during the normal fertile time if their intention remains to avoid pregnancy.

• **Periodic abstinence.** The current knowledge about a woman's alternating phases of fertility and infertility makes it possible for a repentant sterilized couple to restrict intercourse to those times when she is naturally infertile. In this way, they will not be taking advantage of their sterilized state, enjoying the fruits of their sin. Their behavior will be consistent with their present desire that they would not have had the sterilization in the first place. In my opinion, such periodic abstinence during the normally fertile time is required of repentant sterilized couples.

I acknowledge the disagreement of some traditional moralists on this point, but I do not find their reasoning persuasive. For example, Father Thomas O'Donnell, S.J., addresses this situation and first agrees that "if the cost were reasonable and the success rate high, an unwillingness to seek it [reversal surgery] would seem to at least imply a perduring contraceptive intention. And it is clear that such an intention would render subsequent acts of marital intercourse morally wrong."[4]

However, Fr. O'Donnell then reverses his practical conclusion as follows:

"At this time, however, the cost seems sufficiently high and the expectation of success sufficiently equivocal as not to support the obligation to undertake it."[5]

I have no problem with that, but I am not at all persuaded by the practical conclusion as follows, and I quote in full lest anything appear taken out of context.

Thus, as Father Farraher puts it: "If the couple are truly repentant and willing to do what is reasonably possible in reversing what has been done, they may legitimately have marital relations."

The theological reason behind this generally accepted opinion is quite clear. Sterility by itself does not render marriage illicit nor would sterility itself render the marital act illicit. Thus, even though the sterility in this particular case was sinfully induced, the marriage act would be rendered immoral only by the perduring contraceptive intention of the individuals.

212

When this contraceptive will has been abandoned and replaced by genuine contrition and repentance, the marital act is no longer illicit. It is not vitiated by any contraceptive intent (as this has been retracted by contrition and purpose of amendment) nor by the physical circumstance of sterility (because this, of itself, does not make marital intercourse illicit).[6]

I am not persuaded by this line of reasoning for three reasons.

First of all, it must be understood that the article quoted was written in response to the idea that abstinence during the normally fertile time is required of sterilized couples. Essentially what the authors cited above have said is this: If reversal surgery is feasible, then you must do it, and then, of course, if you do not want more children, you must practice abstinence during the fertile time. Call the surgery "A" and the abstinence "B." That means that you must do A *and* B.

The point is this: if one is obliged to do the greater, A plus B, then one is certainly obliged to do the lesser, just B without A.

Second, the authors agree that post-sterilization marital relations would be rendered immoral by the perduring contraceptive intention of the individuals. Furthermore, they agree that, as quoted above, "if the cost were reasonable and the success rate high, an unwillingness to seek it would to at least imply a perduring contraceptive intention." The identical words and principle can be applied to overcoming the practical effects of sterilization. For the practical effect and the whole purpose of the sterilization in the first place was to achieve a state of not-becoming-pregnant **while having unlimited sex**. That situation can be overcome by the very low cost and highly effective means of learning natural family planning and abstaining from relations during the normally fertile times. It must be remembered that even if a woman has had a tubal ligation, she will continue to ovulate and to produce the normal signs of fertility and infertility.

Third, the authors note that the couple must "do what is reasonably possible in reversing what has been done" before they can "legitimately have marital relations." Clearly, two things have been done by sterilization surgery 1) the mutilation of a bodily organ and 2) the removal of the practice of periodic abstinence required of all normally fertile couples who have a sufficient reason to avoid pregnancy. If a couple cannot undo the mutilation, it is still "reasonably possible"—extremely possible—to reverse the removal of periodic abstinence by the simple process of changing their behavior to accept it.

Having reviewed the reasons given for the other view, I remain convinced that it is necessary for the repentant sterilized couple to refrain from sexual relations during the fertile time even if they cannot reverse the sterilization. First of all, as I have indicated above, I think it is psychologically impossible for a couple to enjoy sterilized sexual relations during the fertile time without reaffirming a contraceptive will, and that the refusal to practice the normal periodic abstinence of normally fertile couples (who have sufficiently serious reasons to avoid pregnancy) is a sign of "a perduring contraceptive intention."

Second, the requirement of abstinence during the normally fertile time simply takes seriously a statement which is at the heart of repentance: "If I had it to do over, I would not become sterilized but instead would practice periodic abstinence." In the third place, the requirement that a sterilized couple must refrain from sexual intercourse during the normally fertile time does not impose a severe or extraordinary penance upon the repentant sterilized couple. Far from it, such periodic abstinence is simply the normal behavior of couples who believe they have a serious reason to avoid pregnancy.

It must be remembered that the whole purpose of sexual sterilization is to enable the sterilized couple to have dishonest intercourse—permanently contraceptive sex—at the normally fertile time. That purpose is pursued each and every time a sterilized couple have relations at the normally fertile time. In my opinion, the requirement that the sterilized couple refrain from relations during the normally fertile time is no different from that of Jesus to the woman caught in adultery: "Go and sin no more."

I think it would be moral rigorism to say that a sterilized couple must either undergo reversal surgery, regardless of circumstances, or permanently abstain from sexual relations. However, I believe that requiring them to act no differently from an unsterilized couple who have a serious reason to avoid pregnancy is a moderate position, the true *via media*.

To be sure, there will sometimes be a temptation for sterilized couples to cheat on the rules, to cut corners in order to reduce abstinence, knowing that they cannot become pregnant. However, this is essentially no different from the temptation experienced by many fertile couples to have recourse to contraceptives or other immoral actions during the fertile time. If either type of couple fail to overcome these temptations, the counsel of Pope Paul VI applies to both: "And if sin should still keep its hold over them, let them not be discouraged, but rather let them have recourse with humble perseverance to the mercy of God, which is poured forth in the sacrament of Penance" (*Humanae Vitae,* n.25).

Lastly, I think confessors and counselors who are reluctant to tell the repentant sterilized couples of the obligation of periodic abstinence need to examine themselves for an unconscious elitism. In a thoroughly contraceptive culture, it is very easy to start thinking that in the real world, ordinary people aren't capable of practicing periodic abstinence; i.e., that only a few dedicated, conservative, orthodox, pious souls are capable of practicing sexual self-control. No orthodox Catholic priest or counselor would put it that way consciously, but we are all subject to the influence of our subconscious elements which soak up the spirit of the times.

2. Very serious reasons to avoid pregnancy

When people tell you they have a very serious reason to avoid pregnancy, you will do them a significant favor by getting them to question the reasons. Sometimes the "serious reason" is purely subjective: they have been so brainwashed by the culture that the idea of having more than "X" children is a huge psychological barrier.

At other times, a woman will tell you that her physician says she shouldn't have any more children. Today such a statement needs to be questioned. In general, though with some wonderful exceptions, doctors are thoroughly immersed in the contraceptive culture, and such comments may reflect anything from his or her own ideas about family size to a genuinely very serious reason to avoid pregnancy. Even in the latter case, life or death cases are either non-existent or almost non-existent; the abortion controversy has made it clear that with adequate assistance, any woman can make it through pregnancy. I have repeatedly been told first hand accounts of women of faith ignoring their physician's fearful or legalistic advice and having both healthy pregnancies and healthy babies.

I say you will be doing people a favor by getting them to question their alleged very serious reasons for several reasons. First of all, they may come to realize that their reasons are not really so serious. Secondly, even if they are faced with a truly serious reason, such questioning may help to put it in perspective. For example, the realization that with proper medical care every woman can make it through pregnancy may bring relief for some.

When faced with the situation of a truly very serious reason to avoid pregnancy, you may need to review the counseling principles (above) with the couple.

Second, you should be aware that NFP can be used more conservatively than the standard rules indicate. The vast majority of unplanned pregnancies with the Sympto-Thermal Method come from relations in the time of *pre-ovulation* infertility (Phase I). Frequently the couple engage in wishful thinking and ignore the Phase I rules; sometimes they use the most liberal rule. Only with great rarity do couples become pregnant following the standard conservative Phase I rules. In cases where it is desirable to reduce the chance of pregnancy below the level of 1 in 100 woman-years of use, couples can either abstain during Phase I (as well as during Phase II—the fertile time) or they can apply the rules more conservatively.

The couple with a most serious reason to avoid pregnancy can also apply the postovulation (Phase III) rules more conservatively. For example, I think that couples who have a most serious reason to avoid pregnancy should always use the full STM rather than a mucus-only system. The standard Phase III STM rules call for three days of elevated temperatures. The most-serious-reason couple can add one or two days and go well beyond the 1 per 100 woman-years chance of pregnancy. The late Rudolph Vollman, M.D., noted that pregnancies simply are not observed when couples wait until the evening of the fourth day of well elevated temperatures. I cannot prove it, because it would take an enormous study, but I think that each day added to a standard STM Phase III rule raises the effectiveness by a factor of at least ten. Thus, the chance of pregnancy on the fourth day of well-elevated temperatures is probably less than 1 per 1,000 woman-years of exposure; on the fifth day, it is probably less than 1 per 10,000 woman-years of exposure.

My personal feeling is that I would not counsel additional abstinence beyond the evening of the fourth or fifth day of well elevated temperatures. I think that at some point a couple have to say, "We have done what is reasonable and very cautious in avoiding the pregnancy we think we should avoid; however, if God wants to work a miracle in giving us a baby, then we will have to trust Him to work the other miracles required in our situation."

The point of all this is not to try to make you into an NFP counselor. Rather the point is that as a pro-chastity counselor you need to realize that even the most serious reasons to avoid pregnancy almost never require permanent abstinence but only a more conservative application of the standard rules.

216

3. Severely irregular cycles

One of the most common excuses given for not using NFP is "irregular cycles." The truth is two-fold. First of all, almost no women consistently have the same cycle length, one cycle after another. Almost every woman has some cycle irregularity. Secondly, the amount of variation varies. We consider a woman to be regular if her cycle variation is seven days or less, moderately irregular if her cycle variation is eight to twenty days, and very irregular if the difference between her shortest and longest cycles is 21 days or more, not counting early postpartum cycles.

Much cycle irregularity is self-induced—the results of improper diet, nutrition and exercise. Some of this yields quite easily to common sense changes including common dietary supplements.[7]

Other cycle irregularity is self-induced from taking birth control pills or injections. **Note: the Pill does not "regularize" irregular cycles.** It is true that the Pill will make "periods" (actually Pill-induced withdrawal bleeding) come at regular intervals, but this is completely Pill-controlled. The Pill does not assist the normal fertility cycle but completely overrides it. When a woman stops taking the Pill, it is not at all uncommon for any previous cycle irregularity to be worse than it was before the Pill.

Significant cycle irregularity indicates there may be underlying irregularities or even pathologies. One young woman was alerted by her severe irregularity to have a thorough endocrine check, and the physician discovered cancer of the thyroid gland. After surgery and thyroid supplementation, she resumed extremely regular cycles.

In other cases, couples simply learn to live with cycle irregularity; frequently they rely upon the Phase I "last dry day rules" so that abstinence is reduced to a minimum.

For pastoral counseling, it is not necessary for you to know the details of "managing" irregular cycles. Suffice it to say that several types of help have been worked out to assist couples in this situation. While sometimes a cross, cycle irregularity is bearable, it is frequently made more regular by improved nutrition, and it certainly provides no justification for resorting to immoral forms of birth control or sexual behavior.

4. The demanding spouse

The term "demanding spouse" must be distinguished from the term "the threatening spouse." In both cases, we are talking about

spouses, almost always husbands, who want their wives to participate in immoral sex, but in the "threatening" case, the husband is
threatening to leave her or to go to a prostitute. Such threats are not
a part of the "demanding" situation.

As an aside, I want to mention that in a few rare cases, the
demands of the husband for morally good sex may be legitimate.
One wife wrote me that since she had become more "spiritual" her
interest in sex was almost nil while her husband's remained the
same. Such a person needs to be reminded that the purpose of sex
is not self-pleasure but 1) for having babies and 2) to renew and
symbolize the self-giving of the original marriage act. Other wives
may take out their disillusionment with their husbands by showing
no interest in sexual relations. These problems, are, of course, not
unique to NFP couples and probably occur much less frequently
among them. However, if a wife wants to use NFP as an excuse not
to have marital relations, she can become very sloppy in her
observations so that no one can say when she is fertile or infertile.

Fortunately, these cases are rare among NFP couples; the
feeling of being used for sex is greatly diminished by periodic
abstinence, and if he has a much greater interest in sex during the
infertile times than she does, she frequently grows in admiration
and respect for his self-control during the fertile times.

In the real case of the demanding spouse, the husband demands
sex all throughout the cycle, and during the fertile time he either
wants to use—or have her use—a contraceptive device or to engage
in other contraceptive behaviors such as mutual masturbation, or
complete oral/anal copulation.

It should be obvious that such demands or requests for sex have
absolutely nothing to do with marital love and affection. The wife
should be counseled not to participate in such actions. Rather
obviously, she cannot physically stop him from self-masturbation,
but it is a lesser evil for him to self-masturbate than for her to
help him simply because one objectively mortal sin is less evil than
two of the same kind.

It is doubtful that you as a counselor will be able to speak with
the offending husband unless he is really convinced that marriage
exists primarily for unlimited sex, that he's being cheated, and he's
ready to argue. Regardless, whether you are counseling a wife or a
couple, your task, after you have counseled against such activity, is
to provide a basis for your counsel.

First, you can state the common teaching of the Church, and you
would do well to give her a copy of the Vatican's 1975 *Declaration*

218

on Certain Questions Concerning Sexual Ethics.[8] You might point out sections eight and nine dealing with homosexual acts and masturbation.

Second, you will have to instruct her or them in the marital meaning of sex. Obviously, I hope you find the basic thesis of this book helpful. I believe that even the most aggressive husband, if he still loves his wife, can come to understand that their sex acts are meant to be a symbolic renewal of the self-giving they pledged at marriage. His aggressive behavior is the result, not of hormones, but of wrong thinking about sex, so he has to start thinking rightly about sex if he is to develop the virtue of marital chastity and place his sexual urges at the service of authentic marital love.

The success of your counseling can be assisted by short and readable brochures and pamphlets. Sometimes, a proud man will not listen to his wife; in fact, he may think she is singularly not-with-it. However, he may be willing to look at a short brochure or pamphlet; at the least he may come to realize that the problem of marital chastity is not unique to him or them. *Creative Continence* by Oscar and Susan Staudt[9] discusses the problems of marital chastity in a way that every married couple can relate to. The Staudts write out of their own personal experience in a light-hearted and practical way, and they are successful in relating to others. My own *Holy Communion: Eucharistic and Marital*[10] might be helpful to those who are open to theological reasoning, but it may be more helpful as a handout to normal couples rather than to spouses in deeply troubled marriages. There may be other brochures and pamphlets available, and if you read a good article on this subject, be sure to clip and copy it.

5. The threatening husband

Theoretically, a wife could threaten her chaste husband with infidelity if he didn't have immoral sex with her; but since every case I've ever heard of has been the husband as the aggressor, I'll use the term "threatening husband."

In most respects, this case is identical to that of the "demanding spouse" above, and to that extent, the counsel will be identical. However, what makes it different is the threat of infidelity—whether permanent by way of desertion and divorce or temporary by way of an affair or a prostitute. It is in this context that the question of material cooperation with his contraceptive sex arises.

Catholic moral theology distinguishes between formal and

material cooperation. In formal cooperation, your heart and mind are with what you are doing at least to the extent that you could **not** be doing it. For example, if a nurse participates in a scheduled abortion, she gives *formal* cooperation. However, the president and officers of the utility companies that provide electricity, gas, telephone service, and water to abortion clinics are involved in *material* cooperation. If they tried to cut off the supply, they would be forced by the courts to provide it, etc.

It is generally agreed by Catholic moral theologians that when a wife is threatened by infidelity if she does not allow her husband to have contraceptive sex with her, she may allow him to use her body in that way without her sinning. The idea is that she is allowing one evil to happen in order to avoid a greater evil.

As indicated in the section on counseling principles, such cooperation should be purely passive; she should insist that if it is contraceptive sex, he is the one who should wear a condom, and she should not be an active participant in the sexual action.

My personal opinion is that counsel allowing material cooperation is highly theoretical, unrealistic, and ineffective in achieving its goals of preventing infidelity. First of all, such a husband will not be interested in passive material cooperation. He is not interested just in sexual release; if he were, he would engage in solitary masturbation. No, there is something demonic in such threats. What he wants is her participation in sin; he wants her full hearted cooperation in loveless contraceptive sex.

Second, the husband has already sinned by infidelity in his mind and heart, so such cooperation cannot prevent that sin on his part. Third, I doubt very much that it will be effective. No man who loves his wife will threaten infidelity, and such material cooperation will erode whatever respect he might have for her. With neither love nor respect for his wife, how long will a husband stay around? And if there are children in the house, how can he be trusted not to abuse them in her absence?

I think it would be much more appropriate for a wife threatened by infidelity to say something like this to her errant husband.

"We married each other for better and for worse, and this is certainly part of the 'worse.' We also married each other before God with the idea of helping each other on the narrow path to heaven. If you leave, neither one of us is free to remarry, or we will be living in adultery. However, I will not participate in unnatural forms of birth control or other unnatural sex acts because they are wrong, and sinning together isn't going to help either one of us get to

220

heaven. I love you, but you are being unfaithful to me even by making such threats. If you carry through with your threats of infidelity, I am open to forgive you when you repent, but I cannot risk catching AIDS or some other disease from you, so we will have to live as brother and sister until all risk of incubation is past and you are tested 'clean.' I love you and promise to participate fully in chaste sexual relations, but I can have no part in mutual sin. I pray for both of us."

6. Marital rape

In marital rape, there may be no demands for contraceptive sex or for sexual perversities, and there may be no threats of infidelity, although, on the other hand, all of these elements may be present to some degree. Marital rape is bully behavior, very frequently associated with drinking. When he goes out for a night with the boys, she knows he will be coming back half-drunk, demanding sex, and will slap her around if he doesn't get it. In a day and age of women's liberation and women's shelters, this scenario may seem unlikely, but the daily newspapers lead me to believe it is still an agonizing reality. The wife may truly love him; he may be reasonable most of the time; she has small children to support and few marketable skills, etc.

The moral issues are two-fold. First of all, such an action is not a true marital act because a true marriage act at least implicitly reflects the caring love pledged at marriage. Even if there is no contraceptive behavior on his part, the act of marital rape is a sin on his part. Pope Paul VI said it this way: "It is in fact justly observed that a conjugal act imposed upon one's partner without regard for his or her conditions and legitimate desires is not a true act of love, and therefore denies a requirement of the right moral order in the relations between husband and wife" (*Humanae Vitae*, n.13).

The second moral issue is whether a wife who anticipates marital rape may use a true contraceptive to protect herself from pregnancy. Fr. Edward Bayer has successfully defended his doctoral thesis that it is not immoral for a woman to use a true contraceptive to protect herself against the consequences of rape—whether on the streets or in the marital bedroom.[11] In the case at hand, a wife's use of a true contraceptive—in this case a cervical cap or a diaphragm—would not add the grave matter of a mortal sin to the already sinful action of marital rape. I think this follows logically from the basic covenant theology that the evil of contraception is that it invalidates the sex act as a renewal of the marriage covenant. Thus, when the act is already immoral and invalid as a renewal of the marriage covenant, there is no obligation to allow it to remain open to the transmission of life as if it were a true marriage act which morally **must not** be closed to life.

Other moral theologies allow for efforts to destroy the sperm after rape under the theory that they represent the unjust aggressor whom it is right to repel. While that may be helpful for unforeseen rape, I think that the covenant theology provides an equally plausible basis for protection against foreseeable rape.

*   *   *

In these cases of marital disharmony, the Christian counselor will want to go way beyond the bare moral principles to assisting the couple to develop a truly Christian marriage. The task is sometimes huge, for by the time the problem reaches you, it may be the fruit of years of compulsive sex, pornography, substance abuse, and anti-Christian notions of marriage.

I have neither the talent nor the space to pretend to provide adequate counseling. However, I have one recommendation which I think will help you and those you counsel. I suggest that your counsel be solidly biblical. Books come and go, counseling theories come and go, but the Word of the Lord remains forever. Its teaching about love, marriage, sexuality and human relations provide the perennial basis for sound Christian counseling and for bringing both parties to Christian discipleship.

Part IV

The Context of the Controversy

11

The Historical Context

Some controversies are easier to understand if you can see them in context, and that's the goal of this and the next three chapters. This chapter outlines the historical context, and the next two chapters provide the theological context in which the birth control debate occurred in the years immediately before and after *Humanae Vitae*. Chapter 14 describes a more recent debate among those who accept the teaching of *Humanae Vitae* as true but who differ about the best way to explain the evil of marital contraception.

The presently definitive work on the history of the doctrine of non-contraception has been written by John T. Noonan, Jr.[1] Though not without its editorial defects, it is a comprehensive study of the treatment of the question over the centuries by Catholic theologians and the magisterium. The history is so extensive that any attempt to provide a resume is bound to be inadequate. Nevertheless, it may be worthwhile to note a few points in passing.

First of all, the practice of contraception is nothing new to mankind. Records dating from **1,900 B.C.** show the contraceptive effort in the Mediterranean world of that time. There is every indication that it was an accepted practice in the Roman empire during the beginnings of the Christian era. I mention this because at the popular level there is a common misconception that only through modern science have we found contraception. The popular argument sees in this almost a divine guidance of science, a new cure for a population problem that didn't exist previously. Noonan makes it quite clear that although modern science has greatly improved the technique, the practice of contraception is ancient.

Second, the question about contraceptive acts has been raised in a number of different ways over the centuries of the Christian era. The Gnostics in the **first century** were teaching an extreme doctrine which permitted intercourse for anyone provided that procreation was avoided. Marriage was either attacked or ignored as the stable means of continuing the human race. Sexual intercourse was seen both as the supreme good (and therefore mandatory for everyone regardless of marital status) or as an abominable evil in a dualistic system of spirit and matter. The Cathars of the **Middle Ages** condemned marriage and especially sexual relations in marriage as evil. They did not, however, practice complete continence but had non-marital liaisons which they regarded as permissible. Procreation was seen as evil.

Third, the response of the magisterium and of all Catholic theologians until the middle of the 1960s to these various doctrines was constant in its emphasis that intercourse is moral only within marriage and that intercourse must remain open to procreation. It is fair to say that in various ways the question of contraception has been with us since the beginning of Christianity and that for nineteen centuries the Church has provided a constant answer forbidding unnatural forms of birth control regardless of how the question was raised. For one who believes that the Church is led by the Holy Spirit, it is quite believable that this constant teaching of the Church is the fruit of the Spirit. Such a belief does not say that our philosophizing and theologizing cannot be improved, but it does conclude that God has made it very clear that marital contraception is a serious moral evil.

Pius XI: *Casti Connubii*

The Catholic teaching of non-contraception has always been spelled out in response to the philosophy and the practice of the age. The statement of Pius XI was no exception. The modern birth control movement started with the neo-Malthusians in the 1860s. Anglican clergyman Thomas Malthus had written in **1798** his gloomy prediction that population increase would outstrip increases in the food supply, but Malthus had counseled self-control to hold population in check. However, the accidental discovery of vulcanized rubber by Charles Goodyear in **1839** facilitated the manufacture of condoms, and this new technology may helped the neo-Malthusians to promote contraception in the **1860s** just as the Pill helped their philosophical heirs a century later. In response to such birth control agitation, in **1873** an American evangelical reformer, Anthony Comstock, convinced the U.S. Congress to legislate against the manufacture, distribution and sale of birth control devices, and most states passed similar legislation which became known collectively as the Comstock laws. In passing, it should be noted that these anti-contraceptive laws were passed by essentially Protestant legislatures for a largely Protestant America, thus reflecting the universality of Christian belief at that time.

About **1914** Margaret Sanger founded her National Birth Control League and soon teamed up with England's Havelock Ellis to agitate for contraceptive birth control on both sides of the Atlantic.

In response to the neo-Malthusians, the bishops of the Church of England in **1908** had reaffirmed the traditional teaching against unnatural forms of birth control, and in **1920** they issued another reaffirmation in response to the renewed Sanger-Ellis agitation. It was far more prophetic than they could have realized. After stating, "We urge the paramount importance in married life of deliberate and thoughtful self-control..." they solemnly declared:

> We utter an emphatic warning against the use of unnatural means for the avoidance of conception, together with the grave dangers—physical, moral and religious—thereby incurred, and against the evil with which the extension of such use threatens the race.[2]

It should be noted that when the Anglican bishops so clearly and strongly condemned unnatural forms of birth control, the alternatives for spacing children were ecological breastfeeding which was not well understood at the time, total abstinence, or periodic abstinence based on unscientific guesswork. In 1920 the physiological bases for natural family planning had not yet been discovered.

Thus in the years immediately before *Casti Connubii,* birth control had been the subject of conferences, some national hierarchies had issued statements, and questions of confessional policy with regard to contraception were frequently asked of Rome. In **1930** matters reached a climax. In the June issue of *Hochland,* a German Catholic periodical, a call was issued for a change in the teaching on contraception. On **14 August** the Lambeth Conference of Anglican bishops, which had condemned contraception in both 1908 and 1920, broke away from its own teaching, and permitted contraception. Thus the Church of England became the first body calling itself a Christian church to accept contraception as morally licit, an unhappy but historic first. On **31 December**, the reply of Pope Pius XI renewed in a formal way the tradition of the Catholic Church in his encyclical *Casti Connubii:*

> Since, therefore, openly departing from the uninterrupted Christian tradition some recently have judged it possible solemnly to declare another doctrine regarding this question, the Catholic Church, to whom God has entrusted the defense of the integrity and purity of morals, standing erect in the midst of the moral ruin which surrounds her, in order that she may

preserve the chastity of the nuptial union from being defiled by this foul stain, raises her voice in token of her divine ambassadorship and through Our mouth proclaims anew: any use whatsoever of matrimony exercised in such a way that the act is deliberately frustrated in its natural power to generate life is an offense against the law of God and of nature, and those who indulge in such are branded with the guilt of a grave sin (Section 4, para. 4).

During the period of the thirties through much of the fifties, the statement of *Casti Connubii* was generally taken by Catholics as a truth proposed by the magisterium in the name of Christ, i.e., true beyond any doubt. Some would regard it technically as a formally infallible teaching. However, as the question was raised with new urgency in the Sixties, it was thought that the Pope had not spoken with such formality that it must be considered a *de fide* proposition. Thus it was possible, many thought, to hope for a change in the doctrine. Although Pius XI spoke about nature and acts against nature, he did not, it should be noted, speak from a purely biological point of view. Rather he confined himself to the interpersonal communion of marriage by speaking of "the conjugal act" and the "use of matrimony." A completely biological approach would have necessitated a universal statement such as "the act of sexual partners" and the "use of sexual intercourse." I believe his statement is open to a more personalistic interpretation than is usually given it, one which will still be non-contraceptive, and that is what I tried to do in Chapters 1 through 4.

Probabilism and the Pill

The medical discovery in **1953** of a hormonal pill that would make pregnancy almost impossible raised a new question for moral theology. The customary way of explaining the evil character of contraception had been an effort to show the unnatural character of the physical interference with the reproductive process at the time of intercourse. However, the Pill acted in a hidden, chemical way. It did nothing in the way of physical obstruction of the process of the sex act itself, for it had accomplished its work already by impeding ovulation. Therefore the door seemed open to arguments allowing the use of the Pill as "natural" while retaining the formal condemnation of physical, mechanical contraception. (It should be noted that in the debate triggered by the Pill, the abortifacient potential of the Pill was strangely ignored; the Pill was treated almost exclusively as an anovulant.)

Only two years before the development of this new form of birth control, Pius XII had reaffirmed the teaching of *Casti Connubii* in his **1951** address to the Italian Catholic Society of Midwives. He noted that Pius XI

> solemnly proclaimed again the fundamental law of the marital act and relations: any attempt by the spouses in the completion of the conjugal act or in the development of its natural consequences, having the aim of depriving the act of the force inherent in it and of impeding the procreation of a new life, is immoral; and no alleged indication or need can convert an intrinsically immoral act into a moral and lawful one.
>
> This precept is as valid today as it was yesterday; and it will be the same tomorrow and always, because it does not imply a precept of the human law, but is the expression of law which is natural and divine (AAS 43:843).

Noonan notes that "the important clause here is . . . 'in the development of its natural consequences.' By these words, Pius XII asserted that not only did Pius XI condemn the impeding of coitus— a prohibition of coitus interruptus, the condom, and the pseudo-vagina—but he condemned such means as the douche and other post-coital efforts to destroy or expel the spermatozoa."[3] The statement was not interpreted as an *ex cathedra* definition but it was treated with great respect.

In 1958 Pius XII spoke again. In June of that year Louis Janssens argued that the theory of correcting the defects of the natural mechanism could be used to justify the use of the anovulant Pill. Pius XII answered on **12 September 1958**.

> But one provokes a direct sterilization and therefore an illicit one, whenever one stops ovulation in order to preserve the uterus and the organism from the consequences of a pregnancy which they are not capable of supporting. Certain moralists assert that it is permitted to take drugs to this end, but this is a mistake. It is equally necessary to reject the opinion of several doctors and moralists who permit their use whenever a medical indication renders an early conception undesirable or in other similar cases which it would not be possible to mention here; in these cases the employment of drugs has as its end the preventing of conception in preventing ovulation; it is therefore a matter of direct sterilization.
>
> To justify it they quote at times the moral principle, correct in itself, but wrongly interpreted: "It is lawful to correct the defects of nature." Since, in practice, it suffices, in order to use this principle, to have reasonable probability, they assert that it is a matter here of correcting a natural defect. If this principle had unqualified validity, eugenics could without hesitation utilize the drug method to stop the transmission of a

defective heredity. But it is still necessary to consider by what means the natural defect is corrected and to take care not to violate in any respect other principles of morality.[4]

The 1958 statement of Pius XII, though not given or received under the formality of infallibility, became the generally accepted authoritative norm regarding the Pill until 1963.

In **1963**, Dr. John Rock of Boston, a Catholic physician who had helped to develop the progesterone pill, published a book in which he argued for the morality of the Pill.[5] Either as a result of the Rock book or as a simultaneous reflection of Dutch opinion, Bishop Bekkers of 's Hertogenbosch made a television broadcast on 21 March 1963 in which he spoke of "true love, expressing itself spontaneously. . . The Christian should draw his own conclusions from this view of marriage regarding the difficult question of birth regulation. Each technique for that purpose is somehow unsatisfactory. . . And while we know that periodic continence is a solution for many people, we are also aware that it presents others with really insuperable obstacles."[6] Drawing attention to the Pill, he said that "Most commentators have forgotten, it appears, to ask themselves seriously whether these progestative hormone products really belong to the same category as the more traditional, well-known contraceptives."[7]

Since it is likely that the commentators *had* asked themselves this question and answered affirmatively, Bishop Bekkers statement had the effect of denying it, thus adding theological weight to the contraceptive use of the Pill. He was followed in this by Mgr. J. M. Reuss and Canon Janssens in 1963, both of whom distinguished between physical, mechanical contraception and the Pill and favored the permissibility of the Pill. The debate was now in full swing. The advocates of contraception could point to one, then another, and then another respectable Catholic figure who favored a change in the doctrine to allow an unnatural form of birth control, at least in the form of the Pill.

With respectable voices on both sides of the question, it seemed to become subject to the **theory of probabilism.** According to probabilism, if a "law" is in doubt, then the person who must make the choice should weigh the arguments advanced by both sides and choose the side that seems the more likely. When the law is uncertain, the presumption is for freedom. For the theory of probabilism to apply, it is necessary first of all that the question be in doubt. Thus it became necessary for the advocates of contraception to try to show this doubt. The fact that a bishop and theologians were speaking out contrary to the previous statements of Pius XII and were not drawing down upon themselves a condemnation from Rome was interpreted as an indication that Rome was in a state of doubt.

This was heightened by the fact that John XXIII had appointed a special commission to investigate the problem and by the fact that Paul VI had reserved the question from the debate of Vatican II. However, the formation of a birth control commission by John XXIII should not be interpreted as indicating that Pope John XXIII was open to contraception. In his 1961 encyclical, *Mater et Magistra,* he had clearly reaffirmed Christian teaching against unnatural methods of birth control as follows:

A course of action is not indeed to be followed whereby, contrary to the moral law laid down by God, procreative function also is violated. Rather, man should, by the use of his skills and science of every kind, acquire an intimate knowledge of the forces of nature and control them ever more extensively (n.89).

Because the life of man is passed on to other men deliberately and knowingly, it therefore follows that this should be done in accord with the most sacred, permanent, inviolate prescriptions of God. Everyone without exception is bound to recognize and observe these laws. Wherefore, in this matter, no one is permitted to use methods and procedures which may indeed be permissible to check the life of plants and animals" (n.193).

Paul VI began to speak on **23 June 1964**. He announced an enlarged Papal Birth Control Commission and accompanied his announcement with this statement:

But meanwhile we say frankly that up to now we do not have sufficient motive to consider out of date and therefore not binding the norms given by Pope Pius XII in this regard. Therefore they must be considered valid, at least until we feel obliged in conscience to change them.[8]

Vatican II did not deal directly with the problem of contraception because Paul VI had reserved the question to himself. However in the *Pastoral Constitution on the Church in the Modern World,* usually referred to by its Latin title, *Gaudium et Spes,* the Fathers of the Council reflected both sides of the question. From a personalist point of view, it held that the parents must make the decision about future offspring taking into consideration a number of personal factors. On the other hand, their decision to postpone or avoid pregnancy must make sure that any procedure is conformed to

230

objective standards and to the authoritative teaching of the Church.

The promulgation of *Gaudium et Spes* (**7 December 1965**) served to provide more matter for debate, and ever more frequently it became customary to speak in terms of probabilism. In this cloudy atmosphere, Pope Paul VI spoke again addressing the delegates of the Italian Society of Obstetrics and Gynecology on **29 October 1966**. After some remarks about the complexity of the birth control problem, he went on to state that the magisterium was not in doubt.

> Meanwhile, as we have already said in the above mentioned discourse [23 June 1964], the norm until now taught by the Church, integrated by the wise instructions of the Council, demands faithful and generous observance. It cannot be considered not binding as if the magisterium of the Church were in a state of doubt at the present time, whereas it is rather in a moment of study and reflection concerning matters which have been put before it as worthy of the most attentive consideration.[9]

Paul's statement, apparently intended to curb the invocation of probabilism by denying a state of doubt, brought him a torrent of bitter criticism. Even his supporters found it difficult to explain what was meant by a "moment of study and reflection" and to show how this was different from a state of doubt. It seems to me that the statement must be taken as a clarification of his statement of 23 June 1964. His phrase at that time, "at least until we feel obliged in conscience to change them [the norms given by Pope Pius XII]" did not have a resounding ring of unshakeable conviction that these norms were imbedded in the very nature of man and woman and were therefore unchangeable. The phraseology of 23 June 1964 gave rise to speculation that the norms might be changeable. Sensing this, the Pope acted in 1966 to clarify what he had meant in 1964, and this time he had the advantage of reviewing the birth control commission reports.

The Papal Birth Control Commission had submitted its reports on 28 June 1966, and thus by 29 October, Paul VI had studied them well. Quite obviously, the argumentation on behalf of contraception had failed to convince Paul VI of its own inherent value; he knew that the teaching could not be changed and was not the least in doubt. What he needed was some time to find the best way to reaffirm the teaching of *Casti Connubii*. With hindsight, we can say that in his talk on 29 October 1966, the Pope should have said: "I have reviewed the work of the Commission. There will be no change in the teaching. In due time I will issue an encyclical which reaffirms *Casti Connubii,* but let there be no doubt: all unnatural forms of birth control are immoral and that includes the recently developed anovulant drugs."

Thus his words on 29 October 1966 must be taken to mean that the magisterium was not in doubt but simply needed more time to study and reflect upon the appropriate arguments to use in reaffirming the traditional teaching to a world that was not anxious to hear it.

Why didn't Pope Paul VI use the speech in October 1966 as an opportunity to make a strong, unequivocal reaffirmation of *Casti Connubii*? My opinion is that Paul VI was still looking for a way to persuade at least the Catholic world of the merits of the Church's teaching against unnatural forms of birth control. I think that his reluctance to crack down on dissidents after *Humanae Vitae* showed a decided preference to continued dialogue and that this may have influenced his thinking in 1966. Second, he was fully aware that anything he would say about birth control would be stretched to the limit in the immediate context and would be quoted for centuries. Therefore, he had to be careful and extremely judicious in speaking. Third, although the two years between the submission of the Reports (28 June 1966) and the formal issuance of *Humanae Vitae* (25 July 1968) seemed agonizingly long to us involved in the controversy at the time, two years is not long at all in the life of the Church; it is not even very long in secular terms for the production of a major teaching document considering the various drafts, reviews by confidential advisors, and translations before the actual issuance.

The Papal Birth Control Commission report

The Pope did not make an unequivocal reaffirmation of *Casti Connubii* in October of 1966, so the theory of probabilism was enhanced with the publication of the reports of the Papal Birth Control Commission in April, 1967. Although the members of the Commission were pledged to secrecy, one of them leaked the reports to the press. To be sure, it wasn't the authority of the magisterium, but to many who thought in purely political terms a "majority" was an authority of a tangible sort. If the Commission members appointed by the Pope didn't go along with the tradition, how could the couple in a Paris apartment or a Los Angeles subdivision be expected to abide by it? To more and more it seemed that there was a real state of doubt in the teaching of the Church.

Interestingly enough, the publication of the Birth Control reports put the argumentation much more on the level of authority than on the level of rational argument about contraception itself. The so-called minority report was criticized for avoiding the issue of birth control itself and for stressing primarily the tradition of the Church's teaching and the authority of this tradition. However, since the publication of the reports, there has been very little praise for the *argumentation* of the majority position. Instead, the emphasis has been on the fact that a *majority* of the Commission recommended change. Ironically, such an emphasis is an argument from authority, pure and simple. My personal reaction to the majority position was surprise that the Pope himself had not made it public immediately. I found the argumentation unconvincing, as I explain in Chapter 13, and I am still convinced that Paul VI would have done well to share with the world immediately his reasons for being unpersuaded.

To the advocates of contraception, it now seemed that the battle was over. They had won. The practice of great numbers of Catholics had in fact changed; they thought it was just a matter of time until the Pope gave the official seal of approval to the *de facto* change that had already taken place. There appeared to be such confidence that they had succeeded in changing the teaching of the Church that very few bothered to meet in advance the possibility that Pope Paul would actually reaffirm the doctrine of non-contraception in an authoritative way. Gregory Baum, O.S.A., was an exception. He had written long before this time that "since the conscience of the Church is so deeply divided on this issue and since the solution is in no way contained in divine revelation, the authoritative norms which the Pope himself, as universal teacher, will propose in due time, shall not be a definitive interpretation of divine law, binding under all circumstances, but rather offer an indispensable and precious guide for the Christian conscience."[10]

The encyclical *Humanae Vitae*

It became apparent that Pope Paul's statements of June, 1964 and October, 1966 did not have the intended effect of retaining the norms of non-contraception. On the contrary, since he had not said anything in the authoritative manner of Pius XI and Pius XII, it became a common interpretation that the Pope was doubtful; if he was in doubt, what about the rest of the world? Probabilism was gaining such a firm foothold that allowing unnatural forms of birth control could almost be argued as the *more* probable or even more certain side of the question. Into this atmosphere, Pope Paul VI introduced *Humanae Vitae.* Its teaching that "each and every marriage act must remain open to the transmission of life" (n. 11) clarified the aura of uncertainty regarding the official teaching of the magisterium and triggered a reaction greater than anything the Church had seen in at least 400 years. The application of probabilism was eliminated, for no longer could it be argued that the magisterium was in a state of doubt.

However, as with the publication of the Birth Control Commission reports in 1967, the question of authority was raised. The arguments brought forward by the majority position were so poor they are almost never mentioned. However, emphasis was laid on the authority of the Commission majority, although from the point of view of ecclesiology, it had absolutely no teaching authority. The natural law arguments used in *Humanae Vitae* were considered inconclusive by many. On the other hand, the arguments of the dissenters were disastrous, unable to say a firm "No" to any imaginable behavior between consenting persons. Ultimately the birth control "debate" reverted to the question of divine teaching authority: who spoke in the name of Christ and therefore spoke the truth—the Pope or the dissident theologians?

This chapter has attempted only to present briefly the historical context in which *Humanae Vitae* was promulgated. Several things should stand out. The teaching of the magisterium against unnatural forms of birth control has been constant for twenty centuries. The customary natural law arguments of those defending the magisterium have failed to convince many. The personalist arguments of those advocating contraception fail to convince many others and have been, in fact, disastrous—as indicated above. The debate since *Humanae Vitae* has shifted from argumentation about the meaning of the married sexual union to a debate about authority and conscience. What is clearly needed is a theology of sex which remains true to the Christian faith as revealed in Sacred Scripture and kept alive by the Teaching Church for twenty centuries **and** which upholds the values of Christian personalism. Such an effort was made in Part I of this book.

12

The People of God

Introduction

It was common in the 1960s to read that some priest or bishop had said that married people were better experts on marriage than the Pope. Despite the horrendous rate of divorce that has occurred among Catholics since their almost universal rejection of *Humanae Vitae,* that attitude appeared to be still widespread at the opening of the 1990s. If it were not, then would not the vast majority of priests and bishops have been actively and visibly promoting the teaching of that encyclical? And would not married Catholics have been living out those truths and staying married?

What I want to show in this chapter is that saying or thinking that married people are better experts on marriage than the Pope is no more meaningful than these statements: "Employers are the experts on the moral aspects of the employment relationship." "The police are the experts on human rights." Such statements are questionable because they assume that the people named have developed the virtues necessary for the Christian fulfillment of their respective duties. Each of those statements is widely denied because it has become apparent that too often the people who hold the various positions have a warped and one-sided view of reality; too often they look at the matter through eye-glasses of self-interest.

Saying that married people are better experts on marriage than the Pope is equally as questionable as those other statements. It assumes that these married people have developed the necessary virtues and attitudes—chastity, spiritual prudence, trust, the spirit of poverty, and the obedience of faith. It makes this assumption in the face of widespread evidence that the virtue of chastity is generally undeveloped and that materialism affects Christian peoples no less than non-Christian, that the specifically "Christianized" world is called the source of economic exploitation of the undeveloped nations, and that it is also labeled "post-Christian" by its own theologians. There is ample evidence suggesting that the spirit of the age is not that of the Holy Spirit and that we Christians, in our sexual lives as well as in all other areas of life, stand in need of a strong prophetic voice calling us back to a renewed living of the Covenant in which we can be saved.

Every well instructed Catholic knows that the sacrament of Matrimony is not a magical rite; it does not automatically bring with it the virtue of chastity. Everyone would agree in theory that if we were not chaste before marriage, it is very likely that we will experience difficulty with authentic norms of Christian chastity within marriage.

There seems to be a problem, however, in going from theory to practice. Despite a general recognition that premarital unchastity seems to be horribly common—even with obvious living together arrangements, when those same couples marry and practice contraception, it is somehow assumed that their marital contraception is in full accord with the norms of chastity within Christian marriage.

The reason is not hard to see. When the newlyweds practice contraception, they join the vast majority of others, both Catholics and atheistic humanists, who are doing anything about conception control. It is difficult for Catholic priests and Protestant ministers to think that the vast majority of their fertile married couples are living immorally. In fact, there has been a certain popular appeal to the idea that if a large portion of the laity and the clergy see nothing wrong with using unnatural forms of birth control, then that's a sign that God doesn't see anything wrong with it either. After all, are not the laity and the clergy the "People of God"? This is not the sort of an argument that Catholic academic theologians signed their names to in the 1980s because it simply doesn't hold up under critical examination. Nevertheless, the idea has been pervasive; it amounts to a popular argument, and it needs to be examined.

Such an examination has to be grounded in Scripture and in the history of the Church. If we try to look at the birth control question from the perspective of the God of revelation Who has become actively involved in human history, the question becomes this: which does the biblical doctrine of the faithful remnant and God's faithful people better describe—those who have remained faithful to the teaching of *Humanae Vitae* or those who have ignored or repudiated it? And if, in the West, only a minority of Catholics believe and practice in accord with the teaching of the Church, is this once again the "faithful remnant" of biblical doctrine?

The People of God: Old Covenant

1. The Beginnings. Although the beginnings of Jewish belief go back to Abraham who is still regarded as the father of both Jews and Christians, it is with Moses that we see the real formation of a recognizable nation, a People of God. Moses was the organizer, the law-giver, the greatest of the prophets, and Moses had problems. A cursory look at the Mosaic beginnings will be sufficient to illustrate that even from the outset the doctrine of the "People of God" has been a two-edged sword.

The sacred author of the Book of Exodus tells that the first announcement to the world that Yahweh had a special people was greeted with derision by the world powers (the Pharaoh). It immediately brought hardship upon the people as they were forced to try to make the same number of bricks while now supplying their own straw. Their fellow Hebrew foremen found themselves in a difficult position and complained bitterly to Moses and Aaron. "The Lord look upon you and judge," they said to them. "You have made us offensive in the sight of Pharaoh and his servants, and have put a sword into their hand to kill us."

Moses in turn passed on the complaint. "Lord," he said to Him, "Why have you done evil to this people? Why did you ever send me?" (Ex 5:19-23).

The sacred author then shows us that the people "turned Moses off" because of their hardships. "Moses spoke thus to the people of Israel but they did not listen to Moses, because of their broken spirit and their cruel bondage" (Ex 6:9).

The sacred author continues to show us the problems of the People of God. The ancient equivalent of "Better Red than dead" is expressed by a worried people, "Better for us to serve the Egyptians than to die in the wilderness" (Ex 14:12). After the deliverance through the Red Sea," the people danced, but shortly the complaint began again. First it centered on water. So Yahweh gave them water (Ex 15:25). Then they complained about the lack of food so Yahweh fed them with quail and manna (Ex 16). Then the people lost heart and built for themselves a more visible religious symbol, the golden calf, thereby breaking their covenant promise. Later on, the author of Numbers recounts the reconnaissance of the land of Canaan. It was a land of milk and honey but also filled with big people and fortified cities. "And the people wept that night. And all the people of Israel murmured against Moses and Aaron; the whole congregation said to them 'Would that we had died in the land of Egypt! Or would that we had died in this wilderness! Why does the Lord bring us into this land, to fall by the sword? Our wives and our little ones will become a prey; would it not be better for us to go back to Egypt?' And they said to one another, 'Let us choose a captain, and go back to Egypt'" (Nb 14:1-4).[1]

From the very beginning the People of God proved to be a very "human" people. When we read the account of the exodus we actually wonder about their lack of "religion." The reader of the Book of the Covenant and other sections finds lists of sins prohibited that may well leave him astonished that a "People of God" would even think of such things. Certainly the average parent today in instructing his children wouldn't think of telling them to avoid sexual relations with animals, but it's all there for the people of the Old Covenant.

Also, from the very beginning, there was a problem of faith in God and the corresponding problem of faithfulness to Him. The practical problems looked so great, so insurmountable, so very real, and so tangible, connected as they were with their very survival. Why this life of faith? Why this necessity of trusting Yahweh when they could have food and drink back in Egypt? Security in Egypt? Yes, at the price of their freedom and at great cost and risk to their faith!

These, then, are the beginnings of the People of God as seen through the eyes of the sacred authors. The people, though God's people, are still very much people in this world and of this world. Their interest is in the "now"—today's food and drink, today's security, and tomorrow was not considered in the light of an after-life but simply in terms of physical needs and expectations. Faith was planted but very much in need of constant nourishment in the way of signs and wonders showing the providential and saving character of their God.

2. Through the eyes of the prophets. One has to be careful when speaking about the people as seen through the eyes of the prophets, for there were prophets and prophets. We have to distinguish between the popular prophets and the classical prophet whose works have reached us in the Scriptures. In the middle of the eighth century before Christ, the word prophet had the connotation of someone attached officially to the temple; his message was invariably one pleasing to the people. So heavy was this connotation that when Amaziah, the priest of Bethel told Amos to leave, Amos replied, "I was no prophet, neither did I belong to any of the brotherhoods of prophets" (Am 7:14). The message of Amos was blunt, clear and unpleasant: This people is a sinful people. Change! Come back to the Lord or your enemies will overtake you. When Jeremiah over a century later began prophesying to submit to Nebuchadnezzar, he was opposed by Hananiah who prophesied peace and immediate restoration. Jeremiah replied, "The prophets who preceded you and me from ancient times prophesied war, famine, and pestilence against many countries and great kingdoms. As for the prophet who prophesies peace, when the word of that prophet comes to pass, then it will be known that the Lord has truly sent the prophet" (Jr 28:8-9). The verdict of Scripture is that the prophets of peace, the propagators of the status quo, the Amaziahs and Hananiahs were false prophets, and so we are led to look at the People of God through the eyes of less sanguine men, the men who had the unpopular calling to be the true prophets of Yahweh.

Three elements in the prophetic message are particularly relevant to our time and to the discussion of the total picture in which the contraception controversy is situated.

1) The first of these is the fact that the People of God is a covenanted and *therefore* sinful people. The prophetic message lays heavy emphasis on the fact that this people is a covenanted people. It is their violation of the covenant which makes them so sinful to Yahweh. Objectively speaking their actions weren't much different from those of their neighbor, and that is precisely the trouble. Yahweh had called them to a higher way of life, a life of faith in him, fidelity to him, and humaneness to their fellow man.

Hear this word that the Lord has spoken against you, O people of Israel, against the whole family which I brought up out of the land of Egypt: "You only have I known of all the families of the earth; therefore I will punish you for all your iniquities" (Am 3:1-2).

The same message is found running through all the prophetic works. A particularly beautiful passage shows the fatherhood of God contrasted with the consequences of rejecting his care.

When Israel was a child, I loved him,
And out of Egypt I called my son.
The more I called them,
the more they went from me; . . .
They shall return to the land of Egypt
And Assyria shall be their king,

because they have refused to return to me (Ho 11:1, 2, 5).

The sin of Israel was that it had abandoned Yahweh, it had deserted the covenant. Hosea relates this desertion to the marriage covenant and could scarcely speak in stronger terms: "The land commits great harlotry by forsaking the Lord" (Ho 1:2).

2) The second element in the prophetic message worth noting is the people's rejection of authentic reform. This rejection of the covenant was not accomplished in so many words. That is, the people didn't sign a petition or take a vote formally rejecting Yahweh as their God. It was their actions that spoke; indeed their words could and did remain very "religious."

The covenant bound them together as one people, a brotherhood. They were to love their neighbor; at the least, they were not to harm him. But what do we find in the prophets? We find as sorry a catalogue of injustices to one's fellow man as we would want to find anywhere. Slavery, oppression of the poor, prostitution, refusal to give a hearing to a man who had a grievance, getting rich through the exploitation of the weak, bribery, legal injustices, and the women caring only for their drink, encouraging their husbands to exploit others in their business dealings.

All of this was condemned repeatedly by the prophets, and they in turn were called troublemakers and accordingly rejected. The prophets, however, were not just negative; they pleaded passionately for reform, for a return to Yahweh, for a renewal of trust in Him and a sense of brotherhood toward their fellow man. In spite of their efforts, authentic reform was consistently rejected.

3) A third important element has to do with liturgical reform. One of the earliest and best known of such reforms was that of King Josiah (640-609 B.C.). It was aimed at destroying the idolatry that plagued Israel, and 2 Kings 23 relates how Josiah set about eliminating the idolatrous shrines and sanctuaries throughout the country. For his work in this regard, he received one of the three favorable mentions by the historians of the kings in Scripture. Aside from the resentment that he earned from the priests who were now unemployed as a result of his liturgical reform, Josiah did not seem to stir up much popular feelings one way or the other. It was an external reform; it didn't require an inner change; it was imposed by force by the king.

The prophets, too, were interested in liturgical reform. It was their constant and unpleasant task to chastise the people for their false, idolatrous worship and to call them back to the worship of Yahweh. However, when it came to the worship of God, they were interested in authentic worship.

The people on the other hand found it easier to concentrate on fulfilling the letter of the law in carrying out their liturgical duties. They could assign to these practices a real "religious" value in their own right regardless of personal dispositions. It took a man like the prophet Amos to provide them with the stinging, classical reminder that liturgy which was just external was unprofitable for the soul.

> I hate, I despise your feasts,
> and I take no delight in your solemn assemblies.
> Even though you offer me your burnt offerings and your
> cereal offerings,
> I will not accept them, and the peace offerings of your
> fatted beasts, I will not look upon.
> Take away from me the noise of your songs;
> to the melody of your harps I will not listen.
> But let justice roll down like waters,
> and righteousness like an ever-flowing stream (Am 5:21ff).

God is still revealing his will to us through Amos, the other prophets, and our own times. Since 1963 there has been great concern about liturgical format in the Catholic Church—at least in the West. We can read with amusement about "the noise of your songs" and the "melody of your harps" and easily find our modern substitutes. Whether we use pipe organs, or electronic organs, or pianos, or guitars, or everything or nothing, what difference does it make? It is all in vain unless we worship God with justice and integrity.

I have heard the answer: "We are arriving at a sense of community. The fact that this is our own thing, the fact that we can do our thing in the liturgy is what counts; it helps us individually and as a community." So be it. I won't question for a moment the psychological effect upon a certain number, and I will omit consideration of those who are alienated by irregular liturgies. My only question is, "To what avail?" There are all sorts of communities; certainly the worshipers of Baal formed a community and certainly the practice of cult prostitution could have been argued as fostering togetherness. The relevant point is this: Is today's liturgical concern with community-building equally concerned with building a community that is Christian? I suspect that almost everyone who is trying to change the liturgical format to foster community would answer with an emphatic "Yes." Therefore it is necessary as always to explain what one means by "Christian." In this particular regard, I think that Karl Rahner remains unsurpassed in pointing out that it is of prime importance for the Christian in his life—liturgical and otherwise—to enter into the sacrificial disposition of Christ at the Last Supper.[2]

In line with the thought of Amos, it seems to me that if a particular liturgical format assists the believer to enter more fully into communion with the mind and heart and obediential will of Christ at the Last Supper, then that format is basically valid. If it does not contribute to that authentic communion or even impedes it, such a liturgical format is in need of reform, no matter how enjoyable it may be. The question about today's liturgical formats is: Do they assist the worshiper in entering into a real spirit of sacrifice, of giving of himself for the benefit of the other? Do they have this same carry-over value in everyday life, even in such areas as birth control? Let us be very clear. We know today that both the IUD and the birth control Pill, both the combination estrogen-progestin Pill and the progestin-only mini-pill (plus implants such as Norplant), have the potential to prevent the implantation of a newly conceived baby in its mother's uterus. Does it assist the building up of the Church to allow a woman on the Pill or IUD—or her husband—to be distributing Holy Communion? What sort of liturgical reform is it that permits a woman to be saying "the Body of Christ" at the same time she is destroying a new child's life within her?

I have mentioned three key elements in the prophetic message which I think are relevant and valid for today: 1) the importance of being mindful of the Covenant and of being faithful to it, 2) the need and the difficulty of achieving authentic reform in one's life, and 3) the realization that a change in liturgical format cannot be equated with this authentic reform. These three elements have their parallel in the controversy over contraception and that is why they have been included here.

3. Doctrine of the remnant. To speak of the doctrine of the remnant in such a way as to imply that it may be applicable once again in our time is to run the risk of being labeled a pessimist. Yet in drawing a picture of the People of God, it seems necessary to include this even though it takes on different colors in historical perspective.

To the prophets the remnant was a sign of hope, a ray of sunshine in an otherwise bleak and hopeless horizon. From a people who departed from Yahweh and were punished by captivity, the Lord would gather up a remnant who would receive the fruit of the promise. Yahweh was still watching over them. He would not allow his people to fall into extinction.

What makes the doctrine of the remnant seem dark and pessimistic from our present point of view is the fact that today we have huge numbers in the visible Church. Certainly there is a restlessness not present in recent former years, and certainly Sunday Mass attendance has been dropped seriously between 1960 and 1990; but to those outside, the Catholic Church seems big and healthy. When it comes to birth control, it is clear that only a remnant within the Church still believe and practice what the Church teaches. Data from 1982 indicated that only six percent of Catholics who used any form of birth control used a form of natural family planning,[3] and the 1988 version of that data showed that only three percent of Catholic "family planners" were using natural family planning.[4] This reported 50% drop in only six years is reflected in the experience of the natural family planning movement in the United States; in the Couple to Couple League we experienced a 47% decrease from 1982 through 1988, and my contacts in the field lead me to think it is a common problem. I have no reason to think the figures are unrealistic.

From a human perspective, it is ridiculous to hope that such a small remnant can be the leaven of authentic renewal within the Church; but from a biblical perspective, the doctrine of the remnant remains a doctrine of faith-based realistic hope.

The People of God: New Covenant

The Covenant foretold by Jeremiah has come into being. Christ has fulfilled the Covenant of old and instituted a New Covenant which is meant to be written in the hearts of men and gladly accepted by each and all. No longer can it ever suffice to say that you are one of God's people, that you "know the Lord" if you perform the rituals. Now there must be an inner response to grace so that the externalization becomes an authentic representation of the whole person's acceptance of the Covenant with Christ.

In commenting on the doctrine of the People of God in the New Covenant, I am restricting myself to those aspects which I think are relevant to the contraception controversy and perhaps can offer some balance to what has been written elsewhere in plenitude.

1. The gospel for the poor. In the early to mid-Sixties, there was frequent reference in religious literature to the *anawim,* the Hebrew expression for God's poor, the little ones, the lowly. Today it is less prevalent. I suggest that the *anawim* is a significant biblical theme which supports traditional Christian teaching against unnatural forms of birth control—and also against the selfish use of NFP—especially in an age of materialism. Perhaps that helps to account for the infrequency of reference to this theme today.

Mary was the prime example of the *anawim.* Her *Magnificat* is a beautiful expression of what it meant to her to be one of God's poor.

My soul shows forth the greatness the Lord, and my spirit rejoices in God my Savior, for He has regarded the low estate of His handmaid . . . He has shown strength with his arm, He has scattered the proud in the imagination of their hearts, He has put down the mighty from their thrones, and exalted those of low degree; He has filled the hungry with good things, and the rich He has sent empty away (Lk 1:46ff).

Because Mary was lowly, because she was not proud of heart, God did great things to her. When Luke tells us that she knew that all generations would call her blessed, we are likewise told that this was not Mary's work but God's. Mary looked to God completely for her salvation; she acknowledged completely her dependence upon Him; she provides the model for the Christian who wants God to do great things in all believers.

Luke elaborates on the theme of the *anawim* in his account of the beatitudes which he balances with the prophetic woes.

Blessed are you poor, for yours is the kingdom of God.
Blessed are you that hunger now, for you shall be satisfied.
Blessed are you that weep now, for you shall laugh.
Blessed are you when men hate you, and when they exclude you and revile you, and cast out your name as evil, on account of the Son of man. Rejoice in that day, and leap for joy, for behold, your reward is great in heaven; for so their fathers did to the prophets.
But woe to you that are rich, for you have received your consolation.
Woe to you that are full now, for you shall hunger.
Woe to you that laugh now, for you shall mourn and weep.
Woe to you, when all men speak well of you, for so their fathers did to the false prophets (Lk 6:20-26).

This message forms a major theme in the gospel of Luke. He

244

relates the dangers of storing up wealth (12:13ff), the importance of realizing that "where your treasure is, there will your heart be also" (12:34). The renunciation of possessions for discipleship (14:28-33), the impossibility of being the slave of both God and money (16:13), the parable of the rich man and Lazarus who was poor (16:19ff), and the saying that "it is easier for a camel to go through the eye of a needle than for a rich man to enter the kingdom of God" (18:25) all permeate the gospel according to Luke. It is common for the gospel of Luke to be called "biased in favor of the poor."

So what's so great about being poor? Isn't this emphasis on the theme of the danger of wealth awfully archaic and retrogressive? Don't we all know that what is really important is that we have the *spirit* of poverty while doing all in our power to put as large a gap as possible between actual poorness and ourselves?

It seems to me that the gospel of Luke is telling us that the man of means is in danger of putting his faith in his money, or at least in his own ability to make money, to provide for himself. In doing so, he becomes independent of God. He no longer has the spirit of poverty which would prompt him to put his trust in God, but he has become spiritually poor by putting his trust in himself.

The gospel theme of the danger of riches is most difficult to talk about today in any public gathering. The chances are that in any advertised meeting of Catholic laity you will have a large proportion of Catholics who have spent large sums of money for an education that has one main purpose: to enable him or her to earn good money. His whole education has been geared to making him as independent as possible. It is one more aspect of man's growing control of his environment, and every step towards control of his environment carries with it the risk of feeling independent of God. It is a risk that cannot be avoided, but one which must be recognized in order to be coped with.

Is the doctrine of the *anawim,* God's poor, relevant to the contraception controversy? It seems to me that the biblical theme of God's poor does indeed have a bearing on at least two of the popular arguments advanced on behalf of contraception. First of all, it would appear that there might be a contradiction between putting one's trust in God and doing all that one can to understand and control nature. Of course, such is not the case, for both are part of the biblical message. However, what can happen is that the effort to "subdue the earth" can become so much of a preoccupation that trust in God is gradually left behind so that eventually it is informally considered something only for the poor who cannot help themselves.

The sociological argument is, at least in the northern part of the Western world where the contraception debate rings the loudest, largely a financial argument. "We can't afford to have another child." There is no denying the pressing financial condition of many people even in the Western world, but there is also no denying the financial prosperity of perhaps even more people in this same section of our globe. What bothers me is that the biblical doctrine of the People of God tells us that God's people are the poor, the *anawim*. On the other hand we have the new doctrine that a practice (non-contraception) which may not advance the material prosperity of this particular family and may even lessen it can hardly be the will of God.

It seems to me that we are in danger of trying to have our cake and eat it too. If we want to bask in the realization that we are all God's people according to sound biblical doctrine, then we have to subject ourselves to a constant re-examination of conscience on how well we are accepting the fullness of the doctrine of God's people— including the fact that they are the *anawim*. Certainly it makes no sense at all, biblically speaking, to assert that since the doctrine of non-contraception may bring economic hardship, it cannot be the adequate expression of the will of God for our times. The realization that the People of God are characterized by being God's little ones, His poor ones, His trusting ones would seem rather to indicate that a practice (contraception) whose purpose was to avoid the risk of the *anawim* would be contrary to the will of God for our time and for any time—especially when the alternative courses of action call for much reliance on help from God and trust in His loving care.

The above argument is valid even though the possibility is very slim that the practice of natural family planning (especially the cross-checking sympto-thermal method) will result in an unexpectedly large family. For many, it requires a huge amount of trust in God to trust natural family planning. For others, the challenge is to trust God by choosing to be generous in the service of life.

2. Some New Testament passages. The prophetic tradition of reminding the people of their greatness because of God's election and then recalling their corresponding obligations is replete in the New Testament. The classic statement of being God's people is found in 1 Peter 2:9ff.

But you are a chosen race, a royal priesthood, a holy nation, God's own people, that you may declare the wonderful deeds of Him who called you out of darkness into His marvelous light. Once you were no people but now you are God's people; once you had not received mercy but now you have received mercy.

Every phrase recalls the People of Israel, and now these Gentile Christians are told that they are the New Israel, the People of God. Along with this privilege of election, they have the corresponding privilege and duty of proclaiming the work of God: they are given a missionary mandate as a people, not just as isolated individuals.

Paul's first letter to the Corinthians is a clear witness to the pilgrim nature of this new People of God: "You are still of the flesh. For while there is jealousy and strife among you, are you not of the flesh, and behaving like ordinary men?" (1 Cor 3:3). He writes to bring the people to their senses (1 Cor 4:14) and shames them for condoning the incest of one of the brethren (5:1ff). He reminds them that being the People of God as a community is by no means any guarantee of their individual holiness, for such was the case with Israel.

I want you to know, brethren, that our fathers were all under the cloud, and all passed through the sea, and all were baptized into Moses in the cloud and in the sea, and all ate the same supernatural food and all drank the same supernatural drink. For they drank from the supernatural Rock which followed them, and the Rock was Christ. Nevertheless with most of them God was not pleased; for they were overthrown in the wilderness . . .

Now these things happened to them as a warning, but they were written down for our instruction, upon whom the end of the ages has come. Therefore let any one who thinks that he stands take heed lest he fall. No temptation has overtaken you that is not common to man. God is faithful, and He will not let you be tempted beyond your strength, but with the temptation will also provide the way of escape, that you may be able to endure it (1 Cor 10:1ff).

The followers of the Way were privileged, but this privilege was no guarantee that they would find the way of the Spirit to their liking or would follow it. They were subject just as their spiritual forefathers to a double judgment: the judgment of man for violating right order among men and the judgment of God both for breaking the order of his creation and for violating the Covenant.

My purpose is not a treatise about the Church as the People of God. Rather my mention can be brief because I want to illustrate just one thing in reference to the controversy on contraception. The evidence of both the Old Testament and the New points to the reality that the popular instincts of the people have no guarantee of being the work of the Spirit. On the contrary, the biblical evidence is that the mass of the people regardless of their educational level are in constant need of the prophetic voice.

3. Consensus fidelium: the Arian question. We have seen that the fact that great numbers of the People of God may see no wrong in contraception is no guarantee that this is the work of the Spirit. Paul tells us that most of the people under Moses were not pleasing to God, and he uses this as a very pointed argument to humble the people at Corinth. Yet the phrase, *consensus fidelium,* the sense of the faithful, remains with us as a popular argument— actually more of a slogan than a true argument—advanced by the contraceptionists who persist in seeing in large numbers the evidence of the Holy Spirit.

In the birth control controversy, the terms "consensus fidelium" and "sensus fidelium" have been referred to their use by Cardinal Newman in the middle of the nineteenth century. Therefore it seems important to understand what Newman meant in using these terms.

In July of 1859, John Henry Cardinal Newman published an essay titled "On Consulting the Faithful in Matters of Doctrine" in the *Rambler,* an English Catholic periodical. Its publication at a time when participation by the laity in the whole work of the Church was discouraged caused Newman to fall from favor as a middle-man between left and right in the Church of his day in England.

Newman had written in the *Rambler* for May of that year that "in the preparation of a dogmatic definition, the faithful are consulted, as lately in the instance of the Immaculate Conception."[5] The statement drew theological objections and he answered them with the article "On Consulting the Faithful . . ."

In this essay Newman explains how the witness of the faithful makes up for the absence of clear, authoritative teaching on the part of the magisterium and/or the theologians. He notes the thinking of a number of ancient Christian writers giving great weight to the consent of the faithful in matters of doctrinal controversy. Such consent and pious belief is really a reflection of what they have been taught by the "teaching Church."

The greater part of the essay is devoted to showing how the faithful were the primary voice of Tradition during the sixty years following the Council of Nicea in 325. Newman notes case after case to illustrate his conviction that the great mass of the bishops were unfaithful to their commission, that general (non-ecumenical) councils erred, and that the Pope weakened and "communicated with the Arians and confirmed the sentence passed against Athanasius" (Coulson, 82). He notes that all of this went on at a time which was marked by the presence of a good number of men who would later be canonized as saints—"Athanasius, Hilary, the two Gregories, Basil, Chrysostom, Ambrose, Jerome, Augustine, and all of these saints bishops also, except one . . ." (75).

Yet it was the faithful who remained the bulwark of orthodoxy, and he cites a number of cases to illustrate this. The faithful were subjected to all sorts of persecutions and by and large refused to enter the Arian communion although undoubtedly a number of them did. Their faith was that of the Council of Nicea, and they would have no part with the theological tamperings and weakenings of the next sixty years.

Newman notes that an age similar to that of the Arian controversy may never come again. Speaking of his own times, just before the American Civil War, he could write in glowing terms, "As to the present, certainly, if there ever was an age which might dispense with the testimony of the faithful, and leave the maintenance of the truth to the pastors of the Church, it is the age in which we live. Never was the Episcopate of Christendom so devoted to the Holy See, so religious, so earnest in the discharge of its special duties, so little disposed to innovate, so superior to the temptation of theological sophistry—and perhaps this is the reason why the *consensus fidelium* has, in the minds of many, fallen into the background" (103).

He concludes his essay by noting that "if ever there be an instance when they ought to be consulted, it is in the case of doctrines which bear directly upon devotional sentiments" (104).

It seems to me that there are several points in Newman's explanation of the *consensus fidelium* which are relevant to the application of it to the contraception controversy.

1) He uses as his examples only those cases which are a matter of dogmatic faith. He emphasizes that the sense of the faithful will be especially relevant in those matters of doctrine which have devotional connotations. He mentions in particular those dogmas concerned with the persons of Christ and His mother Mary.

2) His "faithful" are those who reflect the tradition and who reject tampering with the tradition especially after it had been confirmed by the Council of Nicea. They are not the sophisticated, the theologians, the innovators; they are rather those who form a faithful reflection of what had been taught.

3) The faithful by remaining faithful were subject to persecution. They had every material reason to go along with the times and the example of great numbers of priests and bishops who opted either for confusion or for denial of Nicea. The faithful had only spiritual, non-temporal reasons for remaining true to the doctrine of Nicea.

4) The criterion for being counted among the faithful was simple: fidelity to the doctrine of Nicea.[6]

By way of contrast, the situation today seems quite different from the one that Newman used to exemplify his theory on the witness of the faithful.

1) While the Nicea controversy dealt with a matter of dogmatic faith, the present controversy deals with a matter of morals or lived doctrine. The former tended to be more of an "essential" question, i.e., it centered around the essence of Jesus Christ: what sort of a person was and is He? The question today tends to be more of an existential question: how should I live out the doctrine of Christian love in my marriage with regard to the sexual act? Certainly the questions are related, but at least today the immediacy of the two questions is felt differently. Perhaps we might say that the Nicene question is more important while the contraception question is more urgent.

2) While Newman's case is built upon a fidelity to official doctrine by a Catholic people who seem to represent the humbler classes, the advocates of contraception use the witness of the most sophisticated section of the world to build a case for departing from the official doctrine. Newman's faithful were a reflection of the action of the Spirit sustaining in the *anawim* His work which had already been expressed through the official teaching of the Catholic Church. The argument today takes the twist that through the voice of a large segment of the Catholic laity, and perhaps a majority of

those who have been baptized as Christian, we have a reflection of the Spirit working what He has been unable to promulgate through the official teaching of the Catholic Church. Newman painted a sorry picture of the many clerics who abandoned fidelity to Nicea or at least temporized, while today a tabulation of clerics and others who oppose the teaching of the Church is often looked upon with a sense of pride.

3) The "conflict of interest" situation today argues against the contraceptionists. Those who remained fully Catholic and loyal to Nicea did so against their material interests. Today the same holds true for those who accept as binding the traditional doctrine of the Church on contraception as reaffirmed in *Humanae Vitae*. There can be no real doubt that those who remain faithful to the centuries' old teaching reaffirmed by *Humanae Vitae* constitute the *consensus fidelium* as well as the remnant.

However, those who advocate contraception make use of the voice of those who stand to gain from a change in the doctrine. Nobody really "likes" sexual self-control and that's what the birth control debate is all about. If we have a sufficient reason to postpone or avoid pregnancy, does fidelity to the God who made us require that we practice periodic abstinence and sexual self-control? It is easy to see the tremendous conflict of interest involved for married couples in the "debate" because they stand to gain the imagined pleasures of sex whenever they feel like it if they can find a way to think the Church is wrong in its teaching of *Humanae Vitae*. Even theologians have a conflict of interest because, for the most part, theologians are very sensitive to the human condition and very sympathetic with those who claim difficulties with periodic abstinence.

Therefore, it is incongruous that at a time when public officials are scrutinized for a possible conflict of interest, theologians should be basing a popular argument in favor of contraception on the judgment of people who are rather obviously involved in a conflict of interest. If it is thought that judgment may be impaired because of a conflict of interest at the level of the Supreme Court of the United States, should we not ask ourselves to what extent judgment may be impaired because of a conflict of interest in matters of personal morality? The question is simply to what extent the voice of the laity who advocate contraception bears authentic witness to the Spirit of Christ and to what extent it partakes of the nature of a lobby for a vested interest. The fact that opposition to the teaching involves a conflict of interest does not add credibility to such opposition and certainly makes the case far different from that which Newman described in the Arian conflict.

4) A last and rather obvious difference between the situation described by Newman and the present is that in the Nicene period the *consensus fidelium* supported the official doctrine while today it is purported by the contraceptionists to oppose such official doctrine. Nor is it sufficient to say that the faithful of that time were adhering to a teaching that had been promulgated as *de fide,* as a defined dogma, while today we are treating of something taught with a lesser degree of formality and certitude. The present distinctions were not known then. Certainly most of the Catholics in the Nicene period did not regard the Council's teaching as a "definition"; rather, they had fidelity to it simply because it was the clarified teaching of the Church. Then as now a case could be made for opposition. In retrospect today, we and Newman regard as the *consensus fidelium* the witness of the rank and file who accepted the Nicene clarification of the Tradition in spite of the example set by much of the leadership of the Church.The foregoing comments do not absolutely prove that those who advocate contraception are in error. However, the analysis of the *consensus fidelium* shows that it is certainly erroneous to argue that the historical argument of Cardinal Newman can be used in any way to support the dissenters. On the contrary, Cardinal Newman's argument clearly shows by analogy that today's *consensus fidelium* is the witness of the laity who have remained faithful to the Tradition reaffirmed by *Humanae Vitae* despite dissent or equivocation on the part of many clerics—just as it happened in the aftermath of Nicea.

The People of God: Today

The People of God of the Old Covenant present us with a picture of the Church of God always in need of reform in its humanity. The New Testament presents a similar view. The history of the Arian controversy shows that the faithful, the *anawim,* can be the steady vessel of election even when many a leader is opting for confusion or denial. What about the Church today? Do we find in it a clear picture that the people as a whole today are a visible manifestation of the workings of the Holy Spirit? Or is the scene so mixed or even so un-Christian that an argument from the thought and practice of a numerically significant section of this people is meaningless?

252

What indications do we have that show a response or lack of response to the inspiration of the Holy Spirit? I suggest that a review of the general reception of the social teaching of the Church does not support the view that the overwhelming numbers of the laity have so overcome their self-interest that they can likewise be considered to have overcome self-interest in thinking about sex and birth control.

1. The people and the social doctrine of the Church. For a century, there has been an active promulgation of a social doctrine by the Church beginning with *Rerum Novarum* of Leo XIII in 1891. This was followed after forty years by *Quadragesimo Anno* of Pius XI in 1931. Thirty years later, Pope John XXIII issued *Mater et Magistra* (1961), and then he issued the more political document that won world-wide acclaim, *Pacem in Terris* (1963). Pope Paul VI continued this tradition with *Populorum Progessio* issued in 1967 and Pope John Paul II further developed it with *Solicitudo Rei Socialis* (1988). How have these affected the Church as a whole? Specifically, how have the laity responded to these practical calls to love our neighbor?

Only the broadest sort of generalizations are possible in answer to such broad questions, and I will leave it to others either to refute my general answers or to back them up with detailed research. However, I expect very little criticism of the following comments.

1) The Church's membership as a whole has not become a sign of love and concern for others. A chronicler of the twentieth-century struggle for the rights of the working man would not include the efforts of the mass of Catholic laity or clergy on behalf of the oppressed except when **they** were the oppressed. We can point to some wonderful exceptions to this general rule—the self-sacrificing individual missionaries, Msgr. John A. Ryan, Dorothy Day, and a few others like them—but we will search in vain for any long tradition of the laity accepting the social doctrine of the Church and trying to apply it in the world.

Much of this can be explained in North America by the fact that prior to World War II the Catholic population was numerically and politically insignificant in terms of the power it wielded. Many Catholics were recent immigrants and even the second generation of immigrants found themselves disadvantaged economically and educationally.

However, in our own era the reaction of the laity as a whole to the doctrine of social justice has been mixed, to say the least. The reaction to the racial problem by Catholics has found a few leading the way and a great many more unenthusiastic, to say the least. Frequently, those white Catholics in the vanguard of the black civil rights movement had nothing to lose economically while those opposed or unenthusiastic feared economic loss.

Even the great and obvious evil of abortion has failed to stir many Catholics—and other Christians as well; and it is apparent that many such people vote repeatedly for candidates who favor pro-abortion legislation. On the plus side, the pro-life and related issues have secured the involvement of thousands of grass roots Catholics, and to the best of my knowlege the entire Catholic leadership in the pro-life movement—at least at the national level—are people who also accept the teaching of *Humanae Vitae* as true.

2) The Church as a whole in our times has not been noted for its sense of community. The social doctrine promulgated by the Church stresses both the dignity of the individual person and the community of man. It teaches the obligation of those who have a sufficient amount of this world's goods to share generously with those who do not. Yet the statistics on how the affluent section of the Church helps the poor Church are sorry indeed. To be sure, much of this can be explained away by the fact that the primary form of giving, the Sunday contribution, gives distribution control to clerics who too frequently have had a narrow sense of their responsibility. Yet, the special collections for the missions and the missioners' own begging has pitiful per-household results.

3) Those Catholics who have stood to lose economically by a more just distribution of wealth and a more just social order have generally ignored or opposed the social doctrine of the Church. Latin America is a classic example. Both rich and poor are Catholics. The educated are Catholic. Yet Catholic Latin America is now the scene of grave social evils. For a century the social doctrine of the Church too often has been pointedly ignored by those who had the physical freedom to put it into effect. To be sure, the social doctrine has never been taught with the theological note of infallibility. However, the way in which affluent Catholics have formed and followed their consciences in this matter raises some very serious questions about the effort they have put into searching after the truth.

254

4) The reaction of affluent Catholicism to *Mater et Magistra* (1961), *Populorum Progressio* (1967), *Humanae Vitae* (1968) and *Solicitudo Rei Socialis* (1988) can be read as indicating that the People of God are motivated much more by self-interest than by self-giving. Columnist William Buckley spoke for many of the affluent with his infamous retort in 1961—"mater, *si;* magistra, no." The Churches of the poor have acclaimed *Populorum Progressio* and said relatively little about *Humanae Vitae*. I remember a letter to the editor in the summer of 1968 in which the writer told of an international conference. Delegates from Europe and North America were upset by *Humanae Vitae;* delegates from the under-developed countries were almost unconcerned. They said they didn't fear "exploitation" from Rome anywhere near as much as economic exploitation from Europe and North America.

5) Despite the tradition of ignoring or opposing the social doctrine of the magisterium by the People of God who would have something to lose by practicing it, dialoging Catholics still point to this social doctrine with great pride. It remains on the documentary level a sign that Popes, at least, were interested in teaching about the dignity and brotherhood of man. It will remain for historians a sign of at least verbal effort at reform in a Church always in need of reform.

My comments on the People of God with regard to the papal social doctrine have been negative and pessimistic. Perhaps somebody will refute them; I hope so, but I doubt it. Certainly, there have been glorious exceptions, but by and large self-interest seems to have dominated, love has been cast out by fear, and the overall response of the People of God has not been sufficiently different from that of "the world."

2. "Post-Christianity." Another difficulty in accepting the testimony of large numbers of Christians about the permissibility of contraception is that these Christians are living in an age which is being called "post-Christian" by its own theologians. Presumably, this means that the spirit of the day is not that of the Spirit of God, that skepticism and rationalism have crowded out faith, and that the teaching of Christ is either discounted or accepted piecemeal—insofar as it coincides with other philosophies about man but devoid of its constant reference to heaven, the Father, and the cross.

In some formerly "Catholic areas," churches are known for the absence of adult males. In the United States some recent statistics show that total Church membership (Protestant and Catholic) is up while total attendance is down, suggesting that more and more people are going to church less and less.

The question is, in an era being called post-Christian by its contemporary theologians, how do we tell the **real** Christians from the **apparent ones?** I have no answer but only a suggestion from biblical history. The biblical doctrine of the People of God would indicate that when the people become indistinguishable from the men of the world, taken in a pejorative sense, then perhaps we are at a time when the doctrine of the remnant will again give us hope. However the doctrine of the remnant suggests small numbers, not large.

Contraception has certainly been accepted by that section of the world called post-Christian. It has been accepted by the formally non-religious as well as by that segment bearing the name of Christian. It has been attempted by man for at least four thousand years and has reached a high degree of "effectiveness perfection." Our question is whether its use helps the Christian to attain that moral perfection to which Christ is calling him.

The advocates of contraception point to the numbers of Protestants and Catholics who see nothing wrong and lots of good in contraception as a sign that the Spirit of God is speaking through them to the magisterium which must listen and change. My remarks about post-Christianity have been intended only to show the danger of assuming that large numbers indicate the work of the Holy Spirit. The witness of these Christians must be balanced by the fact that (1) they are witnessing to something in perfect accord with the spirit of the day; (2) the spirit of the day is labelled post-Christian by many religious writers; (3) the doctrines of the remnant and the *anawim* should make us wary of the testimony of large numbers about a matter that is to their material benefit and requires no faith to live it.

Look at the numbers once again. In 1965, 32% of Catholic "family planners" used some form of natural family planning,[7] a rate that was undoubtedly down from higher levels in the 1950s. However, the 1988 National Family Growth Survey showed that among "family planners" only 3% of Catholics, 2% of Protestants, and 1% of No Religion used any form of NFP.[8] Thus in a period of less than 25 years, Catholic practice of marital chastity had fallen to a level only one-tenth its previous recorded level. Now when Catholic practice in a matter of sexual morality has become almost identical with that of atheists and other non-religious people, what reason is there to believe that this is the work of the Spirit of God? How can a Catholic theologian say with a straight face that the atheists have been right and the Church established by Christ has been wrong about marital sexuality all these many years?

3. The virtue of chastity. A third question that deserves our attention is, "Are Christian people today developing the virtue of chastity?" There is no way that I can point to one person or another and say, "That person has this virtue; that one doesn't." We'll have to leave the individual judgments to God. There are, however, some public indications that are at least thought provoking although admittedly not conclusive. Harvey Cox has written some pages that are particularly relevant to our effort to judge whether Christian peoples today are developing the virtue of chastity, and I think it best to quote rather liberally.[9]

Remember also that dating (and with it various types of petting) now reaches down to the sixth grade. Youngsters are thus exposed for a longer period and much more intensely to the mutual exploitation of erogenous regions which is the American courtship pattern. The only advice they get is, "Don't go too far," and it is usually the girl who is expected to draw the line.

By the time a girl who begins petting at thirteen has reached marriageable age, she has drawn an awful lot of lines. If she is especially impressed with her religious duty to avoid sexual intercourse, she will probably have mastered, by twenty-one, all the strategems for achieving a kind of sexual climax while simultaneously preventing herself and her partner from crossing the sacrosanct line.

Cox then asks why young people do not hear the Christian sexual ethic as "evangelical," as good news. He believes it has been dissolved into a myth, frozen into a Law. He then proceeds to free it from the myth.

Both the romantic ideal and the identification of intercourse with coitus are cultural accretions that have been coalesced with the rule of premarital chastity . . .

The ideal of romantic love is the most obvious mythical excrescence. It leads often to the belief, especially among girls, that certain forms of intimacy become progressively less objectionable the more you love the boy . . . Among adolescents of all ages *love* has come to mean nothing more than a vague emotional glow (208).

Cox then proceeds to zero in on what I believe is one of the firmest indications that our Christian people are not developing the virtue of chastity.

A more stubborn and deceptive segment of folklore that has been equated with the doctrine of premarital chastity is one that is rarely discussed openly: the curious presumption that a person who has not experienced coital intercourse remains a virgin—no matter what else he or she has done. This popular piece of legerdemain explains in part the discovery by Kinsey that, although the incidence of premarital intercourse among women has merely mounted steadily, premarital petting of all varieties has skyrocketed.

Kinsey's finding could be substantiated by the most casual observer of the American college scene. The number of students who do not pet at all is negligible. An increasing number regularly carry their necking to the point of heavy sex play and orgasm. A pert young graduate of a denominational college assured me recently that although she had necked to orgasm every week-end for two years, she had never "gone all the way." Her premarital chastity was intact.

Or was it? Only, I submit, by the most technical definition of what is meant by preserving virginity. True, some writers actually advocate such noncoital orgasm as the safest way for unmarried people to achieve sexual climax. However distasteful this idea may seem to some, it is extremely important to realize that the Church's traditional teaching actually functions in such a fashion as to give considerable support to this view.

The ideal of premarital chastity is generally understood to mean that, although necking is somewhat questionable, the fragile gem of virginity remains intact so long as coitus is avoided. This myth has helped open the floodgate to a tidal wave of noncoital promiscuity (210-211).

If the above quotation provides a fair estimate of the premarital patterns for the American people as a whole, then there is ample reason to doubt that our Christian people are developing the virtue of chastity. Perhaps certain religious groups are above this average, perhaps Catholics in the late 1940s were not interviewed in sufficient numbers by Kinsey. However, if the picture is valid and if it applies to Christians as well as to non-Christians, then we can trace the following development of a typical couple.

In our day and age, even before the onset of puberty, social pressures including much in-school sex education are being used to break down the natural reserve that most young people have towards members of the opposite sex. At the onslaught of puberty with all its strong drives, social pressures multiply the biological drives. To prove himself, the boy is practically forced to do some-

258

thing to some girl that will show that he's not pure, not sissy. Similar pressures are brought to bear on many girls. Then as our young boy and girl advance from the pressures of the peer group to an area of greater self-assertion, they find that sexual permissiveness provides a way of showing your special liking for one another. Frequently a spiraling round of affective behavior is set in motion. At first a goodnight kiss communicates their liking. Then just a little sitting together and a few kisses. Then impassioned embraces and finally the use of each other's bodies for purely sexual ends. The petting has but one or two purposes: (1) either to lead to a form of mutual masturbation in which at least one or perhaps both seek non-coital orgasm, or (2) to lead to sexual intercourse.

By the time our young man and young woman are ready to marry they have very likely developed sexual habits which are designed to cope with sexual tension only through the seeking of sexual relief in orgasm. If they are Christian, they cloak all this under the myth that pre-marital chastity is synonymous with non-coitus.

It should be obvious to anyone that Christian people who form this sort of view of chastity are scarcely going to see anything wrong with contraception. For them for some years, sex has become a means of personal expression, of regular practice, and of regular relief. If there was no one available from the opposite sex, masturbation provided an easy form of getting rid of the problem; for they had long been told that the only thing wrong about masturbation was that it showed a lack of maturity. The virtue of chastity, a power that controls the sex drive to put it at the service of authentic love according to one's state in life, simply has not been developed. The preservation of virginity in the technical sense of non-coitus, where done at all, is due much less to the development of the virtue of chastity than to a very practical form of prudence. Fear of disease or pregnancy, not love, has been the motive.

If spouses have not individually developed the virtue of chastity during their pre-marital years, the demands of marital chastity taught by the magisterium are going to seem unreasonable and unbearable. If these people have thought that by engaging in all sorts of deliberately stimulating sexual activity in their dating years they were behaving in a Christian manner, then the doctrine of non-contraception with its corollary of self-control is bound to seem un-Christian to them.

Thus when we read that Protestants and many Catholics see

nothing wrong with contraception, we should be wary of attributing this witness to the Holy Spirit. We need to know first of all whether these are the voices of persons who have really developed the virtue of chastity or whether they are themselves in need of reform and renewal. The witness of Kinsey and Cox would indicate that non-coital promiscuity is by no means confined to the non-baptized and that heavy petting habits of unchastity are to be found on almost all campuses, religious and secular.

4. Sociology and morality. For the Christian and the Jew, it should be obvious that what "the nations," the people of the world, are doing is not the criterion for morality. The prophets of old chastized the people of the Old Covenant for slipping into the ways of their neighbors. For the people of the New Covenant, the norm is Christ, the way is the life of the Spirit, not that of the self-interested flesh.

Yet in the entire sexual revolution which has taken place in this century, the sociological survey has replaced the gospel. For many the criterion is the "average" behavior of mankind. If 51 percent are doing it, it can't be too bad; in fact, it must be okay.

The contraception controversy has seen repeated use of sociology as a subtle substitute for the Church in determining the norm. The sociological survey has indicated that Protestants (with some exceptions) and Jews (and the completely secular irreligious, too) see nothing wrong with contraception. Then the surveys showed that a large proportion of Long Island Catholic housewives used some form of birth control; then other surveys showed a certain Catholic acceptance of the Pill, and then of other contraceptives. The issuance of *Humanae Vitae* brought a regular weekly tally of the number of priests who disagreed with the Pope.

This amounts to an argument from authority, the authority of the masses. "How can the masses be wrong?" it asks. I can only respond that the biblical evidence shows us that the masses have been wrong before and have stood in urgent need of God's word to which all men must render obedience in faith if they are to be saved. The norm is Christ; we have no guarantee whatsoever that the voice of the people, be they Jewish, Protestant, Catholic or pagan, provides us with the voice of the Spirit.

5. The need for the prophetic voice. Scripture shows us the need of God's people for the prophetic voice. Moses was raised up to lead the people out of the slavery of Egypt and through the confusion and trials of the wilderness. The prophets of the eighth and sixth centuries before Christ called the people to leave a new type of slavery, one which they had made for themselves out of their own material self-interest. The people of the new Christian churches were also the beneficiaries of some distinctive prophets—Peter, Paul and others. Once again, the people proved themselves in need of a prophetic reminder to be faithful to the Covenant in which they had been raised to the life and the way of the Spirit.

The word of Scripture remains normative for the people of every age. Of itself it provides God's constant call to communal and individual *metanoia,* that change of heart so necessary to live out the gospel. So important is the word of Scripture that it might seem that there would be no further need for the prophetic word. Christ, the fullness of the prophets, has come and has spoken. He has structured a living Church so that the Word of God in Scripture could be transmitted in a living way to all generations. To His Church as a whole He entrusted the mission of being His voice to all the nations: "You are God's people...to proclaim His wonderful work..." (1 Pet 2:9ff).

The history of the Church has shown that the Spirit has raised up men and women from time to time in a very prophetic role, e.g., Athanasius, Catherine of Siena, Francis of Assisi, Savanarola, and other great figures in the life of the Church. It was their responsibility to call for a reform, a renewal, a return to the Covenant of the Lord.

Today, who can question the fact that the People of God are in need of a strong and clear prophetic voice? Too many problems beset the Church to allow complacency in any area of her life. But where is that voice to be found? Will God raise up some person who will be recognized by all or by many as some sort of a prophetic figure? Even if this did happen, the odds are that he or she wouldn't be recognized as such until later generations, so the present age would still be confused—perhaps even more so by an additional debate over personalities.

I submit that one of the charismatic functions of the Petrine office is to be the steadying, prophetic voice for the entire People of God. I realize full well that the Old Testament prophets of the eighth and sixth centuries before Christ were outside the official structure, and the prophetic figures I have mentioned from the history of the Catholic Church have likewise been outside them. It would seem at first that there is almost a contrariness, if not a contradiction, between being used by the Spirit as a prophetic voice and being a member of the hierarchy. However, wouldn't we be thinking in excessively narrow categories to assume that such a contrariness was inevitable or the norm?

Scripture shows us in a very clear fashion that Christ joined in Peter both the structural role of headship and the role of prophet, spokesman for the Lord. Peter is the Lord's prophet on the day of Pentecost and on the succeeding days in the Acts. He is also the Lord's prophet in admitting the first Gentile, Cornelius, into the Church. The fact that he is not the only prophetic voice certainly proves that this charism is by no means exclusive; but the fact that he fulfills both the leadership and prophetic roles also proves that in the Petrine office the two have been combined.

The definition of papal infallibility by Vatican I in 1870 teaches us that under some very specific conditions we can have the certainty of divinely illuminated faith that the Petrine office is exercising its prophetic role as a teacher of the truth. It is commonly thought that the conditions for the exercise of that extraordinary authority in an **ex cathedra** definition of faith have been met only twice, and both concerned Mary.[10] The first was the definition of her Immaculate Conception in 1854 and the second was the definition of her Assumption in 1950. However, the question on people's minds today concerns the role of the Petrine office in the exercise of the **ordinary magisterium.** Is the apparent loneliness of the Pope on the birth control question the loneliness of the prophet of God? Is the rejection of his call to a high and difficult way of marital life the rejection usually accorded to the prophets of old?

I would like to offer at this point three reasons why I think that Pope Paul VI was used in a prophetic role. First of all, I believe that in *Humanae Vitae,* especially sections 7-18, the Pope is calling the people to live up to the demands of the Covenant—the marriage Covenant which sacramentalizes the Covenant of Christ and his Church. If this is in fact what he is doing, he is firmly in the tradition of the classical prophets whose primary mission was to call the people back to the living of the Covenant. Secondly, he is obviously asking the people to be faithful to the tradition. This again was a prime function of the prophet. Thirdly, the Popes of recent years have been fulfilling, in my opinion, a genuine prophetic role in the promulgation of the social gospel. They have likewise been constant in their call to marital chastity.

I realize that none of these three reasons **proves** anything about the truth of *Humanae Vitae;* I offer them only as reasons that

262

incline me to believe that it is more likely than not that the prophetic role of Peter was exercised in the Petrine office by Paul VI and continues to be exercised by Pope John Paul II in his unrelenting emphasis on the truth of *Humanae Vitae*.

This chapter has been an analysis of the appeal to the voice of the People of God. The appeal raises the question about where we can find the voice of the Spirit in the controversy over contraception. The biblical evidence shows us that we should not be surprised in the least if, in a matter of morality closely tied in with one's material interests, the voice of the people should err. We should not be surprised if the bearer of the voice of the Spirit, the prophetic figure for our times, seems alienated from the people to whom he speaks; for such was the case with the prophets of old.

13

A Critique of the Contraceptive Arguments

It would be impossible in less than several volumes to offer a critique of all the contraceptive "theology" that has been written or popularized since the beginning of Vatican II (October, 1962). However, as one who has tried to keep somewhat abreast of the major currents of thought, I think I have assimilated certain main lines of argumentation, and it is these that I hope to criticize. Some of them would be uttered by no responsible theologian today; yet in this controversy they have become part of the popular arsenal and need to be examined even if only very briefly.

Since this chapter deals with arguments put forward under the name of theology, I hope I will not be out of order in offering some comment about theology and the role of the theologian in Part I; in Part II, I address various arguments that have been made in the birth control controversy.

I: Theology and Theologians

Theology and faith

As a teacher of theology, I had the uncomfortable experience of talking with students who were taking a course so that they could have more knowledge and *less* faith. They seemed to be thinking that "faith" was for the unlearned and that as soon as they became learned, their faith would be replaced by understanding and comprehension. Their approach to religion was much the same as would be their approach to any other "problem" area of Twentieth century life.

The study of theology differs significantly from other organized areas of knowledge, nor is it identical with philosophy. Since the theologian and the philosopher do, however, deal with many of the same areas of life, its nature, ends and problems, etc., it might be well to make a brief comparison of these two fields of thought.

The work of a philosopher is judged on the basis of the cogency of his arguments and of the evidence he marshals. The philosopher must first of all be an acute observer of all that is and he must do his best to relate it. He forms his premises, and from these he draws his conclusions. His conclusions are judged (or should be) *entirely* on how well they are contained in his premises, and his premises are open for all other philosophers to criticize. The philosopher does not and cannot ask us to believe him. He must be able to prove the correctness of his premises and his conclusions, and he only asks us to reason with him. It is this process of formulation and criticism, reformation and reasoned debate that forms the basis for the dialogue of philosophers and keeps their journals and publishers in business. It is healthy and necessary.

The Christian believer on the other hand does not approach something (or better yet, someone) he believes with the same critical and even skeptical attitude as the philosopher approaches a philosophical conclusion. The Christian believer believes that somehow the One creative God has revealed Himself through the prophets and finally in Jesus Christ. He believes the "something" of his faith solely because the Someone has revealed it. He does not demand proof from God, for to do so would amount to saying that God was not believable on His own word but had to approach us in the same way as any one of the philosophers.

However, the believer still seeks to understand as much as possible. He likes to think about what God has revealed. He wants to know what it means for him; he wants to know how one aspect of God's revelation is related to another; he wants to know if he can or must draw from this revelation some conclusions which are not themselves the primary "something revealed" but seem to flow from it.

As he begins thinking about his faith he becomes a theologian in the sense that every believer who has ever thought about his religion is a theologian. Theology, after all, in the classic and still valid definition, is simply faith seeking understanding. Theology does not seek to *replace* one's faith but rather to enlighten it, to show the unity among its various parts or facets, and hopefully to deepen it.

The professional theologian differs from the ordinary inquiring believer not in kind but rather by degree and intensity. He devotes time, perhaps his full time, to the study of his faith. He is aware that whenever someone begins to think about anything, he does so in terms of his own background. He therefore seeks to learn from the theologians of the past, filter out that which has a timeless value and to leave behind that which was only a reflection of the mode of their day. This, of course, is tricky business, for the theologian of today is just as much a prisoner of the thought patterns of his times as was the theologian of yesteryear. For this reason, even if for no other, there will never be an end to theology. The theologian brings to bear whatever is useful from the other sciences and attempts to enlarge the frontiers of theological knowledge and religious understanding.

The role of the theologian

Sometimes it is easier to say what someone's role is *not* rather than to specify what it is, and I think that this applies quite well to the role of the theologian in the contraception controversy. Thus at the outset, before I attempt to state what the theologian should be doing, I will list some of the pitfalls he should avoid.

Being a politician. First of all the theologian is not a politician and he should not engage in demagoguery. He must be extremely aware of all the conscious and unconscious pressures being brought to bear on him to advocate contraception, and he should be extremely vigilant to avoid teaching something simply because that is what many want to hear. In the same vein he should be wary of grandstanding, making a big play for public opinion.

Lack of charity. Another approach that we can dispense with is that which suggests that those who accept the authoritative teaching of the Church must thereby suggest that those who do not are corrupt. For example, one theologian has written that "it is difficult to explain how a rule of life that is based on natural law and hence corresponds to the universal moral experience of man is advocated in the present culture only by the Catholic Church, unless one wanted to suggest that the consciences of other men and even other Churches are so corrupt that they are no longer in touch with the foundation of human morality."[1] What that author failed to realize in 1968 was the National Council of Churches had already accepted abortion for the health of the mother in 1961; nor could he foresee that during the Seventies and Eighties the mainline Protestant Churches would be practically unanimous in their support for the abortion-on-demand ruling of the 1973 U. S. Supreme Court in *Roe vs. Wade*. Yet I have never read of any Catholic theologians using the language of corruption suggested by this dissenting theologian.

266

Inconsistency. A third pitfall for the theologian to avoid is talking out of both sides of his mouth. That is, he should not quote the "experience of the laity" as an experience of virtue in one area of morality and then use the "experience of the laity" as an example of sin in another. To be specific, the argument from the experience of some of the laity who see no wrong in their use of contraceptives has been used frequently in the debate. At the same time, however, theologians tell us that we are living in a "post-Christian" society. We are reminded that these same Christians for whom contraception supposedly is loving behavior are likewise guilty of racism and that collectively they refuse to give even one per cent of their gross national product to help the poor and starving. One wonders at the consistency of calling these Christians experts on what constitutes authentic love within marriage and blind on what it means to love our neighbor outside the context of marriage.

Eclecticism. Fourth, theologians must try to avoid the pick and choose method of using the social sciences. This is most difficult, perhaps psychologically impossible in controversy, for the debater soon seeks to make points instead of simply searching for the truth. For example, the advocate of contraception should not limit himself to quoting philosophers, sociologists, and psychologists who describe the harmful effects of tension in our lives. He should also quote those philosophers, sociologists, and psychologists who believe that tension is a necessary part of becoming human, who teach that only in situations of anguish, or "shipwreck," or suffering and stress do we come to grips with ourselves, the meaning of our lives, and our relationship with God.

Absolutizing relativity. As a fifth point, in the theologian's current emphasis on anthropology, he must avoid forming a firm conclusion on the tentative and partial insights of one or more of the social sciences. The social sciences are in a state of continuing development; they are subject to fads; what seems beyond question today may be discarded as obsolete tomorrow. To form a theology on this is to build on shifting sand.

Pride. Then he should avoid the belief in his own personal infallibility; he should avoid becoming so attached to the contraceptive culture and perhaps his own pulpit and confessional pronouncements that he cannot change, and he should avoid concluding that vocal theologians have replaced the Pope.

If the theologian who takes up the task of clarifying the

contraception controversy manages to avoid the above and other pitfalls, what should he be doing in a more positive vein? Again, these are my personal reflections; I am not quoting eminent authorities; I can only appeal to common sense.

Openness. I believe that the theologian in his search for the truth should develop the "both this...and this" approach. No heresy has ever started with sheer negation. Rather, every heresy began with an emphasis on the truth—but only one aspect of the truth. That aspect became more and more emphasized until at last there came a formal denial of some other aspect of the total truth. In the contraception controversy, if a theologian finds himself strongly advocating one aspect, he should be asking himself if he is actually denying another valid aspect of the truth.

I am not suggesting that the theologian whose conviction is based on his faith that the Church's teaching is true should be open to arguments to the contrary. Who would want a Catholic theologian "hanging loose," open to arguments seeking to justify rape or pederasty or the killing of the innocent? On the other hand, I am suggesting that there may be more than one way to explain the truth of a teaching and that theologians should be open to such arguments.

Loyalty. The theologian of today, simply because he is a theologian and not a philosopher, must give his qualified assent to the magisterium. He cannot brush off 19 centuries of anti-contraceptive teaching with glib phrases about a new culture or a new understanding of man. Now that Pope Paul VI and Pope John Paul II have reaffirmed the tradition in an authoritative way, the theologian is required to give the presumption of truth to the tradition. *If he is disposed to seek its change, he must realize that the* **burden of proof** *is upon him rather than upon the philosophy or the theology of* Humanae Vitae.

Perspective. The theologian should be perceptive and judge things in their proper perspective. He must place his search for the meaning of sexual morality in marriage within the framework of the larger search for a better explanation of the total meaning of man. Is it not simply double-talk to tell us that the *anawim,* God's poor, will inherit the kingdom of God and then to tell us that a justifying reason for contraception is that it will enable us to avoid becoming poor?

In context. The theologian must place the explanation of sexual morality in marriage within the context of the call to perfection that Christ extends to married people. He must place the search for the meaning of sexual interpersonal relationships in the context of the Incarnation and in the context of the interpersonal relationships of the Triune God in whose image man is created and is meant to live.

He should keep his theologizing about married sexual morality within the context of all sexual morality. This he has not always done. What we have witnessed in the contraception controversy is a reasoning process that has gone something like this: "Now that we've shown that we were wrong in the past about contraception, the presumption is that we were possibly (or probably) wrong about some other areas of sexuality in the past"; or, "We showed that non-contraception was wrong because it interfered with the spontaneous expression of love. By the same token, isn't the ban on pre-marital relations a similar interference with the spontaneous expression of love? And what about so-called extra-marital relations between two people who are truly loving toward each other, who want to help each other overcome loneliness, frustration and a sense of emptiness? We used to call this adultery when we had a static concept of man's nature and his inter-personal relationships. But now, with our new understanding of man's dynamic nature and the self-determining of his own relationships, might it not be better to say that these two temporary lovers are more virtuous in their love-making, in their self-structured relationship of affective love, than they would be with their own spouses in their static contractual marriages? If we were wrong on contraception, we may be just as wrong about everything else in the sexual sphere."

Needless to say this is not the specific quote of any particular author. Nor, on the other hand, is it just a straw man. It rather seems to me to be a pretty fair representation of some of the current Catholic thinking on sex.[2] I disagree with it completely, preferring to approach the question from an entirely different direction. That is, since I believe that the evil of adultery and fornication is revealed much more clearly than the evil of contraception, I prefer to look for the quality that makes the former an evil and then to see if this quality is also relevant to contraception. I think that the evil central to all is the denial of a covenant, as I explained in Part I of this book.

Practicality. The theologian writing about sexuality should also be working to develop a better understanding of the entire moral order. In doing so, he must be aware—critically aware—that any principles that he develops and advocates to support a particular conclusion will likewise be used in other areas of human morality. Thus, principles which are over-extended to "solve" the contraception controversy can be expected to be applied in their erroneously over-extended position to other matters, especially those dealing with sex and human life.

The burden of proof. The Catholic who is disposed to seek a change in the teaching about marital contraception must accept the burden of proof. Given the enormous theological weight of nineteen centuries of teaching and the papal reaffirmations since 1930, the presumption of truth is clearly on the side of the teaching of the magisterium. The contraceptive theologian has to prove that his position is both internally consistent and that it does not advocate or use moral principles in such a way that they will wreak havoc when applied to other areas of human relationships.

As a matter of fact, this has not been done. In 1971 I demonstrated that the moral principles of arch-dissenter Fr. Charles Curran could not say "no" even to spouse-swapping, and my argument was never challenged.[3]

II: The Arguments

The preceding chapter analyzed the pervasive feeling or argument from the practice of the "People of God." The remainder of this chapter deals with other arguments in a much briefer way.

The argument from science

This argument is typically phrased along these lines. "Until recently man has not known about efficient means of contraception. New medical knowledge has given us extremely efficient ways of contraception, especially the Pill. God gave man a brain to use it to control nature. Therefore God permits contraception, and intelligent man should use the means most efficient for him."

The worth of the argument is easily seen by substituting another value. "Until recently man has not known about efficient means of mass killing. New scientific knowledge has given us extremely efficient ways of mass killing, especially the hydrogen bomb. God gave man a brain to use it to control nature. Therefore God permits mass killing and intelligent man should use the means most efficient for him—in this case the H-bomb."

No one, I hope, would subscribe to the "logic" of the second argument. Everybody, I hope, would say that the argument says nothing about the morality of mass killing and that the *use* of our new scientific knowledge has to be evaluated according to moral principles. The fact that we know **how** to do something, even if it has taken the work of geniuses to discover it, does not mean that it is *good* to do it. And that is equally true about contraception, the use of the Pill or any other device. Knowledge of newer and more efficient means of contraception, even though the work of brilliant scientists, is of itself no indication that it is good to practice contraception, either in the older forms such as Onan's withdrawal before ejaculation or the newer forms such as the Pill. The argument from science is simply no argument.

A new concept of man

Somewhat related to the argument from science, the theory of a new concept of man stresses man's dynamism. Man is no longer content to look upon nature as a static thing of which he is the passive subject. Rather, he seeks to control nature. Now that he knows more about fertility it is natural for him to control it so that he can be true to his role as a dynamic, self-determining being. He may and should therefore use whatever scientific means he can to control the fertility aspect of nature.

It is true that modern man is probably considerably more aware, self-consciously aware, of being dynamic and self-determining than previous generations have been. It is equally true that man has always been dynamic, he always sought to "control nature" in one way or another. Ancient civilizations had well-planned and well-functioning irrigation systems. Probably every war that was ever fought was a result of somebody's dissatisfaction with the "natural" boundaries of his tribe or kingdom. The building of boats (and how primitive is that?) is evidence of man's desire to master the "natural" boundary of water.

Change has been noted as a fact of life ever since Heraclitus immortalized it in his teaching that the only constant is change. What is new about change today is that it is 1) much more rapid than ever before, 2) more self-consciously sought by agents of change, and 3) found influencing almost every facet of life. Yet the emphasis on man's self-conscious dynamism leaves unexplained that which remains the same. Why is it that I can read the Old Testament and relate to the people there? Why is it that I can read the plays and the epics of the ancient Greeks and see myself and others there? Is it not because at the same time that man is by nature dynamic he is also by that same nature unchanging in the essence—the real guts—of what it means to be a human person?

I can hear the critics now. "Kippley has a static concept of nature, and if you can abide anyone so archaic . . . etc." What the critics fail to see is that the truth lies in a philosophy of "both . . . and." Man is unchanging in some ways and changing in others. Man is basically unchanging with regard to his inter-personal relationships, but he is changing with regard to his self-conscious awareness of those relationships. Man has always been a social being, and he has always known that he has certain rights and that others have certain rights. He has had to grow—evolve, if you please—into a conscious understanding that all men are one community, that the community exists for the sake of the individual person, etc. The conflict with statist philosophies such as communism in which the individual is absolutely subordinated to a Supreme State shows the difficulty with which this latter consciousness has evolved.

The idea that man has changed in some way that would affect the moral law that derives from the very order of creation is also at odds with both experience and Christian faith. The reason we can experience empathy with peoples of other lands and cultures and centuries is that we recognize that for them and for us the basic goods of humanity are the same—life itself, knowledge of the truth, the value of doing what is right, friendship, peace, and even the appreciation of beauty. This fundamental experience is in accord with the Christian faith which teaches that all human beings have a common origin and the same calling, and that we are all redeemed by Christ who took on the human nature which we all have in common. To say that there is a real change in the very nature of man is to rupture the solidarity of the human race with Christ. The argument from a new concept of man says nothing at all about the morality of contraception. It is one-sided in its emphasis on man's self-determining dynamism, and **even if this were the full truth, it still would not be a *reason* for contraception.** At the best it would be a reason for investigating further whether married sexual intercourse is a proper subject for willful interference.

The argument from sociology

The sociological argument might well be called the argument

from present difficulties. This line of thought reminds us that in the immediate past we were more of an agrarian culture where children were an economic asset, but that's a narrow perspective which overlooks 1) the Irish rural economy in which a large family was certainly no economic asset and 2) the history of civilization which is basically a history of the cities. It seems to me that this argument places too much emphasis on what has happened in North America during the Twentieth century. After the frontiers were settled, machinery came in, and people began migrating to urban centers. If the majority of people once lived on farms, there have always been a great number of people who lived in the cities where large families have never been an economic asset.

The sociological argument forcefully reminds us of the population expansion. It tends to center on global population, while individual married couples tend to center on the population within their own family. The sociological argument reminds us also of the desirability of higher education for all and the expense of this for the large family. We cannot help but become aware of the difficulties for both nations and individual families.

The argument seems to run something like this: 1. Today there are tremendous, even unprecedented sociological difficulties in our world. 2. The economy of the rich nations seems geared for a family of not over three children. The economy of the poor nations leads many to starvation. 3. Man has a duty to better his whole world. He has created part of the problem by lowering the natural death rate. 4. He has the physical power to limit population through contraception. 5. Therefore it is permissible, even perhaps mandatory, to practice contraception in the present sociological circumstances.

The argument is extremely attractive. Let us suppose that every statement up to the "therefore" conclusion is true. The problem is that the conclusion is by no means contained in the preceding statements. The argument assumes what needs to be proved, i.e., that contraception is in itself a morally permissible way of expressing married love. To prove to yourself the error of the "therefore" statement, simply substitute other means in statement 4: "He has the physical power to limit population through _____" Put in contraception, genocide, infanticide, abortion, the destruction of the incurably sick, the killing of the old, the sterilization of non-contracepting parents, and you can see that what remains to be proved is that any one of these is morally acceptable. That is, the existence of external pressures is no sure sign at all that either contraception or any other method of population control is morally permissible. The existence of the external pressures is, of course, a sure sign that we should take a very close look at what is involved in each one of these and other physically possible methods.

Certainly contraception is a lesser evil than any of the other methods of population control mentioned above. It alone does not violate the rights of a third person. However, what should concern us is that the sociological argument, first used to justify contraception, is now being used to justify abortion, and it is being used in this way by spokesmen for Christian Churches. What has happened, it seems, is that the method of reasoning from external difficulty has led too many to stop asking themselves, "What is it that I am doing right now, regardless of my intention? Am I invalidating an act of love? Am I killing a person who has just as much right to live as I do?"

This argument or line of reasoning still avoids the issue of what is involved in contraception. It assumes that contraceptive sexual intercourse is an indifferent biologism whose moral character is ascertained solely by reference to the external economic and other sociological circumstances. Thus it assumes what needs to be proved; this argument provides, at best, a good reason to examine more closely the morality of contraception itself.

The love union

The most potent of the arguments for contraception centers around the affective love that can be expressed in sexual intercourse. Married couples witness to the fact that they have various felt needs—affective, psychological, physiological—which are satisfied through the expression of their affection and love in the sexual union. Married couples testify to the tension that occurs when they wish to have relations and yet are fearful of pregnancy. They want to express their love in the sexual union, and it seems so natural to do so that it seems unnatural to refrain. It is generally agreed that when there are physical indications that the couple should refrain from sexual intercourse, it would not be loving for the husband or the wife to insist upon "making love." Here there seems to be an understanding that the processes of "nature" sometimes exclude doing "what comes naturally" in the way of affective love. Still, these are regarded as the exceptions which only serve to point up the rule that "normal" married behavior between two people who love each other is to have relations when they feel like it.

In the earlier stages of the controversy it seemed to be argued that the married sexual union was an expression of married *agape,* a self-giving love. As orthodox theologians pointed out that contraception was sexual relations with severe reservation, that there could not be a complete self-giving in contraceptive intercourse, the argument shifted; we heard that man was never capable of complete self-giving at any time, that he always loved with reservation. Then we began to see that the uniquely Christian word for love, *agape* was dropped by some in favor of *eros,* and the values of erotic love were said to be worthy to be sought or enjoyed for their own sake; these too were the works of God.

There is no use denying that the personalist, affective, and erotic values of sex were not emphasized in, say, pre-1960 moral theology and marriage texts. There is no denying that the emphasis on the procreative aspects of sex as "primary" had the effect of putting the "secondary" aspects of marriage in an entirely inferior position. It was as if both could not be maintained as purposes or values within marriage, as if to admit both would exclude one or the other. This still remains a valid question: can people psychologically hold both the procreative and unitive aspects in a creative tension, or will they not in fact actually deny one in their emphasis of the other? I think that a much stronger historical case can be made for the latter, but I believe that the truth lies in keeping both elements in a creative tension. Barrels of ink have described the alleged ecclesiastical repression of the personalist, affective, erotic values, so no space has to be devoted to that here. However, has not the current contraceptive mentality done the same thing to the procreative values?

The proponents of contraception who strive to give due credit to the procreative aspects of the sexual union while emphasizing the unitive aspects sometimes give the impression that the procreative aspects may be denied for a time because the marriage is basically open to life. Without saying it in so many words, they imply that a marriage is basically open to life because most of the time the procreative and unitive aspects of the marital union are not positively separated. If this is what they mean by being basically open to life, I fear they have not taken a good reading on what is going on in the average contraceptive marriage. Young people are being urged not to have over two children, three at the maximum. If a couple decides upon this course and fall into a somewhat average pattern of sexual relations about two or three times a week, over the course of their fertile years they will have allowed well under ten percent of their sexual acts to be not positively closed to the possibility of procreation. When over ninety percent of marital sex acts contraceptively separate the unitive and procreative aspects of marriage, is it realistic to say that such a marriage is basically open to life? Would it not be more realistic to admit that such marriages represent a *de facto* denial of the procreative values of sex?

The difficulty of saying that you are respecting the procreative dimension of marital relations while contradicting that dimension most of the time is illustrated by applying the same reasoning to the unitive dimension of marital sex. Would the advocates of contraception approve of mutual adultery for the sake of building future unity? Would they approve of his forcing her to engage in perverse sex acts *any* percent of the time so he would stay with her and practice normal sex the other times? Absurd! Likewise, it is sheer rationalization to say that one is honoring the procreative good of marriage by deliberately opposing this good in numerous marital acts. Note also that Pope Paul VI clearly rejected this argument in *Humanae Vitae:* "It is an error to think that a conjugal act which is deliberately made infertile and so is intrinsically wrong could be made right by a fertile conjugal life considered as a whole" (n.14).

Furthermore, the love union approach cannot make an adequate distinction between casual, pre-marital, marital, and extra-marital affections. If the new sin is denial of one's affective love, on what philosophical grounds can we ask young lovers to deny themselves? Scripture is of only limited help, for it can be interpreted into meaninglessness, and everybody knows that the Church has defined only a half dozen or so passages of Scripture. Ethicians counsel against exploiting each other. Others bring in a Kantian motive; consider that your actions are the norm for everybody else. But what if a young couple, well read in the philosophy of the love union, come to their parents and say that they are simply so fond of each other, so full of love, that full sexual expression seems natural, that they are not exploiting each other, that they hope every young couple feels the same way, and that they don't feel that a fundamentalist interpretation of Scripture is relevant to their case? What if they should then ask, "If denial of strong affective love is bad for you, why isn't it bad for us too?" How do the parents with the love-union contraceptive mentality answer? I have given an answer based on the marriage covenant in an earlier chapter, but on the basis of affective love, I am at a loss. The "Wait and it will be more meaningful" answer only brings the question, "Why can't married people wait ten days or two weeks? You're asking me to wait for years." If spontaneity is so important in married life, why isn't it equally valid among the unmarried whose psychological needs for affection may be considerably greater than those of a happily married couple? This application of the principle to an area of moral life outside of marital contraception seems logical enough. It also carries the seed of moral chaos, and it illustrates the danger of the principles used by contraceptionists to solve the birth control question.

Nor is it of any value for the advocates of the contraceptive love-union to state that sex outside of marriage is illicit and that they are adamantly opposed to casual, premarital, and extramarital sex. Their argument from their own authority is gratuitous. They must be able to explain **why** the principle of the affective love-union may not be applied universally wherever there is a strong affective love that desires to express itself in the sexual union.

Implicit in the "love union" argument is the belief that having sex whenever the spouses feel like it and having a relatively small family will build marital happiness and stability. That was the public philosophy of Margaret Sanger, foundress of Planned Parenthood. (I say "public philosophy" because she also believed that sex with anybody was permissible and that abortion was an acceptable means of birth control, but these views were not widely promulgated during her career which stretched from pre-WWI through the 1950s.[4])

Is there any evidence to support the notion that unlimited contraceptive sex and very limited family size produce marital happiness and stability? The overall evidence suggests the opposite. The American divorce rate in 1910 was one in ten marriages. Sanger formed her National Birth Control League about 1914 to promote her philosophy of sex and succeeded immensely in promoting what is now called the sexual revolution. However, despite the almost universal acceptance of her philosophy, the divorce rate has risen 500 percent, an obvious indication of widespread marital unhappiness. Whatever other factors have contributed to the high divorce rate, the Sanger philosophy of sex and birth control has to be recognized as a major cause, perhaps **the** most significant factor.

In summary, the argument from the affective love-union reflects the feelings of many married couples. At the same time it fails to distinguish adequately between married and unmarried love. It also fails to hold a real balance between the procreative and affective values in marriage. It fails to relate adequately the Christian *agape,* self-giving love with the seemingly universal tendency to *eros,* pleasurable love; and its promise of marital happiness flies in the face of the reality of a 50 percent divorce rate in the American contracepting society.

The principle of the total human act

I have commented on several of the chief lines of argumentation that seem to be popular today—the emphases on our new scientific knowledge, a new understanding of man, the sociological difficulties and the personal love-union. I would characterize these as "new subject matter" approaches to the problem. They seem to say, "Look at this. This has changed, this is new, this is different, this is better. Our non-contraceptive tradition was formed before we had these new insights. The traditional insights have been replaced. Therefore contraception is good or at least permissible." Other approaches are based more on principle rather than on subject matter, and I offer a critique of three of these.

End and means. We have all learned that it is false to say that the end justifies the means. This has been so ingrained in most of us that even the most radical of the new Catholic theologians feel uneasy about flatly contradicting it. Thus I cannot remember having seen in print yet the statement that "we were wrong before, but now we know that the end does justify the means." Another way of stating the principle is to say that intention does not justify an action which is morally wrong in the objective order. Likewise the theologians of the new morality have not yet, to my knowledge, made the good intention the sole criteria of morality although everyone recognizes that a good intention with invincible ignorance can remove an otherwise evil act from the realm of subjective sin and guilt.

However, despite the verbal repetition that morality does not consist just in good intentions, there is a way of explaining our actions which does in fact make morality (and not just culpability) dependent solely upon the intention while proclaiming all the while that it does not. For lack of a better term, I will label this way of reasoning "the principle of the total human act."[5] In using this term, I am combining what is sometimes called "the principle of totality" with the theory of the truly human act. In my opinion, the two are inseparably linked.

The proponents of the principle of the "total human act" say it is misleading to speak of "end" and "means" because to do so

278

separates an inseparably unified human act. They criticize the language of "end" and "means" as dividing into neat but unrealistic categories what is really a unified action of a person. They say there is no simple material substratum which is made good or bad by the "end." There is only the human act which is matter-spirit in particular circumstances and has to be evaluated as a totality, not just a physical thing.

Examples abound. Take this knife held by this hand slitting this skin. What's going on? Much more than just skin-slitting. It can be a medical operation by a skilled surgeon, or torture, murder, etc. Or again, suppose that the knife is being thrust into this person in such a way as to end his life. What is the human value of the act? Is it murder or self-defense or capital punishment? The anatomical description does not do justice to the action as a truly human act. So far, no problem.

This line of reasoning then points to the history of Catholic moral theology as having been excessively materialistic and devisive of the total human act. Here a favored example is the development of the doctrine concerning human transplants. When the question first arose, primarily after World War II, many moralists regarded it as unjustified, even if done to help another person. The end was seen as good but the means was bad. Therefore, it was forbidden. At the same time, it became apparent to many that excessive attention paid to anatomical integrity of the one person was interfering with a great act of inter-personal giving. If a person could give up his whole life for a friend, could he not also give up a kidney?

The problem was solved by the recognition that a kidney transplantation could be a great act of charity on behalf of a conscious, willing donor, not a self-harming mutilation in the common, pejorative sense of ordinary language. The donor still had one healthy kidney which could fulfill his or her bodily needs. The moral principle against mutilation still stood, and a kidney transplantation was seen as an act of charity.

In analyzing what has happened here, we have to realize that certain words already define the human act; that is, they already have attached a value to the action. For example, murder, rape, arson, and mutilation. To describe an act as a mutilation in ordinary language is to say that there is something wrong with it, that it's bad as a totality. This is important, for if in answer to the question, "What's going on here?" the doctor answered, "I'm mutilating one person, but it's for a good purpose. We're saving somebody else's life," we would have a clear example of the classic "bad means" for a "good end." That's why it was necessary to be able to see the transplant operation 1) not as a mutilation in the common pejorative sense and 2) then a life-saver but rather as one inter-personal act which really did no moral evil and accomplished much good. Again, so far no problem.

The problem comes in the extension of the principle of the "total human act."

"What's going on here?"
"I'm making the world a better place to live."
"Could you be a bit more specific?"
"Sure, I just sent 500 inmates of a mental institution to their heavenly reward. Yesterday I eliminated quite a bit of suffering, worry, and even some despair by speeding up the journey to heaven for 54 people in an old folks home..."

"What's going on here?"
"I'm making the world peaceful."
"Could you be a bit more specific?"
"Sure, I just sent off some H-bombs to eliminate all the political centers of Russia, China, Iran and Libya."
"Oh no! Your good purpose just can't justify your means!"
"Are you ever old fashioned! You're dividing up into unrealistic categories my total human act which is really one of peacemaking."

These examples may seem too far-fetched. Let's take a look at what actually has happened.

"What's going on here?"
"We're just following orders."
"Could you be more specific?"
"Sure. We're eliminating a problem?"
"What sort of a problem?"
"The 'Jewish problem.' You're looking at 5,000 Jews about to be eliminated." (Actual total: 6,000,000.)

Or again, listen to the proponents of abortion.

"What's going on here?"
"I'm building family happiness."
"Could you be more specific?"

"Sure. I'm a doctor; I'm performing a perfectly legal abortion."

"That's building family happiness?"

"Sure. This woman figured that the family budget was already tight enough. She didn't take the pill one day, got pregnant and very unhappy. She began to take out her unhappiness on the rest of the family. Everybody got unhappy. So by aborting her, I'm building family happiness."

"Yes, but what about the right of the unborn baby?"

"Look. Today you've got to look at the big picture, the total human act. We're not takers of innocent human life. We're builders of happiness...."

To bring in these examples is not to bring in a red herring. They illustrate the actual evil that has come from misapplication of this principle of the total human act. One can say that there is no intrinsic connection between contraception and abortion, but there is a bridge, and that bridge is the approach to the problem. An approach which glides over the evil of certain specific actions by saying that they take their morality from the larger, total human act is erroneous, misleading, and ultimately destructive of morality.

Human acceptability. Nor is it an adequate answer to imply that the limiting criteria is human acceptability. W. Van der Marck writes: "If doctors decide that the removal of a fetus is medically necessary, and if this is humanly acceptable, then it *is not* abortion (except perhaps in purely medical or physiological terms), and the principle that abortion is murder, still applies."[6] What is "humanly acceptable?" In a mid-Sixties book, Msgr. Paul Furfey[7] admirably demonstrated the gross evils that have become "humanly acceptable" to people well-educated in the western (Judeo-Christian?) culture. I shall never forget an abortion symposium held at the University of Santa Clara in early 1967. A respectable doctor said he wanted abortion legalized to make legal what he and his colleagues were already doing. A respectable sociologist told us about his gardening—how you have to thin out the rows of carrots so the survivors will have more room to grow. He didn't verbalize his conclusion about humans—he didn't have to. Finally, an Episcopalian priest (Rev. Charles Carroll) who had been at the Nuremberg trials arose to express his shock at such reasoning and to express his fears concerning the similarity between the solution of the problem of the undesired child in the womb and the solution of the problem of the undesired Jews (by the Nazis) in Germany.

To keep discourse about morality from degenerating into a broadbrush morality of good intentions, we have to use the distinction of St. Thomas concerning the **proximate and remote ends or intentions.** Imagine that you have a big exam coming up. You've got to get ready to pass it. What do you do? Study hard or design a cheat system? Your remote intention is to pass the exam; you might also introduce even more remote ends or intentions—to graduate, to earn money to support works of charity, etc. But right now you have to choose between two proximate ends or intentions— to study or to cheat. The specific material things you use—pen and paper—may be the same, but the morality of their use is determined by your proximate intention.

St. Thomas, following Catholic tradition, says, "An act is good in its integrity and is wicked by reason of any defect" (bonum ex integra causa, malum ex quocumque defectu). That means that if any part of the total action—such as the means chosen or the proximate intention or the remote intention—is bad, the whole human act is bad. The proponents of the "total human act," however, have chosen to ignore the "present intention" or "proximate end" and to focus on the "further intention" or "remote end," claiming that if the latter is good, then the whole human act is good. Of course, that amounts to saying that the end justifies the means.

Furthermore, isn't that just begging the question? That is, doesn't concentration only upon the remote end just assume that the here and now action—the action which is in question—is morally right in itself?

Thus **the task of moral discourse** is to talk about the action which is really intended and to evaluate that intended action. Would any honest person say that "using a pencil and paper" was an adequate moral description of preparing cheat notes? Or "button pushing" for sending H-bombs to their destination? Or "doing a procedure" for killing an unborn baby? Equally important, what honest person could say that an adequate moral evaluation of cheating was "to support charities later on in life," that an adequate evaluation of firing H-bombs was "making peace" or that an adequate evaluation of abortion was "relieving stress"?

What does this have to do with the controversy on contraception?

The problem of contraception really boils down to how we should answer the question, "What's going on here?" about the act of sexual intercourse. It would be an error on the side of materiality to describe the act as the insertion of the penis into the vagina with subsequent ejaculation of semen therein. It is an error on the side of intentionality to describe the action as one of making love, for love is what is hoped for or intended. The same would be true of a description which called the action one of developing our personalities, expressing our affection, expressing our love.

An accurate description must include the relevant moral information. Each of the above intentional descriptions could have been said by a couple not married to each other. At the minimum then, an accurate description must include whether or not the sex act takes place within marriage.

The key question in the contraceptive controversy is whether or not an accurate description of marital intercourse also needs to include the circumstance of contraception; that is, is the morality of marital intercourse affected by the particular circumstance of contraception?

The entire weight of the teaching of the Church says that it is. A valid description of morally good marital sexual intercourse has to read something like this: "an act of sexual, mutually genital, intercourse which is intended to express marital feelings of affection and which does not positively exclude the possibility of procreation." I have deliberately omitted the word love, for to insert it would be begging the question, "When is sexual activity truly human love activity?"

The advocates of the total human act have not shown us that we can discard the "end and means approach." Certainly it is necessary to see an action in its totality; but it is equally necessary to limit that totality to the lowest meaningful level of material human activity. It is likewise necessary, when thinking about human actions to distinguish between the materiality and the intention, the physical means and the human intention. Without such distinctions we will have a fuzzy morality of good intentions in which the grand over-all purpose will be seen to specify all the lesser level acts. This "grand purpose morality" is clearly rejected by those who object to immoral acts in a war which may be "justified" on the whole; it must also be rejected in other areas of interpersonal relations including sex.

Applied to masturbation. A favorite application of good intentions while ignoring the morality of a specific and meaningful human action is found in the typical revisionists' treatment of masturbation. "One moralist maintains that masturbation for seminal analysis is not morally wrong. Just a human consideration, now buttressed by modern psychology, indicates that such an act is not the human act of masturbation. Even though the act has the same material substratum as masturbation, the human act in this case is an act of obtaining semen for analysis." The quotation is from Charles Curran.[8] He identifies the theologian as Bernard Haring, C.Ss.R., who proposed such an opinion as probable at Regis College, Toronto, July, 1963. However, this is word changing without reality changing. No longer is the act of self-stimulus for orgasm seen as masturbation. It is judged only on the basis of the overall purpose— semen analysis, fertility study, etc. If this is the case, then the act of self-stimulus for orgasm is not wrong in itself. Only when it is done for "selfish" reasons is it called by the negative value word of "masturbation." But if it is not selfish to obtain semen through voluntary orgasm instead of more bothersome methods, then how could it be termed selfish for a man to seek masturbatory relief from sexual tension rather than the more bothersome way of exercising sexual self-control?

The problem is that selfishness has been erroneously elevated to the sole criterion of morality. However, selfishness is a purely intentional aspect, and a morality of "selfishness" errs by neglecting the material (means) and stressing only the intention (end). This leaves me all the more convinced that all willful sexual activity is at the level of a meaningful human act whose morality is to be judged by the marriage covenant, not by other circumstances such as seminal analysis and relief of tensions.

A double standard. A further problem with the "total human act" approach is that it unwittingly establishes a new "double standard" in sexual morality. The individual act is seen as significant from the point of view of personal love but not significant from the point of view of procreation. In the latter case it would seem that this theory regards as significant only the totality of the marriage.

The error of this double standard can be illustrated by another violation of the marriage covenant. Is fidelity to be judged only by the totality of the marriage or by individual acts? If the spouses engage in occasional acts of mutual adultery (say a monthly spouse swapping club), are those spouses guilty of wrong-doing, of infidelity? Or should these individual acts be considered as an insignificant level of activity because the only significant level is the "total human act of the whole marriage" which was faithful most of the time? Granted the importance of the "most of the time" fidelity, does this make the individual act of adultery not significant, not objectively immoral?

284

Setting a double standard for the evaluation of individual sex acts is an erroneous solution to the problem. If it is argued that there is no double standard, that the individual sex act is not seen as important or significant from the point of view of personal love (just as it is not seen as significant from the point of view of procreation), two things need to be asked: 1) If it is not important, then why be concerned about not having it? 2) On what basis does one assume or prove that the individual sex act is not a significant total human act?

The assumption that the individual act of sexual intercourse does not need to be regarded as a significant level of human action, a total inter-personal human act in its own right may be the weakest point in this line of reasoning. From the most cursory survey of modern literature, theatre and movies, it would seem self-evident that sexual activity, in its individual acts, has caused and continues to cause so much concern that it needs to be considered always as significant. I cannot see how its significance is lessened by its commonness, nor can I agree that its basic significance is reduced by such obvious distortions as rape and prostitution. The reason why these are abhorrent is that we understand that in the order of creation the sex act is **meant to be** a significant inter-personal activity and that these are gross contradictions of the intended meaning.

The principle of the overriding right

Among the efforts to provide a way out of the apparent impasse between the doctrine of marital non-contraception and the difficulties of married couples in living it, some attempts have been made in the way of formulating general principles that would be applicable to moral behavior as a whole. These efforts keep the traditional moral doctrines intact but limit their applicability. This approach does not treat contraception as a unique case and then develop principles for it alone, principles which can cause havoc when applied to other areas of human life. Instead it starts with the treatment of contraception as one problem among many.

One such effort has been made by Denis E. Hurley, O.M.I., Archbishop of Durban, in his formulation of the principle of overriding right.[9] In his own words,

The principle of the overriding right boils down to this. Situations arise in life when a right clashes with a duty. For instance, when I am attacked, my right to life clashes with my duty to respect the life of another;

when I am in dire need, my right to life clashes with my duty to respect the property of another; when an infected organ threatens my life, my right to life clashes with my duty to preserve my bodily integrity; when I am bound by secrecy, my right to preserve the secret may clash with my duty to tell the truth. In all these cases we admit that the right predominates over the duty. This seems to indicate that we need to formulate the general principle underlying these various particular convictions. The formulation I proposed was "When the infringement of an obligation is necessarily involved in the exercise of a proportionate right, the obligation ceases." I suggested that this principle might be useful in solving the moral problems of contraception, sterilization, and transplantation of organs from living people.[10]

The principle had been criticized by Richard A. McCormick, S.J., who did not see it as the answer to the contraception dilemma.[11] My own criticism is that I think Archbishop Hurley makes a false antithesis between rights and duties. In each of the examples he uses, it would have been just as proper to speak of the clash between *my duty* "to preserve my own life" and *my duty* "to respect the life of another"; . . . *my duty* "to preserve my life and my duty to preserve my bodily integrity"; . . . *my duty* "to preserve the secret" and *my duty* "to tell the truth." I don't think this is just a matter of splitting hairs but of trying to put the contrasting elements of a human situation in terms of a common denominator so that evaluation can proceed more rationally and without the emotional connotations involved in the statement of a dilemma in terms of rights versus duties.

Archbishop Hurley criticizes the application of the principle of totality to the corporate person of the family. He wonders: is there "anything to prevent its being applied to the corporate person of the state? Unless it is very carefully formulated, it may very well become a principle of totalitarianism. We should beware, therefore, of invoking the principle of totality in respect of collectivities until we have discovered a foolproof formulation—which I suspect will be very hard to find."[12]

The same criticism is to be made of his own formulation, and he admits as much. Just at the principle of totality is accepted in theory by all but disputed in its application, so also with the principle of the overriding right (or duty). The only thing I find helpful about Archbishop Hurley's effort is that it doesn't want simply to change the teaching or to treat contraception as an isolated ethical problem. Rather he attempts to formulate a broad principle, which may or may not ever be applicable to the contraception question, but which at least recognizes that moral principles are universal in their application; i.e., you can't have one set of principles for birth control and another set for the rest of human actions.

The principle of compromise

Other efforts to arrive at a way out of the dilemma of many couples include formulations of a principle of compromise (Charles Curran)[13] and a principle of tension (Peter Chirico, SS.).[14] Both of these efforts share the value that they are not isolated treatments of the contraceptive problem but rather the formulation of wider principles that can be applied to a whole range of moral issues. On the other hand, both share the common difficulty of being an interpretation of how people **have made** their decisions rather than being a guide as to how one **should** make decisions. That is, neither attempt offers much practical guidance in forming one's conscience. Neither helps in the determination of right and wrong. They are principles insofar as they provide a guide for the analysis of moral guilt but not insofar as they provide a guide for determining the right and obligatory thing to do.[15]

Both Curran and Chirico lay emphasis on man's sinful condition in an imperfect world. They recognize that contraception is an evil, and they attempt to justify it on the basis of man's state of imperfection and other evils in his situation. However, such an emphasis can tend towards a mystique of sin, a feeling that there is really no point in developing the virtues because the more we sin, the more we have to admit our need of God and the more we feel his gracious, forgiving presence.

Proportionalism

The reigning attempt to justify contraception, fornication, homosexual acts, and masturbation is called proportionalism. Its principle theoretical advocate has been Richard A. McCormick, S.J., but Philip S. Keane, S.S., has openly applied this theory to various sexual acts so his book is our primary reference.[16] It should be noted that although his book is titled *Sexual Morality: A Catholic Perspective,* it is mistitled because it is not an authentic Catholic perspective on sexual behavior. The author openly dissents from official and traditional teaching. It initially carried the *Nihil Obstat* of Peter F. Chirico, S.S., mentioned above, and the *Imprimatur* of Archbishop Raymond G. Hunthausen of Seattle; however, the Vatican required the removal of the *Imprimatur* because the book is replete with moral error.

In essence, the theory of proprotionalism is a very fancy and erudite way of teaching that the end justifies the means although its advocates deny this. Says Keane: "But neither tradition nor newer Catholic theological patterns of thought would justify the use of a morally evil means to accomplish a good end" (46).

However, that tribute to traditional moral principles is neatly undermined by the key element in this theory, for the proportionalists say that no act is morally evil if you have a proportionate reason for doing it.

Rather obviously, this theory rejects the notion of universal negative moral absolutes, and such rejection makes it a form of situation ethics.

A key element in this theory is the distinction between **ontic** evil and **moral** evil. The proportionists would call having sex outside marriage, using contraception, and engaging in homosexual acts and masturbation examples of ontic evil. In the ideal world, they shouldn't happen. But in our world, say the proportionalists, the morality of doing such actions depends on your circumstances. If you have a proportionate reason for doing such an action, then, so they say, you can do it without being guilty of doing a moral evil. "Moral objectivity in sexual matters—and in all matters—is based on the interaction of fundamental moral values and the real concrete circumstances that are inherently part of people's actions. These circumstances may be so significant that they change the nature of the moral objectivity in given cases" (190). "Circumstances" is simply another word for "situation." Substitute "situation" for "circumstances" in the preceding quotation, and you will readily see that proportionalism is simply an erudite form of situation ethics.

Keane tries to argue that proportionalism is not a form of **subjectivism**: "Subjectivity does not make for proportionality unless the proportionality is there in the first place"(50). However, in a system that denies universal negative absolutes, the bottom line of subjectivism is quickly reached. It is somewhat comforting to learn that Keane personally thinks that there are a number of sexual actions that are *almost* always moral evils, but he cannot say an absolute "No, never, not under any circumstances." His list of almost always wrong "includes rape, prostitution, incest, the sexual abuse of children, and any form of sexual activity involving cruelty" (171). However, aside from prostitution and certain forms of incest among adults, the rest of the list involves various forms of assault.

288

When it comes to adultery, contraception—including early abortifacients such as the Pill and the IUD, fornication, and sodomy, whether marital or by homosexuals—well, it all depends on the circumstances.

Such are the opinions of one proportionalist. Another might have a different list. The point is that if the proportionalists claim a right to dissent from the clear teaching of the magisterium, as Keane does, then that same right extends to anyone who wants to dissent from any particular list of "near absolutes" or "justifying circumstances" drawn up by one or a group of dissenting proportionalists. Subjectivism is inherent to the whole theory.

In summary, the system of proportionalism evacuates the strength of the moral principle "You may not use morally evil means to attain a good end" by calling "not morally evil" all sorts of actions taught by Sacred Scripture, Tradition and the Church to be morally evil. By its overwhelming emphasis on circumstances, it earns the dishonored title of "situation ethics." And by its very nature as a system to provide a rationale for dissent from the authoritative teaching of the Church, it reduces itself ultimately to a radical subjectivism. It is hardly surprising that the *Imprimatur* was withdrawn from a book promoting both the theory and its practical applications as indicated above.

Students desiring a more thorough examination of proportionalism should study William May's *Contraception, Humanae Vitae and Catholic Moral Thought*.[17]

The Papal Birth Control Commission Report

Some of the previous controversies are reflected in the contrasting reports by members of the Papal Birth Control Commission; one could say that the core of the controversy is brought into sharp focus in one paragraph in the "position paper" signed by Revs. Joseph Fuchs, S.J., Canon Phillippe Delhaye, and Raymond Sigmond, O.P. It is inserted as an *Explanatory Note* in "Section III. *Intervention is well explained within the limits of the classic doctrine.*"

Not every act which proceeds from man is a complete human act. The subject of morality for St. Thomas is always the human act whose master is man (determined from a knowledge of the object or end). But this human act which has one moral specification can be composed of several particular acts **if these partial acts do not have some object in itself already morally specified.** And this is the case for matrimonial acts which are composed of several fertile and infertile acts; they constitute one totality because they are referred to one deliberate choice (emphasis added).[18]

I don't think it any sort of an oversimplification to say that the controversy is summed up in the last sentence. Is it true that all the matrimonial acts—fertile, naturally infertile, and deliberately infertile (contraceptive) are all just one totality? I have already shown why the advocates of contraception do not have a valid application of the principle of totality, and Paul VI specifically rejected the argument from totality in *Humanae Vitae* (n.14). In terms of their own philosophy, I would answer that **the individual sex act is not a partial act but in itself is already morally specified.** I believe that this specification is conferred first of all by the marriage covenant which makes of the sex act a sacramental encounter. As such, each and every exercise of the sex act in marriage has its own particular value and structure; each and every sex act is meaningful in itself, or at least meant to be meaningful in itself.

Aside from the inadequacy of the argument from totality in this regard, the majority reports carry other interesting features. Regarding abstinence, married people are said to recognize that they must abstain sometimes for lengthy periods of time because of various conditions of their lives including "professional necessities." However according to an alleged sense of the faithful, "condemnation of a couple to a long and often heroic abstinence as the means to regulate conception cannot be founded on the truth." Abstinence for professional reasons is acceptable; abstinence for religious reasons is questioned, while the debatable "sense of the faithful" seems to be accepted as determinative.

Another interesting feature is the analysis of the objective criteria of morality. *Gaudium et Spes* (n.51) states the necessity of objective criteria "based on the nature of the human person and his acts, which preserve the full sense of mutual self-giving and human procreation in the context of true love."

The majority papers twice list their interpretation of objective criteria. In the first instance they are given as follows:

3. *Objective criteria for the moral decision concerning methods.*

1) Infecundity of the act, when this is required by right reason, should be accomplished by an intervention with lesser inconveniences to the subject. Man can use his body in such a way as to render it more apt to attain its proper ends but he cannot manipulate his body and organs in an arbitrary fashion.
2) If nature ought to be perfected, then it should be perfected in the

manner more fitting and connatural.

3) On the other hand, this intervention ought to be done in a way more conformed to the expression of love and to respect for the dignity of the partner.

4) Finally, efficacity should also be considered. If there is privation of conception for the sake of procuring other goods, these must be sought in a more secure and apt manner. In this matter the rhythm method is very deficient. Besides only 60 per cent of women have a regular cycle.[19]

The second instance occurs in the final report.

1) The action must correspond to the nature of the person and of his acts so that the whole meaning of the mutual giving and of human procreation is kept in a context of true love.

2) The means which are chosen should have an effectiveness proportionate to the degree of right or necessity of averting a new conception temporarily or permanently.

3) The means to be chosen, where several are possible, is that which carries with it the least possible negative element, according to the concrete situation of the couple.

4) Then, in choosing concretely among means, much depends on what means may be available in a certain region or at a certain time or for a certain couple; and this may depend on the economic situation.[20]

In the first list, we are told (1) to choose the method most convenient, (2) to choose the method most fitting and connatural, (3) to be dignified and loving and (4) to be efficient.

In the second list, #1 is almost a verbatim quotation from *Gaudium et Spes*. As such it offers no interpretation; #2 says to be as efficient as you have to be; #3 says to choose the means that are the least obnoxious; #4 says to choose what you can afford from what's available.

First of all, how can these be considered any realistic sort of objective criteria? In the second list, numbers 2, 3 and 4 are really as much subjective as objective. The individual couple decide how efficient they want to be, what seems least negative and what they can afford. In the first list, "lesser inconveniences" is surely a subjective element. What is "fitting and connatural" and "conformed to the expression of love . . ." is begging the question. As such they offer no objective criteria. Lastly efficiency is both subjective and objective, but it has nothing to do with chastity. Argumentation which confuses objective with subjective and comes out with a totality that is in perfect agreement with hard-core pragmatism and then calls this the criterion for chastity surely does not recommend itself to a Christian people searching for truth and virtue.

The minority position paper signed by Revs. John Ford,S.J., Jan Visser, C.Ss.R., Marcelino Zalba, S.J., and Stanislaus de Lestapis, S.J., has been amply criticized. The primary criticism has been that their report skipped over the problem of birth control and focused only on the fact of the tradition and the teaching authority of the Church. The criticism is not wholly accurate. Their report is divided into two sections. Part I is concerned with the tradition and authority. Part II, almost as long as Part I, is concerned with the argumentation of the advocates of contraception. It includes references to the magisterium but is primarily concerned with philosophical and moral questions. One may disagree with the authors' treatment, but it is not fair to say that they have not handled the problem.

Furthermore, the minority paper of Ford and others raises some questions to which the position paper of Fuchs and others failed to give an adequate response. For example, the Ford paper alleges that the reasoning process of the contraception theorists logically opened the door to permitting non-marital relations, oral and anal intercourse, masturbation and direct sterilization. The Fuchs paper apparently accepts the charge about direct sterilization as falling under the objective criteria of efficiency. The other Fuchs' replies to Ford are worth looking at in quotation.[21]

b. The so-called new theory is extremely strict, as is that of the casuists, with regards to oral and anal copulation, *since it does not permit them.* For in these acts there is preserved neither the dignity of love nor the dignity of the spouse as human persons created according to the image of God (emphasis added).

The answer of Fuchs and company is inadequate because it is arbitrary, authoritarian, and reneges on their basic argument from totality. On what criterion is it established that in these acts the dignity of love and of the spouses is not preserved? If a couple thinks fellatio, for example, helps their interpersonal relationship, how can one who accepts contraception fault them? Or again, under the principle of totality, such acts would have to be seen as taking their virtue from the overall totality of all the sex acts. Of themselves, they would only be a partial act, not a true human act, so there would be no reason not to permit them.

c. Human intervention in the process of conception is not permitted, as we have said, unless it favors the stability of the family. Therefore there is no parity with the question of extra-marital relations. These relations lack the sense of complete and irrevocable giving and the possibility of normally accepting and educating children. These extra-marital relations contradict the norms already given concerning the habitual ordination of the institution of marriage towards offspring and love.

Yes, but why? If, under the principle of totality, individual sex acts are only partial human acts and get their specific morality from the totality of marriage acts, why become concerned about a "little" bit of adultery? The contraception theory has already admitted the acceptability of individual contraceptive acts which by definition "lack the sense of complete and irrevocable giving and the possibility of normally accepting and educating children." It sees these as imperfect acts made perfect by the overall fecundity and self-giving of the total marriage. If the authors of the theory had spoken with the prostitutes interviewed by one of the San Francisco papers some time ago, they would have become aware that a fair share of the clientele are happily married men whose wives are pregnant and who felt that for family stability it would be good to have relief from sexual tensions. Furthermore, it is very questionable whether a marriage which is positively contraceptive in some ninety percent of its sexual acts can really be described as having an "habitual ordination...towards offspring." Whether we like it or not, that is the real alternative to the traditional doctrine.

d. The affirmation of the permissibility of intervention [contraception] does not lead to an indulgent attitude towards masturbation since intervention preserves the intersubjectivity of sexuality (they shall be two in one flesh). Masturbation rather negates that intersubjectivity. Masturbation inasmuch as it turns the individual on himself and seeks mere egocentric satisfaction, totally perverts the essential intentionality of sexuality whereby man is directed out of himself towards another. For intercourse even with intervention is self-giving and heterosexual. If a question is to be raised about masturbation, this should be done independently of the question of the regulation of birth, even should the classic teaching on this matter remain in force.

The answer fails to meet the objection. First of all, the objection by Ford et al didn't raise the question of masturbation for egocentric satisfaction but rather as motivated by the same reasons given for the licitness of contraception. The objection envisioned a situation wherein physical illness might preclude any marital relations and where the sexual tensions that play such a big part in the contraceptive theory would build up. Masturbation would then be used to release sexual tension in order to have better family stability. If the marriage was usually characterized by normal marital relations, the theory that individual acts are only partial acts receiving their morality from the totality would certainly seem to allow the "partial" act of masturbation.

The statement that "intercourse even with intervention is self-giving and heterosexual" is most unfortunate. Obviously the contracepted marital act is heterosexual, but it is erroneous to say that it is self-giving. Contraceptive or open to life, it is simply naive to assume that all intercourse, even between married people, is self-giving. It is **meant to be** that, but the whole question of the morality of any given sex act in marriage is whether or not it is **actually** an act of self-giving. The contraceptive question itself can be stated in terms of self-giving: is an act which by positive intervention excludes any possibility of new life a real self-giving or is it rather a form of mutual enjoyment or even use? Does the reality (contraception) make a mockery of the sign (self-giving)?

It is almost humorous that the so-called Minority Report was criticized for its explanation of the theological authority of the Tradition because the most popular argument **for** contraception has been the reference to the alleged authority of the dissenters. However, the dissenters have no theological authority, and their individual arguments and principles lead to moral chaos.

Lastly, contrary to the gratuitous assertions by the so-called Majority Report of Fuchs et al. in 1966 against oral and anal sex, in the immediate aftermath of *Humanae Vitae* (1970), one dissenter openly proclaimed that dissent from *Humanae Vitae* **logically** entailed the acceptance of any imaginable sexual activity between two consenting persons or by one person—even bestiality.[22] And, as previously indicated, I showed in 1971 that the principles of Fr. Charles Curran are open to anything of mutual consent, even spouse-swapping[23], and no one has ever challenged that analysis. By 1977, the dissenters were openly showing that the acceptance of contraception entailed the acceptance of almost any imaginable behavior. A decade after Fuchs rejected oral and anal copulation, Keane was showing how proportionalism could accept such activity,[24] and Kosnik was arguing that there was no moral difference between homosexuals engaging in sodomy and married couples engaging in contraceptive intercourse.[25] If that isn't moral chaos, what is?

Summary

With the case for contraception based on an unacceptable extension of the principle of totality and upon naive and erroneous statements about the sex act itself, it should hardly be surprising that Pope Paul VI knew he had to reject the contraceptive conclusion. To overturn the tradition on the basis of arguments that could be faulted as easily as those presented him by members of the birth control commission would be theologically irresponsible.

On the other hand, one can object that the natural law reasoning advanced by Ford and by others has failed to convince many of its own value. To an objective onlooker who did not feel qualified to pass judgment on the values of the arguments of either side, it would seem that the reasoning advanced by each position met with criticism and rejection by the other. It would seem that the dispute could not be settled on the grounds of reasoning alone. With an apparent holdoff at the philosophical level (at least in the sense that each side's reasoning was unacceptable to the other), the issue needed clarification at some other level, the level of authority. Only an authoritative statement could break the apparent deadlock, and only through faith could this authoritative statement be accepted.

The function of *Humanae Vitae* was to reaffirm the doctrine of marital non-contraception. The prevailing consensus in the first twenty years after its issuance has been that it did not ask for that highest type of faith, the faith given a dogmatic definition. Rather it asked for faith that the universal "No" given to the contraceptive question raised in a number of ways over a period of some 1,900 years was guided by the Holy Spirit. (However, see Chapter 7, "Is the teaching infallible," for the case for the infallibility of the teaching affirmed by *Humanae Vitae*.) The issuance of *Humanae Vitae* said, at a minimum, that the presumption of divine guidance had to be given to the tradition both because of the importance of that tradition, theologically speaking, and because the advocates of contraception had failed to produce logical and theologically convincing reasons for change. Instead, their reasons introduced principles which threatened to and did create general moral havoc.

The agony of the promulgation of *Humanae Vitae* was that the advocates of contraception had produced argument after argument to win the emotions and sympathies of all men. No one can deny the dimensions of the question, the great concern about population, and the problems that go on in the homes of many married couples.

Everyone would like to alleviate these problems, especially if they could be alleviated by such a simple device as mechanical or chemical contraception. But instead of a teaching that would have been hailed as modern, scientific, and simple, we are left with a teaching that has no more sex appeal than the cross—folly to some and a stumbling block to others, but salvation to those who walk the narrow road with the Lord Jesus.

At the same time that I mention the cross and the narrow way, I would be negligent not to state that countless couples have discovered the truth of another teaching of Jesus, that His yoke is easy and His burden is light (Mt 11:30). These couples have found for themselves that natural family planning with its chaste periodic abstinence and friendly courtship during the fertile times has been a key to marital happiness and stability. Such couples and their families are, at the human level, the hope for the future of the Church in the West.

14

Different Approaches

I have stated repeatedly that theologies are different from the teaching of the Church and that different theologians or schools of thought have developed different ways of understanding the teaching of the Church. Thus it should come as no surprise that there are different ways of explaining the evil of marital contraception. Nor should it be any surprise that proponents of one approach may point to alleged weaknesses in another approach. As with adultery and fornication, God has not revealed precisely **why** it is evil to practice marital contraception; God has left plenty of work to be done by believing philosophers, teachers, and theologians.

Physical integrity

The traditional argument of longest standing focuses on the readily observed truth that the human male and female genital organs are by nature made for each other. This argument then notes that we are body and soul by nature, and we act against our very nature as human beings when we contradict our natural acts, especially those heavy with human significance. Contraception contradicts the natural integrity of the act of intercourse. Therefore it acts against the nature of the persons involved and is evil.

I make no claim that the above paragraph is an adequate explanation of the traditional argument, but it is realistic enough to point out at least one thing: the traditional argument focused upon the physiological integrity of sexual intercourse.

Pro-contraceptionists label the traditional argument "physicalist" and err in the opposite direction of "dualism." Dualists view the body as just a mechanical thing which the all-important mind uses for its various purposes. Thus, for the contraceptive dualist, the physical integrity of sexual intercourse counts for almost nothing; all that really matters is the person's intentions. Neither the physicalism of the traditional argument nor the dualism of the contraceptionists distinguish between marital or non-marital intercourse and contraception. While the traditional argument doesn't distinguish between marital and non-marital *contraception*, the reactionary dualism of the contraceptionists cannot distinguish between marital and non-marital *intercourse*. If all that really counts is your intention, then presumably you can have good enough intentions to engage—morally—in actions called adultery and fornication by Sacred Scripture. I think it bears repeating that just days before I wrote these pages, the following quotation appeared in one of the Cincinnati daily papers concerning Fr. Charles Curran, dean of the American dissent movement:

And while admitting to mistakes in church traditions, the hierarchy should admit the Bible contains mistakes, too, he said. For example, biblical teachings that sex outside of marriage is sinful must be seen as out of date—evidence of a less sophisticated age, Father Curran said.[1]

Since 1968, Fr. Curran has believed that he is above the Pope as an authority on morality; now he openly puts himself above Sacred Scripture. In normal times, his "above-Scripture" posture would enable every Catholic to recognize him as theologically absurd, and his pro-contraception views would be recognized as coming from the same mentality and as equally absurd. But in 1989, theological absurdity was still rampant, so one has to wonder if Fr. Curran did not guarantee himself further speaking engagements at allegedly "Catholic" colleges and symposia by putting himself above Scripture.

Critique

The quotation of Fr. Lorenzo Albacete is worth repeating in this context: "Let us keep in mind that the dissenting position is the natural product of the manualist moral theology of the preconciliar period."[2]

The pre-conciliar, textbook moral theology explained the evil of contraception in terms of a violation of the physical integrity of the marriage act. In fact, its explanations of the evil of contraception focused so much on how the barrier methods of contraception physically degraded the natural beauty of marital intercourse that such explanations were not equipped to respond to the evil of a *chemical* contraceptive whose action did not degrade the marriage act in a *physical* way.

The traditional "physical integrity" theology was so ill-prepared to handle the Pill that the real reason for the two papal birth control commissions set up by Pope John XXIII and Pope Paul VI was to study the Pill from a moral perspective.

My personal opinion is that there is much to be said for the traditional "physical integrity" arguments. It **is** true that the male and female sexual organs are made for each other. It **is** true that procreation of new life is a basic purpose of sexual intercourse. And the analogy between the lust of contraceptive behavior and the gluttony of the vomitorium still makes a lot of sense to many people today.

It also needs to be said that proponents of the physical integrity arguments were, by and large, not absolutists in its application. I think it is fair to say that all such proponents would allow true contraceptive measures such as a douche (but not abortifacient measures) to be used after rape. I think most such proponents would allow the use of a true contraceptive in the case of foreseeable possible rape. In my opinion, a logical conclusion of a strict physical integrity argument would not allow the use of a contraceptive even in the case of foreseeable rape. However, for at least the last three centuries, such logic has not been followed.[3] There has been increasing recognition that the subject of the Church's anti-contraception teaching is not biological intercourse which would be *coitus* in Latin but *marital* sexual intercourse, called *usus matrimonii* in *Casti Connubii* and *Humanae Vitae*. That is, there has been an increasing awareness that the physical integrity argument was becoming inadequate to convey the fullness of the Church's teaching on this subject.

The limitations of the strict physical integrity approach became apparent in the confusion caused initially by the Pill and by an apparent exception to allow a contraceptive defense against the consequences of rape. In theory, it also can make no distinction between contraception used within marriage and contraception used in acts that are already the grave matter of mortal sin such as adultery, fornication and incest. For these and other reasons, alternative approaches or theologies have been developed.

The contralife will

A considerably different approach has been published in *The Thomist* (July 1988) by Professor Germain Grisez and others.[4] This approach focuses on the will of the couple practicing contraception, and it notes that contraception involves a decision against one of creation's most basic human goods—human life itself. It involves a positive willing that this basic human good not be realized. This is a contralife will, the positive will that a possible person should never come into being.

The strongest statement of this approach draws a comparison between contraception and homicide.

Insofar as contraception is contralife, it is similar to deliberate homicide . . . An essential condition of the immorality of deliberate homicide is that it involves a contralife will (372) . . . Deliberate homicide is immoral primarily because the contralife will which it involves cannot be a loving heart . . . [The contraceptive will] is a practical (though not necessarily an emotional) hatred of the possible baby they project and reject . . . In short, contraception is similar to deliberate homicide, despite their important differences, precisely inasmuch as both involve a contralife *will*. Our thesis is that that the contralife will which contraception involves also is morally evil, although we do not claim that it is usually as evil as a homicidal will (373-374).

The authors of this approach recognize that a couple can use natural family planning (NFP) with a contralife will, and thus they take pains to distinguish the morally appropriate use of NFP from the contralife use of NFP.

The first element in the proper use of NFP is that there must be a good reason; just selfishly not wanting another baby or a general hatred of children would not be good reasons. However, couples could have good reasons not to have another child and still decide to use contraception.

Thus the key element in the contraceptive, contralife will is the "choice *to do something,* with the intent that the baby not be, as a means to a further end"(402), namely, that the baby not come into existence.

The authors contrast that positive action against the existence of the child with the choice "not to do something—namely, not to engage in possibly fertile sexual intercourse—with the intent that the bad consequences of the baby's coming to be will be avoided and with the *acceptance as side effects* of both the baby's not-coming-to-be and the bad consequences of his or her not-coming-to-be" (402).

Critique

In my opinion, Professor Grisez and associates have done a real service by showing the connection between contraception and abortion at the level of the individual person's will. They have shown that if a couple practice **any** form of birth control with a real intent against the very **being** of a new baby, then the abortion decision would be a "logical" next step in the event of a surprise pregnancy.

They have also shown the need for purity of intention for the morally good use of natural family planning. A couple needs sufficient reason to avoid pregnancy, and then their choice can be reasonable. Second, their reason will have to do with the avoiding what they think will be the bad effects of having another baby such as insufficient food, personal inability to care for more children, etc. The desire to avoid the bad effects and additional responsibilities is entirely different from the contralife will. The decision to avoid pregnancy through NFP, in order to be morally good, has to be a decision with regrets. "We would welcome another baby if . . . we weren't so exhausted educating the children we already have . . . if the wife's health were better . . ." The morally good NFP decision for avoiding pregnancy must have this clause: "but if You send us the unrequested gift of a new baby, we will do our best to care for him or her."

I find one of the most important distinctions made by the authors of the contralife approach to be this: the distinction between 1) *"not willing* that the good *be realized"* and 2) *"willing* that the good *not be realized"* (402, italics in original).

At first, that sounds like a distinction without difference, but there's more to it than appears at a first reading. In the context of family planning, it's the difference between 1) choosing not to pursue pregnancy and 2) setting your heart and will against the very existence of a new baby. The first choice must be based on good reasons and is made regretfully; the second choice comes from a hardened heart, involves a contralife will, and explains why pregnant women kill their unborn children.

On the other hand, it is not clear to me that the thesis of the contralife will explain the evil of contraception in the way claimed by its proponents. That is, while they acknowledge that "contraception is wrong for several reasons," they claim that "it is wrong *primarily and essentially* because it is contralife" (368, emphasis added). Thus any criticism of the contralife thesis is not of the general statement that contraception is contralife; rather any critique seeks to probe only the assertion that the contralife thesis offers the primary and essential reason why contraception is wrong.

First of all, there can be no quarrel with the general statement that contraception is contralife. Rather obviously, the whole purpose of contraceptive behavior is to prevent a new life from coming into being from behavior whose natural consequences make possible the procreation of new life. The only question is whether the contralife will as described by this thesis provides the primary and essential reason why contraception is wrong.

Second, the important difference between **taking positive action** to prevent conception through contraceptive behavior and **simply not acting** by not having intercourse is not unique to the contralife explanations. It is fundamental to every explanation of the difference between contraception and natural family planning. If you talk to a high school or college class about these things, you simply must establish the huge and irreconcilable difference between 1) doing something and then doing something else to contradict the first action and 2) not doing something in the first place. This huge difference must also be maintained in any teaching about the difference between killing the terminally ill (euthanasia) and not killing them but simply doing what you can to alleviate their suffering without doing everything possible to prolong their lives.

Third, it is not clear to me that every contralife will put into contraceptive practice is intrinsically evil. For example, take the case of a woman who is in danger of being raped, e.g., a public health nurse working in a notoriously high crime area. May she use a true contraceptive device—a diaphragm or cervical cap—to prevent pregnancy from rape? I think the common answer of orthodox Catholic theologians is that it would be morally permissible for her to use such a true contraceptive device.

Granted, she does not possess the contralife will envisioned by the contralife thesis which envisions contraceptive behavior between consenting persons. Nevertheless, she possesses a contralife will insofar as she could choose the contrary, i.e., to allow forced relations the possibility of causing a new life which she would carry to term.

I suppose that some may argue that in using a contraceptive device to protect against pregnancy she is not engaging in the human act of contraception. I think it's obvious that protection from the consequences of rape is hardly what the contraception controversy is all about; and I would certainly agree that such protective action is not the marital action considered and condemned by *Humanae Vitae*, etc. Nevertheless, I think it is still a premeditated contraceptive action, the human act of contraception. The authors of the contralife thesis allow post-rape contraceptive actions to seek

302

and destroy sperm on the grounds that they are the continuation of an act of unjust aggression, and I am not aware of any Catholic theologian who would disagree with that practice. However, such actions are, in fact, contraceptive in intent and would appear to be motivated by a contralife will—the will to take positive although limited steps against the coming-to-be of a new human being. Thus it appears to me that there is an inconsistency which does not assist the claim that contraception "is wrong primarily and essentially because it is contralife" (368).

An alternative argument might admit that this was a contraceptive action but that it did not entail a contralife will in the sense envisioned by the thesis of the contralife will. That serves to raise the question whether every contraceptive act—including that which is associated with voluntary intercourse—necessarily entails the contralife will against the very being of a new life. For example, John and Mary already have five children and they hope to have three or four more. However, Mary just hates the idea of having babies in the winter. So, they use contraceptives during the spring months. Recognizing that their barrier contraceptives may fail and that conception may result, they have already decided to accept any such baby as coming on God's timing, not theirs. They don't mind babies; what they refuse to tolerate is sexual abstinence, especially during the romantic spring months.

It is clear to me that John and Mary have an unchaste will; they refuse to practice sexual self control when necessary to avoid pregnancy. It is also clear that John and Mary have a contralife will insofar as every act of contraception is contra-new-life right here and now. However, it is not entirely clear that the will which is already disposed to accept any unplanned babies as gifts of God is the contralife will that can be even remotely compared to a homicidal will.

At the other end of the spectrum, it is not clear to me how the contralife thesis supports standard Catholic teaching against using contraceptives or masturbating as part of a strategy to **achieve** pregnancy when the couple has an infertility problem. In one case, a husband may be asked by a doctor to use a condom to collect sperm for analysis; the standard answer is the use of a perforated condom because then the basic symbolism of self-giving is preserved. More typically, the husband will be told to masturbate into a glass container to obtain sperm for analysis. Masturbation is wrong, even when done out of a pro-life will; and it seems to me that the traditional approach, Pope John Paul II's theology of the body, and the covenant theology of sex are more helpful in explaining the wrongness of masturbation for seminal analysis than the contralife approach.

In another case, a physician may hypothesize (guess) that infertility is caused by a cervical mucus reaction to sperm and may suggest using condoms for several months. It is difficult to see any sort of contralife will in this case, but the action itself degrades the symbolism of self-giving. (As an aside, I was once consulted by a couple in such a predicament. I could not counsel using condoms, so they abstained for six months, at the end of which they still did not become pregnant. Later conceptions did occur by using an over-the-counter cough syrup containing guaifenesin, an ingredient which liquifies bronchial mucus—and has the same effect on cervical mucus, thus sometimes assisting sperm migration.)

Which Commandment? If I am correct in thinking that the contralife thesis is not applicable to the cases of masturbation for seminal analysis and intercourse with condoms as part of a long range strategy for seeking pregnancy, it is because the authors of the contralife thesis readily acknowledge that their approach does not view contraception as a sexual sin. "Assuming contraception is a sin, it is not a sexual sin, such as masturbation, fornication, adultery, homosexual behavior, and so on" (369).

The authors also recognize that the contralife thesis departs from the approach taken by the Church in recent years. First of all they note that those who advocate contraception generally allege that the end homogenizes the means. "Homogenize" is a term I am using here to mean the allegation that a common purpose or end makes morally the same all the different means to get there. As I have shown in earlier chapters, that sort of thinking is absurd; it is utterly destructive of morality; it would be thrown out of any courtroom in the country; no parent would accept it from a child or from a business associate; but it still remains one of the most popular "arguments" against Catholic teaching about the immorality of using unnatural forms of birth control. The specific allegation that the end homogenizes the means regarding birth control is that there is no moral difference between using contraceptive behavior or NFP within marriage when both have the common purpose of preventing pregnancy.

Whether you are writing a book or discussing these matters in a high school religion class, you have to be able to show the difference between married couples using contraceptives and using NFP. The authors of the contralife thesis put it this way:

> Confronted with this argument [about the homogenization of the means], one defending the tradition either must show that contraception differs morally from NFP precisely in its relationship to the value of life, or must avoid grounding the immorality of contraception in its contralife character (367).

Then they note that they take the former approach while recent Church teaching has taken the latter approach. The authors of the contralife thesis believe that while "contraception is wrong for several reasons, it is wrong primarily and essentially because it is contralife" (368).

In other words, if you want to use the Ten Commandments for classifying all the different types of sins, the authors of the contralife thesis see contraception as a type of sin against the Fifth Commandment, "Thou shalt not kill," which includes not just murder but all other sins against life. On the other hand, the teaching of the Popes and theologians has generally treated the sin of contraception as a sin against the Sixth Commandment, "Thou shalt not commit adultery," which includes not just adultery but fornication, incest and all other sins of impurity. The three major papal teachings, *Casti Connubii, Humanae Vitae*, and *Familiaris Consortio* have all taught the necessity of the virtue of chastity in order to practice natural family planning, and that would indicate that they have seen the sin of contraception to be primarily a sin of unchastity.

Furthermore, Pope John Paul II has repeatedly taught that the evil of contraception is rooted in its violation of the marital meaning of conjugal relations. For example: "In the conjugal act it is not licit to separate the unitive aspect from the procreative aspect, *because both one and the other pertain to the intimate truth of the conjugal act.*" This truth has to do with the mutual gift of self to the other, and contraception violates that gift-meaning of marital relations. "Such a violation of the interior order of conjugal union, which is rooted in the very order of the person, **constitutes the essential evil of the contraceptive act.**"[5] In short, John Paul II locates the evil of marital contraception in the very nature of the sex act, not in the contralife will of the contraceptors.

Si aliquis. While acknowledging that recent Catholic teaching and theology have not treated the sin of contraception primarily as a sin against the Fifth Commandment, the authors of the contralife thesis believe that their thesis does have a basis in an older theological tradition embodied in a Thirteenth century document known by its first two Latin words, "Si aliquis"—"If anyone." Their translation reads as follows:

> If anyone for the sake of fulfilling sexual desire or with premeditated hatred does something to a man or to a woman, or gives something to drink, so that he cannot generate, or she cannot conceive, or offspring be born, let it be held as homicide (366).

It is recognized by everyone that *Si aliquis* does not say that contraception is homicide. However, there is a difference of opinion as to what it says about the immorality of contraception. The authors of the contralife thesis believe that "to regard contraception as homicide is regarded is not only to make it clear that contraception is wrong, but also to point to its being contralife as the reason why it is wrong" (366). On the other hand, others have pointed out that *Si aliquis* is part of a body of teaching called "The Penitentials," which guided priests in assigning penances for different types of sins. Thus, in this opinion, what *Si aliquis* was saying was that when someone confessed a sin of contraception, the priest should give him or her the same kind of penance he would give to someone confessing a sin of homicide.

* * *

Certainly the advocate of one approach is not an impartial evaluator of another approach, and that has to be applied to myself. I have the highest personal regard for the authors of the contralife thesis, and I regard them not only as friends of the Church but as personal friends (the three whom I know personally) and advisors. However, while we are in 100 percent agreement with the teaching of the Catholic Church against marital contraception, we find ourselves in respectful disagreement as to the ultimate evil of marital contraception.

This is not unhealthy, and such differences provide utterly no reason for not accepting the teaching which I think many orthodox Catholic theologians now believe has been proposed infallibly by the universal ordinary magisterium of the Church. As I have pointed out repeatedly, different reasons have been proposed as to the ultimate evil of adultery, fornication and sodomy, but such differences do not detract in the least from the teaching of the Church that these actions are immoral.

Different starting points. One of the reasons for different approaches is undoubtedly different starting points. The theology of the body of Pope John Paul II reflects a system of philosophy called phenomenology, a system in which the Pope was trained and an expert years before becoming Pope. Three of the scholars who have authored the contralife thesis are professional philosophers and are deeply rooted in natural law philosophy.

My own background is considerably less academic. Working as a parish lay theologian in the mid-Sixties, I was on the firing line or the hot seat. I was simply giving instructions in the Catholic faith, transmitting the Church's teaching on birth control, and looking for a more personalist way to explain that teaching. I needed a way of explaining the evil of marital contraception that would allow my married students to see that contraceptive intercourse contradicted what they themselves had done in "committing marriage." I am in a roughly comparable situation as I write this in 1990, for the people I serve—married couples using natural family planning—want an easily understood explanation of the Christian Tradition on birth control. In short, my starting point has been the search for a very usable theology of sex that can be understood by ordinary people.

Agreement within differences. It also needs to be pointed out that there are basic agreements between the different approaches. For example, it is hard to imagine anyone disagreeing that very frequently the decision to use contraception stems from a contralife will. However the question remains as to whether the contralife will is *always* present among those using contraception and whether such a will constitutes the precise or ultimate evil of contraception.

Similarly, the covenant theology of sex has been spelled out since 1967, and I have never received a challenge to its basic thesis that God intends sex to be at least implicitly a renewal of the marriage covenant. However, some may disagree that such a thesis explains the precise or ultimate evil of contraception.

Perhaps the truth is that the evil of all of these actions— adultery, contraception, fornication, and sodomy—is so enormous and such an affront to the holiness of God that no single approach will ever capture the ultimate evil but that almost every approach will capture some of the evil of these actions.

That immediately raises the question as to how actions that are taken so much for granted today can be such serious and horrible evils, and that is the question which I addressed in Section III dealing with pastoral considerations.

Part V

The Historical-Traditional Teaching

15

Biblical Foundations

In his Apostolic Exhortation on the Family (*Familiaris Consortio*) Pope John Paul II extended a "pressing invitation" to theologians "to commit themselves to the task of illustrating ever more clearly the biblical foundations, the ethical grounds and the personalistic reasons behind this doctrine" [on birth regulation affirmed by *Humanae Vitae*] (n.31).

The Holy Father did not explicitly call for explanations of particular verses of Sacred Scripture that prove a particular point of moral teaching, and I think he avoided such an approach for two reasons. First, he has to deal with the theological milieu within the Church, and for whatever reasons, the "proof-text" approach has not been much in favor since the mid-Sixties. Secondly, I think the Holy Father wants it recognized that the doctrine of marital non-contraception is grounded upon the entire biblical teaching about sex and marriage, not just upon an isolated text, and I tried to develop such an approach in Chapter 1, "A Covenant Theology of Sex."

Nevertheless, the Onan account cannot be ignored. This, of course, refers to the account in Genesis 38 in which Onan practices *coitus interruptus* (withdrawal and ejaculation) and is killed by God for doing so. For centuries, the most common form of contraceptive behavior was *coitus interruptus,* and Onanism was the general term for all forms of contraception. However, during the birth control debate of the mid-Sixties, the anti-contraceptive interpretation of the Onan account was challenged by some of those who thought the Church could and should change its teaching to allow contraceptive behaviors. They have alleged that the sin of Onan was not his contraceptive behavior but only his failure to do his duty to his deceased brother, i.e., a sin against charity or justice. Thus this chapter of Sacred Scripture needs a closer review.

The Onan account: Genesis 38

In Genesis 38, the sacred author relates the account of Onan, one of the sons of Judah. In this account, Onan follows an ancient Near Eastern custom known as the Law of the Levirate. According to this custom, if a married man died before he had children, his brother was obliged to marry the widow; their children would be considered as the deceased brother's children.

Onan's brother died, so Onan married the widow Tamar. However, he practiced the contraceptive behavior called withdrawal and deliberately ejaculated outside the vagina. "When he went in to his brother's wife, he spilled his seed on the ground, lest he should give offspring to his brother. But what he did was evil in the sight of the Lord, and He slew him also" (Gn 38:9-10).

Interpretation. What is the meaning of this text? How should it be interpreted?

The first rule of biblical interpretation is that a text must be considered in itself. In the case at hand, the key sentence is, "What he did was evil in the sight of the Lord, and He slew him also."

Second, the text must be interpreted in the immediate context of the entire account, namely, all of Chapter 38.

Third, it must also be seen in the wider context of other biblical condemnations for violations of the Law of the Levirate.

Fourth, the text must be interpreted in the context of related teaching.

Fifth, but not least, the text must be seen in the context of the Church's traditional teaching over the centuries lest a person think that the Holy Spirit became operative only today in His guidance of the Church.

1. Biblical scholar Manuel Miguens has pointed out that a close examination of the text shows that God condemned Onan for the specific action he performed, not for his anti-Levirate intentions. He notes that the translation "he spilled his seed on the ground" fails to do full justice to the Hebrew expression. The Hebrew verb *shichet* never means to spill or waste. Rather, it means to act perversely. The text also makes it clear that his perverse action was related towards the ground, not against his brother. "...His perversion or corruption consists in his action itself, not precisely in the result and goal of his act . . . In a strict interpretation the text says that what was evil in the sight of the Lord was what Onan actually did (*asher asah*); the emphasis in this sentence of verse 10 does not fall on what he intended to achieve, but on what he **did**."[1]

2. In the context of the entire chapter, Genesis 38, it is clear that Onan is only one of three persons who violated the Levirate. His

father, Judah, and his younger brother, Shelah, also violated the Levirate law, and Judah openly admitted his guilt in verse 26. After Tamar had tricked Judah into having intercourse with her and getting her pregnant, thus getting Tamar accused of harlotry, he admitted, "She is in the right rather than I. This comes of my not giving her to my son Shelah to be his wife."

When three people are guilty of the same crime but only one of them receives the death penalty from God, common sense requires that we ask if that one did something the others did not do. The answer is obvious: only Onan went through the motions of the covenantal act of intercourse but then defrauded its purpose and meaning; only Onan engaged in the contraceptive behavior of withdrawal.

3. The traditional anti-contraception interpretation is reinforced by the wider context of the Bible. The Law of the Levirate and the punishment for violators are spelled out in Deuteronomy 25:5-10. An aggrieved widow could bring the offending brother-in-law before the elders; if he still refused to do his duty, she could "take the sandal off his foot, spit in his face, and pronounce the following words. 'This is what we do to the man who does not restore his brother's house,' and the man shall be surnamed in Israel, House-of-the-Unshod" (Dt 25:9-10). That would be embarrassing, but it is a far cry from the death penalty meted out by God to Onan. It must be remembered, also, that Deuteronomy has no hesitation about the death penalty for serious sexual sins: chapter 22:22-23 prescribes the death penalty for adultery and for rape. Thus the context of Deuteronomy provides utterly no support for the Levirate-only interpretation of Genesis 38:10. On the contrary, it supports the traditional interpretation that the crime for which Onan received the death penalty was his directly contraceptive behavior.

The anti-contraception interpretation is given further indirect support by the only instance in the New Testament when God metes out an immediate death penalty. In Acts 5:1-11, Ananias and Sapphira went through the motions of a covenantal act but defrauded it, and both were stricken dead after they each engaged in this deception. Onan's responsibility to Tamar was a covenantal obligation; so was the obligation of Ananias and Sapphira to be honest with the apostles. The act of marital intercourse is also a covenantal act intended by the Creator to be a renewal of the faith and caring love pledged at marriage. The Onan account directly supports the Christian Tradition that we are obliged not to defraud this covenantal act by contraception, and the Ananias-Sapphira account shows how seriously God takes the defrauding of covenantal acts.

4. The text must be interpreted in the context of the rest of the Bible's teaching about love, marriage and sexuality. It can be stated without fear of contradiction that the teaching against unnatural forms of birth control is in perfect harmony with the Biblical teaching against immoral forms of sex such as sodomy, fornication, and adultery. It is also in the most perfect harmony with the biblical teaching on love, marriage and discipleship.

On the other hand, the intellectual acceptance of the unnatural sexual behavior of Onan, deliberate ejaculation outside the vagina, has disastrous consequences. Acceptance of one unnatural sexual act as morally permissible provides a sexual logic that cannot say "no" to any imaginable sexual behavior between consenting persons.[2] It is most unpleasant to think about these logical consequences; the number who follow out the sexual logic are still relatively few, but their number is growing. At least since 1964, homosexuals have been calling theirs a preferred way of life because their sexual activity is 100% effective as a method of birth control.

In the New Testament, it is possible that the Greek "pharmakeia" may refer to the birth control issue. "Pharmakeia" in general was the mixing of various potions for secret purposes, and it is known that potions were mixed in the first century A.D. to prevent or stop a pregnancy. The typical translation as "sorcery" may not reveal all of the specific practices condemned by the New Testament. In all three of the passages in which it appears, it is in a context condemning sexual immorality; two of the three passages also condemn murder (Gal 5:19-26; Rev 9:21, 21:8). Thus it is very possible that there are three New Testament passages condemning the use of the products of "pharmakeia" for birth control purposes. Interestingly enough, there were the same questions about those potions as about the modern pharmaceutical product, the Pill: abortifacient or contraceptive? However, since the Christian Tradition used the term "Onanism" for condemning all forms of unnatural birth control throughout the centuries, our primary emphasis has been on the Onan text.

5. For all practical purposes, the way in which the Church has understood the Scriptures throughout the centuries is the most important part of interpretation. It is this which enables us to

distinguish between Old Testament affirmations of the natural moral law ("Thou shalt not commit adultery") and mere uncleanness rules, between discipline open to change and truth that is unchangeable. For example, St. Paul spends more words on women's veils in church (1 Cor 11) than he does on sodomy (Romans 1), but the Church has always held that sodomy is a very serious offense against the natural moral law while the matter of veils has been seen only as a matter of discipline.

There is no question that the anti-contraceptive interpretation of Genesis 38 has been *the* interpretation over the centuries, and not just by Roman Catholics. A rabbi in the third century of the Christian era noted "the deadly sin of Onan," and in the context the sin is clearly his contraceptive behavior.[3] John Calvin noted that Onan had sinned both by defrauding his deceased brother and by his act of coitus interruptus.[4] Martin Luther never allowed contraception of any sort but instead noted that the purposes of marriage were for husband and wife "to live together, to be fruitful, to beget children, to nourish them, and to bring them up to the glory of God."[5]

The strength and universality of the anti-contraceptive interpretation of Genesis 38 is reflected in the American Protestant Christianity of the late nineteenth century. In response to the neo-Malthusian efforts to promote unnatural methods of birth control, American Protestants passed a federal law against the manufacture, sale, or possession of contraceptives in the District of Columbia and federal territories; it also forbade the mailing of contraceptives or advertisements for them. Passed on March 3, 1873 and known as the Comstock law after its chief backer, Anthony Comstock, a young Protestant reformer, it was followed by many similar state laws. Catholics in the United States at this time were a small and quiet minority. There is no doubt about it: the anti-contraception laws of the late 19th century were passed by Protestants for a largely Protestant America. It was also during this same period that the states passed anti-abortion legislation.

The strength and universality of the anti-contraceptive interpretation of Genesis 38 by Protestants is further illustrated by Charles Provan in his 1989 book, *The Bible and Birth Control.*[6] About one-third of this little book consists of quotations from 66 Protestant theologians in favor of the anti-contraception interpretation of the Onan account; it also contains a list of 33 additional Protestant theologians who spoke or wrote to support the anti-contraception interpretation of Genesis 38 but without quotation. The author introduces this section by noting that in his extensive research "we have found not one orthodox theologian to defend Birth Control before the 1900s. NOT ONE! On the other hand, we have found that many highly regarded Protestant theologians were enthusiastically opposed to it, all the way back to the very beginning of the Reformation."[6] Provan's quotations indicate that Calvin regarded Onanism as a form of homocide (68); Luther regarded Onanism as "far more atrocious than incest and adultery. We call it unchastity, yes, a Sodomitic sin" (81).

The Catholic anti-contraceptive interpretation of Genesis 38 has been so strong and so universal that it is difficult to separate it from the received teaching. Pope Pius XI quoted St. Augustine's anti-contraceptive interpretation in *Casti Connubii* (part 4). Nevertheless, no claims are being made that the Church has defined the interpretation of Genesis 38, and Pope Paul VI did not base *Humanae Vitae* upon Genesis 38. In fact, he did not even directly refer to it, only indirectly through his reference to *Casti Connubii.*

Commentary

I think it is clear that Onan sinned in two ways—both against the law of the Levirate and against the natural moral law. The sacred author of Genesis 38 makes it clear that God is punishing Onan for one or both of these offenses, but are they both equal or is one more serious than the other? And if one is more serious, which one? Christian common sense requires us to say that in levying capital punishment, God did it to punish a sin that was truly serious, a sin that was a grave violation of the natural moral law.

Three factors militate mightily against the interpretation that Onan was punished only for his violation of the law of the Levirate and not for his contraceptive behavior or that both were equally serious.

1. There is utterly no support for the Levirate-only interpretation either in Scripture or Tradition. As noted above, Deuteronomy 25:9-10 treats such a violation as a relatively minor offense, not a grave offense against the natural moral law.

2. No one claims that the law of the Levirate is part of the natural moral law. Far from that, it was simply part of the ancient Near Eastern customs that had developed to insure the survival of family lines.

3. There has been an almost universal tradition, at least in the Christian era, that interpreted the punished sin as the sin of contraceptive behavior which was seen as a sin against the natural moral law.

Realistically, I think we have in the Levirate-only interpretation a classic example of an interpretation for expediency. Given the weight of centuries of teaching against Onanism, the simplest way to undermine the teaching at the popular level is to say it was based on a misinterpretation of Scripture. Of course, such a statement cannot be proved, but just the mere assertion was all that was necessary for many who had those itching ears spoken of by St. Paul (2 Tim 4:3).

When I was doing my initial research for the forerunner of this book in late 1968, I spent several hours in a seminary library searching for scholarly articles that would explain the switch in interpretation. Frustrated at not finding a single reference, I phoned a scripture professor for help. However, in response to my inquiry for references, he gave me none but simply told me, "We just don't *do* it that way anymore." It would be hard to imagine a reply that gave more evidence that the Levirate-only interpretation is without merit, an interpretation of expediency.

However, what may seem to be an expedient interpretation is very uncharitable to God. Such interpreters have God punishing only one man—when three were guilty of violating the Levirate; they have God giving capital punishment to Onan for an offense that did not violate either the natural moral law or revealed positive law, and which was regarded as a light offense by the sacred author of Deuteronomy 25. They make God to be arbitrary and capricious, and that is truly outrageous. Expediency is a poor principle in politics; it is disastrous and irreligious in theology.

The weakest thing that can be said about the Onan account from the perspective of one who believes the doctrine of marital non-contraception is true is that it played a part in forming the universal Christian teaching against contraception.[7] The strongest thing that can be said is that in Genesis 38 God revealed part of the natural moral law against contraception.[8]

I think there are sound reasons for the latter conviction, but the teaching Church has chosen not to make that statement at the present time. However, even without such a definition, I think it is clear that once you review the extreme weakness of the Levirate-only interpretation, the Onan account contributes to the overall biblical foundations for the Church's teaching about sexuality, including contraceptive behaviors. If it is not definitive, it is at least illustrative and supportive.

Other biblical foundations

In the development of the covenant theology of sex in the first part of this book, I noted that by a process of elimination we arrive at the conclusion that God intends that sexual intercourse is meant to be a marriage act which is open to the transmission of life at least in the sense of not being deliberately and positively closed to the transmission of life. That process of elimination is a review of the biblical treatment of other sexual behaviors. I will review them in alphabetical order.

Adultery. Every Christian and Jew knows that adultery is forbidden in the Ten Commandments (Ex 20:14). However, precisely what constitutes adultery was debated in the time of Christ as it is today. Jesus utterly shocked even his disciples by teaching that remarriage after a divorce constitutes living in adultery (Mt 5:31-32; 19:3-12; Mk 10:2-12; Lk 16:18; 1 Cor 7:10-11.) Countless words have been written about the text in Matthew, "except for sexual immorality" (Mt 5:32; 19:9). *Porneia* is sometimes translated as "adultery," but it is a far broader term, so I have used "sexual immorality."

This brief review is no place to discuss the scholarly articles, books, and prejudices on this text. However, two brief comments may be in order. First, it is clear that the Pharisees were trying to bait Jesus, to get him to take sides in a dispute. "The school of Rabbi Shammai regarded adultery and moral misconduct as the only acceptable grounds for divorce; but the school of Rabbi Hillel held that all kinds of reasons, even quite trivial ones, were sufficient grounds for legal divorce, and it was this second interpretation of the law which was in fact practiced."[9]

Second, it is equally clear from Mt 19:10 that his disciples were surprised to learn that Jesus had not sided with either school of thought. Note that for anyone to say today that sexual immorality on the part of one spouse is moral grounds for divorce and remarriage is to side with Rabbi Shammai, and that is precisely what Jesus did not do.

I have found helpful the summary of E. Schillebeeckx who was orthodox when he wrote in 1963. First I will quote Matthew 19:8-

12 because he refers to these verses, and then I will quote his summary comments.

8. He said to them: "Moses permitted you to put away your wives because of the hardness of your hearts, but it was not so in the beginning. 9. And I say to you, that whoever puts away his wife, except for sexual immorality and marries another, commits adultery; and he who marries a woman who has been divorced commits adultery." 10. His disciples said to him, "If that is the case of a man with his wife, it is not expedient to marry." 11. And he said, "Not all can accept this teaching, but those to whom it has been given. 12. For there are eunuchs who were born so from their mother's womb; and there are eunuchs who were made so by men; and there are eunuchs who have made themselves so for the sake of the kingdom of heaven. Let him accept it who can."

After discussing and rejecting the idea that the "except for *porneia*" clause is a true exception to the permanence of marriage, Schillebeeckx concludes:

The whole passage would have become quite meaningless if the evangelist had included this exception in the verse that followed. What is more, if Mt 19:9 is taken to mean that Jesus was siding with the followers of the school of Shammai, who permitted divorce on grounds of adultery, then the astonishment expressed in the apostles' answer would be incomprehensible—"then it is not expedient to marry" (19:10). Their astonishment is only explicable if Christ in fact rejected all possibility of the dissolution of marriage . . . Christ not only expressly condemned divorce (showing, in other words, that the indissolubility of marriage is a moral imperative); he also said that any divorce which might possibly take place had no effect whatever on the bond of marriage itself (pointing out, in other words, that the indissolubility of marriage is an objective bond).[10]

It may be worth noting that as soon as the dissenters had won the battle for public opinion on the contraception issue, they began a heavy campaign for the Church to change its teaching to allow divorce and remarriage. Also, though precise statistics are not available, it is generalized common knowledge that as soon as contraception was widely embraced by Catholic couples, the Catholic divorce rate began rising horrendously.[11]

Bestiality. Sexual relations with animals is not a subject of common concern today. Nevertheless, it is related to the *Humanae Vitae* "debate" because at least one outspoken dissenter noted that dissent from *Humanae Vitae* logically entailed rejection of the teaching against bestiality, as follows:

It seems unreasonable to maintain that there is a difference between allowing a husband and wife to use the condom and allowing them to have anal intercourse since neither fulfills the natural law doctrine's requirement of insemination in the vagina. Likewise there is no difference between using the condom and coitus interruptus [withdrawal] or any of the other so-called sins prohibited under the doctrine such as masturbation, homosexuality, and bestiality.[12]

For the record, bestiality is condemned in Sacred Scripture. "Anyone who lies with an animal shall be put to death" (Ex. 22:18); "If a man has carnal relations with an animal, the man shall be put to death, and the animal shall be slain. If a woman goes up to any animal to mate with it, the woman and the animal shall be slain..." (Lv 20:15-16).

Fornication and prostitution. Fornication is the biblical and theological word for sexual relations between two people who are both unmarried. If one person is married, and the other single, it is adultery for each of them. Sacred Scripture makes little distinction between fornication and prostitution; the Greek *porneia* can mean prostitution as well as fornication. Interestingly, St. Jerome in his famous translation from Greek to Latin known as the Latin Vulgate, translated *porneia* as *fornicatio*. Some of those who dissent from the entire Christian Tradition on sexuality try to allege or infer that St. Jerome didn't handle this translation very well and that only prostitution is really condemned by Sacred Scripture, but such an allegation remains simply that—wishful thinking that can never be proved.[13]

I suggest that the reason Sacred Scripture makes few distinctions between fornication and prostitution is because they are essentially the same. The Greek *porneia* came from a word meaning "to sell,"[14] and the selling of self is what is involved in both fornication and prostitution. It is more obvious in the latter, but endless articles about fornication have made it very clear that the fornicating girl or woman is selling herself. She submits to sex in order to receive attention or to keep a man. What she gets is more precious to her than money, namely, his time and attention. Generally she fears that if she did not give sex, she would not receive his time and attention. Furthermore, as I pointed out in more detail in Chapter 2 dealing with sex outside of marriage, both fornication and prostitution are equally dishonest and fail equally to be a renewal of the marriage covenant. Perhaps it is time to learn from the Scriptures and to cease making huge distinctions between these two immoral actions. And perhaps prostitution is actually the lesser evil because the transaction is more open and "honest."

For the record, fornication is condemned repeatedly in the New Testament. "Do not err: neither fornicators, nor idolaters, nor adulterers, nor the effeminate, nor sodomites, nor thieves, nor the covetous, nor drunkards, nor the evil-tongued, nor the greedy will possess the kingdom of God" (1 Cor 6:9). See also Gal 5:19, Eph 5:5, Col 3:5, Heb 13:4, and Rev 2:14. Both 1 Cor 6:9 and Heb 13:4 distinguish between fornication and adultery. Prostitution is singled out in 1 Cor 6:15: "Do you not know that your bodies are members of Christ? Shall I then take the members of Christ and make them members of a prostitute? By no means!!"

In short, there are ample biblical foundations for the Christian Tradition against both fornication and prostitution.

Incest. We commonly think of incest as sexual relations between parents and children or between the children themselves, but the Old Testament had a wider view. Starting with the general injunction, "None of you shall approach a close relative to have sexual intercourse with her" (Lv 18:6), the sacred author of Leviticus continues to spell out a large number of possible relationships (Lv 18:7-18). Some of the major incestuous relationships are included in a list of twelve curses in Deuteronomy (Dt 27:20, 22-23).

I am not aware of anyone who is publicly advocating that the Church should change its teaching on incest, but there is nothing in the principles of the major dissenters that can absolutely prohibit incest between consenting adults. If the dissenters were honest and responsible, they would be openly admitting that any alleged "justification" for marital contraception is at the same time the "justification" for incest.

Masturbation. Masturbation refers to the practice of sexual stimulation with intent of achieving orgasm completely apart from completed genital-genital, heterosexual intercourse. Masturbation can be either solitary or mutual, either heterosexual or homosexual, and of the latter, either between men or between women.

Thus *coitus interruptus* or Onanism is one form of masturbation, and the Onan account (Gen 38:9-10) has been traditionally seen as a biblical foundation for the universal Catholic Tradition against masturbation. Fellatio and cunnilingus, aside from foreplay to complete heterosexual relations, are both forms of mutual masturbation.

Intellectual acceptance of masturbation in any one of its forms logically entails the intellectual acceptance of the principle that it is morally permissible for a man or woman to deliberately seek orgasm apart from genital-genital intercourse including ejaculation outside the vagina. However, if you accept that principle, then you are logically required to accept as morally permissible any and all forms of masturbation including homosexual sex. The Catholic Church is consistent in its rejection of masturbation as well as contraception and sodomy.

Sodomy. The fate of the cities of Sodom and Gomorrah after the homosexuals of Sodom tried to abuse the guests of Lot has been traditionally seen as a divine condemnation of homosexual behavior (Gen 19:1-29). Homosexual sex is specifically forbidden in Leviticus 18:22 and is awarded the death penalty in Leviticus 20:13. It is described as against nature and the results of shameful lust in Romans 1:24-27, and as an action excluding one from the kingdom of God in 1 Corinthians 6:10. However, all of this is ignored as irrelevant by those who advocate the moral permissibility of homosexual acts as is explained below.

Foundations, not proof-texts

The wisdom of Pope John Paul II's call for biblical foundations rather than biblical proofs is apparent when you consider how the dissenters handle the anti-sodomy texts. They dismiss the Genesis sodomy account as irrelevant to homosexual behavior because, they say, the sin of the men of Sodom was their inhospitality, not their homosexual intentions. The death penalty of Leviticus for homosexual acts is explained away as being a cultic not an ethical judgment. What that means is that it was allegedly only a judgment against homosexual acts because of a supposed connection with the Canaanite fertility rites.[15] The fact that such rites involved male-female cultic prostitution is less important than the more obvious fact that what was so horrible about the Canaanites is *what they were doing*. That is, what they were doing was objectively wrong; it wasn't wrong just because they were Canaanites; and what they were doing disfigured their religion; cultic prostitution isn't condemned by Scripture just because it was practiced by the Canaanites but because it always and everywhere disfigures authentic religion. However, that distinction escapes the dissenters who are on the alert for any possible way to explain away the force of texts which support the traditional Catholic teaching of the natural moral law.

The texts of St. Paul against homosexual activity are neatly undermined by the allegation that St. Paul wasn't condemning homosexual behavior in itself, only promiscuous sodomy or sodomy by those who deliberately choose to be homosexuals. Dissenters also attempt to undermine the force of the Pauline texts by stating that St. Paul knew nothing about inversion regarded "either as an inherited trait or a condition fixed in childhood,"[16] thus removing St. Paul's condemnation from those whose sexual orientation is not heterosexual. Such an interpretation, of course, eliminates God from the picture; it forgets that God is not subject to the limitation of human knowledge and that God can use the limited knowledge of a sacred writer to convey a truly universal judgment. It also ignores the fact that heterosexual sex outside of marriage is also condemned.

However, such sentences as the immediately preceding two are examples of rising to the bait offered by the dissenters, of arguing the meaning of particular texts. Such arguments then invite counter-arguments, and such overall argumentation gives the general impression that the debaters think that the problem will be solved by biblical scholarship, if not tomorrow, then perhaps in 20 or 50 years.

Such endless debate illustrates the wisdom of God in not leaving us just a Book but rather a living Church with a living teaching authority—which we call the **magisterium**.

The treatment of the anti-sodomy texts is also helpful in considering the Onan account. Sometimes I have wished that there was a clear and unmistakable teaching in the New Testament against all unnatural forms of birth control. However, it wouldn't make any difference. You could scarcely ask for more explicit anti-sodomy texts than those in Romans 1 and 1 Cor 6:9, and the dissenters dismiss them. The same thing would happen to any additional texts condemning unnatural forms of birth control. As indicated in the preceding chapter, the dean of American dissenters from *Humanae Vitae* has blithely dismissed all biblical condemnations of sex outside of marriage as mistaken and simply out-of-date.

If the twentieth century debate on sexuality has made one thing clear, it is the absolute need for a living magisterium. The magisterium has spoken authoritatively and clearly about birth regulation. "He that has ears to hear, let him listen" (Mt 11:15).

16

Ecclesial Documentation

The purpose of this chapter is to put in one place some of the primary texts by which the magisterium of the Roman Catholic Church has taught on the issue of birth control. There are also a few texts from other sources for purposes of illustration.

Two things must be noted. First of all, the reading of a few paragraphs from a document is no substitute for reading the entire document; this is particularly the case when the document is devoted to the issues of marriage, the family, love and sexuality as is the case with *Casti Connubii, Humanae Vitae* and *Familiaris Consortio*. Secondly, this chapter is greatly supplemented by Chapter 6, "Forming a Correct Conscience," which contains many quotations from talks by Pope John Paul II.

Before and around *Casti Connubii*

The modern, well organized and well funded effort to promote unnatural methods of birth control had its start in 1914 when Margaret Sanger established her National Birth Control League in the United States. Very early in her birth control career, perhaps even before 1914, she teamed up with one of her many lovers, Havelock Ellis, to promote contraception in England. Their activity definitely had an effect which is reflected in the following two statements from the Church of England's Lambeth conference of 1920.

Lambeth committee report, 1920

We recognize that the physical union of husband and wife has a sacramental value by which is expressed and strengthened the love that the one ought to have for the other. At the same time we urge the paramount importance in married life of deliberate and thoughtful self-control and we feel called upon to utter an earnest warning against the use of any unnatural means by which conception is frustrated. We are aware that many persons of undoubted sincerity, whose opinions are entitled to respect, do not share this view, considering the whole matter as chiefly a question of expediency to be determined on medical, financial and social grounds. This contention we cannot admit, as we believe that the question cannot be separated from the moral and religious issues involved.[1]

Anglican Lambeth Conference, Resolution 68, 1920

The Conference, while declining to lay down rules which will meet the needs of every abnormal case, regards with grave concern the spread in modern society of theories and practices hostile to the family. We utter an emphatic warning against the use of unnatural means for the avoidance of conception.[2]

However, the pressures continued within the Anglican Church, and ten years later the Church of England broke what had been a unanimous front by Christian churches against unnatural forms of birth control.

Anglican Lambeth Conference, 14 August 1930

Where there is a clearly felt moral obligation to limit or avoid parenthood, the method must be decided on Christian principles. The primary and obvious method is complete abstinence from intercourse (as far as may be necessary) in a life of discipleship and self-control lived in the power of the Holy Spirit. Nevertheless in those cases where there is such a clearly felt moral obligation to limit or avoid parenthood, and where there is a morally sound reason for avoiding complete abstinence, the Conference agrees that other methods may be used, provided that this is done in the light of the same Christian principles. The Conference records its strong condemnation of the use of any methods of conception-control from motives of selfishness, luxury, or mere convenience.[3]

This was preceded by a committee report which recognized the previously strong Anglican teaching "that the use of preventive methods is in all cases unlawful for a Christian."[4] It was followed four and one-half months later by the historic response of Pope Pius XI in *Casti Connubii*.

Casti Connubii, 31 December 1930

Since, therefore, openly departing from the uninterrupted Christian tradition, some recently have judged it possible solemnly to declare another doctrine regarding this question, the Catholic Church, to whom God has entrusted the defense of the integrity and purity of morals, standing erect in the midst of the moral ruin which surrounds her, in order that she may preserve the chastity of the nuptial union from being defiled by this foul stain, raises her voice in token of her divine ambassadorship and through our mouth proclaims anew: any use whatsoever of matrimony exercised in such a way that the act is deliberately frustrated in its natural power to generate life is an offense against the law of God and of nature, and those who indulge in such are branded with the guilt of a grave sin.[5]

The Federal Council of Churches (USA), 1931

Within a few months, the Anglican break was echoed in the United States. On 21 March 1931, the majority of a committee of the Federal Council of Churches, a forerunner of today's National Council of Churches, endorsed "the careful and restrained use of contraceptives by married people," at the same time admitting that "serious evils, such as extramarital sex relations, may be increased by general knowledge of contraceptives."[6]

The reaction was immediate and provides a good reflection of that day's leadership opinion. Note the tone of an editorial in the *Washington Post,* 22 March 1931:

Carried to its logical conclusion, the committee's report if carried into effect would sound the death-knell of marriage as a holy institution, by establishing degrading practices which would encourage indiscriminate immorality. The suggestion that the use of legalized contraceptives would be "careful and restrained" is preposterous.

It is the misfortune of the churches that they are too often misused by visionaries for the promotion of "reforms" in fields foreign to religion. The departures from Christian teachings are astounding in many cases, leaving the beholder aghast at the willingness of some churches to discard the ancient injunction to teach "Christ and Him crucified." If the churches are to become organizations for political and "scientific" propaganda, they should be honest and reject the Bible, scoff at Christ as an obsolete and unscientific teacher, and strike out boldly as champions of politics and science as modern substitutes for the old-time religion.[7]

Strong criticism followed in Protestant church monthlies and from leading spokesmen. I have quoted them elsewhere[8] and repeat them here because I think they give a certain flavor, a certain understanding of the strength of the traditional Christian teaching against unnatural forms of birth control. I found most of them in a booklet written about 1939 by "J.F.N.," almost certainly Bishop John Francis Noll.[9]

Birth Control, as popularly understood today and involving the use of contraceptives, is one of the most repugnant of modern aberrations, representing a 20th century renewal of pagan bankruptcy. —*Dr. Walter A. Maier, Concordia Lutheran Theological Seminary, St. Louis*

The whole disgusting movement rests on the assumption of man's sameness with the brutes. —*Bishop Warren Candler, Methodist Episcopal Church South, 13 April 1931*

It is of prime significance that the present agitation for birth control occurs at a period which is notorious for looseness in sexual morality. This fact creates suspicion as to the motives for the agitation, and should warn true-minded men and women against the surrender of themselves as tools for unholy purposes. The duty of the Church is now possibly more than ever to proclaim the holiness of the sexual relation as well as temperance in the use thereof. There will then be no need for birth control. —*Dr. F. H. Knubel, President, Lutheran Church in America,* New York Times, *21 March 1931, 13.*

A second line of attack was directed towards the Federal Council of Churches for allowing such a committee endorsement.

Its recent pronouncement on birth control should be enough reason, if there were no other, to withdraw from the support of that body, which declares that it speaks for the Presbyterian and other Protestant churches in ex cathedra pronouncements. —The Presbyterian, *2 April 1931*

Its deliverance on the matter of birth control has no authorization from any churches supporting it, and what it has said I regard as most unfortunate, not to use any stronger words. It certainly does not represent the Methodist Church, and I doubt if it represents any other Protestant Church in what it has said on this subject.—*Bishop Warren Candler, letter to* The Atlantic Constitution *11 April 1931. First sentence carried in* New York Times, *12 April 1931, 1.*

According to the J.F.N. booklet, "the Northern Baptist Convention at Kansas City and the General Synod of the Reformed Church also denounced the Federal Council for its surrender to human weakness," and *The Lutheran* of 2 April 1931 noted that "the report of the Federal Council should have been labeled 'The Opinions of Twenty-Eight Persons Belonging to Portions of the Christian Church Commonly Called Protestant.' "

The teaching of Pope Pius XII

Fathers John Ford and Gerald Kelly note that Pope Pius XII "reiterated his teaching about contraceptive acts and contraceptive sterilization" many times during his reign (1939-1958), but his 1951 address to Italian midwives is generally referred to as his primary statement.[10]

Contraception against natural and divine law; 1951

Our predecessor, Pius XI, of happy memory, in his encyclical *Casti Connubii,* December 31, 1930, solemnly proclaimed anew the fundamental law governing the marital act and conjugal relations: that any attempt on the part of married people to deprive this act of its inherent force and to impede the procreation of new life, either in the performance of the act itself or in the course of the development of its natural consequences, is immoral; and no alleged "indication" or need can convert an intrinsically immoral act into a moral and lawful one.

This precept is as valid today as it was yesterday; and it will be the same tomorrow and always, because it does not imply a precept of the human law but is the expression of a law which is natural and divine.

In the same address to the Italian midwives, Pius XII also condemned **sexual sterilization**:

Direct sterilization—that is, sterilization which aims, either as a means or as an end at rendering procreation impossible—is a grave violation of the moral law and therefore illicit. Even public authority has no right, whatever "indication" it may use as an excuse, to permit it, and much less to prescribe it or have it done to the detriment of innocent human beings. This principle has already been enunciated in the above-mentioned encyclical of Pius XI on marriage. Therefore, ten years ago, when sterilization came to be more widely used, the Holy See found it necessary to make an explicit and public declaration that direct sterilization, whether permanent or temporary, of the man or of the woman, is illicit, and this by virtue of the natural law, from which the Church herself, as you well know, has no power to dispense.

Concerning the Pill

Ford and Kelly also noted that in the month before he died in 1958, Pius XII applied the same moral principles "to the new anovulant drugs: the use of such drugs to prevent conception is direct sterilization; their use for therapeutic purposes, with incidental loss of fertility, can be squared with the principle of the double effect and thus be justified."[11]

Two things should be noted about that statement. First of all, Pius XII was probably unaware in 1958 that the Pill could act as an early abortion agent; he was viewing it strictly as an ovulation suppressing drug. Secondly, (and I write here from my experience in the field of natural family planning and consultation with physicians) the use of the Pill to "regularize" couples is nonsense, not therapy, for ovulation is not regulated but is generally suppressed, and the irregularity is usually worse after the Pill is discontinued.

The teaching of Pope John XXIII

In the third year of his pontificate Pope John XXIII issued *Mater et Magistra,* an encyclical "On Recent Developments of the Social Question in the Light of Christian Teaching."[12] The occasion was the 70th anniversary of *Rerum Novarum*, the landmark social encyclical by Pope Leo XIII in 1891. Paragraphs 185-199 constitute a section titled "Population Increase and Economic Development." The issue of birth regulation is addressed, and the principles of Catholic teaching are reaffirmed.

The Terms of the Problem

188. Now to tell the truth, the interrelationships on a global scale between the number of births and available resources are such that we can infer grave difficulties in this matter do not arise at present, nor will in the immediate future. The arguments advanced in this connection are so inconclusive and controversial that nothing certain can be drawn from them.

189. Besides, God in His goodness and wisdom has, on the one hand, provided nature with almost inexhaustible productive capacity; and, on the other hand, has endowed man with such ingenuity that, by using suitable means, he can apply nature's resources to the needs and requirements of existence. Accordingly, that the question posed may be clearly resolved, a course of action is not indeed to be followed whereby, contrary to the moral law laid down by God, procreative function also is violated.

Respect for the Laws of Life

193. In this connection, we strongly affirm that human life is transmitted and propagated through the instrumentality of the family which rests on marriage, one and indissoluble, and, so far as Christians are concerned, elevated to the dignity of a sacrament. Because the life of man is passed on to other men deliberately and knowingly, it therefore follows that this

should be done in accord with the most sacred, permanent, inviolate prescriptions of God. Everyone without exception is bound to recognize and observe these laws. Wherefore, in this matter, no one is permitted to use methods and procedures which may indeed be permissible to check the life of plants and animals.

194. Indeed, all must regard the life of man as sacred, since from its inception, it requires the action of God the Creator. Those who depart from this plan of God not only offend His divine majesty and dishonor themselves and the human race, but they also weaken the inner fiber of the commonwealth.

Creation for Man's Benefit

196. When God, as we read in the book of Genesis, imparted human nature to our first parents, He assigned them two tasks, one of which complements the other. For He first directed: "Be fruitful and multiply,"(Gen 1:28) and then immediately added: "Fill the earth and subdue it."

197. The second of these tasks, far from anticipating a destruction of goods, rather assigns them to the service of human life.

198. Accordingly, with great sadness we note two conflicting trends: on the one hand, the scarcity of goods is vaguely described as such that the life of men reportedly is in danger of perishing from misery and hunger; on the other hand, the recent discoveries of science, technical advances, and economic productivity are transformed into means whereby the human race is led toward ruin and a horrible death.

199. Now the provident God has bestowed upon humanity sufficient goods wherewith to bear with dignity the burdens associated with procreation of children. But this task will be difficult or even impossible if men, straying from the right road and with a perverse outlook, use the means mentioned above in a manner contrary to human reason or to their social nature, and hence, contrary to the directives of God Himself.

The teaching of Vatican II

It is sometimes alleged that the Second Vatican Council (1962-1965) changed Catholic teaching about the purposes of sex and marriage and opened the way for a change in the Church's teaching on birth control. Neither allegation is true, but each has a story that helps to keep the false allegations alive.

The purposes of marriage

It is true that Vatican II did not use the traditional terminology about the primary and secondary purposes of marriage, but section 50 of *Gaudium et Spes* carries an unmistakable emphasis on the procreation and education of children. The following is the entire text of Section 50 plus my paragraph numbering, 50.1, 50.2, etc.[13]

THE FRUITFULNESS OF MARRIAGE

50.1 Marriage and conjugal love are by their nature ordained toward the begetting and educating of children. Children are really the supreme gift of marriage and contribute very substantially to the welfare of their parents. The God Himself who said, "It is not good for man to be alone" (Gen. 2:18) and "who made man from the beginning male and female" (Mt. 19:4), wished to share with man a certain special participation in His own creative work. Thus He blessed male and female, saying: "Increase and multiply" (Gen. 1:28).

50.2 Hence, while not making the other purposes of matrimony of less account, the true practice of conjugal love, and the whole meaning of the family life which results from it, have this aim: that the couple be ready with stout hearts to cooperate with the love of the Creator and the Savior, who through them will enlarge and enrich His own family day by day.

50.3 Parents should regard as their proper mission the task of transmitting human life and educating those to whom it has been transmitted. They should realize that they are thereby cooperators with the love of God the Creator, and are, so to speak, the interpreters of that love. Thus they will fulfill their task with human and Christian responsibility. With docile reverence toward God, they will come to the right decision by common counsel and effort.

50.4 They will thoughtfully take into account both their own welfare and that of their children, those already born and those which may be foreseen. For this accounting they will reckon with both the material and the spiritual conditions of the times as well as of their state in life. Finally, they will consult the interests of the family group, of temporal society, and of the Church herself.

50.5 The parents themselves should ultimately make this judgment, in the sight of God. But in their manner of acting, spouses should be aware that they cannot proceed arbitrarily. They must always be governed according to a conscience dutifully conformed to the divine law itself, and should be submissive toward the Church's teaching office, which authentically interprets that law in the light of the gospel. That divine law reveals and protects the integral meaning of conjugal love, and impels it toward a truly human fulfillment.

50.6 Thus, trusting in divine Providence and refining the spirit of sacrifice, married Christians glorify the Creator and strive toward fulfillment in Christ when, with a generous human and Christian sense of responsibility, they acquit themselves of the duty to procreate. Among the couples who fulfill their God-given task in this way, those merit special mention who with wise and common deliberation, and with a gallant heart, undertake to bring up suitably even a relatively large family.

50.7 Marriage to be sure is not instituted solely for procreation. Rather, its very nature as an unbreakable compact between persons, and the welfare of the children, both demand that the mutual love of the spouses, too, be embodied in a rightly ordered manner, that it grow and ripen. Therefore, marriage persists as a whole manner and communion of life, and maintains its value and indissolubility, even when offspring are lacking—despite, rather often, the very intense desire of the couple.

The reaffirmation of *Casti Connubii*

It is also true that the text of *Gaudium et Spes* did not directly quote or reaffirm *Casti Connubii*. However, the **complete** text did two things which can only be interpreted as reaffirming the received teaching, and the complete text includes the footnotes. Official Catholic teaching documents simply cannot be interpreted accurately aside from any footnote references, and bishops and theologians know this—both in writing the document and in interpreting them. Thus, the first thing to be noted is that at the end of paragraph 51.4, footnote number 14 refers to *Casti Connubii,* the address of Pius XII to the midwives, and the address of Paul VI on June 23, 1964. These references were inserted at the specific insistence of Pope Paul VI.[14]

The second thing to note are the references to the objective nature of sexual acts, the criterion that such acts must "preserve the full sense of mutual self-giving and human procreation in the control of true love," (51.4 below) and the need for the virtue of marital chastity. Just the last element would preclude any openness to contraception because, by definition, if it is permissible to engage in contraceptive behaviors, there is no need for the virtue of marital chastity between the spouses. I strongly recommend reading all of sections 47-52 of *Gaudium et Spes*; what follows is the entire text of section 51.

HARMONIZING CONJUGAL LOVE WITH RESPECT FOR HUMAN LIFE

51.1 This Council realizes that certain modern conditions often keep couples from arranging their married lives harmoniously, and that they find themselves in circumstances where at least temporarily the size of their families should not be increased. As a result, the faithful exercise of love and the full intimacy of their lives are hard to maintain. But where the intimacy of married life is broken off, it is not rare for its faithfulness to be imperiled and its quality of fruitfulness ruined. For then the upbringing of the children and the courage to accept new ones are both endangered.

51.2 To these problems there are those who presume to offer dishonorable solutions. Indeed, they do not recoil from the taking of life. But the Church issues the reminder that a true contradiction cannot exist between the divine laws pertaining to the transmission of life and those pertaining to the fostering of authentic conjugal love.

51.3 For God, the Lord of life, has conferred on men the surpassing ministry of safeguarding life—a ministry which must be fulfilled in a manner which is worthy of man. Therefore from the moment of its conception life must be guarded with the greatest care, while abortion and infanticide are unspeakable crimes. The sexual characteristics of man and the human faculty of reproduction wonderfully exceed the dispositions of lower forms of life. Hence the acts themselves which are proper to conjugal love and which are exercised in accord with genuine human dignity must be honored with great reverence.

51.4 Therefore when there is question of harmonizing conjugal love with the responsible transmission of life, the moral aspect of any procedure does not depend solely on sincere intentions or on an evaluation of motives. It must be determined by objective standards. These, based on the nature of the human person and his acts, preserve the full sense of mutual self-giving and human procreation in the context of true love. Such a goal cannot be achieved unless the virtue of conjugal chastity is sincerely practiced. Relying on these principles, sons of the Church may not undertake methods of regulating procreation which are found blameworthy by the teaching authority of the Church in its unfolding of the divine law. [Original footnote no. 14 occurs here.]

51.5 Everyone should be persuaded that human life and the task of transmitting it are not realities bound up with this world alone. Hence they cannot be measured or perceived only in terms of it, but always have a bearing on the eternal destiny of men.

Footnote 14: *Cf. Pius XI, encyclical letter "Casti Connubii":* AAS 22 (1930), Denz-Schoen., 3716-3718; Pius XII, Allocutio Conventui Unionis Italicae inter Obstetrices, Oct. 29, 1951: AAS 43 (1951), pp. 835-854; Paul VI, address to a group of cardinals, June 23, 1964: AAS 56 (1964), pp. 581-589. Certain questions which need further and more careful investigation have been handed over, at the command of the Supreme Pontiff, to a commission for the study of population, family, and births, in order that, after it fulfills its function, the Supreme Pontiff may pass judgment. With the doctrine of the magisterium in this state, this holy Synod does not intend to propose immediately concrete solutions.[15]

The teaching of Pope Paul VI

The legacy of Pope Paul VI will always be associated with his landmark encyclical, *Humanae Vitae*. However one might be mystified by his prudence in assigning a signer of the pro-contraceptive Majority Report, Mgr. Lambruschini, as his initial spokesman for the encyclical, and whatever one might think of the prudence of his decision to suppress the Tridentine Rite, the fact remains that he will be known as the author of *Humanae Vitae*. To some it is a stumbling block, but to an ever increasing number it is the prophetic work that is a sign that the papacy enjoys the special guidance of the Holy Spirit.

Sections 10, 11 and 14 of *Humanae Vitae* dated 25 July 1968 are quoted in full below.[16] The usual short quotation is the last sentence of section 11, but I have also included section 10 because of its teaching about conforming to the very nature of marital sexuality. Lastly, section 14 is quoted because 1) it completes section 11, 2) it answers the argument from totality, and 3) it figures heavily in the theology of Fr. Ermenegildo Lio as reviewed in Chapter 7.

Responsible parenthood

10. Hence, conjugal love requires in both husband and wife an awareness of their mission of "responsible parenthood," which today is rightly insisted upon, and which also must be correctly understood. It must be considered under its various legitimate and interrelated aspects.

In relation to the biological processes, responsible parenthood means knowing and respecting the functions of these processes; the intellect discovers in the power of giving life biological laws that are part of the human person.

In relation to the tendencies of instinct and of the passions, responsible parenthood means the necessary mastery that reason and will must exercise over them.

In relation to physical, economic, psychological and social conditions, responsible parenthood is exercised either by the thoughtfully made and generous decision to raise a large family, or by the decision, made for grave motives and with respect for the moral law, to avoid a new birth for the time being, or even for an indeterminate period.

Responsible parenthood also and above all implies a more profound relationship to the objective moral order established by God, and of which a right conscience is the faithful interpreter. The responsible exercise of parenthood implies, therefore, that husband and wife recognize fully their duties toward God, toward themselves, toward the family and toward society, in a correct hierarchy of values.

In the task of transmitting life, they are not free, therefore, to proceed at will, as if they could determine with complete autonomy the right paths to follow; but they must conform their actions to the creative intention of God, expressed in the very nature of marriage and of its acts, and manifested by the constant teaching of the Church.

Respect for the nature and finality of the marriage act

11. These acts, by which husband and wife are united in chaste intimacy and by means of which human life is transmitted, are, as the Council recalled, "good and honorable," and they do not cease to be legitimate if, for causes independent of the will of husband and wife, they are foreseen to be infertile, because they remain ordained to expressing and strengthening their union. In fact, as experience bears witness, not every act of marital intercourse is followed by a new life. God has wisely arranged natural laws and rhythms of fertility, which already of themselves bring about a separation in the succession of births. But the Church, calling men back to the observance of the norms of the natural law, interpreted by her constant teaching, teaches that each and every marriage act must remain open to the transmission of life.

Unlawful means of birth regulation

14. In conformity with these fundamental elements of the human and Christian vision of marriage, we must once again declare that the direct interruption of the generative process already begun, and, above all, directly willed and procured abortion, even if for therapeutic reasons, are to be absolutely excluded as lawful means of birth regulation.

Also, to be excluded, as the Magisterium of the Church has on a number of occasions declared, is direct sterilization, whether perpetual or temporary, whether of the man or of the woman.

Similarly excluded is every action that, either in anticipation of the conjugal act or in its accomplishment or in the development of its natural

334

consequences, would have as an end or as a means, to render procreation impossible.

And to justify conjugal acts made intentionally infertile one cannot invoke as valid reasons the lesser evil, or the fact that when taken together with the fertile acts already performed or to follow later, such acts would coalesce into a whole and hence would share in one and the same moral goodness. In truth, if it is sometimes permissible to tolerate a lesser moral evil in order to avoid a greater evil or to promote a greater good, it is not permissible, not even for the gravest reasons, to do evil so that good may follow therefrom. One may not, in other words, make into the object of a positive act of the will something that is intrinsically disordered and hence unworthy of the human person, even when the intention is to safeguard or promote individual, family or social goods. Consequently it is an error to think that a conjugal act which is deliberately made infertile and so is intrinsically wrong could be made right by a fertile conjugal life considered as a whole.

The teaching of Pope John Paul II in *Familiaris Consortio*

Pope John Paul II has been unceasing in his efforts to teach the truth about the demands of love, and Chapter 6 records parts of over 40 talks in which he has reaffirmed the teaching of *Humanae Vitae*. However, *Familiaris Consortio,* issued on 22 November 1981, remains his chief, formal teaching document. It is somewhat long because it addresses the whole range of family issues. Of particular interest to the student of the birth control and marital chastity issue is the part titled "Serving Life," sections 28-41.[17] (The section numbers (e.g.,n.29) are part of the official text, but the headings and the individual paragraph numbers (e.g., 29.1 are not.)

Reaffirming the traditional teaching

29.1 Precisely because the love of husband and wife is a unique participation in the mystery of life and of the love of God Himself, the Church knows that she has received the special mission of guarding and protecting the lofty dignity of marriage and the most serious responsibility of the transmission of human life.

29.2 Thus, in continuity with the living tradition of the ecclesial community throughout history, the recent Second Vatican Council and the magisterium of my predecessor Paul VI, expressed above all in the encyclical *Humanae Vitae*, have handed on to our times a truly prophetic proclamation, which reaffirms and reproposes with clarity the church's teaching and norm, always old yet always new, regarding marriage and regarding the transmission of human life.

29.3 For this reason the synod Fathers made the following declaration at their last assembly:

29.4 "This sacred synod, gathered together with the successor of Peter in the unity of faith, firmly holds what has been set forth in the Second Vatican Council (cf. *Gaudium et Spes,* 50) and afterward in the encyclical *Humanae Vitae,* particularly that love between husband and wife must be fully human, exclusive and open to new life (*Humanae Vitae,* 11; cf. 9, 12)."

The call to theologians

31.1 The church is certainly aware of the many complex problems which couples in many countries face today in their task of transmitting life in a responsible way. She also recognizes the serious problem of population growth in the form it has taken in many parts of the world and its moral implications.

31.2 However, she holds that consideration in depth of all the aspects of these problems offers a new and stronger confirmation of the importance of the authentic teaching on birth regulation reproposed in the Second Vatican Council and in the encyclical *Humanae Vitae.*

31.3 For this reason, together with the synod Fathers I feel it is my duty to extend a pressing invitation to theologians, asking them to unite their efforts in order to collaborate with the hierarchical magisterium and to commit themselves to the task of illustrating ever more clearly the biblical foundations, the ethical grounds and the personalistic reasons behind this doctrine. Thus it will be possible, in the context of an organic exposition, to render the teaching of the church on this fundamental question truly accessible to all people of good will, fostering a daily more enlightened and profound understanding of it: in this way God's plan will be ever more completely fulfilled for the salvation of humanity and for the glory of the Creator.

31.4 A united effort by theologians in this regard, inspired by a convinced adherence to the magisterium, which is the one authentic guide for the people of God, is particularly urgent for reasons that include the close link between Catholic teaching on this matter and the view of the human person that the church proposes: doubt or error in the field of marriage or the family involves obscuring to a serious extent the integral truth about the human person in a cultural situation that is already so often confused and contradictory. In fulfillment of their specific role theologians are called upon to provide enlightenment and a deeper understanding, and their contribution is of incomparable value and represents a unique and highly meritorious service to the family and humanity.

On the difference between contraception and NFP

32.4 When couples, by means of recourse to contraception, separate these two meanings that God the creator has inscribed in the being of man and woman and in the dynamism of their sexual communion, they act as "arbiters" of the divine plan and they "manipulate" and degrade human sexuality and with it themselves and their married partner by altering its value of "total" self-giving. Thus the innate language that expresses the total reciprocal self-giving of husband and wife is overlaid, through contraception, by an objectively contradictory language, namely, that of not giving oneself totally to the other. This leads not only to a positive refusal to be open to life, but also to a falsification of the inner truth of conjugal love, which is called upon to give itself in personal totality.

32.5 When, instead, by means of recourse to periods of infertility, the couple respect the inseparable connection between the unitive and pro-creative meanings of human sexuality, they are acting as "ministers" of God's plan and they "benefit from" their sexuality according to the original dynamism of "total" self-giving, without manipulation or alteration.

32.6 In the light of the experience of many couples and of the data provided by the different human sciences, theological reflection is able to perceive and is called to study further the difference, both anthropological and moral, between contraception and recourse to the rhythm of the cycle: It is a difference which is much wider and deeper than is usually thought, one which involves in the final analysis two irreconcilable concepts of the human person and of human sexuality. The choice of the natural rhythms involves accepting the cycle of the person, that is, the woman, and thereby accepting dialogue, reciprocal respect, shared responsibility and self-control . . . In this way sexuality is respected and promoted in its truly and fully human dimension and is never "used" as an "object" that, by breaking the personal unity of soul and body, strikes at God's creation itself at the level of the deepest interaction of nature and person.

Education in chastity

33.4 And so the church never ceases to exhort and encourage all to resolve whatever conjugal difficulties may arise without ever falsifying or compromising the truth: she is convinced that there can be no true contradiction between the divine law on transmitting life and that on fostering authentic married love. Accordingly, the concrete pedagogy of the church must always remain linked with her doctrine and never be separated from it. With the same conviction as my predecessor, I therefore repeat: "To diminish in no way the saving teaching of Christ constitutes an eminent form of charity for souls."

33.5 On the other hand, authentic ecclesial pedagogy displays its realism and wisdom only by making a tenacious and courageous effort to create and uphold all the human conditions—psychological, moral and spiritual—indispensable for understanding and living the moral value and norm.

33.6 There is no doubt that these conditions must include persistence and patience, humility and strength of mind, filial trust in God and in his grace, and frequent recourse to prayer and to the sacraments of the eucharist and of reconciliation. Thus strengthened, Christian husbands and wives will be able to keep alive their awareness of the unique influence that the grace of the sacrament of marriage has on every aspect of married life, including therefore their sexuality: the gift of the Spirit, accepted and responded to by husband and wife, helps them to live their human sexuality in accordance with God's plan and as a sign of the unitive and fruitful love of Christ for His church.

33.7 But the necessary conditions also include knowledge of the bodily aspect and the body's rhythms of fertility. Accordingly, every effort must be made to render such knowledge accessible to all married people and also to young adults before marriage through clear, timely and serious instruction and education given by married couples, doctors and experts. Knowledge must then lead to education in self-control: **hence the absolute necessity for the virtue of chastity and for permanent education in it.** In the Christian view, chastity by no means signifies rejection of human sexuality or lack of esteem for it; rather it signifies spiritual energy capable of defending love from the perils of selfishness and aggressiveness, and able to advance it toward its full realization (emphasis added).

Instilling conviction and offering practical help

35.1 With regard to the question of lawful birth regulation, the ecclesial community at the present time must take on the task of instilling conviction and offering practical help to those who wish to live out their parenthood in a truly responsible way.

35.2 In this matter, while the church notes with satisfaction the results achieved by scientific research aimed at a more precise knowledge of the rhythms of women's fertility, and while it encourages a more decisive and wide-ranging extension of that research, it cannot fail to call with renewed vigor on the responsibility of all—doctors, experts, marriage counselors, teachers and married couples—who can actually help married people to live their love with respect for the structure and finalities of the conjugal act which expresses that love. This implies a broader, more decisive and more systematic effort to make the natural methods of regulating fertility known, respected and applied.

Education

36.1 As the Second Vatican Council recalled, "Since parents have conferred life on their children, they have a most solemn obligation to educate their offspring. Hence, parents must be acknowledged as the first and foremost educators of their children. Their role as educators is so decisive that scarcely anything can compensate for their failure in it. For it devolves on parents to create a family atmosphere so animated with love and reverence for God and others that well-rounded personal and social development will be fostered among the children. Hence, the family is the first school for those social virtues which every society needs."

36.2 The right and duty of parents to give education is essential, since it is connected with the transmission of human life; it is *original and primary* with regard to the educational role of others on account of the uniqueness of the loving relationship between parents and children; and it is *irreplaceable and inalienable,* and therefore incapable of being entirely delegated to others or usurped by others.

Sex education

37.3 Education in love as self-giving is also the indispensable premise for parents called to give their children a clear and delicate *sex education.* Faced with a culture that largely reduces human sexuality to the level of something commonplace, since it interprets and lives it in a reductive and impoverished way by linking it solely with the body and with selfish pleasure, the educational service of parents must aim firmly at a training in the area of sex that is truly and fully personal: for sexuality is an enrichment of the whole person—body, emotions and soul—and it manifests its inmost meaning in leading the person to the gift of self in love.

37.4 Sex education, which is a basic right and duty of parents, must always be carried out under their attentive guidance whether at home or in educational centers chosen and controlled by them. In this regard, the church reaffirms the law of subsidiarity, which the school is bound to observe when it cooperates in sex education, by entering into the same spirit that animates the parents.

37.5 **In this context *education for chastity* is absolutely essential, for it is a virtue that develops a person's authentic maturity and makes him or her capable of respecting and fostering the "nuptial meaning" of the body.** Indeed Christian parents, discerning the signs of God's call, will devote special attention and care to education in virginity or celibacy as the supreme form of that self-giving that constitutes the very meaning of human sexuality (emphasis added).

37.6 In view of the close links between the sexual dimension of the person and his or her ethical values, education must bring the children to a knowledge of and respect for the moral norms as the necessary and highly valuable guarantee for responsible personal growth in human sexuality.

37.7 For this reason the church is firmly opposed to an often widespread form of imparting sex information dissociated from moral principles. That would merely be an introduction to the experience of pleasure and a stimulus leading to the loss of serenity—while still in the years of innocence—by opening the way to vice.

The purpose of this chapter has been to provide in one convenient place the principal sources of the Popes and Vatican II dealing with the birth control issue. As mentioned previously, even more extensive documentation of the many addresses of Pope John Paul II is provided in Chapter 6.

References

Introduction

1. John F. Kippley, *Birth Control and the Marriage Covenant.* First published under the title *Covenant, Christ and Contraception* (Staten Island: Alba House, 1970); republished under the newer title by Liturgical Press (MN) in 1976.

Chapter 1, A Covenant Theology of Human Sexuality

1. Many of the ideas in this section appeared in a previous article: John F. Kippley, "A covenant theology of sex," *Homiletic and Pastoral Review* August-September 1983, 22-32.
2. Charles D. Provan, *The Bible and Birth Control* (Monongahela, PA: Zimmer Printing, 1989) 63.
3. Michele M. McCarty, *Relating* (Dubuque: Wm. C. Brown, 1979) 56.
4. McCarty, 50.
5. Richard R. Roach, S.J., "From What Are They Dissenting?" *International Review of Natural Family Planning* VI:4 (Winter 1982) 338.
6. McCarty, 49.
7. McCarty, 49.

Chapter 2, Sex Outside of Marriage

1. Leon J. Cardinal Suenens, *Love and Control* (Paramus, NJ: Paulist/Newman Press, 1961).
2. James A. Pike, *You and the New Morality: 74 Cases* (New York: Harper and Row, 1967.)
3. John F. Kippley, "Continued Dissent: Is It Responsible Loyalty?" *Theological Studies* (32:1 March 1971) 48-65.
4. Thomas Dubay, S.M., "The State of Moral Theology: A Critical Appraisal," *Theological Studies* 35:3 (September 1974) 482-506.
5. Anthony Kosnik, chairperson, William Carroll, Agnes Cunningham, Ronald Modras, and James Schulte, *Human Sexuality: New Directions in American Catholic Thought* (New York: Paulist Press, 1977) 86.
6. Kosnik et al, 149.
7. Sigmund Freud, *A General Introduction to Psycho-Analysis,* translated by Joan Riviere (New York: Liverwright, 1935).
8. Franjo Cardinal Seper, *Declaration on Certain Questions Concerning Sexual Ethics* (Vatican City: Sacred Congregation for the Doctrine of the Faith, 29 December 1975) n.9.
9. Joseph Cardinal Ratzinger, Prefect of the Sacred Congregation for the Doctrine of the Faith, *Instruction on Respect for Human Life in Its Origin and on the Dignity of Procreation: Replies to Certain Questions of the Day* (Vatican City: SCDF, 22 February 1987). Available in English from St. Paul Editions, 50 St. Paul's Avenue, Boston MA 02130, 45 page booklet.
10. John F. Harvey O.S.F.S., personal correspondence dated 9 February 1989.
11. John F. Harvey, O.S.F.S. The national headquarters of Courage is located at St. Michael's Rectory, 424 W. 34th Street, New York NY 10001. Phone: (212) 421-0426. In late 1990, chapters existed in California, District of Columbia, Massachusetts, Missouri, New York, Ohio, Pennsylvania, Texas; and in British Columbia and Ontario in Canada. Information about establishing new chapters may be obtained from the national headquarters.

12. Joseph Cardinal Ratzinger, *On the Pastoral Care of Homosexual Persons* (Vatican City: SCDF, 1 October 1986).

13. "Man commits this adultery 'in the heart' also with regard to his own wife, if he treats her only as an object to satisfy instinct." John Paul II, "Interpreting the Concept of Concupiscence," General Audience of 8 October 1980, *Blessed Are the Pure of Heart* (Boston: St. Paul Editions, 1983) 145.

Chapter 3, Birth Control and the Marriage Covenant

1. Edward J. Bayer, *Rape within Marriage: A Moral Analysis Delayed* (Lanham, MD: University Press of America, 1985). This book reflects the doctoral thesis of Father Bayer, who accepts the teaching of *Humanae Vitae* as true, that if a woman is in danger of rape she may use a non-abortifacient contraceptive device to prevent pregnancy. He holds that this applies to marital rape, because, as he argues, marital rape is not the "marriage act" that is the subject of the Church's teaching in *Humanae Vitae*, etc. He further argues that in the absence of any specific Church teaching against the marital rape thesis, it may be held as a probable opinion according to the theological theory of probabilism.

2. John Paul II, "Pope calls spouses to a sense of responsibility for love and for life," *L'Osservatore Romano*, 17 December 1990, 3, n. 5.

3. John Paul II, above, n. 4.

4. John Paul II, above, n. 5.

Chapter 4, Holy Communion: Eucharistic and Marital

1. John F. Kippley, "Holy Communion: Eucharistic and Marital," *Ave Maria* (105:8) 25 February 1967, 9-12.

2. John Paul II, "The reality of Christian marriage is transfigured by the New Covenant," *L'Osservatore Romano*, English edition, 15 November 1982, 8.

3. Michael Novak, "Rome, Spur of Intellectual Freedom," *Crisis* (7:6) June 1989, 2ff.

Chapter 5, Fundamentals about Conscience

1. John Paul II, "The diligent search for truth requires the teaching of the Magisterium," *L'Osservatore Romano*, 19-26 December 1988, 6.

2. Germain Grisez, "The duty and right to follow one's judgment of conscience," *Homiletic and Pastoral Review* 89:7 (April 1989) 10.

Chapter 6, Forming a Correct Conscience

1. John F. Clarkson, S.J., John H. Edwards, S.J., William J. Kelly, S.J., and John J. Welch, S.J., editors, *The Church Teaches: Documents of the Church in English Translation* (St. Louis: B. Herder, 1955), n.219; Denziger 1839.

2. *The Code of Canon Law in English Translation,* prepared by The Canon Law Society of Great Britain and Ireland et al. (London: Collins Liturgical Publications, 1983) Canon 749.

3. As reported by Terry Mattingly, "Fighting an uphill battle," *The Cincinnati Post,* 25 February, 1989, 4A. I personally talked with Mr. Mattingly who assured me he had personally checked the quote with Father Curran immediately after his lecture.

4. Karl Rahner, *Nature and Grace: Dilemmas in the Modern Church* (New York: Sheed and Ward, 1964) 52.

5. John Paul II, *Origins* 9:18, 18 October 1979, 289.

6. John Paul II, *L'Osservatore Romano,* 3 December 1979, 2.

7. For an analysis of these sixty-two talks see Richard M. Hogan, "A Theology of the Body," *Fidelity* 1:1 (December 1981) 10.

8. "The man-person becomes a gift in the freedom of love," LOR* 21 January 1980, 1.

9. Synod Proposition 21, cited in *Familiaris Consortio*, 22 November 1981, n.29.

10. *The Cincinnati Enquirer*, 20 February 1981, A-5.

11. "Vocation of married couples to the interior truth of love," LOR 11 May 1981, 1.

12. "The Church is grateful for the help you offer married couples," LOR 12 July 1982, 4.

13. "Pope repeats strict policy on abortion, birth control," *Cincinnati Post,* 4 November 1982, 2A.

14. Stephen Kinzer, "Pope attacks divorce, abortion, contraception in Panama visit," *Cincinnati Enquirer,* 6 March 1983, A-1.

15. Nancy Frazier, "Pope urges fidelity to birth control teachings," *Catholic Telegraph,* 10 June 1983, 2.

16. "The bishop, a living sign of Jesus Christ," LOR 12 September 1983, 3.

17. "Christian vocation of spouses may demand even heroism," LOR 10 October 1983, 7.

18. "The 'Professio fidei' and the 'Iusiurandum Fidelitatis'," LOR 13 March 1989, 3.

19. "Marriage and the family linked to the Paschal Mystery of Jesus," LOR 17 October 1983, 10.

20. "Cooperate consciously in the work of Creation in Christ's love," LOR 24 October 1983, 3.

21. "Anti-family policies are highly destructive," LOR 16 January 1984, 4.

22. *Educational Guidance in Human Love: Outlines for Sex Education,* LOR 5 December 1983, 5-9, n.62.

23. "Church must lead couples to the truth about themselves and their love," LOR 2 April 1984, 7.

24. "Joy and gratitude for abundant vocations," LOR 12 March 1984, 9.

25. "Diverse family situations are resolved in the light of the Church's doctrine," LOR 16 April 1984, 8.

26. "Responsible procreation requires dialogue between science, faith and theology," LOR 18 June 1984, 5.

27. *Reflections on Humanae Vitae: Conjugal Morality and Spirituality* (Boston: St. Paul Editions, 1984) 96pp.

28. The catechesis referred to is found in two books: 1) John Paul II, *Original Unity of Man and Woman: Catechesis on the Book of Genesis* (Boston: St. Paul Editions, 1981) 184pp. This is a series of 23 talks given by the Pope between 5 September 1979 and 2 April 1980. 2) John Paul II, *Blessed Are the Pure of Heart: Catechesis on the Sermon on the Mount and Writings of St. Paul* (Boston: St. Paul Editions, 1983) 305pp. This is a series of 41 talks given by the Pope between 16 April 1980 and 6 May 1981.

29. Most Rev. Edouard Gagnon, "The Pope's Catechesis," LOR 28 January 1985, 10.

30. "Rediscover the relationship of truth, goodness and freedom," LOR 28 April 1986, 12.

31. "The Church's teaching on contraception is not a matter for free discussion among theologians," LOR 6 July 1987, 12.

32. Address to the bishops of the United States, Los Angeles, 16 September 1987, *The Pope in America II* (St. Paul: Wanderer Press, 1987) 87.

• LOR = *L'Osservatore Romano,* English edition.

33. "Spouses called to live the entire truth of *Humanae Vitae*; pastors are to teach it without calling it into question," LOR 11 April 1988, 6.

34. "Pope to U. S. bishops on 'ad limina' visit," LOR 14 November 1988, 5-6.

35. "Revive awareness of conjugal love as a gift of the Spirit through the Sacrament of Marriage," LOR 5 December 1988, 8.

36. "The diligent search for truth requires the teaching of the Magisterium," LOR 19-26 December 1988, 6, n.3.

37. *Origins,* 18 October 1979, 289.

38. "Christian vocation of spouses may demand even heroism," LOR 10 October 1983, 7.

39. Most Rev. Costanzo Micci, "Responsible Parenthood: A discourse that one needs to understand," LOR 12 December 1983, 9.

40. Fr. Lino Ciccone, C.M., "Contraception and the rejection of God," LOR 12 December 1983, 9.

41. "Church must lead couples to the truth about themselves and their love," LOR 2 April 1984, 7.

42. "Rediscover the relationship of truth, goodness and freedom," LOR 28 April 1986, 12.

43. John Paul II, "The Church's teaching on contraception is not a matter for free discussion among theologians," LOR 6 July 1987, 12.

44. John Paul II, "Spouses are called to live the entire truth of *Humanae Vitae*; pastors are to teach it without calling it into question," LOR 11 April 1988, 6.

45. John Paul II, "The universal ordinary magisterium can be considered to be the usual expression of the Church's infallibility," LOR 24 October 1988, 22.

46. Rahner, *Nature and Grace,* 52.

47. John Paul II, "The diligent search for truth requires the teaching of the Magisterium," LOR 19-26 December 1988, 6.

48. Canadian Catholic Conference, *Statement on the Formation of Conscience,* 12 December 1973, sections 40-41. Available in pamphlet form from Daughters of St. Paul.

Chapter 7, Is the Teaching Infallible?

1. Ingrid Trobisch, *The Joy of Being a Woman...And What a Man Can Do* (New York: Harper & Row, 1975).

2. Larry and Nordis Christenson, *The Christian Couple* (Minneapolis: Bethany Fellowship, 1977). "I would not go back to using a contraceptive device even if the alternative were having twenty-one children." p. 74

3. Siegfried Ernst, *Man, the Greatest of Miracles* (Collegeville, MN: Liturgical Press, 1976).

4. Mary Pride, *The Way Home: Beyond Feminism, Back to Reality* (Westchester, IL: Crossway, 1985).

5. Mary Pride, *All the Way Home* (Westchester, IL: Crossway, 1989) 35.

6. Charles Provan, *What the Bible Says about Birth Control* (Monongahela, PA: Zimmer Printing, 1989).

7. John T. Noonan, Jr., *Contraception: A History of Its Treatment by Catholic Theologians and Canonists* (Cambridge, MA: The Belknap Press of Harvard University Press, 1965).

8. "Papal infallibility has to do with what Jesus Christ taught us to believe and to do (faith and morals). But the evaluation of birth control has to do with human wisdom...In this area the Church has the authority to teach but here its teaching is always non-infallible and changeable." Gregory Baum, *Toronto Globe and Mail,* 1 August 1968.

9. John Paul II, "The universal ordinary magisterium can be considered to be the usual expression of the Church's infallibility," LOR 24 October 1988, 22.

10. William E. May, personal correspondence, June 20, 1989.

11. John C. Ford, S.J., Germain Grisez, Joseph Boyle, John Finnis, and William E. May, *The Teaching of Humanae Vitae: A Defense* (San Francisco: Ignatius, 1988). Original article: John C. Ford, S.J. and Germain Grisez, "Contraception and the Infallibility of the Ordinary Magisterium," *Theological Studies* (39:2) June 1978, 258-312.

12. Francis Sullivan, S.J., *Magisterium: Teaching Authority in the Catholic Church* (Dublin: Gill and Macmillan, 1983) 3-6.

13. Noonan, 6.

14. Brian Harrison, *Living Tradition* 2 (December 1985) 3-6.

15. Germain Grisez, "Infallibility and Specific Norms: A Review Discussion," *The Thomist* 49:2 (April 1985) 248-287.

16. Ermenegildo Lio, O.F.M., *Humanae Vitae e Infallibilita: il Concilio, Paolo VI e Giovanni Paolo II* (Vatican City: Libreria Editrice Vaticana, 1986).

17. Brian W. Harrison, "*Humanae Vitae* and Infallibility," *Fidelity* (November 1987) 43-48.

Chapter 8, Natural Family Planning

1. John F. Kippley and Sheila K. Kippley, "The Relation between Breastfeeding and Amenorrhea: Report of a Survey," *JOGN Nursing* 1:4 (November-December) 1972.

2. Sheila Kippley, "Breastfeeding Survey Results Similar to 1971 Study," *The CCL News* 13:3 (November-December 1986) 10 and 13:4 (January-February 1987) 5.

3. Sheila K. and John F. Kippley, "The Spacing of Babies with Ecological Breastfeeding," *International Review* XIII; 1 & 2 (Spring/Summer 1989) 107-116.

4. Harry William Taylor, Jr., *Effect of Nursing Pattern on Postpartum Anovulatory Interval*, Doctoral dissertation, (Davis, CA: University of California, 1989).

5. Sheila Kippley, *Breastfeeding and Natural Child Spacing: How Natural Mothering Spaces Babies,* second revised edition, (Cincinnati: Couple to Couple League, 1989).

6. John F. and Sheila K. Kippley, *The Art of Natural Family Planning* (Cincinnati: The Couple to Couple League, 1972, 1984).

7. Marlyn E. Wade, Phyllis McCarthy, et al., "A Randomized Prospective Study of the Use-Effectiveness of Two Methods of Natural Family Planning," *Am. J. Ob. and Gyn* 141:4 (October 15, 1981) 368-376. Among couples who followed the rules for avoiding pregnancy, the STM users had a 100% method-effectiveness rate; the OM users had a 94% method-effectiveness rate. Among couples who said they wanted to avoid pregnancy but did not always follow the rules, the STM users had an 85% user-effectiveness rate; the OM users had a 63% user-effectiveness rate. Two things must be noted. First, no couples were allowed in this study if they had a serious reason to avoid pregnancy; the resulting group was biased towards those who would "take chances." Second, both systems have shown higher user-effectiveness rates in other studies. For a more complete treatment of effectiveness, see pages 14-17 of *The Art of Natural Family Planning*[6] and CCL's pamphlet, *The Effectiveness of Natural Family Planning.*[8]

8. John F. Kippley, *The Effectiveness of Natural Family Planning* (Cincinnati: Couple to Couple League, 1986) 15 pages.

Chapter 9, Practical Pastoral Policies

1. I am certain that using any unnatural form of birth control within marriage mocks God. On the other hand, as I have indicated in the first part of this book, I do not think such mockery is involved in the use of a true contraceptive device as

protection against the invasion of sperm from foreseeable rape. It is not entirely clear to me whether additional mockery is involved by using a true contraceptive when the act is one of adultery or fornication, acts which already mock God's design for love and sexuality.

2. "Marital Sexuality: Moral Considerations," (Cincinnati, Couple to Couple League, 1989).

3. John F. Kippley, *Last Supper Themes Applied to Love and Marriage: A Series of Seven Homilies* (Cincinnati: The Couple to Couple League, 1982).

4. Kippley, "Preaching about Natural Family Planning," *Homiletic and Pastoral Review* January 1983, 56-61.

5. Human Life Center, Steubenville, OH 43952, (614) 282-9953.

6. Kippley, *Birth Control and Christian Discipleship* (Cincinnati: Couple to Couple League, 1985) 1-14.

7. John Paul II, "The bishop, a living sign of Christ," to U. S. bishops on "ad limina" visit, 5 September 1983, n.3, LOR, 12 September 1983, 3.

8. Kippley, *Birth Control and the Marriage Covenant,* 154.

9. Kippley, *Birth Control and the Marriage Covenant,* 155-156.

Chapter 10, Hard Cases

1. Karl Rahner, *Nature and Grace,* 55-56.

2. Victor Frankl, *Man's Search for Meaning,* 3rd ed. (New York: Washington Square Press, 1984).

3. "Some of the most respected theologians of the first quarter of this century considered this situation. The opinions of Arthur Vermeersch, S.J. (Professor at the Gregorian University in Rome and consultor to three Vatican congregations) and Hieronymus Noldin, S.J. (Professor of Moral Theology at the Jesuit Theologate in Innsbruck) are accurately reflected by Joseph J. Farraher, S.J., in the *Homiletic and Pastoral Review* (July 1979). With them, Father Farraher holds that a sign of true contrition 'would seem to include an attitude that if the sterilization can be safely, effectively and relatively easily repaired, it should be repaired'." Thomas O'Donnell, S.J., "Repentance Following Directly Willed Contraceptive Sterilization," *The Medical-Moral Newsletter* 26:1 (January 1989) 4.

4. O"Donnell, 4.

5. O"Donnell, 4.

6. O"Donnell, 4.

7. See Marilyn Shannon, *Fertility, Cycles and Nutrition* (Cincinnati: Couple to Couple League, 1990). This book provides scientific analyses of a number of irregularities that can affect fertility, both female and male, and offers practical non-medical suggestions for improvement.

8. Franjo Cardinal Seper, Sacred Congregation for the Doctrine of the Faith, 29 December 1975.

9. Oscar and Susan Staudt, *Creative Continence* (Cincinnati: Couple to Couple League, 1989) brochure. Its complement is *Marital Sexuality: Moral Considerations,* another CCL brochure.

10. John F. Kippley, *Holy Communion: Eucharistic and Marital* (Cincinnati: Couple to Couple League, 1975) 12 page brochure, and chapter 4 in this book.

11. Edward F. Bayer, (see Chapter 3, reference 1) 5.

Chapter 11, The Historical Context

1. Noonan: see Chapter 7, reference 7.

2. Noonan, 427.

3. Noonan, 467.

4. *Address to the Seventh International Congress of Hematology,* AAS 50: 735-

736 (Noonan, 466).

5. John Rock, *The Time Has Come* (New York: Alfred A. Knopf, 1963).

6. *Herder Correspondence,* October 1963, p. 28; quoted in *The Pill* by Leo Pyle (Helicon, 1964) 6.

7. *Herder* p. 30, in Pyle, 7.

8. "The Times," June 24, 1964. Quoted by Pyle, 212.

9. As quoted by Leo Pyle, *Pope and Pill* (London: Darton, Longmann and Todd, 1968) 212.

10. Gregory Baum, O.S.A., "Birth Control—What Happened?" *Commonweal* December 24, 1965, 370.

Chapter 12, The People of God

1. The point of recalling these accounts is to show that the sacred authors regularly view the People of God as less than faithful to Yahweh.

2. Karl Rahner, S.J., *Theological Investigations,* Vol. 3 (Baltimore, Md.: Helicon Press, 1967) 164.

3. William F. Pratt, William D. Mosher, et al., "Understanding U. S. Fertility: Findings from the National Survey of Family Growth, Cycle III," *Population Bulletin* 39:5 (December, 1984) Table 7: Current Contraceptive Use: 1982. This table indicates that of the 54,099 women aged 15-44 surveyed, 31, 298 said they were Protestant and 17,377 said they were Catholic. Of those, 54.6% of Protestants and 52.5% of Catholics said they were using some form of birth control. These percentages appear low for several reasons. 1) They include women aged 15-19, of whom as a whole, only 24.2% used any form of birth control. They also include women who are single and chaste, women who are pregnant, post-partum, or seeking pregnancy, and even women who are sterile for noncontraceptive reasons. Thus these figures most certainly do not indicate that only 52.5% of Catholic married women are using some form of birth control. What they say is that after you eliminate chaste single women, those who are pregnant, postpartum, seeking pregnancy and naturally sterile, there are left 52.5% of Catholic women who practice some form of birth control and of that group, only 6.0% in 1982 and only 3.0% (see next reference) in 1988 used any form of natural family planning.

4. Calvin Goldsheider and William D. Mosher, "Patterns of Contraception in the United States: How Important are Religious Factors?" Table 2 - Current contraceptive status and method by religious affiliation: white non-Hispanic women of all marital statuses aged 15-44, United States, 1982 and 1988. Draft version, unpublished, received 10 August 1990.

5. John Henry Newman, *On Consulting the Faithful in Matters of Doctrine,* John Coulson, ed. (New York: Sheed & Ward, 1961) 8, 13.

6. See also: Joseph Cardinal Ratzinger, *Instruction on the Ecclesial Vocation of the Theologian* (Rome: Sacred Congregation for the Doctrine of the Faith, 24 May 1990), n. 35. This document is essential reading for every student of theology. Section 34 provides a rationale for Chapter 13 of this book by noting the danger of dissent: "When dissent succeeds in extending its influence to the point of shaping a common opinion, it tends to become a rule of conduct." Therefore, the errors of dissent must be exposed.

7. *Trends in Contraceptive Practice: United States, 1965-1976* (U.S. Dept. of HHS, Publication No (PHS) 82-1986, 1982) Table 13.

8. Goldsheider and Mosher.

9. Harvey Cox, *The Secular City* (New York: Macmillan, 1965) 206-207.

10. See Chapter 7, "Is the teaching infallible?" for the thoughtful view of Fr. Ermenegildo Lio that the conditions have also been met in *Casti Connubii* and *Humanae Vitae.*

Chapter 13,
A Critique of Arguments for Contraception

1. Father Gregory Baum, O.S.A., *Toronto Globe and Mail,* of August 1, 1968. Of more importance than authorship is the fact that such a statement reflects badly and unfairly on those Catholics who not only adhere to the teachings of the Holy Father on contraception but likewise follow him in his example of charity. Our Blessed Lord himself gave us the norm when he told us to "judge not." It is applicable even here.

2. I am aware that Bernard Haring and some others disavow this. However, in reading their disavowals, I cannot help but conclude that their assertions fail to block the logical flow of the conclusions from the premises from which they argue. The entirety of *Human Sexuality* (Anthony Kosnik et al., 1977) illustrates that the acceptance of contraception leads to the acceptance of other immoral behaviors: "All else being equal, a homosexual engaging in homosexual acts in good conscience has the same rights of conscience and the same rights to the sacraments as a married couple practicing birth control in good conscience" (216).

3. John F. Kippley, "Continued Dissent: Is It Responsible Loyalty?" *Theological Studies,* 32:1 (March 1971) 48-65.

4. See Elasah Drogin, *Margaret Sanger: Father of Modern Society* (New Hope, KY: CUL Publications, 1986).

5. For descriptions of this, see W. H. Van der Marck, O.P., *Love and Fertility* (London: Sheed & Ward, 1965), and *Toward a Christian Ethic* (Paramus, NJ: Paulist/Newman Press, 1967).

6. W. H. Van der Marck, *Love and Fertility,* 60.

7. Paul Furfey, *The Respectable Murderers* (New York: Herder & Herder, 1965).

8. Charles Curran, *Christian Morality Today* (Notre Dame, IN: Fides, 1966) 129.

9. Denis E. Hurley, O.M.I., *Furrow,* 17 (October 1966) 619-622.

10. Hurley, "In Defense of the Principle of Overriding Right," *Theological Studies* 29 (June 1968) 301.

11. Richard A. McCormick, S.J. *Theological Studies* 28(December 1967) 757-758.

12. Hurley, *Theological Studies,* 305.

13. Charles E. Curran, "Dialogue with Joseph Fletcher," *Homiletic and Pastoral Review* 67(1967) 821-829.

14. Peter Chirico, SS., "Tension, Morality, and Birth Control," *Theological Studies* 28(1967) 258-285.

15. Richard A. McCormick, S.J., *Theological Studies* 28(December 1967) 759-760.

16. Philip S. Keane, S.S., *Sexual Morality: A Catholic Perspective* (New York: Paulist Press, 1977).

17. William May, *Contraception, Humanae Vitae and Catholic Moral Thought* (Chicago: Franciscan Herald Press, 1987).

18. Quoted in Robert G. Hoyt (ed.), *The Birth Control Debate* (Kansas City, MO: National Catholic Reporter, 1968) 72.

19. Hoyt, 75.

20. Hoyt, 94.

21. Hoyt, 76-77.

22. Michael Valente, *Sex: The Radical View of a Catholic Theologian* (New York: Bruce, 1970). After describing himself as a revisionist, Valente notes: "To accept the revisionist position on the liceity of contraceptive use in marriage is not merely to find an exception to the natural law doctrine, but to destroy it. In view of this, it seems unreasonable to maintain that there is a difference between allowing a husband and wife to use the condom and allowing them to have anal intercourse, since neither fulfills the natural law doctrine's requirement of insemination in the

vagina. Likewise there is no difference between using the condom and *coitus interruptus* or any of the so-called sins prohibited under the doctrine, such as masturbation, homosexuality, and bestiality." p. 126. Well, at least he's honest about the "sexual logic" of contraception. (JFK)

23. Kippley, 48-65.
24. Keane, 117-118.
25. Kosnik, 214-217. See quotation in reference 2 above.

Chapter 14, Different Approaches

1. Terry Mattingly, "Fighting an Uphill Battle," *The Cincinnati Post*, 25 February 1989, 4A.

2. Lorenzo Albacete, quoted by Marina Ricci, "Human Life between the Pill and the Test Tube: The Future of Moral Theology," *30 Days* (December 1988) 9.

3. Father Edward Bayer (*Rape within Marriage*) relates the historical development of this subject over the last three centuries.

4. Germain Grisez, Joseph Boyle, John Finnis and William E. May, "'Every Marital Act Ought to Be Open to New Life': Toward a Clearer Understanding," *The Thomist* 52:3 (July 1988) 365-426. This essay is reprinted in *The Teaching of "Humanae Vitae": A Defense* (San Francisco: Ignatius, 1988). Page references are to the original article.

5. John Paul II, General audience, 22 August 1984. See *Reflections on Humanae Vitae: Conjugal Morality and Spirituality* (Boston: St. Paul Editions, 1984) 33-34.

Chapter 15, Biblical Foundations

1. Manuel Miguens, "Biblical Thoughts on Human Sexuality," *Human Sexuality in Our Time,* ed. George A Kelly (Boston: St. Paul Editions, 1979) 112-115.

2. It is accepted by both dissenters and orthodox theologians that intellectual acceptance of contraceptive behaviors logically entails the intellectual acceptance of other actions traditionally called perversities. More on this was spelled out in Chapters 2 and 13. See also reference 12.

3. Noonan, 10.

4. Noonan, 353.

5. Noonan, 353.

6. Charles D. Provan, *The Bible and Birth Control* (Monongahela, PA: Zimmer, 1989) 83.

7. John C. Ford, S.J., and Germain Grisez, "Contraception and the Infallibility of the Ordinary Magisterium," *Theological Studies* 39:2 (June 1978) 282.

8. See John C. Ford, S.J., and Gerald Kelly, S.J., "Is this revealed doctrine?" *Contemporary Moral Theology, Vol. II: Marriage Questions* (Westminster, MD: Newman, 1964) 271-278.

9. E. Schillebeeckx, O.P., *Marriage: Human Reality and Saving Mystery* (New York: Sheed and Ward, 1965) 143.

10. Schillebeeckx, 153-154.

11. I suggest that a student could write an interesting M.A. level paper describing the post-*Humanae Vitae* attack on indissolubility just in the pages of *America* magazine, 1968 to 1973. A doctoral thesis might tackle the Catholic divorce rates pre-and post-*Humanae Vitae*.

12. Valente, 126.

13. Kosnik, 24.

14. Kosnik, 23.

15. Kosnik 189-190.

16. Kosnik 195.

Chapter 16, Ecclesial Documentation

1. *The Lambeth Conferences—1867-1930* (London: S.P.C.K., 1948) 102-103. Quoted in Ford and Kelly, 247.

2. *The Lambeth Conferences,* 50-51; Ford and Kelly, 247.

3. *Lambeth Conferences,* 166; Ford and Kelly, 246.

4. *The Lambeth Conferences,* 199; Ford and Kelly, 246.

5. Pius XI, *Casti Connubii,* Section 4, para. 4, 31 December 1930.

6. *New York Times,* 21 March 1931, 13.

7. Editorial, *The Washington Post,* 22 March 1931.

8. John F. Kippley, *Birth Control and Christian Discipleship* (Cincinnati: CCL, 1985).

9. J.F.N., *A Catechism on Birth Control,* Sixth edition (Huntington: OSV Press, ca 1939) 30-31. Additional reports of the battles within Protestant Churches are carried in the *New York Times* for several months including strong criticism by Baptist and Lutheran assemblies in early June.

10. Ford and Kelly, 240-241, quoting the Address to Italian Midwives, 29 October 1951; AAS, 43 (1951) 843-844.

11. Ford and Kelly, 242, citing the Address to Hematologists, 12 September 1958; AAS, 50 (1958) 732-740.

12. John XXIII, *Mater et Magistra,* 15 May 1961, N.C.W.C. translation (Boston: St. Paul Editions). The headings and the paragraph numbers were in the NCWC text.

13. *The Documents of Vatican II,* Walter M. Abbott, S.J., editor (New York: Herder and Herder, 1966).

14. Brian Harrison, "*Humanae Vitae* and Infallibility," *Fidelity,* November 1987, 46.

15. Abbott edition.

16. Translation by Rev. Marc Calegari, S.J., copyright 1978 by Ignatius Press, San Francisco.

17. The Official Vatican translation of *Familiaris Consortio* from the Vatican Polyglot Press is available in its entirety from the Daughters of St. Paul (Boston: St. Paul Editions).

Index

Index

354

About the Author . . .

John F. Kippley holds Masters degrees in Theology (University of San Francisco), Applied Theology (Graduate Theological Union, Berkeley), and Industrial Relations (University of Minnesota); his undergraduate degree was in philosophy (St. Paul Seminary, Minnesota). After military service and a half-dozen years in the business world, Mr. Kippley worked for five years in Catholic parish programs of outreach to the uncommitted. It was out of this experience that he first developed the "covenant theology of sex" in the mid-Sixties.

When Pope Paul VI reaffirmed the traditional Christian teaching against unnatural forms of birth control in 1968 through his encyclical *Humanae Vitae* (*Concerning Human Life*), he recommended that married couples help other married couples with natural family planning. In response, John and Sheila Kippley founded the Couple to Couple League for that purpose in 1971.

After several years of teaching college theology, Mr. Kippley become the full-time director of the League in 1974 and has held that position ever since. With his wife Sheila, he has co-authored *The Art of Natural Family Planning*, and he has written a wide range of articles, brochures and booklets related to natural family planning and the traditional Christian truths about human love.